563

THE BOOK OF
THE DUFFS

COMPILED BY ALISTAIR AND

HENRIETTA TAYLER

v. I

VOLUME I

EDINBURGH

PRINTED BY T. & A. CONSTABLE, AND
PUBLISHED BY WILLIAM BROWN
5 CASTLE STREET

1914

ADAM DUFF OF CLUNYBEG

By G. van Houthorst.

Tayler, Alistair Norwich, 1870–

    The book of the Duffs; comp. by Alistair and Henrietta Tayler ... Edinburgh, W. Brown, 1914.

    2 v. fronts, illus, ports, map, facsim, fold geneal, tables. 26ᶜᵐ

    Title vignette (coat of arms)

53171

    1. Duff family   i Tayler, Helen Agnes Henrietta, 1869–   joint author. II. Title 2.Gordon fam. 3.Urquhart fam.

15–1476

PREFACE

As long ago as the year 1889 it was pointed out, in the pages of the *Genealogist*, that there existed no proper history of the Duff family in ancient times.

Again, in subsequent years, the present writers have frequently been asked by members of this large and scattered family to compile an account of ' the nineteenth century Duffs,' showing their connections with each other.

It was determined to combine the two objects, and while providing a record of a long-lived and energetic family from the earliest days, to collect at the same time, from all possible sources, printed and otherwise, interesting details of what may be called the ' mediæval' and modern members, and to bring the history of the family and the genealogical tables thoroughly up to date.

The present volume, therefore, aims at providing a record, complete as far as possible, of those Scotsmen who have borne, and now bear, the name of Duff, giving the legendary lore connected with this family (even though some of it may be discredited by modern historians), as well as a full personal history of those Duffs who have distinguished themselves in any way (and brief mention of the others), with their intermarriages and their matrimonial connections with other families.

The only attempt previously made at anything of the kind is the *Memoirs of the Duffs*, written about the year 1770, by William Baird of Auchmedden (whose wife was one of the daughters of William Duff of Dipple), and privately printed in 1869 by Major Lachlan Gordon Duff of Drummuir.[1]

Several original manuscripts of this work exist   One, belonging to

---

[1] *Genealogical Memoirs of the Duffs.* Printed for private circulation. D Wyllie and Son, Aberdeen, 1869.

Miss Fyffe Duff of Corsindae, bears date September 24, 1772, which presumably was the date of the completion of one portion, as some births and deaths, etc., connected with the families dealt with, occurring in 1773, are recorded. William Baird himself died in 1775.

Baird's original manuscripts contain frequent blanks for names both of persons and of places, and there are many inaccurate statements and conjectures, due doubtless to enforced reliance upon hearsay evidence, to the difficulty of communications, and the impossibility at that period of verifying references and dates, or obtaining access to original documents.

When we consider the expenditure of time and energy involved, even now, in correspondence with outlying members of the family, and in research in public offices at home and abroad, we are filled with admiration for the courage and energy displayed, and the large amount of information collected by our forerunner, a hundred and forty years ago

For permission to make copious extracts from this chronicle we are indebted to Thomas Gordon Duff, son of the original editor, among whose papers is also preserved a schedule of questions sent by William Baird to various members of the family, showing the meagre response he sometimes elicited.

The arrangement of the first few chapters of the present history explains itself, as it is purely chronological. After that, it has been found best to carry the elder line down to the present day, and then revert to the younger sons, in order. It is hoped that the full genealogical tables and the smaller key tables will make this plain.

After tracing the descendants of John of Muldavit and his son, Adam of Clunybeg, in over twenty separate lines of descent,[1] the later chapters deal with other branches of the Duff family (which it has been found impossible to correlate with the Muldavit stock), and with one or two other families with which the Duffs have intermarried so frequently as to make some account necessary.

Other sources, besides Baird, which have been found of great value, are the family trees preserved in various branches of the family, old family

---

[1] The chart of these will be found at end of Volume I.

papers, letters and manuscript records, wherever existing and obtainable, the Decennial List of Heirs for Scotland, parish and local registers,[1] and records of every kind, in London and Edinburgh, as well as all over the United Kingdom.

Innumerable histories of other families, and historical and genealogical collections of every sort have been laid under contribution; wills, records of sasines, hornings, deeds and decreets, commissariat records, school chronicles, files of old newspapers, everything which might yield the smallest scrap of information, has been consulted, and the writers would further like to place on record their debt to the personal recollections and traditional information of several old friends in every walk of life, some of whom have, unfortunately, not lived to see the appearance of the book.

> 'All which doth require
> Briareus his hundred hands,
> Argus his hundred eyes,
> And Nestor's century of years to marshal'

This volume represents the results of many years of congenial labour, in which the writers have received valuable assistance from relations and friends almost too numerous to mention.

Special thanks are due to:

H.R.H. the Princess Royal and Her Highness the Duchess of Fife, Princess Arthur of Connaught, for permission to examine and print selections from the documents long preserved at Duff House, and now in the

---

[1] Though these do not invariably give all details, for, as is well known, the parish registers in Scotland suffered, like everything else, from the wars and tumults. Those in the Episcopal Church in Banff stop abruptly in 1746, when Cumberland on his way to Culloden burnt the church, and, it is said, carried off the books. While those in Brechin suffered a century earlier, as is then noted by the clerk:

'In the month of March 1645, the scrolls were lying in the book, but the book being taken by the cruel enemie, the scrolls were lost and leaves ryven out of the book, as evidentlie appears' And two months later, he notes 'There, six or seven leaves following, being clean paper, were cutt out be som of Montrose followers.'

And the parish clerk of Inverness protects himself from the charge of inaccuracy by the following entry:

'If there be any blanks here, know that it is not the fault of the clerk, but such as did not pay their christening money'

One of these reasons must account for the fact that exhaustive search has failed to discover any record of the baptisms of the thirty-six children of Patrick Duff of Craigston (q.v.), except those of his eldest son and eldest daughter, chronicled at Grange

charter room at Montcoffer,[1] and for permission to reproduce ten family portraits.

To Her Highness Princess Maud, for the loan of the portrait of her father, her sister, and herself.

To the Duke of Richmond and Gordon and the Earl of Seafield, for permission to make extracts from their charter chests.

To Thomas Gordon Duff of Drummuir, for the unrestricted use of all his family papers, dating from the sixteenth century downwards, without which some chapters of this history could never have been written.

To Mrs. Chancellor and J. Wharton Duff, for permission to use the large collection of family letters at Orton, from which a great part of the personal history of Lord Braco's family has been reconstructed. To Mrs. Chancellor also for kindly supplying photographs of the family portraits in her possession.

To Edward Gordon Duff, for the loan of the Rose MSS. now in his possession.[2]

To Edward Alexander Duff, for the use of all his papers, and permission to reproduce two portraits and the facsimile letter in chapter xvii.

To Garden Alexander Duff of Hatton for the loan of documents, etc.

To General Sir Beauchamp Duff, G.C.B., for an invaluable list, prepared for us from official sources, of all Duffs who have served in the Army[3] or Navy, and for his kindly criticism and help on many points, particularly wherever in our history we have touched on military matters.

To Walter B. Blaikie, LL.D., for expert assistance and advice in the production.

---

[1] In the *Historical Manuscripts Commission* these papers are thus noted

' The extensive series of documents in the charter room at Duff House were scheduled in 1872, the entries numbering over 1000 They consist wholly of the title-deeds and relative papers of the vast estates belonging to Lord Fife in the countries of Banff, Moray, and Aberdeen, and none of them call for detailed description.'

Besides these there are also innumerable family letters

[2] William Rose was long factor to the second Earl Fife, and in that capacity a great deal of very interesting correspondence was addressed to him. He also became possessed of many other family letters and papers, and amassed, on his own behalf, a large collection of genealogical and other notes All these were left untouched at his death and long afterwards, but were eventually scattered, Mr. Edward Gordon Duff of Liverpool purchasing the greater part, while some were acquired for the Spalding Club, but were never utilised.

[3] Since 1755 over a hundred men of the name of Duff have held commissions in the British Army.

PREFACE

To H. Inglis Lindsay, W.S., for his unwearied kindness and energy in undertaking researches in Edinburgh.

To William MacIntosh, Fife Estates Office, for much help in dealing with matters regarding the Earls Fife.

To the Hon. Henry Hannen, for help in the elucidation of obsolete words and phrases.

To J. Malcolm Bulloch, for useful advice as to the sources to consult, and for much information.

To the Rev. Stephen Ree, for various important notes supplied.

To James Grant, LL.B., for permission to make use of the books in Banff.

To the authorities of the Advocates' Library, the Public Library, and the University Library, Aberdeen, for permission to examine manuscripts in their hands.

To the authorities of the office of the Lord Lyon, of the Advocates' Library, and of the Signet Library, Edinburgh, for similar permissions.

To the officials of the India Office, Record Office, Somerset House, College of Arms, and the British Museum Library and Manuscript Room.

And to the following relatives and friends for the loan of letters and pictures, and for information and corrections connected with their own branches of the family :

Mrs. Darwin of Muirtown and Colonel A. R Warrand; Lady Duff and the Misses Duff of Fetteresso; Major Adrian Grant Duff, C.B.; the late General A. G. Duff; Miss Fyffe Duff of Corsindae; Miss Jane Clerk Duff; Major-General R. W. Duff; Adam Gordon Duff; Mrs. Duff Dunbar; Miss Marjory Kate Duff; Miss Louisa Duff; Professor Archibald Duff; John Duff, Dublin; Mrs. Petre and Captain Granville Duff; Miss Mary Ramsay; Colonel Sir Aubone Fife; George Duff, Towiemore; Stanley Duff Muttlebury.

Thanks are also due to the late William Cramond, LL.D.; the late Alexander Ramsay, LL.D.; David Littlejohn, LL.D.; Mr. J. A. Henderson; and to Frances Cathcart, Annie Clark, and John Wyatt.

ALISTAIR N. TAYLER.
HENRIETTA TAYLER.

EDINBURGH, *December* 29, 1913

NOTE

In order to differentiate the family letters,
drawn from various sources, they are
marked thus :

Letters from the Duff House papers, now
at Montcoffer, . (*D*).

Letters from the Rose MSS., in the collection of Mr. E G Duff, (*R*)

Letters from the Orton papers, . (*O*)

Letters from other sources are acknowledged
in full.

CONTENTS

VOLUME I

CONTENTS

VOLUME II

ILLUSTRATIONS
PORTRAITS AND PLATES
VOLUME I

VOLUME II

SKETCHES IN THE TEXT

VOLUME I

VOLUME II

GENEALOGICAL TABLES

VOLUME I

VOLUME II

THE BOOK OF THE DUFFS

CHAPTER I

LEGENDARY HISTORY

THE Duff family claims an origin veiled in the mists of antiquity, and there are preserved many and curious old family trees, some even going back to the days of Darius the Mede ; but perhaps those trees starting from the ninth century, with the first thanes of Fife, take us as far as we need seek to penetrate.

The first mention of Fife is in the verses ascribed to St. Columba,[1] wherein the seven great sons of Cruthne are given as Fib, Fidach, etc., and Fib, of course, is the same as Fife.

Again, Fibh, or Fiv, was one of the seven provinces into which Scotland was divided before the thirteenth century, and the first of the fourteen Pictish tribes, that called Cinid, occupied this province which later became the earldom and county of Fife.[2]

Until quite recently, Burke's *Peerage* was wont to state that ' the noble family of Duff derives from Fyfe Macduff, a chief of great wealth and power, who lived about the year 834, and afforded to Kenneth II., King of Scotland, strong aid against his enemies the Picts.' An old MS. at Drummuir calls him ' Fife Duff, a royal young man, cousin-german of Kenneth the Second, and one of his generals, and in the year 838 is made Thane.'

Another version, which has the authority of Hector Boece, first Principal of Aberdeen University,[3] gives the name of the hero as Fifus Duffus, and says that he was granted the county of Otholenia as a reward for his

---

[1] *Pictish Chronicle*, translated by Pinkerton.   [2] Skene's *Highlanders of Scotland*.
[3] History of Scotland, published 1526.

A

services, and that this became the kingdom of Fife (*Macfarlane's Genea-logical Collections*).[1]

Yet another legend ascribes the origin of the family to Duff (or Dubh, the Black) son of Malcolm I., King of Scotland, who succeeded to the throne in 962, having first defeated Colin, son of Indulph, the last king. Subsequently Colin defeated King Duff, who was murdered by a band of assassins, hired by Donald, Governor of Forres, at the castle of Forres, and his body was hidden under a bridge at Kinloss, tradition stating that the sun did not shine again until the body had been found and buried Skene, in his *Celtic Scotland*, suggests that the eclipse of the sun on July 10, 967, originated (or confirmed) this story. The elder son of King Duff was Kenneth III., and the younger became McDuff, first Thane of Fife, from whom an un-broken line of thanes and earls would bring us to the Countess Isabel, died 1389, ' of whom presently.'

The more usual form of the legend, not, of course, incompatible with the two first already mentioned, makes the first *authentic* ancestor to be Macduff, the eighth Thane of Fife, who married Beatrice Banquo, daughter of the Thane of Lochaber, about 1040.[2]

This, of course, is the ' dear Duff ' of Shakespeare (*Macbeth*, act ii. sc 3), and the Makduf of John of Fordun's *Scotichronicon* (book v.), and Andrew de Wyntoun's *Chronicles* (book v. chapter xviii.), and the hero of the little burgh of Earlsferry in Fife.[3]

He is thus described by John of Fordun :

' Macduff Thanus de Fyfe, qui cautius ceteris atque diutius incognitum animi celavit propositum,' which phrase is thus translated · ' Macduff,

---

[1] But, according to Pinkerton, the name of the hero was Odo, and he was called Dubh, or Black, by the Celtic part of his subjects, the soubriquet descending to his family

[2] Though eight thanes of Fife in two hundred years seems a large number even for those troublous and bloodthirsty times Moreover, Skene in his *Celtic Scotland* says there never were any thanes of Fife, thane being a Saxon title

The seven thanes after ' Fife Duff ' (*sic*) are thus given in the Drummuir MS. .

' Duff Mc Duff, a man like unto his father, who was killed fighting against the Danes Infgaous, that is the warlike Fife

Dufaganus, that is the Little Duff, '' a man little in body but great in virtue ''

Colbanus, that is the white Prince or Thane '' He did not degenerate from his ancestors '' Malcolm, dyed in the year 918.

Constantine his son and heir did govern that province of Fife and dyed in the tyme of King Duncan the first, that mild king who was barbarously murdered by Mc Beth the Tyran Duncan the first, called the great Macduff, a man beyond all praise, who killed Macbeth and settled Malcolm on the throne of his predecessors.'

[3] 'South of this upon the sea is Earls ferry, a little Fisher town which, as is said, Mc Duff, Earl of Fife, got erected into a royal Burgh because the Fishers here transported him over the Firth when he made his escape from Macbeth. They are said to have only 3 fishing boats ' (Sibbald's *Natural History of Fife and Kinross*, 1710)

who kept the unknown purpose of his heart (which was inimical to Macbeth) hidden longer and more carefully than the others.'

This extreme caution may be held to have been inherited by some of his descendants.

Modern Scottish critics, such as Dr. Skene in his edition of Fordun's *Chronicles*, and Robertson in his *Scotland under her Early Kings*, now throw doubt on the very existence of Macduff, treating him as an invention of Fordun, and they, moreover, seek to whitewash the grim Macbeth, who is held to have had a ' tanistic ' [1] right to the throne of Scotland.

Andrew Lang's *History of Scotland*, chapter iii., sets forth clearly how Malcolm II. himself was by some looked on as a usurper, and Lulach, son of Gruach (otherwise Lady Macbeth) was considered to have a better right to the throne than Duncan (grandson of Malcolm II., and father of Malcolm III.), who was ' assassinated ' by Macbeth, Maormor of Moray, the guardian of Lulach, Macbeth then reigning for nine years. The murder by Macbeth is stated, in the register of St. Andrews, to have taken place at Bothgowanan (the smith's house), supposed to be near the village of Auldearn, and not at Cawdor Castle. Lang does not mention Macduff.

Skene says: ' I consider Fordun to be wholly responsible for the ingeniously imagined interview of Macduff with Malcolm, and am also inclined to credit him with the entire invention of Macduff Thane of Fife, and the part which he plays in the reigns of Macbeth and Malcolm ' (Note in his edition of Fordun *Historians of Scotland*).[2]

Early Scottish history has not, as yet, been quite finally remodelled to exclude the old legends, and though Sir James Balfour Paul in his new *Scots Peerage*, and the writer in the *Dictionary of National Biography*, both speak of Macduff as a mythical character, the present writers, with the tacit support of Professor David Laing, continue to believe in the existence of this attractive personage and possible ancestor, who, according to John of Fordun, was mainly instrumental in placing Malcolm on the throne

---

[1] Tanistry : from Gaelic *Tana*, a chief, was the Celtic system of succession, whereby the king or chief of the clan was the ablest male of the family in his generation, not necessarily the eldest.

[2] Other critics have advanced the theory that Fordun's *Chronicle* itself was a forgery of post-reformation times, but in any case it is not usually held to be possible that Andrew de Wynton, writing about 1420, could have copied from him, and *his* account of Macduff is at least as detailed as that of Fordun, occupying ten pages in Laing's edition, *Historians of Scotland*. It is true that nothing is known personally of the writer called John of Fordun, save the tradition as to the date of his death, but this alone could not serve to annihilate the claim of his work to authenticity The long account of the conversation between Malcolm and Macduff, to which, through the medium of Boece and Hollinshed, Shakespeare was so much indebted, is, of course, a fiction, though possibly founded on a traditional fact, and even such writers as Xenophon and Thucydides have used this method of giving life to authentic chronicles, nor been thereby discredited.

which had been usurped by Macbeth,[1] or, as he is called in the *Latin Chronicles*, ' Maccabeus.' [2]

According, then, to legendary history, Macduff defeated Macbeth at the battle of Lumphanan, 1056, and in reward Malcolm, King of Scotland, bestowed upon him the following privileges (Andrew de Wynton, book vi. chapter xix.) :

1. That he should be created Earl of Fife, and that he and his successors as Lords of Fife should have the right of placing the kings of Scotland on the throne at their coronation. This right, and also that of crowning the king, was exercised by Isabel Duff, Countess of Buchan, who crowned King Robert Bruce in 1306, and was in consequence imprisoned by the English Edward in a cage (or dungeon so-called) at Berwick Castle, for three years.

2. That he and his successors should lead the van of the Scots army whenever the royal banner was displayed.

3. That if he or any of his kindred ' committed slaughter of suddenty ' [3] they should have peculiar sanctuary and obtain remission on payment of an atonement in money. (Some versions of the legend limit this right of sanctuary to the waters of the Firth of Forth between Macduff's own burgh of Earlsferry (Elie) and the Haddington coast, and say that if any fugitive embarked from the Fifeshire coast, the pursuers were not allowed to start until the boat was half-way across the Firth.)

These privileges must be quoted in Wyntoun's [4] own words :

' Quken Makbeth Fynlayk thus wes slane
Offe Fyffe Makduff that tyme the Thane
For his traivaille till his bounte
At Malcolme as Kyng askyd these thre

1 Fyrst, till hys sete fra the awtare [5]
That he sulde be the Kynge's ledare
And in that set, thare set hym downe
Till take his Coronatyowne,

---

[1] From the old *Irish Peerage* .

' The family of Duff or Macduf is of great antiquity in Scotland   Macduff Thane of Fife, one of the most powerful subjects in Scotland, excited a formidable revolt against the usurper Macbeth in the year 1056, which terminated in the defeat and death of Macbeth at Lunfanan in Aberdeenshire 5 Dec and the restoration of King Malcolm iii to the throne of his ancestors   In reward Malcolm created him Earl of Fife, and bestowed on him many privileges to be enjoyed by himself and his successors. By the forfeiture of Murdoc D of Albus 1425 the title of Earl of Fife was vested in the Crown until it was revived in the person of William Duff, Lord Braco of Kilbryde '

[2] There was a Machabeus Duff in Cullen in 1312.

[3] Lord Hailes' *Annals of Scotland*, 1776   [4] Andro de Wyntoun, 1350-1422.

[5] Altar.

For hym and hys posteryte
Quhen-evyre the Kyng suld crownyd be

2 Efftyre that, the secound thyng
Wes, that he askyd at the Kyng
Till haue the waward[1] oft hys bataylle
Qwhat-evyr thai waie, wold it assaylle
That he and hys suld haive always
Quhen that the Kyng suld banare[2] rays
Or, gyff the Thane oft Fyff in were[3]
Or in till ost[4] wyth his powere
Ware, the waward suld governyd be
Be hym and his posteryte.

3 Efltyre this, the thryd askyng
That he askyt at the Kyng,
Gyve ony be suddane chawdmelle[5]
Hapnyd swa slayne to be
Be ony off the Thaynys kyne
Off Fyff the kynryk[6] all wyth-in
Gyve he swa slayne were gentill-man
Four and twenty markys than
For a yhwman[7] twelf markys ay
The slaare suld for kynbwt[8] pay,
And haive full remyssyone
Fra thin for all that actyowne.
Gyve ony hapyd hym to sla
That to that lawch[9] were bwndyn swa
Off that prvylage evyrmare
Partles[10] suld be the slaare
Off this lawch are thre capytale
That is the Blak Prest off Weddale
The Thayne off Fyffe, and the thryd syne
Quha ewyre be Lord off Abbyrnethyne.'

The existence of some special privileges is authenticated by the fact that in the Acts of the Scots Parliament of 1384, the Earl of Fife agrees to cause the new laws to be observed in his capacity as principal of the Law of Clan Macduff (*capitalis legis de Clan m'Duffc*).—Skene.

'The King also granted that to the Clan Macduff there should be perpetual regality, that is, that they should have the power of creating any persons in their tribe magistrates, or of appointing judges for administering the law in any action whatever, excepting the crime of *lese majesty*, and of recalling from

---

[1] Van.   [2] Banner.   [3] War   [4] Battle
[5] Brawl.   [6] King's power or jurisdiction   [7] Yeoman
[8] Compensation for slaughter of kindred   [9] Law.   [10] Having no part

any parts of the kingdom any one of the Clan Macduff, or of their country, who might be called in judgment, to their own judges ' (MS. History of Mackintoshes, quoted by Macfarlane in his *Genealogical Collections*).

In 1421, Johnson, as Stewart in Fife, received three gentlemen who had been concerned in the slaughter of Melvil of Glenbervy, to the Lach of Clan Macduff [1] (Macpherson's Notes to Sixth Book, Andro de Wyntoun's *Chronykil*).

The right of peculiar sanctuary is also sometimes associated with Macduff's Cross, near Newburgh, of which only ruins now remain. Sibbald gives an account of this cross, with the Latin inscription said to have been on it, and a rhyming paraphrase of the same, adding, ' If this be not a true account, it is at least ingenious and well invented.'

Sir John Skene, in his *De Verborum Significatione*, says : ' Gif ony man slayes, being within the ninth degree o' bluid to Macduffe, repair to the Cross, an' there declare his kinship,' at the same time presenting Macduff [2] with nine cows ' an' ane *colpendach* ' (a year-old cow), he was, after washing himself in a well near by, declared free ' O' ony sudden chawdmelle,' and could not again be tried.   In every instance the person claiming the protection of Macduff's law had to prove consanguinity or be immediately slain.

In the year 1390, Sir Alexander de Ogilvy was summoned to appear before the Earl of Strathearn's Court, ' holden ' at Fowlis, on December 9, to show cause why he ' spilt the bluid of William de Spalden.' Sir Bernard de Hadden (an ancestor of Lord Haldane) appeared on Sir Alexander's behalf, and pleaded that, as Sir Alexander had stood Macduff's law, he could not be again tried.   The defence was successful, and Sir Alexander got off without pain or penalties.

This early history is a most fascinating subject, but as it has, in truth, very little to do with the Duffs, we must pass on.

MACDUFF, eighth Thane of Fife, according to legend, thus became, in 1057, the first Earl.

His son DUFFAGAN, the second Earl, was, according to Sir James Dalrymple's *Historical Collections*, witness to a charter granted by King Alexander I. to Trinity Church at Scone, 1115.   According to the Drum-

----

[1] The Clan Macduff is therefore sometimes said to be the oldest of the Scottish Clans, and as such is mentioned in one of the Irish genealogical MSS Book of Leinster (Skene's *Celtic Scotland*), although, of course, the Duffs were never, strictly speaking, Highlanders at all, and had no habitation within the Highland line (as drawn by Skene) until after 1715, when some of them established themselves in the forfeited estates of the Earls of Mar

(Those who carried on their business in the town of Inverness in the seventeenth century scarcely form an exception)

[2] He does not explain how this was to be done.

muir MS. he was buried, like his father, in the ' royall buriall place at
Dumfermling.' ¹

The third Earl was CONSTANTINE, died 1127. He was witness to a
charter of the Monastery of Dunfermline.²

GILLMICHAEL, the fourth Earl, appears as a witness to the Foundation Charter of Holyrood Abbey in 1128, and to several other charters
of David I. In King David's Confirmation Charter to Dunfermline he
appears as Gillemichael Macduf. He died 1139.

His eldest son was DUNCAN, the fifth Earl, also frequently employed as
a witness by David I. and Malcolm IV. He died 1154, after having assisted
in 1153 at the coronation of King Malcolm IV., to whom he had been tutor.

The second son of Gillmichael was Hugh or Hugo, ancestor of the Earl
of Wemyss, who may be said to be the only thoroughly authenticated living
representative of the ancient Thanes of Fife, and bears the ancient arms
of the Fifes, ' the Scottish Lyon red and rampant upon a golden shield.'

According to Andrew de Wyntoun (the chronicler who devoted so much
space to the first Macduff), DUNCAN, fifth Earl of Fife, was appointed
Regent of Scotland during the minority of Malcolm IV. From other
younger sons of Gillmichael are said to be descended other branches of
the Duff family, but this statement is also made with regard to the younger

---

¹ But there is also a memorandum of a donation to the Culdees of Loch Leven by Etheldred, son of Malcolm, King of Scotland, Abbot of Dunkeld and Earl of Fife, of the same date
The authenticity of this donation has been questioned, and the possibility of its being a fabrica-
tion of later date is suggested by the fact that the names of Etheldred's two brothers, David
and Alexander, are given in the wrong order, Alexander being in reality the elder   It is this
donation which is used by those who wish to disprove the existence of Macduff the Thane and
first Earl of Fife, and the *Scots Peerage* gives Etheldred as the first earl   The king's son
may, of course, have held the title of earl while the subject was only thane, and may have
resigned it later   This would account for the fact that some ancient trees give to the second
earl, son of Macduff, the thane and first earl, the unusual Saxon name of Etheldred.   As the
name of the son of the Saxon Queen Margaret it is, of course, natural and supported by
history, it is held by some writers that Macduff's son might have taken it out of courtesy.
Lord Hailes suggests that Etheldred had the custody of the earldom of Fife during the
minority of Macduff's son, and hence received the title of Earl of Fife as being ' *custos comitatus* '
The children of Malcolm and Margaret are thus given by Andrew de Wyntoun in book vii
chapter iii of the *Cronykil of Scotland*

> ' Malcolm Kyng be lawchfull get
> Had on hys wyff Saynt Margret,
> Sownnys sex and dowchtrys twa
> Off thir sownnys thre off tha
> Wes Edmund, Edward, Ethelrede
> Kyng off thire nowcht ane we red
> Bot Edgare, Alysawndyre and Dawy *yhyng*,*
> Ilkane off thir wes crownyd a kyng '

' In the *Annals of Ulster*, Constantine is called Constantine Macduffe   * young

sons of the sixth earl   The fifth Earl left two sons, Duncan and a younger one, sometimes called SHAW, from whom descend the Mackintoshes.

DUNCAN, the sixth Earl, succeeded his father in 1154. He was Justiciary of Scotland in the reign of William the Lion, and, as had been the case with former earls of Fife, he was the first to witness all charters, and was one of the peers who treated for the monarch's ransom. He married Ada or Ela, niece of Malcolm IV., ' and got with her in tocher the lands of Strathmiglo, Falkland, Kettle, Rathkillet in Fife, and Strathbran in Perthshire' (Sibbald). He founded the nunnery of North Berwick. He died in 1203, leaving three sons : MALCOLM, DUNCAN, and DAVID.

MALCOLM, the seventh Earl, founded the Abbey of Culross in 1217, and made a donation to the episcopate of Moray to which his brothers, Duncan and David, were witnesses. He married Matilda, daughter of Gilbert, Earl of Strathearn, but died childless in 1229, and was buried in St. Servan's Church, Culross.

His brother DUNCAN, married Alicia Corbet, daughter of Walter Corbet of Makerstoun, and their son was the eighth Earl. Upon the third, DAVID, his father settled the lands of Strathbogie,[1] which he had obtained from William the Lion, and his son John married Ada, heiress of Athole, and from them a (probably mythical) descent has been traced to David Duff of Muldavit who will appear later.

Mr. Malcolm's *Collections*, belonging to the Earl of Wemyss, also affirm that 'the Duffs of Craighead, which is the same as Muldavit,' were descended from Duncan, sixth Earl of Fife, who died 1203, through this third son.

MALCOLM, the eighth Earl, succeeded his uncle in 1228. He married Helen, daughter of Llewellyn, Prince of Wales, and died 1266. He was a member of the regency appointed, in 1255, under the influence of Henry III. of England, and, with his fellow regents, swore an oath that he would restore the Queen of Scotland and her child, when she went to England for her first confinement.

COLBAN, the ninth Earl, died in 1270; he had a younger brother Macduff, who fell gallantly fighting under the standard of Wallace at the battle of Falkirk, July 22, 1298.[2]

---

[1] ' Duncan Meduff, Earl of Fife, got Strathbogie from King William the Lion, who died 1214, and left it to his second son David, and the Duffs were therefore proprietors of the whole county of Strathbogie about a hundred years before the Gordons left the borders of England or the Grants came into Strathspey.'

[2] A MS. history of the Duffs, written in Latin in 1599, states that Duncan or Macduff (he probably had both names), brother of the ninth earl, who was killed at the battle of Falkirk 1298, fighting for Wallace, had a younger son Malcolm, who married a daughter of Duncan, Thane of Cawdor, and was progenitor of the Duffs of the North   It will be noted that no opportunity is lost by the old chroniclers of providing a possible ancestor for these prolific ' Duffs of the North.'   Cf ' Dufforum Stirpe, hodie prepotente inter Borealis Scotos ' (Drummuir MS)

TRADITIONAL DESCENT OF THE OLD EARLS OF FIFE.

I

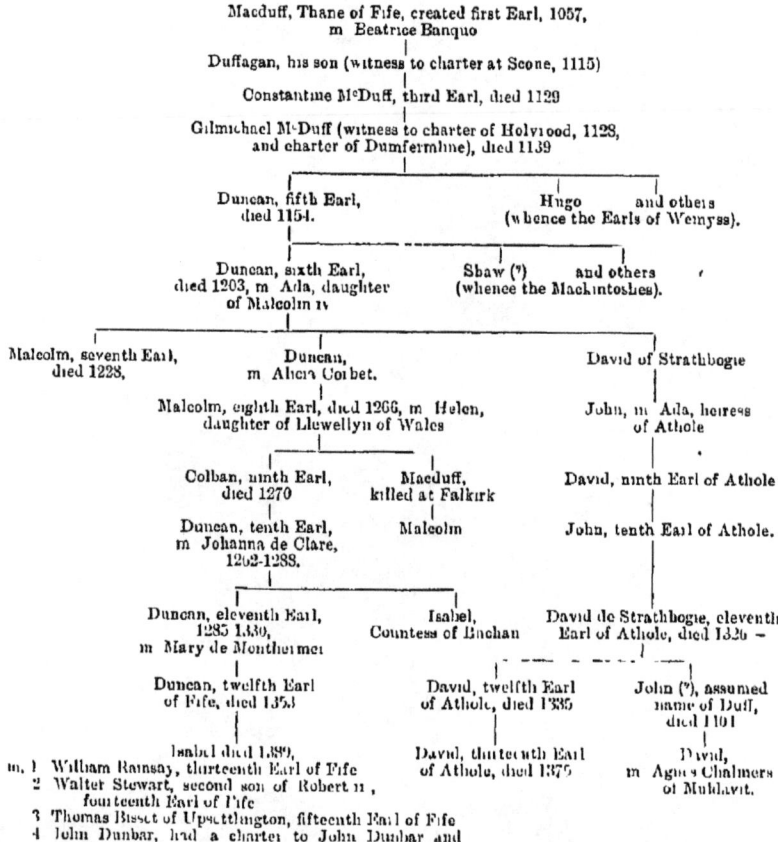

Macduff, Thane of Fife, created first Earl, 1057,
m Beatrice Banquo

Duffagan, his son (witness to charter at Scone, 1115)

Constantine McDuff, third Earl, died 1129

Gilmichael McDuff (witness to charter of Holyrood, 1128,
and charter of Dumfermline), died 1139

Duncan, fifth Earl, died 1154.

Hugo and others
(whence the Earls of Wemyss).

Duncan, sixth Earl, died 1203, m Ada, daughter of Malcolm IV

Shaw (?) and others
(whence the Mackintoshes).

Malcolm, seventh Earl, died 1228,

Duncan, m Alicia Corbet.

David of Strathbogie

Malcolm, eighth Earl, died 1266, m Helen, daughter of Llewellyn of Wales

John, m Ada, heiress of Athole

Colban, ninth Earl, died 1270

Macduff, killed at Falkirk

David, ninth Earl of Athole

Duncan, tenth Earl, m Johanna de Clare, 1262-1288.

Malcolm

John, tenth Earl of Athole.

Duncan, eleventh Earl, 1285 1336, m Mary de Monthermer

Isabel, Countess of Buchan

David de Strathbogie, eleventh Earl of Athole, died 1326 –

Duncan, twelfth Earl of Fife, died 1353

David, twelfth Earl of Athole, died 1335

John (?), assumed name of Duff, died 1401

Isabel died 1389,
m, 1 William Ramsay, thirteenth Earl of Fife
2 Walter Stewart, second son of Robert II,
fourteenth Earl of Fife
3 Thomas Bisset of Upsettlington, fifteenth Earl of Fife
4 John Dunbar, had a charter to John Dunbar and
Isabella, Countess of Fife, of the earldom of Fife

David, thirteenth Earl of Athole, died 1375

David, m Agnes Chalmers of Muldavit.

After Isabel's death (1389), without heirs, the earldom and lands passed (by her will, made in 1371) to Robert, Earl of Menteith, third son of Robert II, and brother to Isabel's second husband. When he and his son, Murdoch, were executed in 1425, the title of Earl of Fife reverted to the Crown, to be revived in 1759.

DUNCAN, the tenth Earl, born 1263, was, during his minority, a ward of Alexander, Prince of Scotland, son to Alexander III. He was admitted to possession of his earldom in 1284. He was chosen one of the six regents on the death of Alexander III. in the Parliament of Scone, April 2, 1286, and took an oath to maintain the rights of the Maid of Norway. He married Johanna de Clare, daughter of the Earl of Gloucester. He was basely murdered at Petpollock, September 25, 1288, by Sir Patrick Abernethy and Sir Walter Percy, the latter being subsequently executed for the murder. ' He was most worthie of a longer life ' (Drummuir MS).

DUNCAN, the eleventh Earl, born in 1285, was therefore only three years old at the time of his father's death, and was brought up at the English Court. At the coronation of John Bahol at Scone in 1292, being a minor (only seven years old) he could not perform the ceremony, and John de St. John was appointed as his deputy.

His sister Isabel, who was a good deal older, subsequently exercised the hereditary family right at the second coronation of Robert Bruce on May 29, 1306, and this in spite of the fact that her husband, John Comyn, third Earl of Buchan, was an enemy of the Bruce.

Duncan married, in 1306, Mary de Monthermer, grand-daughter of Edward I.,[1] and shortly after returned to Scotland, where he espoused the cause of the Bruce, received from him the charters of the earldom of Fife and the baronies of O'Neil in Aberdeenshire, Kinnoul in Perthshire, and Calder in Midlothian. He did good service at the battle of Donnibristle and was the first of the earls who signed the celebrated letter to the Pope from the Parliament of Aberbrothock, asserting the independence of Scotland, April 6, 1320. He was taken prisoner at the fatal battle of Dupplin, August 12, 1332, and assisted at the coronation of Edward Bahol at Scone, on September 24 following, placing him in the regal chair, as his sister had done for Bruce twenty-seven years before. He probably acquired his liberty as the price of his assistance on the occasion, as the presence of the Earl of Fife or his representative was, in those days, considered essential to the validity of a Scottish coronation.

He was killed at the battle of Halidown Hill, 1333 [2]

DUNCAN, the twelfth and last Earl of Fife in the male line from the great Macduff, fought on the side of David II after his return from France, and took for him the castle of St. Andrews. He accompanied him to England

---

[1] On January 28, 1319, King Edward II. granted a safe-conduct to his beloved niece Maria, Countess of Fife, to go to Scotland to join her husband

[2] According to Sir James Balfour Paul's *Peerage*, this Earl and the next are the same, i e Duncan the eleventh Earl, or, as the *Peerage* styles him, the tenth, was not killed at Halidown Hill, but survived until 1353, and left the daughter Isabel

in 1346, where he was taken prisoner at the battle of Durham and tried for treason, but pardoned on account of his relationship on his mother's side to Edward III.[1] He died without male issue in 1353, and with him the Duffs or Macduffs, Earls of Fife, became extinct. He was succeeded in his estates by his daughter Isabel, presumably called after her intrepid great-aunt.[2] While still a child she had been made a prisoner at Perth by Edward Baliol. She was four times married, but had no children :

1. To William Ramsay of Colluthie, styled the thirteenth Earl of Fife. He witnessed a charter of King David II., 1358, and obtained from the king a charter erecting Cupar into a free burgh.

2. To Walter Stewart, second son of King Robert II. He died in 1360 or 1361 ; he was styled the fourteenth Earl.

3. To Thomas Bisset of Upsettlington. He obtained a charter of the earldom from David II., June 8, 1362, and is styled, by Sibbald, the fifteenth Earl.

4. To John Dunbar. Among the missing charters is one to John Dunbar and Isabella, Countess of Fife, of the earldom of Fife.[3] John was the sixteenth Earl.

Isabel, who died in 1389, left all her lands to her brother-in-law by her second husband, Robert, Earl of Menteith, afterwards Duke of Albany, to whom also the title of Earl of Fife seems to have passed by virtue of some shadowy right on the part of his wife, Lady Margaret Menteith, or, more probably, simply by royal favour. In any case, after the execution of Robert, Duke of Albany, and his son Murdoch for treachery, in 1425, the title of Earl of Fife reverted to the Crown, and disappeared from the peerage for over three hundred years, until revived in 1759.[4]

---

[1] See papers at the Record Office

[2] Or aunt. See Note 2, p 10

[3] Robertson's *Index of Missing Charters.*

[4] Many of the above particulars are taken from a very old manuscript tree and other ancient MSS preserved in various branches of the family, and have been carefully collated with all the early historical authorities and modern commentators, but the authors are well aware that their conclusions on various disputed points are open to criticism, and they give them for what they are worth, as embodying the traditions of the family, supported by its own archives.

CHAPTER II

DUFFS OF MULDAVIT

FROM about the same period as that of the extinction of the direct line of the family of the old Earls of Fife dates the appearance of the family of Duffs of Muldavit, which has a well-authenticated record, supported by Crown charters and Privy Council records for two hundred and fifty years. It is, however, difficult to connect it authoritatively with the Thanes of Fife.[1]

The bald statement, found in some old family trees, that 'David Duff of Muldavit, who died in 1375, was grandson of Duncan, thirteenth Earl of Fife,' is obviously false, for the thirteenth Earl was one of the husbands of the childless Countess Isabel, and if Duncan, twelfth Earl, is meant, the question of dates proves a stumbling-block. Moreover, Isabel is generally said to have been the only child.

However, as we have already seen, many of the earlier Earls of Fife had younger sons, and there is a perfectly possible descent for the Muldavit family from the fourth, the sixth, or the eighth Earl. Baird quotes a story of old William Duff of Inverness, son of Adam of Clunybeg, when 'taking a cheerful glass in company with the then Earl of Wemyss and MacIntosh of Moy, Duff's grandson-in-law, who were his guests, and the question was started somehow or other which of them was representative of the old Thanes of Fife. Provost Duff spake not a word till Lord Wemyss and MacIntosh had pled their respective pretensions with a very serious air, but all in good humour; then he said, "Ha, ha! gentlemen, if I had Lord Weems' estate and MacIntosh's following, I think I would have as good title to be Thane of Fife as any of ye."' This, of course, is of no real value as evidence, but he was obviously referring to the linking of the Muldavit family to the old Earls of Fife, and the descent of his own father from the Muldavits, and shows that the claims were well known even in those days. Baird, the only previous historian of the family, says, on the authority of Sibbald, that two younger sons of the family of the Earls of Fife left their own country and came north, 'one to the shire of

[1] Jervise in his well-known book on epitaphs, having gone carefully into the subject with all the data then at his disposal, gives it as his opinion that the connection of the Duffs of Craighead or Muldavit with the ancient Earls of Fife is pure assertion, founded on no evidence

Perth, where he purchast the Lands of Findowie in Stratherle, and the other to Banffshire, where he purchast Craighead or Moldavit in the Boyn.' Dr. Cramond, in his slashing refutation of all claim on the part of the Duke of Fife to antiquity of family, published in the *Scotsman*, July 29, 1889, quotes this with scorn. But obviously neither he nor Baird had taken the trouble to verify the quotation from Sibbald. It really runs thus (edition 1710, Sibbald's *Natural History of Fife and Kinross*): ' There are several cadets of the house, the predecessors of Fanduy, Craigtown and others.' Baird obviously wished to identify this with Craighead, but it is at least equally possible that Sibbald may have been referring to Craigston, belonging in his day to Patrick Duff.[1]

The family of Muldavit has, from the beginning of the fifteenth century, a well-authenticated family tree:

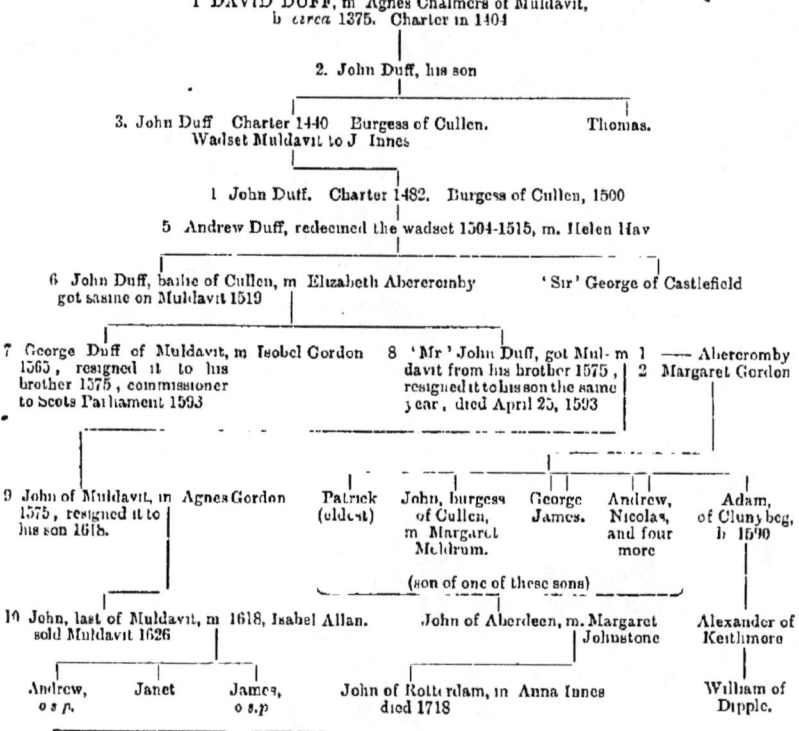

1 DAVID DUFF, m Agnes Chalmers of Muldavit, b *circa* 1375. Charter in 1404

2. John Duff, his son

3. John Duff Charter 1440 Burgess of Cullen. Wadset Muldavit to J Innes Thomas.

4 John Duff. Charter 1482. Burgess of Cullen, 1500

5 Andrew Duff, redeemed the wadset 1504-1515, m. Helen Hay

6 John Duff, bailie of Cullen, m Elizabeth Abercromby got sasine on Muldavit 1519 ' Sir ' George of Castlefield

7 George Duff of Muldavit, m Isobel Gordon 1565 , resigned it to his brother 1575 , commissioner to Scots Parliament 1593

8 ' Mr ' John Duff, got Muldavit from his brother 1575 , resigned it to his son the same year , died April 25, 1593

1 —— Abercromby 2 Margaret Gordon

9 John of Muldavit, m Agnes Gordon 1575 , resigned it to his son 1615.

Patrick (eldest) John, burgess of Cullen, m Margaret Meldrum. George James. Andrew, Nicolas, and four more Adam, of Clunybeg, b 1590

(son of one of these sons)

10 John, last of Muldavit, m 1618, Isabel Allan. sold Muldavit 1626 John of Aberdeen, m. Margaret Johnstone Alexander of Keithmore

Andrew, o s p. Janet James, o s.p John of Rotterdam, m Anna Innes died 1718 William of Dipple.

[1] For Findowie, see chapter xxxv.

1. DAVID DUFF of Muldavit, son of John Duff,[1] for whom the date 1375 is given (and to whom and to his wife Agnes Chalmers ('de Camera'), daughter and heiress of Maud of Muldavit, a charter of the lands of Muldavit was granted in 1404 by Robert III.), is said to have been descended from a younger son of the fifth or sixth Earl, but no proof of this has ever been given, and no one living has seen the above quoted charter, once in the possession of the Earl of Findlater, and given by him to the Earl of Fife. It is quoted in Robertson's *List of Missing Charters*, where the names are given as Maldakatu (Muldavit) and Baldavy [2]

The later charters may be seen in the *Scottish Records* and the *Registrum Magni Sigilli*.

2. JOHN, the second Duff owner of Muldavit, flourished in the reign of King James I. of Scotland, 'as appears by the charter to his son in his lifetime, though it does not appear that he ever expede a charter to himself' (Baird).

3. JOHN, the third of Muldavit, his successor, had a charter from James II. during the lifetime of his father:

'Apud Edinburche, 12 Feb. 1440. Rex concessit Johanni Dufe filio et heredi Joh. Dufe et heredibus ejus terram que vocatur Fyndachtefield, jacentem ex parte occidentali acquae de Culane, quam dictus Joh. pater personaliter in castro de Edinburche resignavit. Reddend annuatim regi, dictus Joh. heredes sui vel assignati i mare et taciend sectum cum bladis dicti tem. ad molendinum burgi de Culane debitam et consuetam. Riservato libero tenemento dicte Joh. patri et rationabili tertia sponse ejus cum contigerit.'

This John had a brother Thomas, as shown by a notarial instrument in the charter room at Cullen House, which narrates that 'in the presence of the notary and witnesses underwritten, in full Court in the Court House, compeared James Ogilvy of Drumnakeith and Thomas Duff, baillies of the burgh of Cullen, with the councillors and fellow-burgesses thereof, and in a high and intelligible, yet sufficiently lamentable voice, deplored the abuses and confusions into which misgovernment had brought the affairs

---

[1] A monument, removed from the church of Cullen in 1792 by James, second Lord Fife, is supposed to represent John Duff, father of David. The date of his death, 1404, being cut in Arabic figures, not in use at that period, points to the hand of the restorer, anxious to emphasise the antiquity of the family, and to give the same date as the charter

[2] In the inventory of charters at Cullen House, the absence of this, the first charter, is noted in the following words

'This charter, at Lord Fife's earnest desire, was given up to him, and his letter of thanks, dated 19th Nov. 1759, is put up in its place.'

The date of the charter is there given as February 5, 1403 (old style).

It was printed in the Spalding Club collections from this 'copy in private hands,' which has now disappeared

of the burgh, and they agreed to elect certain discreet and understanding burgesses, to whom they gave the power of setting in tack all lands, mills, and others belonging to the said burgh, etc., etc. Done on March 16, 1480-1. Witnesses—James Ogilvy of Drumnakeith, John Duff, senior, and Thomas Duff, senior, brother-german to said John.' John Duff wadset (that is, mortgaged), Muldavit to one James Innes

4. JOHN, fourth of Muldavit, his son, had this wadset confirmed in the following terms :

'Apud Edinburghi, 13 April 1482. Rex confirmavit cartam Johannis Duff, burgensis di Culane qua, pro certa summa pecuniæ vendidit et alienavit Jacobo Innes de eodem heredibus ejus et assignatis terras di Maudavat. vic Banff.' [1]

The house of Muldavit, of which no trace now remains, is said to have stood 'upon a cliff just above the burn of Cullen, opposite to the magnificent mansion of Cullen House.' Exactly the same description is given by Gordon of Straloch of the site of Craighead. Possibly the house on the estate of Muldavit was called Craighead. The latter name does not occur until a century later, and may have been applied only to the mansion built on that site by Margaret Gordon of Cairnburrow, wife of the great-grandson of the John Duff who died in 1482.[2] In the Balbithan MS [3] it is stated that ' she built the house of Craighead which is now reazed.' It was in ruins in 1732.[4]

5. John was succeeded in 1500 by ANDREW DUFF, said by Baird to be his son, but the *Registrum Magni Sigilli*, 1504, says nephew (*nepos Johannis*), though the word may mean, as it often does, grandson, and refer to John, third of Muldavit, brother of Thomas, leaving out Andrew's immediate predecessor. In any case, he redeemed the wadset upon Muldavit granted by his grandfather, John Duff :

'Apud Linlithgow, 16 June 1504. Rex conformavit cartam Jac. Innes de Rothybrysbane, filii et heredis quondam Jac. Innes de eodem, qua concessit Andrae Duff et heredibus ejus quibuscunque terras di Muldavet vic Banff ; quae quondam John Duff, avus dicti Andrae, dicto quondam Jac. Innes parti alienavit sub reversione certi summa pecuniæ quam dictus And. persolvebat ' (*Scottish Records : Accounts of the Lord High Treasurer*, 1504).

Andrew married Helen Hay, grandchild of John Hay, Lord of the Forest of Boyne, Enzie and Tillibady. After his death, Helen built the

---

[1] The confirmation is dated March 13, 1481

[2] This John Duff, the burgess of Cullen (see above), raised an action in 1493 against one Ogilvie re the lands of Findachtyfield, which the Duffs claimed under a charter of Robert the Bruce (Acta Audit 170)

[3] Printed in the *House of Gordon*, Spalding Club, 1903   [4] Ramsay

Duff aisle in the church of Cullen, and left some land for its upkeep,[1] and placed the following inscription in the church : ' John Hay, Lord of the Forest Bon, Aze, Tolbovil, gudsir to Elen Hay yt bigit yrs Ile feſt a chaplaii heir to sing personali of his landis of Ordihuf,' with the craftsman's Z mark.

Round the window is also : ' Sant anis chaplan heir dotat yt acre gud croft land in cula sal be a gud singar of hali liſ but odir service dati resident to pray for Elen Hay and hir baimis his fundors at gift of Jon Duf and his aris of Maldavit and faling yarof at gift of ye balzeis and comunite of Cula per Elena Hay.'

On the west side : ' Elene Hay Jon Duffis modr of Maldavit yat maid yis Ile ye chaplanrie,' and on two corner stones : ' per Elena Hay, soli Deo honor et Gloria.' [2]

6. Andrew Duff died in 1519 according to Baird, but according to the Decennial List of Heirs he was dead in 1515, leaving two sons. JOHN, sixth of Muldavit, who succeeded him, was served heir in 1520. Helen Hay, John's mother, had married again, one Alexander Dick, who seems to have been appointed guardian to John Duff, for in the *Register of the Privy Seal, Scotland*, date July 21, 1515, there is :

' Ane letter to Alexander Dyk his airis and assignaris, of the ward of all lands and annualis that pertinct to unquile Andio Duff of Muldavit, and now, be his deecis, being in the kyngis hands be resoun of ward for all the tyme thereof, and the marriage of Johne Duff his sown and are, and failzeand of hym of any other are or airis male or femell,' etc.

---

[1] *Cullen Records*

[2] After the aisle fell into disrepair it appears to have been used for the interments of any who chose to pay for it, and in the next century Agnes Gordon, wife of John Duff, who is summoned as a recusant for refusing to come to church, gives as her reason that ' there was a man buried in her husband's ile without the consent of her and her friends ' In 1624 a process was issued against her 'George Douglas declared that Agnes, having sworn and subscribed to the true religion, refuseth to hear the word in his kirk because there was a man buried in her husband's yle and burial place, upon the night, without the consent of her and her friends ' The process dragged on until 1633, when Agnes is spoken of as of great age, and was therefore treated with lemency 'The Presbyterie, considering that she has been avers from the treuth all her dayes, and that of lait she is induced to hear the word now and then elsequher and to communicat, and that being of greit age she cannot be ane ordinir heiriar, wills him to continue, until the Assemblies adwys be had ' She was, however, still alive in 1641. In 1637 there was further quarrelling about this aisle. Several brethren, namely George Ogilvie in Cullen, James Ogilvie, sometime of Glassa', and certain other parishioners of Cullen, gave in a report that Mr James Hay of Muldavit had erected a double desk on the east side of the Isle reaching further, much of a foot, beyond the pend (arch) of the church, whereas Mr Pat Duff sometime of Darbruich and his predecessors had their burials ' (*Presbytery Records of Fordyce*).

The decision of the bailies was that the desk be removed (*Cullen Court Books*).

Adam Duff of Clunybeg was buried in this aisle See next chapter

The second son was GEORGE DUFF, a priest, Provost of Cullen, chaplain in the parish church there, who in 1562 renders accounts to the bailies of Cullen. He acquired the lands of Castlefield, and left them by a charter (apud Dalkeith, 10 July 1575)[1] to his natural son John, afterwards legitimated, whose heirs were to carry the name and arms of Duff. John Duff of Castlefield appears as a witness to a charter in 1583.

George Duff appears in the family trees as ' Sir ' George.[2]

John, elder brother of George, had a precept of sasine on the lands of Muldavit, apud Banff 1520.[3] He also appears in the roll of the bailies of Cullen in 1521. According to Cullen Records, he married Elizabeth Abercromby.

7. He left two sons, GEORGE and JOHN, seventh and eighth lairds of Muldavit. The first resigned his lands in favour of his brother.[4] He was commissioner for the burgh of Cullen, and, according to the Acts of the Parliament of Scotland, was present with other commissioners at the Tolbooth, Edinburgh, in 1593.

According to Baird he never married, but later researches have elicited the fact that he married Isobel, daughter of Patrick Gordon of Drummoy, and had a daughter Isobel, who married another Patrick Gordon, son of

---

[1] 'Apud Dalkeith, 10 July 1575 Rex confirmavit cartam quondam D Georgio Duff portionam de Castlefield, qua pro servitus et laboribus sibi impensis, consessit Johanni Duff filio suo naturali, quondam bastardo, sed tunc legitimate, quartam et octavum partem terrarum de Castlefield per se modo occupat Tenend dicto Joh et heredibus masc ejus de corpore legit procreandis, quibus deficientibus, heredibus masc Mag Johannis Duff in Connes de corpore legitime procreatis, quibus def heredibus rege Reservato vitali reddito dicto Georgio, cum precepto sasine directo Alexandro Syme, burgensi in Cullane

Test M Jo. Duf in Connes
Geo Duf. filio quondam William D '

Dr David Hay Fleming in his *Reformation in Scotland* gives a list of the sons and daughters of the celibate clergy of Scotland, recorded to have been legitimated at this period, taken from the *Registers of the Great Seal of Scotland*

[2] About 1540 the title ' Sir ' was applied in Scotland to such of the clergy as had not proceeded in the course of their studies at the University to the degree of Master of Arts ' Master ' then implied a higher position than ' Sir,' which was equivalent to a B A (Cramond).

[3] 'Banff, 1520 Vicecomes respondebit pro 40 lib de firmis terrarum de Muldavit cum pertinem jacentium infra belliam suam existentium in manibus regis per spatium 5 annorum ult, elaps, sasina non recuperata et pro 4 ti de relevis earundum regi debitis per sasinam datam Johanni Duff de eisdem apud Edinburgh.'

[4] 'Apud Hammyton, 28 April 1551. Regina confirmavit cartam quondam Georgii Duff de Muldavit' (but Mr Maitland Thomson says the word quondam here is an error) 'qua propter servitium sibi impensum concessit fratri suo germano Johanni Duff heredibus ejus et assignatis, terras de Muldavit cum molendino ejusdem vic Banff Riservato dicto Geo libero tenemento.

Test Jac Duff in Tellemacht
Dom Georgius Duff, preposite college de Culane '

C

Cairnburrow (Gordonstown Tables, *House of Gordon*, ii.). He is not known to have had any sons.

8. JOHN, the eighth owner from the original David, got a charter for himself on Muldavit from Queen Mary, November 26, 1550, and another upon a croft, of which the teindsheaves are said to belong to the vicar of the parish church of Rathven.[1] The witnesses to this charter are George Duff, Muldavit, brother of John, and Andrew Duff, probably another brother, and the same man who had sasine on Clunybeg, 1573. This John Duff, who was evidently an M.A., and is always described as 'Mr.', became a burgess of Aberdeen in 1581. He married, first, Abercromby of Skeith's daughter,[2] and had one son, JOHN, who succeeded to Muldavit; secondly, Margaret Gordon, daughter of Cairnburrow,[3] by whom he is said to have had eleven sons. 'He was servitor to George, Earl of Huntly, and tackman in the lands of Rannes. Service in Chancery gives his death April 25, 1593' (Rose). He lived for some time in Conage in Rannes, and is frequently so described.

In the Balbithan MS., now published as part of the *House of Gordon*, New Spalding Club, Margaret Gordon is thus described:

'Margaret Gordon, second daughter of John Gordon of Cairnburrow, first married the goodman of Craighead (which is the same as Muldavit), Mr. John Duff, who bore to him eleven sons, of whom is come Braccho and all the opulent sirname of Duffs; after the Craighead's death, she married the goodman of Milton Ogilvie in the parish of Keith; she built the house of Craighead, now reazed; she built the house of Milton-Achoynanie and the steeple of Keith; her name and her husband's is on the house of Achoynanie, dated 1601. She was interred in her paternal burying place in the kirk of Botarie.'

The eldest of her sons was PATRICK of Darbruch, who married Janet Ogilvie (thus further complicating the relationships between the families of Duff and Ogilvie)[4]

In one place where William Rose mentions the eleven sons of 'Mr.' John Duff and Margaret Gordon, he adds (for his own future guidance, apparently) 'Collect who they were'—but does not seem to have done so very satisfactorily.

Those we know of were as follows:

---

[1] Pronounced Raffan, near Buckie

[2] No record has been found, but the fact of a first marriage is certain

[3] Margaret's brother, William Gordon of Rothiemay, and his son John Gordon, were burned in Frendraught Castle by Crichton of Frendraught, October 1630. This event is commemorated in a well-known ballad, 'The Burning of Frendraught'

[4] Margaret, widow of John Duff, married Walter Ogilvie. Her eldest son by John Duff, Patrick of Darbruch, married Janet Ogilvie, and her husband's grand-daughter, by the son of his first wife, Margaret Duff, married George Ogilvie of Clunes, 1623

PATRICK, JOHN, GEORGE, JAMES, ANDREW, ALEXANDER, ADAM, and NICHOLAS, with three others (of whom one was possibly WILLIAM and another THOMAS).

PATRICK of Darbruich, actually second son of 'Mr.' John Duff, is always described as the *eldest* son of 'Mr.' John Duff and Margaret Gordon. He would seem to have been nearly grown up at the time of his father's death in 1593. In 1599 he granted a charter of the lands of Badcheir, near Dufftown, to John Gordon of Buckie (*Gordon Castle Charters*), who had in 1580 made them over to Patrick's father, Mr. John Duff (*ibid*). He had a tack of Darbruich (part of the Muldavit property in Deskford, where there was, until recently, a farm of that name) in 1601, and sold it to Andrew Hay of Rannes in 1625, and Tullochallum (which his father had got from Gordon of Auchindoun in 1592) to Leslie in the same year. He was burgess of Cullen 1623.

In 1623 the Master of Deskford resigned to Patrick Duff, burgess of Cullen, lands which had belonged to the second prebendary of Cullen. There was a discharge granted in 1611 by Adam Duff in Ardrone to his brother Mr. Patrick Duff of Darbruich of an obligation for a hundred merks, which the said Adam Duff borrowed. In 1611 Adam also discharged Mr. Patrick, his brother, of the sum of four hundred merks left to him by his father after the decease of Margaret Gordon, his mother, which presumably took place in the year 1611, and the above deed was not registered until nine years afterwards (*Deed Book of Banff*, September 10, 1620).

JOHN DUFF, third son, was servitor to the Laird of Balveny, and witness to a deed of 1630. This is the second John in the family of 'Mr.' John Duff of Muldavit, the other being by his first wife. He is witness to a deed of 1618, and is referred to by his brother, who executes the deed, as 'John Duff, my brother-german.' Either he or his brother was prebendary of St. Anne's in 1617.

GEORGE, described in his old age as 'of Whynty.' 'He did marry Janet Allan' (Rose MS.). '1596 Testis, Geo. Duff, filio quondam M. Joannis Duff de Maldavatt' (*Reg. Mag. Sig.*).

JAMES, in Cullen, also apparently a burgess of Aberdeen. 'He had pertaining to him in Cullen the croft called the straight croft, and the Deip slack and several other crofts. He died on Charitymas in France 1663,' being apparently 'fugitate,' and his record in Cullen does not seem to have been very honourable.[1]

He left one son JOHN, afterwards in Aberdeen (John Duff, burgess of Aberdeen, son of James Duff in Cullen.—Rose MS.).

ANDREW lived in Cullen, and was an elder of the parish (1655-1657),

---

[1] He was frequently cited before the kirk-session and the presbytery for his evil deeds.

in which capacity he attended a meeting of the presbytery of Fordyce. He was possibly the same man who was afterwards a merchant burgess in Elgin, 1655.

Andrew also left descendants.[1]

'Andro' and his brother John were also witnesses for John Gordon of Findlater in 1660.

ALEXANDER is said to have been a messenger in Elgin.

ADAM, the most important of the eleven.

NICHOLAS, whom Rose tries to identify with Nicholas or Nicol Duff, town-clerk of Forres, but as the latter had two sons, Alexander and George, and in 1618 Nicholas Duff and his son George, both burgesses, are witnesses to a charter, it is obvious that this Nicholas cannot be the younger brother of Adam Duff, born in 1590, as that Nicholas could himself havebeen only twenty-six, and could not have had a son a burgess and valid witness.

There was one daughter MARGARET.

9. JOHN, the half-brother of all these, and ninth laird of Muldavit, 'Mr.' John Duff's son by his first wife, was served heir to him in certain lands in 1622, not long before his own death : [2]

'Joannes Duff, hoeres magistri Joannis Duff de Maldavit patris, in terris de Tarbruiche et New fosterseat ex parti orientali silvae di Bynwode ; officio forestariae praefatae silvae de Bynwoode in baronia seu dominis de Culsawerthe ' (From the *Early Scottish Heirs, Record Commission*, May 25, 1622).

This John Duff, ninth laird, the first of the family to be described as ' of Craighead,' got a charter upon the lands of Muldavit, during his father's lifetime, dated July 10, 1575, and another, February 24, 1610.[3] He was a Justice of the Peace for Banffshire, 1611. He married Agnes Gordon.[4]

In the Rose MS. there is the following note : ' John Duff, called younger of Craighead, in 1580 residing in Conas or Conage in Rannes, was not Margaret Gordon's son, but a son of John Duff of Muldavit and a daughter of Abercrombie of Skeith.' It seems obvious that a man who lived on a farm as tenant in 1580, whose son (John Duff, tenth of Muldavit, who married Isabel Allan) was married in 1618, must himself have been born

---

[1] In one of the papers at Drummuir, of the date 1666, referring to the marriage of Provost William and Janet Lockhart, reference is made to lands acquired from James Duff in Cullen, and to Isabel, Janet and James Duff or *Demiduff*, as lawfully charged to enter heirs in general to the deceased Andro Duff, to be holding of the immediate superior as the said William Duff holds. James in Cullen and Andrew were *presumably* these two of the younger uncles of William, sons of ' Mr.' John Duff and Margaret Gordon

[2] In those days, many years often elapsed between the death of the testator and the proving or acting upon the will, or entering upon an inheritance

[3] These two charters are now at Cullen House among the papers of Lord Seafield

[4] Their portraits, by a predecessor of Jamesone, are here reproduced.

JOHN DUFF OF MULDAVIT

Erroneously attributed to James same

before 1560, and could therefore not have been the son of the woman (Margaret Gordon) whose youngest children were born after her second marriage in 1601 to Walter Ogilvie. (She is known to have had two Ogilvie children—one son, John, and the daughter Margaret, married to John Stewart of Ardbreck, who will be mentioned later.) This fact seems to need no demonstration, and clearly proves a first marriage for ' Mr.' John Duff, though no record of it exists. Margaret Duff is first mentioned as wife in 1579 in a reversion to Gordon of Auchindoun. There is an instrument of John Duff's renunciation to Sir Patrick Gordon of Auchindoun of the half town and lands of Clunymore, Milton and Smithston, and the contract of wadset thereon, by payment of five hundred merks, dated February 6, 1584. His wife, Margaret Gordon, does not appear in this instrument, and it has been pointed out that the appearance of her name in the deed of five years earlier probably fixes the date of her marriage as having taken place some years only before that date.[1]

In a document in the charter room at Cullen House, dated March 31, 1612, John Duff of Muldavit (son of ' Mr.' John Duff and husband of Agnes Gordon), Mr. Patrick Duff of Darbruich his brother, Walter Duff, son of John Duff and present prebendary of St. Anne's, and Adam Duff, brother-german to Patrick Duff, confirm the right of James Lawtie, burgess of Cullen, to some lands granted in 1591 by John Duff (father of John, Patrick, and Adam) in liferent, to his son Adam and his own wife Margaret Gordon, and Patrick binds himself to obtain from Margaret Gordon, or her son Adam, all necessary titles to complete the sales. Adam would appear to have been young at the time of his father's death, probably three years old, and Patrick much older. John (ninth laird), eldest son of ' Mr.' John, married Agnes Gordon (the recusant mentioned on page 16), and in 1626 he and his son sold Muldavit to James Hay of Rannes, ' with the consent of Agnes Gordon his spouse, John his eldest son, and Isabel Allan, spouse of the said John, by charter, *apud Cullen.*' The signatures of these four persons may still be seen in the *Court Books of Cullen.* The elder John Duff (ninth laird), who had three other sons, Walter, prebendary of St. Anne's, James, the witness (baillie of Cullen), and William, as well as a daughter Margaret, who married George Ogilvie of Clunes, died in 1627 (Precept of Chancery, September 4, 1627).

From 1626 then the family is no longer ' of Muldavit.'

10. Of JOHN DUFF younger of Muldavit, tenth and last owner, and more properly described as of the Orchard, very little is known, except the following from the Presbytery Records of Fordyce :

---

[1] *Gordon Castle Charters.*

'29 *Sept.* 1624.—John Duffes of Craighead, elder and younger, are ordenet to be spoken to and conferit with, anent their not keeping of the Saboth and heiring of the word, be Mr. David Forester, and Mr. Patrick Darg quha said John Duff elder of Craighead had promessit to amend, and Mr. David Forester promersit to speak John Duff younger and to report his answer the next Presbyterie.'

After the death of the elder John there is another entry:

'10 *Dec.* 1628.—George Douglas, moderator, shews that John Duffe, sometymes of Muldavid is come to be resident in Cullen, wha is a profest Papist and contemner of the word. He is ordained to deal with him privatlie, and with his familie to observe ordour, and to report the fruit of his privat paines the next day of meeting.'

'18 *March* 1629.—George Douglas declares that John Duff being oftentymes desired be him to confer anent his doubts in religion postponed and would enter on no conference thereanent. The said Jhon, being summondit to this day apud acta is called and compeires, affirms that the caus of his not conferring wes his travell and many distractions about his affaires, alwise offered now to confere, to continue in hearing sermons, and to communicat at Pasch.'

'7 *April* 1630.—George Douglas reported that John Duff in Cullen, and Agnes Gordon his mother, had conformed.'

A copy on parchment of his marriage-contract to Isabella Allan exists among the Drummuir papers,[1] dated June 8, 1618, in which John Duff, his father, makes over to him the lands of Muldavit.

The text of the charter, in translation, is here given:

To all who will see or hear this charter, John Duff, of Maldavit, eternal greeting in the Lord.

Know that I, for the fulfilment of a charter on my part for a certain contract entered into and made between me, John Duff, for myself and undertaking the charge for John Duff the younger, my lawful first-born son, and for Agnes Gordon my wife, and John Duff the younger for himself, with the express consent and assent of his said father and mother, of one part, and Katharine Thornton, relict of the late William Allan, burgess of Aberdeen, and Andrew Kelly, burgess of the said city of Aberdeen, for themselves and undertaking the charge for Isabella Allan, lawful daughter born of the said late William Allan and the said Katharine Thornton, and the said Isabella Allan for herself, with the consent of her said

---

[1] One of the witnesses is ' John Duff, burgess of Cullen, my brother-german '; another is ' James Duff, my third lawful son ', and a John Duff, undescribed, also signs the document According to the instrument of sasine, Edinburgh, this John was a burgess of Aberdeen, and ' procurator legitime constitutus pro Issobella Allan futura conjuge dicti Joannis Duff apparan. de Muldavat ' He was, without doubt, a relative, and may have been John Duff of Boghole, who will appear later

AGNES GORDON
WIFE OF JOHN DUFF OF MULDUM

mother, of the other part, the present date at Aberdeen and Craighead, 23rd May and 8th June 1618. Also for the love and filial affection which I bear and have towards my beloved son, the aforesaid John Duff, and his future wife Isabella Allan, I have given, granted, alienated, sold . . . by title of pure sale, and have confirmed by this my present charter, to the aforesaid John Duff and Isabella Allan, his future wife, and the survivor, in joint enfeoffment in tail male, in default of which to the heir and assigns of the said John Duff, the whole and entire my lands of Maldavat, with manors, houses, buildings, dovecote, mill, mill-lands of the same, woods, parks, tofts, crofts . . . parts and appurtenances, lying within the parish of Rathven and the county of Banff ; reserving only the free tenement or liferent of all and singular the aforesaid lands with . . . appurtenances to me, John Duff, senior, of Maldavat, and Agnes Gordon, my wife, for all the days of our lives, To hold and to have wholly and entirely the aforesaid my lands of Maldavat to the aforesaid John Duff and Isabella Allan, and the survivor of them, in joint enfeoffment in tail male, and in default, to the heirs and assigns of the said John, of me, my heirs and assigns, in fee and free white farm ; [1] through all their ancient right boundaries and divisions as they lie in length and breadth, in houses, buildings, gardens, woods, plains, moors, marshes, roads, paths, waters, ponds, rivers, meadows, feedings, pastures, mills, mill tolls, and their suits, bird-catching, hunting, fishing, peat, turf, coal, charcoal, tools, brew-houses, heath, broom, woods, groves, copses, cut-wood, logs, wood-cutting, stone-cutting, stone and chalk, with courts and their issues, scutages, fines, with common pasture, the right of taking fuel, free entrance and exit, and with all and singular other the liberties, commodities, profits, easements and their just appurtenances whatsoever both named and unnamed, above and beneath the earth, far and near, to the aforesaid lands of Muldavat . . . with appurtenances belonging or rightly belonging in any way in the future, freely, quietly, fully, honourably, well and in peace, without any revocation, reclamation or obstacle whatsoever, paying thence annually, that is, the aforesaid John Duff and Isabella Allan, his future wife, and the survivor of them, and their male issue, and in default the heirs and assigns of the said John whosoever they are, to me, my heirs and assigns, one penny in the name of white farm at the feast of Pentecoste, if demanded only, for all other charge, secular service, by action, question or demand, which for the said lands of Maldavat can be justly exacted by any one in any way. And I, the aforesaid John Duff, of Maldavat, my heirs and assigns, will warrant all and singular the aforesaid lands of Maldavat to John Duff and Isabella Allan, his future wife, and the survivor of them, in form alike and effect as is aforesaid, also free and immune from all wages, reliefs, entries, forfeitures, pourprestures, disclaimers, acknowledgments, interdictions, evictions, assignments, resignations, assessments, ' third yearly ' and liferents, etc., bastardies, other alienations, estates and seisins, also from all and singular other dangers, losses and injuries whatso-

---

[1] A yearly rent paid in silver.

ever, will warrant against all mortals, acquitt and defend for ever. Moreover, to our beloved Master Patrick Duff of Darbruich [1] . . . I enjoin and firmly order each of you, jointly and separately, my bailiffs specially appointed in this matter, that you give and deliver estate and seisin alike and possession, actual, real and corporal, of all and singular my aforesaid lands of Maldavat . . . to John Duff and Isabella Allan, by handing and giving earth and stone of the ground to the same according to the force, form, tenor, and effect of my above charter, on sight of these presents, without delay, and omitting nothing. For which purpose I empower you and each of you jointly and separately, my bailiffs aforesaid, fully and irrevocably by the tenor of these presents.

In witness whereof to this my present charter I have subscribed with my hand, and written by the hand of Master John Gellie in Fordyce, I have appended my seal, at Craighead, 8th June 1618, before these witnesses, Paul Gelhe, burgess of Cullane, John Duff, burgess of Cullen, my brother germane, James Duff, my third lawful son, and James Gardner, sergeant in Cullen, and John Duff.

JOHN DUFF of Muldavatt, with my hand

AGNES GORDON.

John Duff, witness to the premises.
Paull Gellie, witness.
James Duff, witness.
James Gairdner, witness.
J. Gelhe, witness and scribe of the premises.

James Duff (' my third lawful son '), brother of John Duff of the Orchard, is afterwards heard of in Cullen as ' a distressed gentleman,' and the rent of a ' mortified croft ' is to be used to pay the maill (*i.e.* rent) of his house in 1670. He makes frequent appearances in the Cullen Session Records as an evil-doer.

' PRESBYTERY OF FORDYCE

' 3rd Sept. 1627. Visitation of Cullen

' The whol presbytrie convent . . . together with elders James Lord Desk-fuird, Mr. George Lesly, James Lawtie, Thomas Lawtie, Johne Hempseid, Alexr. Ogilvie, Mr. Patrick Duff, Johne Duff, George Stemsone.

' Compeirit *James Duff, burgess of Cullen,* quho befor vas privathe admonisht by George Douglas, minister, that he suld not vncharitablie abuse his wyff, *Agnes Geddes,* in beating of her, qlk he promeissit to doe, nevertheless the said James Duff upon one Sabboth the 2 of September did beatt her befor sermon befor noon and vpon the same day, being ane day of publik fast and humiliation, having come to Gods sanctuarie for hearing the afternoon sermon, immedi-

---

[1] Half-brother to the elder John

ntche after the sermon is begun, went out of the kirk in a furie, and came to his house and than did cruelie maisterfully and pitifully vithout commiseration strik and ding his said spous to Gods dishonom, breach off his Sabboth and fast. The said James beeing now personallie present seemit to deny he did strik his wyff befor noon, but confessit that in tyme of the afternoon sermon, and did in wrath and raige that cam vpon him sitting in Gods house he dung his said spous, quhervpon all that vas present vas astonished at the said wicked fact, the tyme manei and circumstances thairoff, in one voice decernit the said James to mak his publick repentance on Sabboth day evir quhill the minister and elders receivit satisfaction with signes off his true repentance to God, and in cause of dissobedience to be processit *secundum canones ecclesiae*, as lykwayes to pay tuentie pounds for his penaltie to the said kirk to be bestowed *ad pios usos*, and to this effect ordanes his person to be vardit vntill he find a cautioner to obeye the premises and for eschewing the lyk enormitie in all tyme comming, quherfor the said James hath frund Alexr. Ogilvie, notar publick and burgess of Cullen, cautioner for fulfilling the premises.'

John Duff and Isabel Allan had a son Andrew,[1] who married Grisel Bell 1647, and a son James, baptised in Cullen April 3, 1629, as well as the daughter Janet (see next chapter), but none of these left descendants—Janet's son dying without issue.

Adam Duff was half-brother to the John Duff who granted this charter of alienation, whole brother to one of the John Duffs who witnessed it, uncle to the John Duff who received it, while his relationship to the other John who witnessed it is unexplained.

Before dealing with Adam Duff of Clunybeg[2] himself, we must consider the last John Duff of the elder Muldavit line, who was presumably his *great*-nephew, and died in 1718, when the headship of the family passed to the heirs of Adam.

---

[1] There is a portrait by Jamesone, erroneously described in Lord Fife's catalogue as John Duff of Muldavit and his sister, which must, from the date of painting, represent Andrew and Janet

[2] Adam Duff, who will be treated of in chapter iv., did not own the estate of Clunybeg, but merely had a wadset of it, and was therefore properly described as *in* this place, but his name occurs so often in contemporary records as Adam of Clunybeg that it seems simpler to allude to him by this title.

CHAPTER III

JOHN DUFF, OF THE FAMILY OF MULDAVIT

(MESSENGER-AT-ARMS AND JACOBITE)

ACCORDING to Baird, John Duff, tenth and last of Muldavit, and his wife Isabel Allan had one son, ' John Duff, who settled in Trade in Aberdeen, and got a charter from that town to John Duff, merchant and burges of Aberdeen, upon the " sun " [1] half of the Lands of Corghall (Boghoill) ' (Baird). There *was* a John Duff, burgess of Aberdeen at this period, and the following points about him are incontestable, but his actual parentage is a matter of uncertainty, beyond the well-ascertained fact that he was *not* the son of John Duff of the Orchard and Isabel Allan. He had a charter on the lands of Bogholl, May 26, 1622,[2] and had a house in Old Aberdeen until December 22, 1625 (Rose), and on June 3, 1642, executed the following ' Renunciation by John Duf, burges of Aberdeen, of 20/- lands of Maldavat with lands of Auchingallan and teinds ' ·

' Me, Jhone Duff, portioner of Borghoill, burges of Aberdeen, forsameikle as John Duff elder of Maldavit and Jhone Duff fiar thairof his eldest lanfull sone and Issobell Allane spouse to said Jhone Duff fiar of Craigheid be ane dispositione of dait 4 Aug 1623 sauld . . . to me, my aires etc. . . . thair twentie schilling land of Muldavet, etc. . . . and because the said Jhone Duff younger fiar of Craigheid hes pay it . . . to me the forsaid sowme of 2400 markis money . . . thairfor wit ye me to have renuncit, etc. . . . at Aberdeen, 1 June, 1624.'

John Duff, merchant, burgess of Aberdeen, is found granting obligations and bonds in 1632, 1634, 1635, 1638, and 1649 (*Aberdeen Records*).

Another fact about him to be found in the records of the period is that in 1624 John Duff, burgess in Aberdeen, entered a complaint against Janet Duff, wife to Andrew Kellie,[3] for violence and assault And in 1631 a counter complaint is recorded on the part of Andrew Kellie for ' illegal warding,' John Duff having ' bought bonds over the complainer's head and holding him now, in respect of them. John Duff not appearing, Kellie is

---

[1] *i e.* the south

[2] Baird could scarcely have been aware of the date of this charter, for any son of John Duff and Isabel Allan could have been, at most, three years old in this year.

[3] Mentioned in Charter of Alienation 1618, quoted in last chapter.

20

liberated (*Privy Council Records of Scotland*).[1] John Duff, burgess of Aberdeen (probably the son of the last-named John Duff, whatever his exact relationship to the last owner of Muldavit), married Margaret Johnstown (*Sheriff Court Records*, 1638), and died in 1672, leaving one son John, who may be identified with the following John, of Baird's history:

'John Duff, a lawyer at Aberdeen, a man very much esteemed in his life, being one of great honour and honesty, of extraordinary good parts and a facetious and agreeable companion. He married a comely, graceful gentlewoman named Innes. He engaged in the rebellion of 1715, and was very zealous in that cause, by which being obnoxious to the government, he slept over to Holland in the beginning of 1716, where he soon fell into a large acquaintance and was treated by them all with the greatest civility and kindness. There he laid himself out to serve all his young countrymen who came over to the continent in the course of their travels and upon mercantile and other private affairs. He died at Rotterdam in 1718, universally regretted. He left no issue.' As regards the earlier ancestors of the Duff family, Baird's statements must be received with great caution, his avowed object being to establish the continuity of the line, but this John Duff died when Baird was seventeen years old, and the facts of his life may be presumed to be reliable. A historically interesting letter from this John Duff to his cousin, William Gordon (of Farskane), is among the King's MSS. at Windsor:

'ROTTERDAM, *Oct.* 12, 1716

'Had I not thought to have been with you before this, I had not been so long in writing, but if Will Drummond passed your way he must have given you an account of my being here, as we came together from Scotland to Bergen, and thence to Amsterdam. I had gone forward, but by all the advices from our master's doers to gentlemen in my circumstances, I find no invitation, provided we are safe where we are, which we have hitherto, but how long that may continue God knows, as in the last two Dutch courants it is said that the English court have ordered their resident at the Hague to give in a memorial to the States-General, either to demand the persons of the gentlemen in this country, or that they will order their removal from their country. What answer this may get time will determine, but next what's to be feared is that G[eorge] is to be in person at the congress, and how far he may prevail is not known. I shall do as others in my circumstances, till I get your advice. I understand our master is like to allow all the gentlemen who escaped, reasonable subsistence according to their posts. I had the honour to be one of the last in the field and garrison

---

[1] There was also a John Duff, merchant in Aberdeen, son of James Duff, in Cullen (Rose MS), therefore cousin to John and Isabel But John has always been a common name in this as in other families

for his father, and was taken out of the castle of Feddeiat [1] with Lord Fren-draught, who commanded the regiment of Footguards in which I was Captain, and suffered 12 months imprisonment.   I leave it to the Duke of Mar and my noble patron, the Earl Marcschal, to inform His Majesty what service I did in the late unfortunate design.   As I know you have much to say about the sub-sistence allowed to gentlemen in our circumstances, I entreat you to endeavour to get me an equal share according to my station.   I should have been one of the last to have accepted any such favour were it not that all my effects are stopped by Government, and my poor wife put from her lodgings.   Had I not been supported by Robert Gerrard since I came here, I should not have known what to do ' (*Historical MSS. Commission*).

In the *Calendar of Stuart Papers*, v. 299, occurs the following :
' William Gordon (of Farskane) to the Duke of Mar.   Paris, Dec. 21, 1717.
Poor John Duff's wife is dead at Rotterdam, and her burial charges will be hard on him in this winter season, if His Majesty is not pleased to allow him something.'
And the Rose papers give the following account of his death :
' John Duff the hen, made a merchant in Aberdeen, failed upon 1700, was a messenger,[2] he engaged in 1715, went to Holland, where Irvine of Cults saw him in the beginning of 1716.   Mr. Forbes, Balbithan, told me he was drowned returning with Taylor of Boyndie in 1718, and both their bodies got clasped with a rope and an oak plank.   Boyndie, in life, got on the shore of Musselburgh, retained the black mark of the log on his head, but Duff drowned.   He married Jane Innes (*her name was really Anna*), daughter of Thomas Innes, Chamberlain to the Earl of Panmuir of the lands of Belhelvie.'   Mr. Alexander Mitchell, sometime minister of Belhelvie, and afterwards of Old Aberdeen, was married to another sister, Christian,[3] and the third sister, Elizabeth, married, on November 7, 1700, Mr. John Maitland, minister of Skene ; John Duff, messenger in Aberdeen, being a witness,[4] so, presumably, he was already married to the sister of Elizabeth, while at the date of the *Aberdeenshire Poll-Book* [5] he is described as ' John Duff, messenger, for himself, no wife or child.'   The Jacobite John Duff *was* at one time a messenger in Aberdeen as well as a lawyer, and the acknow-ledged cousin of Clunybeg's grandsons, as will be seen by his letters, *infra*.

Baird would now take us at once from this John of Rotterdam to Adam

---

[1] In Aberdeenshire, near New Deer, originally Federaught

[2] A messenger, or King's Messenger, at that period was an officer of the law-courts whose duty it was to serve writs and execute other legal business   A messenger ' at arms ' was further an official under the control of the Lyon King of Arms, and was charged with the delivery of letters of horning, letters of diligence, and signet letters

[3] This was July 18, 1699.   [4] *Belhelvie Parish Records*   [5] Date 1696

of Clunybeg, whom he calls his uncle,[1] thus · ' This worthy man had no issue, and as the posterity of the late John Duff of Muldavit by his first wife Isabel Allan ended in him, the representation came next to the heirs of Adam Duff of Clunybeg, his son by his second wife, Margaret Gordon, Cairnburrow's daughter.' This descent is obviously impossible, as John Duff, husband of Isabel Allan, had no second wife, his first having outlived him, for she appears in the *Cullen Court Books* in 1637, ten years after his death, as ' relict of umqull John Duff.' Moreover, Margaret Gordon of Cairnburrow was his grandmother.

John Duff and Isabel Allan did, without doubt, have a son Andrew, and a daughter Janet, who, in 1672, when Andrew was dead, is described as ' daughter of the deceased John Duff of the Orchard, sometime of Muldavit, and whose eldest brother was Andrew Duff, sometime of the Orchard, and air or appeirand air of lyne to her said brother, father and good syre, also that John Duff in Old Aberdeen was appeirand air maill to John Duff his father, John Duff his good syre and cousin-german to Janet Duff.' [2]

The most likely presentment of this tangle is as follows :

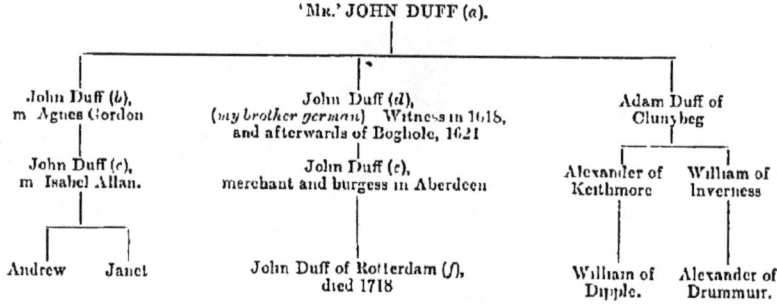

'Mr.' JOHN DUFF (a).

John Duff (b), m Agnes Gordon
John Duff (c), m Isabel Allan.
Andrew   Janet

John Duff (d), (*my brother german*) Witness in 1618, and afterwards of Boghole, 1621
John Duff (e), merchant and burgess in Aberdeen
John Duff of Rotterdam (f), died 1718

Adam Duff of Clunybeg
Alexander of Keithmore   William of Inverness
William of Dipple.   Alexander of Drummuir.

but it involves a loose use of cousin-german as covering second cousin, and is open to possible objection.[3] John Duff of Boghole and John Duff of Rotterdam are, however, both frequently described by Rose (as well as by Baird) as the 'heirs of Muldavit,' and Rose was an industrious and careful genealogist He gives a great many references (but without authorities) to John Duff of Boghole, John Duff, merchant in Aberdeen, John Duff, messenger in Aberdeen, and John Duff, who died in Rotterdam, as heirs and representatives of Muldavit

[1] But they were in reality two generations apart

[2] *Cullen Court Books*

[3] The cousin-german to Janet in 1672 *might* have been John Duff the merchant, called (e) in the above table—cousin-german to her father

The two former and also the two latter he *always* assumes to be the same persons, being apparently not aware that there had been more than one 'messenger' of that name in Aberdeen at the period, one of whom was a near and intimate relative of William of Dipple and Alexander of Drummuir, and that two of them, strange as it may appear, married women of the name of Anna Innes.

Janet, the daughter of John Duff and Isabel Allan, married one Stephen, and had a son Alexander Stephen, after whose death the line was extinct. The Orchard crofts were in possession of Janet, who sold them to Alexander Johnstown, and they were subsequently bought by William, Provost of Inverness, third son of Adam of Clunybeg. Neither Janet, the heir of line, nor her cousin John, the heir-male, was accepted as representing her grandfather John of Muldavit (doubtless because the property had been sold), for in 1670, in a note of the mortifications given up by the minister of Cullen, we find 'Observe this, hence, that since the airs of John Duff of Muldavit are not to be found, the bailie and community of Cullen are undoubted patrons.' This presumably refers to the bequest of Helen Hay, mentioned above. The passage is triumphantly quoted by Dr. Cramond to prove that the family of Muldavit died out completely, but according to his own showing, and by the evidence of the same Cullen books, it had not, at any rate in that year, yet died out—it had merely ceased to be of Muldavit.

The history of the direct line of Duffs of Muldavit and Craighead, then, may be taken as completely authenticated between the limits of 1404 and 1718, after which the representation passed to the descendants of Adam, a younger son. The identification and history of the last representative of the elder line presents some difficulty, and is complicated by the fact that there were, as has been said, apparently two, if not three, John Duffs, messengers in Aberdeen, in the latter half of the seventeenth century.

In a record [1] in the Lyon Office, Edinburgh, there is a brief note that 'John Duff, Messenger at Arms, Aberdeen, died rich, 1700. His fortune went to Braco.' Supposing (as is most likely) the 1700 to be a clerical error for 1718, the John Duff of Rotterdam who died in that year seems to have left whatever he did leave, besides the shadowy headship of the family, to 'Braco,' that is, William of Dipple and Braco, whose son was afterwards Lord Braco, and first Lord Fife. The 'Braco' of 1700 would have been Alexander of Braco (died 1705), who never appears to have made any claim to the headship of the family, being content with becoming the largest landowner.[2]

[1] In MS.

[2] This extract, therefore, is of no great value, beyond having helped the present historians to establish the fact that the 'messenger' of the *Aberdeen Poll-Book*, 1696, was of the Muldavit family—a fact already known to William Rose, and abundantly proved by many letters

The John Duff, messenger, who was the relation and correspondent of William of Dipple and Alexander of Drummuir, was certainly alive until 1718, as letters and papers are in existence from him, bearing dates up to that year, and one, of the year 1715, to William of Dipple, is docketed as ' last letter from John Duff, Messenger ' (*i.e.* before he went to Holland), all of which goes to prove that 1700 should read 1718.

The facts collected by William Rose as to the John Duff, messenger, called by him ' the heir ' are briefly these :

' John Duff, King's Messenger, admitted Burgess of Aberdeen, Sept. 22, 1684.

' John Duff, the heir of Muldavit, made a merchant in Aberdeen,[1] failed upon 1700, and was a messenger. He engaged in the 1715 and went to Holland '—(this followed by the account of his death).

' For John Duff's appointment as messenger, see William Gordon of Farskane.'

The Drummuir papers throw further light upon the matter by an agreement between John Duff, messenger in Aberdeen, and William Gordon of Avochie, before John Gordon of Davidston, date March 1, 1693. This agreement is witnessed by ' George and Robert Duffs, brothers to John,' but no other mention of them has been found

There is another note to the effect that John Duff, messenger in Aberdeen, prepared the sasine for William Gordon of Farskane, 1699.

And the following letters, which conclusively prove the near relationship of John Duff to Alexander of Drummuir and William of Dipple. (If the table on p. 29 be accepted, they were all second cousins.)

The first seven letters come from the archives of Duff House, now preserved at Montcoffer. They show John Duff not only in his business capacity, but also as offering, in his house in Aberdeen, a shelter for all the young sons of his second cousins while pursuing their education at the University there. Another letter on the same subject will be found in the Drummuir chapter, xxiv.

---

[1] It seems probable to the present writers that the John Duff of the '15, ' messenger,' and correspondent of the family, was never a merchant, but was always engaged in legal business, as he seems to have been the recognised man of business both for Dipple and Drummuir prior to 1700 (see his letters both in this chapter and in chapter ix), and was a messenger when he became a burgess in 1684   William Rose seems to be confusing John with his own father, another John, who *was* a merchant, though it is impossible to pronounce with certainty as to which of the Muldavit family was *his* father.

John Duff, Messenger in Aberdeen, to his cousin William Duff of Dipple

'Aᴜᴅ , 8th Jany. 1702

'Dᴇᴀʀ Cᴜsɪɴ, Sɪʀ,—I hade yours from J. Lonoway whereby you alleadge your haveing pressing use for money at Edᵗ which has oblidged me to add to it 600 mʳ I wrott you of in my letter to Mr. Robert flrasers cair others to make up 50 lb. Starr—but cane gett noe Bill for the samen as the Bearer Bailie Forbes cane informe me.   In case the money be disposed of acquaint me of it first and I 'll remitt it for post but if you cane gett the money in Edinʳ for value then it will be better both for you and I.   But for the rest you cane not expect it at Candlemas considering my haveing cleaid with Laidy Spynie at this terme but agᵗ Whyt Sonday you may.   I wish you a happy new year and am, Sir, Your most affectionate Cusine to serve you,   Jo Dᴜꜰꜰ.'

William Duff of Braco to John Duff

'Bᴀʟᴠᴇɴɪꜰ, 9th July 1712.

'Dᴇᴀʀ Sɪʀ,—I have sent this bearer for to get my papers from Mr. Charles Gordon.   I desyre you may give him a crown per sheet because he is my mother's [1] relation, and buy powder and shot with the rest, cause buy the lead of ane good ordinaire syse for moorfouls I intreat you see what you can doe with Edntoire and if you can gett but seven hunder merks in all I would discharge him of Mrs. Laws debt but not of my debt as Superior, for that is a seperate claime.   I hope you will doe what you can for me as to my meall.   I can dispose of 1000 Bolls att five merks, and would not seek mony till Whitsunday next, only I would have a good debitor and acquaint me before you conclude.   I give my service to your selfe and Ladie and I am, Dear Cusine, Your most humble Servant,   Wɪʟʟɪᴀᴍ Dᴜꜰꜰ.' [2]

John Duff, Messenger, Aberdeen, to the Laird of Dipple

'Aʙᴇʀᴅᴇᴇɴ, 21 Jan 1713.

'Dᴇᴀʀ Dɪᴘᴘʟᴇ,—I have your very angry letter anent your sone, which is truely very groundless.   It 's time I have given him a suit of honest cloathes which as your sone I think he ought to have.   But nothing of vanity about him as you may depend ont that then is nothing about the youth But good sober inclinations and whatever I may bestow on him for his education which shall be also good as this place cane affoaid.   You shall in the event have noe ground to grudge, and therefor I 'd have you be easy for you know its a pretty whyll since you promised you would send your sone to me to be my pupill and was not to

---

[1] Margaret Gordon of Lesmoir
[2] This William Duff died in 1718 in the same year as John   See chapter viii.

controll any thing I should happen to bestow on his educatione, and now that
I 'm in possessione doe not resolve to pairt with him untill he is capable of satisfy-
ing you that by his improvement you shall vow all weill bestowd and that their
is nothing either produgall or profuse about him. I give our hearty service to
your self, Laidy, and family. and I continue, Dear Dipple, Your most affectionat
Cusine to serve youe,   Jo. Duff.[1]
  ' To the much Honored The Laird of Dipple.'

William Duff, afterwards Lord Braco, to his father the Laird of Dipple

' Abd , Aprile 21, 1713.

  ' Sir,—I thank you for your affectionat letter. I bless God I am perfectly
well recovered, and as I formerly wrote you was warie much oblidged to my
cousin and his bedfellow [2] for thence care about me. I would have returned you
ansure sooner but we have been warie busie befor the riseing of our Coledge.
My Cousin hath cleared my phisitian and I belive you will not find I have been
aniewise extravagant in my pocatmony, for all I have received from Mr. Scott
is but wary smal. Our Coledge is not as yet given up, but will in a short time.
I refer you to what my cousin wrot in his last conserning me and with my humble
duty to yourself my mother in law [3] is all at present, Sir, Your affect. and most
obedient Son,   Wm Durr.[4]
  ' To the Laird of Dipple at Elgin.'

The same to the same

' Aberdeen, 14th May 1713

  ' Sir,—You see by my Cousins letter and Mr. Scot's that I have had a fever
some days bygone but am now, blessed be God pretty well recovered, and lest
you should be aniewise surprised notwithstanding of the other letters, I have
sent you this from my own hand   I cannot express how much I am bound to
my cousin and his bedfellow for the unspeakable concern and care they hade of
me   I expect to hear from you by the next post. I offer my service to my mother
in law, Sir, your most afft and obedient son,   Wm. Duff.'

---

  [1] The different ways of signing the name John Duff are curious, and have been of great help
in dealing with the vast mass of family correspondence   For though a man's handwriting
alters with advancing age, he rarely changes the contraction of his Christian name, or the form
of his capital letters
  [2] There is an otherwise uninteresting letter to William of Dipple, about his son, signed by
John Duff and Anna Innes, his wife   This proves the curious point as to two John Duffs
having married wives of the same name, for the other Anna Innes was ' relict ' of her John
Duff seventeen years before this date (see Poll-Book and page 37)
  [3] i.e. stepmother.   [4] Aged sixteen.

John Duff, Messenger, Aberdeen, to the Laird of Dipple [1]

'ABERDEEN, 17th May 1714.

'DEAR SIR,—I accknowledge that I am mightiely in the wrong in not returning you ane answer to your last which was mearly occasioned by the Lordes and then advocats being in this place of whom I did not gett free till Saturday last. As to your sons clearing with Mr. Smith you cannot say he has been any wayes extravagant Being he has not exceeded What was given the last year · which with the two gines you gave me to be given that way is only hall ane ginie more and realy even in this he tells me he is behind with his comorads; and I have no mind to cross him, for I never knew him extravagant in any thing.   I am hopefull to make ane haill saill bargan of the bear I bought in Murray and that free of any risck or Charges and for my meall, I am hopefull it will prove no ill bargane being that the meall begins to start both here and in the South firth and I have my barck takeing in the firsth of her Lodeing att Doun [*Macduff*] just now from which place she is to sail to Portsoy and I believe will be their about the midle of this week of which I have acquainted the Lady Glengerrick and Mrs Robertsones to have their meall in readyness that so the barck may not be detamed.   I am sory I cannot answer your demandes att this term but I am hopefull be as it will to gett you cleared againest the next—your sone and governor are in very good health.   Pleas accept of my hearty service to your-self and I continue, Dear Sir, Your most affectionat Cousine and humble servant,

Jo. DUFF.'

The same to the same

'ABD , 21 July 1714

'DEAR SIR,—On Wednesday last your son Will: returned to this place from his milk dyet, which blessed be God hese agreed very weel with him. Albeit it hese not given him any more beef then what he had befor but he is perfectly healthy and weel and I hope will prove as pretty a man as is his name which att meeting you will discover and I hope you will be no worse as your word in comeing this length to see him after your Ladies being brought to bed to whom I wish ane safe and happy delivery.[2]

'According to your desire I have sent you ane sett of Cups ane containing ane Chapin for a tost, ane mutchkin cup and ane half mutchkin which are the bonniest sett I have seen in this place for a long time but we have no Copper Smiths for makeing of copper girths proper for them but you will find when you receive them they deserve silver.   Your son told me he was to write you by this

---

[1] It will be seen in the chapter on William of Dipple that he also was at one time in Rotter-dam, presumably visiting his cousin (and former man of business and correspondent), after the latter's enforced departure from Scotland

[2] Birth of Mary, afterwards wife of General Abercromby

post to which I refer. My wife and I give our humble duty to your Ladie self and family and I continue, Dear Sir, Your most affectionat Cousin and humble servant, Jo. Duff.'

1912260

Letters from among Drummuir papers. (Docketed ' from John Duff, Messenger.')

'Aberdeen, *Dec.* 14, 1700

' To the Much honoured, the Land of Drummuir.

'Honoured Sir,—This day about 12 o'clock, I received yours with discharge and renunciation of Harskane to Gordon of Davidston, and your saisine of the lands of Davidston and Thornebank, which according to order I had duly registrat, and in as great haist as I could, albeit you may think the expense dear enough, the receipt whereof you have, encld, which as you 'll see amounts to £24, whereof received £11. 10. 0. so for the balance you may remit with conveniency. Your servant was in so great haist that it was not possible to get the registers looked for, and what encumbrances are against that estate, and likeways I find them somewhat dear, being they will not look back 20 years neither for seasines, inhibitions nor hornings under 2 or 3 dollars so that till your further order, I don't resolve to give them the trouble. I cannot omitt to tell you that I arrested Arradoull in Tolbooth of Banff, after incarceraing of him at another's man's instance, which I think is easier than apprehending him at yours, however, doe in the matter as seems you good. I shall take caii to acquaint you how soon I come to Banffshire and shall be ready to receive your commands which shall be as far obeyed as in my power. Thus, with my humble service to your father, self, lady and all friends with you, is the present from your most affectionate cusine and servant, Jo Duff.'

To the same

'Aberdeen, 28 *Dec.* 1700.

' Sir,—I have yours just now with £12. 10 in the same, and shall take care to cause look both registers of sasines, inhibitions and hornings for the year you write of, but it is not possible to get it done of hand, being we have as yet Christmas vacance here, but shall cause doe them as soon as possible. Be the by I cannot omitt to tell you that your predecessor is a little out of the road to me,[1] having depursed some money for him, which put him in circumstances too common with you, so that I trust if be anything yet in your hands you 'll help till I be clear of him. Notwithstanding I firmly purpose to be at him with personal dilligence. This is written at a bottle, so that I hope you 'll excuse any escapes [*sic*] and shall only conclude with my respects to your fair self, lady and family wishing you a happy New Year, but that I am, sir, your most affectionate cousin to serve you, Jo. Duff.'

---

[1] This again shows legal business as having been transacted by John for his relatives and others prior to 1700

To the same

'ABERDEEN, 19 *Ap* 1701

'SIR,—My being so long at Edinburgh has retarded the note of inhibitions etc. which I should have sent you from our registers against Davidston which herein receive and am hopeful will yet come in good time, otherwise I fear may come to loss betwixt him and I. being you are the only foundation for my clearing. Albeit what he owes me is but small, yet I intend to have if possible, with your friendship, upon which I very much rely. I think of being in Murray in a very short time, where I am hopeful to see ye and all my friends in Inverness at which time shall write no more of particular, but service to your fair lady and family, not forgetting your own.—I am, sir, your most affectionate cousin and servant,   Jo. DUFF.'

'To the much honoured, the Laird of Drummuir at Inverness.

'ABERDEEN, *Mar.* 20, 1702.

'SIR,—It is none of my fault your Sasine is not yet sent you, but then I beg excuse for the trouble. And would beg you to have this bill discounted for me as it is payable in your town of Inverness, and what expenses you are at on the head shall be thankfully paid you at meeting, which with my service to yourself, Lady,[1] Mistress Anne[2] and family, not forgetting the old gentleman,[3] is all at present from sir, your most affectionate cousin,   Jo. DUFF.'

In 1709 in a mortification by Margaret Gordon, widow of Alexander of Braco, of a sum of money for Aberdeen College, the right of 'supporting it,' goes first to William Duff of Braco, her son, and then to John Duff, messenger in Aberdeen, and William of Dipple.

In April 1714 William Duff of Dipple writes to the Lady Glengerack . 'Affectionate Niece, I have disposed of the meal I bought from you to our Cousin John Duff in Aberdeen.'

There is also a letter from John *re* the ' good and sufficient oat meal at 8 stone per boll.'

A man who *may* be the same 'John Duff, messenger in Aberdeen,' is frequently referred to in the *Aberdeen Sheriff Court Books.*

In 1680 an obligation is granted to him by one Menzies.

In 1681 another by one Hay, another by Mackie, and another by Cruikshank.

In 1683 one by Lumsden, one by Gordon of Terpersie, and one by Alex Fyfe.

In 1710 John Duff, ' Armiger,' Aberdonia, acts for George Mowat in the negotiation for the sale of Balquholly (Hatton).

The title Armiger, which is equivalent to Esq , shows John Duff to have been a man of good family

---

[1] Katherine Duff of Drummuir, born 1669

[2] Her eldest daughter, afterwards Lady Mackintosh, born 1684, and married 1702

[3] Provost William, aged seventy, born 1632, died 1715

Though it is quite possible to identify the John Duff of the letters and John Duff of the *Sheriff Court Books*, as well as he who ' died rich in 1700, whose fortune went to Braco,' with Baird's John, ' who died in Rotterdam in 1718,' and Rose's ' who was drowned on the coast at Musselburgh in the same year,' it is at any rate certain that there was another John Duff, whose widow is thus noted in the *Aberdeenshire Poll-Book*, 1696 : ' Anna Innes, relict of John Duff, messenger, her daughter Janat, servants Elizabeth Gray and Elspit Mitchell.' She occurs among the pollable persons within the burgh of Aberdeen, rated ' at £6 yeirly ' each.[1]

The John Duff who afterwards married Anna Innes of Belhelvie, and died in 1718, is undoubtedly referred to, in the same volume, as ' John Duff, messenger, for himself, no wife nor child, ane servant, James Ritchie, £6 yeirly. While, in the same roll, his future wife appears under ' Thomas Innes, factor to the earl of Panmure . . . 6s. for ilk ane of his daughters in familia, viz : Christane, Elizabeth and Anna Innes.' [2]

As it is obvious that the Duff stock in Aberdeen, in so far as it was connected with Muldavit, died out early in the eighteenth century, it is perhaps unnecessary to endeavour to pursue it further.

---

[1] This must be the John Duff and Anna Innes the births of whose children are found in the Aberdeen Registers.

1677, Elizabeth , 1679, Robert , 1680, Marjorie ; 1683, Thomas.

[2] Other puzzles in the *Aberdeenshire Poll-Book* (a valuable record of the time) may also be placed here.

' George Duff, gentleman tennent in Old Overtone, parish of Belhelvie, payes his proportion of his mother's valovatione, £1 7 8, but being classed as a gentleman it is not to be payed —but £3 as ane gentleman—6s for himself and 6s for his wyfe ' It may be supposed that this George was the brother George, witness, in 1692, to signature of John Duff messenger, who also at one time lived, or at least married, in Belhelvie , but nothing more is known of him. (John Duff in Lochlands of Belhelvie is mentioned in the *Aberdeen Sheriff Court Records*).

A disposition is granted to this George Duff, Old Overtoune of Belhelvie, in 1694, and his marriage with Agnes Montgomery, relict of the deceased Andrew Milne of Old Miln of Foveran, is noted in the *Aberdeen Sheriff Court Books* on October 4, 1721, and is apparently witnessed by John Duff, messenger in Aberdeen But this may be a mistake, as in the next entry, referring to George Duff and Agnes Montgomery his spouse, reference is made to the ' deceased John Duff, messenger in Aberdeen,' who granted a bail-bond to the above George in November 1704

Also in the *Poll-Book* are to be found William Duffes, tenent in Turriffe, with wyfe and sone and John Duffes, tenant in Mill of Dalgaty

James Duffes in Kaines of Blacktoune, King Edward

William Duffes, tennent in Balmade, King Edward

It is perhaps possible to connect these latter with the present family of Bruntyards, King Edward

In the same list we find John Duff, shoemaker, no wife, child, nor servant He may be identified with a John Duff, cordiner in College Bounds, of whom we have record in 1681, but that does not, of course, show whether he was any relation to either of the messengers or to either of the John Duffs, burgesses of Aberdeen

CHAPTER IV

ADAM DUFF OF CLUNYBEG

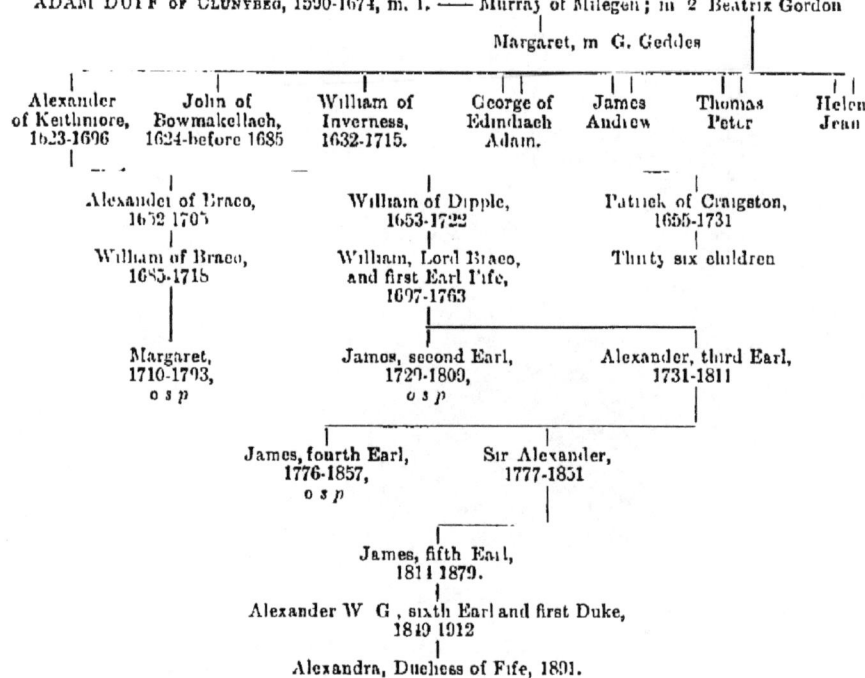

ADAM DUFF OF CLUNYBEG, 1590-1674, m. 1. —— Murray of Milegen; m 2 Beatrix Gordon

Margaret, m G. Geddes

| Alexander of Keithmore, 1623-1696 | John of Bowmakellach, 1624-before 1685 | William of Inverness, 1632-1715. | George of Edinbaeh Adam. | James Andrew | Thomas Peter | Helen Jean |

Alexander of Braco, 1652 1705

William of Braco, 1685-1718

Margaret, 1710-1793, o s p

William of Dipple, 1653-1722

William, Lord Braco, and first Earl Fife, 1697-1763

James, second Earl, 1729-1809, o s p

Patrick of Craigston, 1655-1731

Thirty six children

Alexander, third Earl, 1731-1811

James, fourth Earl, 1776-1857, o s p

Sir Alexander, 1777-1851

James, fifth Earl, 1814 1879.

Alexander W G , sixth Earl and first Duke, 1849 1912

Alexandra, Duchess of Fife, 1891.

THE relationship of Adam Duff in Clunybeg[1] to the family of Muldavit was long a moot point. The only previous family historian, as has been seen, made him the son of the last John Duff of the Orchard, by a mythical second wife, but this relationship, which is impossible on the face of it, as a mere matter of dates, is completely disproved by the entries in the *Cullen Court Books*,[2] and the refutation of it was set forth, with much acerbity, in an article which appeared in the *Scotsman* at the time of the marriage of the late Duke of Fife to Princess Louise of Wales in 1889, which article

---

[1] Correctly so described, as being a tenant, but also often called ' of Clunybeg,' *vide infra*

[2] First brought to light by Dr Cramond in 1883.

attracted, as it was meant to do, a good deal of notice and has had some weight, up to the present day, with pedigree writers and compilers of peerages. But it went a little too far, in trying to prove that the Duff family had no ancestors, and later researches have firmly established the pedigree of Adam Duff, so that the sneers about the 'fatherless Adam' have now quite lost their point. Dr. Cramond was so anxious to show that the duke's ancestor was not the son of that particular John Duff, tenth and last of Muldavit, married in 1618 to Isabel Allan, who certainly never had a second wife called Margaret Gordon, that he wished to show (and seemed to think he had shown) at the same time, the impossibility of *any* connection between Adam in Clunybeg and the Muldavit family. This is not established. In fact, it is now certain that there was clear descent, and the elder line having died out in John of Rotterdam in 1718,[1] it was fully allowed at the time that the descendants of Adam did represent the family, though they were originally only cadets thereof. The inscription on the tomb of Alexander, son of Adam, erected in Mortlach church, stating that he was so descended, appears to have been unchallenged at the time, and arms were granted to him in 1676 as being 'lineally descended from the family of Moldavid and Craighead,' and the note appended to this, in the roll-book in the Lyon Office, Edinburgh (of which Cramond made so much) 'in a different but apparently contemporary hand' to the effect that 'there is good reason to believe that he is not the representer of Craighead,' proves nothing against his relationship, for, of course, while John of Rotterdam lived, he was not 'the representer.'[2]

It has now been *proved* that, instead of being the son of John Duff of the Orchard, who married Isabel Allan, Adam Duff of Clunybeg, father of Alexander Duff of Keithmore, was the uncle of the said John, the Adam mentioned in the last chapter as one of the eleven sons of 'Mr. John Duff of Muldavit' (who died in 1593) and his second wife, Margaret Gordon of Cairnburrow. Margaret Gordon, after the death of John Duff, married (in 1600) Walter Ogilvie of Auchoynany, who in 1573 had bought the property of Clunybeg from Patrick Gordon of Auchindoun, and her son Adam Duff was placed by her 'in Ardrone' in 1611[3] and subsequently in Clunybeg. He was still of Clunybeg in 1656 when his words to Margaret

---

[1] For, whatever his exact relation to John of the Orchard and Isabel Allan (see last chapter), he undoubtedly represented an elder line than Adam

[2] And there may have been, in that year, other first cousins of Clunybeg or Keithmore, sons or grandsons of the other elder sons of 'Mr' John Duff and Margaret Gordon, still alive Even according to Baird it was not until forty-two years later (1718) that Keithmore's son, William of Dipple, was held to be 'head of the family,' or in any way 'representer of Craighead'

[3] *Banff Register of Deeds*

Ogilvie (his half-sister), married to John Stewart of Ardbreck, are quoted as evidence before the Kirk-Session of Botriphnie. These facts were authoritatively brought to light by the Rev. Stephen Ree, whose discovery in the Botriphnie Kirk-Session Records of this strange story of the scandal of a buried cat, first revealed as a *certainty* the identity of Adam in Airdrone with the man afterwards known as Adam of Clunybeg, father of Alexander of Keithmore. The evidence, being curious, is here reprinted in full .

BOTRIPHNIE KIRK-SESSION RECORDS

' 12 Feb. 1656. Compeired Georg Riach in Slagrein and gave in a bill of complaint on Marjorie Baron, bearing that the said Marjorie said his mother, Katharin Neil, in prejudice of her neighbours, buried a cat and her four feet upwards, and gave up witnesses. The partie and witnesses to be summonded to the next day.

' 2 March 1656. Compeired Marjorie Baron and being accused of the former slander complained on by Georg Riach, denyed that she said so, but only said that Agnes Low, spouse to James Mill in Towie, said so.

' 23 March 1656. Compeired Marjorie Baron and gave up Agnes Low for author anent the business of the buried cat. Compeired the said Agnes and declared that Adam Duff of Clunybeg[1] came in on a tyme to John Stewart's barn quher she, the said Agnes, was winnowing with the said John Stewart's wife, and non present but they two, and said to Margaret Ogilvie, spouse to the said John Stewart and sister to him, the said Adam, " Ye cannot thrive heer, for they say ther was a cat yearded[2] heer and her four feet upward," but named no man, and therefor she said it. Being posed quhat if he denyed it, she said he could not, but she knew no way to prove it. The matter referred for advice to the presbyterie.

' 20 April 1656. Anent the matter of slander . . . the minister reported that it was the presbyterie's advice that Agnes Low forsaid, be posed who told her that ther was a cat buried and her feet upward, in Little Towie. The said Agnes being called and posed *ut supra* answered that she heard Adam Duff of Clunybeg say to Margaret Ogilvie, spouse to John Stewart of Ardbreck, ther being non present but she, the said Agnes, that ther was a cat buried ther etc., how could she thrive there. The Session concluded that the said Adam sould be called to come and declare the truth in that matter.

' 29 April 1656. Reported by the minister that he had spoken with Adam Duff of Clunybeg anent the forementioned witchcraft, that the said Adam denyed utterlie that ever he spake any such, yea regrated that Agnes Low sould

---

[1] It is important to note that he is here described as *of* Clunybeg

[2] Earthed, *i e.* buried

slander him with a thing she could not make out, that he was willing to go to the presbyterie and declare so much. The Session did refer the matter to the presbyterie.' [1]

The proofs of Adam Duff of Clunybeg being the son of ' Mr.' John Duff of Muldavit must be recapitulated, to show that the position of Dr. Cramond is no longer tenable.

We have already seen that Adam Duff, son of ' Mr ' John Duff and Margaret Gordon was 'in Ardrone ' in 1611, the proof of this being an entry in the Banff Deed Book, where ' Adam Duff in Ardrone ' on February 2, 1611, grants dischaige to his brother ' Mr. Patrick Duff of Darbruiche ' of money left him by his father after the decease of ' Margaret Gordon his mother. Registered at Banff, September 10, 1620.'

And the identification of Adam Duff in Ardrone, in whom even Cramond was obliged to believe, on the incontestable evidence of the *Cullen Court Books* and other documents, with Adam Duff of Clunybeg, rests on *two* grounds.

Firstly, on the evidence of the Balbithan MS., which says that ' of Mr. John Duff and Margaret Gordon is come Braccho, and all the opulent sur-name of Duffs.' This MS , which is accepted as an undoubted authority on all the matters with which it deals, was of course unknown to Cramond, having been first published in Bulloch's *House of Gordon*, Spalding Club, 1903. The approximate date of the MS. on internal evidence is 1730.[2]

And secondly, on the fact that the mother of Adam Duff in Ardrone married, after the death of Adam's father (which occurred in 1593), Walter Ogilvie of Auchoynany, and had a son John Ogilvie, and a daughter Margaret, married in 1618 to John Stewart of Ardbreck, Adam Duff being procurator, ' Adamus Duff in Ardrone certus procurator et co nomine probe ancillae Margarete Ogilvie, filie legittime Walteri Ogilvie de Miltoun '; and thirty-eight years later, in 1656 Adam Duff of Clunybeg is mentioned in the Kirk-Session Records of Botriphnie (still to be read in the original), together with ' Margaret Ogilvie, spouse to John Stewart in Ardbreck and sister to him, the said Adam,' which is absolutely conclusive that the man known in 1656 to 1674 (when he died) as Adam Duff of Clunybeg, and father of Alexander Duff of Keithmore was the same person as Adam Duff in

---

[1] There is no further mention of the matter in the Session Records, and the Presbytery Records of that period are lost

[2] It is known to have been written subsequent to 1715, as the battle of Sheriffmuir is mentioned, but there is no reference to the troubles of the year 1715 The Braccho (Braco) referred to is therefore William Duff, son of William Duff of Dipple (who himself succeeded to Braco on the death of his nephew in 1718). William Duff, the son, became Lord Braco in 1735, and Earl Fife in 1759. He was the great-grandson of Adam Duff of Clunybeg, and therefore great-great-grandson of ' Mr ' John Duff of Muldavit and Margaret Gordon

Aulrone, and therefore son of 'Mr ' John Duff of Muldavit and Margaret Gordon of Carnburrow.

A large amount of evidence as to the facts of Adam's descent had been collected in the end of the eighteenth century by William Rose of Ballivat, factor to Lord Fife, some of whose notes are now in the Advocates' Library Aberdeen others in Advocates' Library Edinburgh and others again in private hands.[1] All of these have been carefully collated by the present writers, and a fairly complete life history of Adam can now be compiled.

He was certainly born in 1590, and in the following year certain crofts were granted by his father John Duff of Muldavit to his own wife, Margaret Gordon, in liferent, and to Adam in fee.[2] This fact was used by Dr. Cramond to attempt to disprove the identity of this Adam with Adam, father of Keithmore, who lived until 1674, but the infeftment of children in the fee of estates of which the liferent was granted to other persons was, of course, quite usual.[3]

There was an Andrew Duff in Clunybeg, who had a precept of sasine in 1573 which was confirmed in 1580, and a reversion upon the same lands granted by him in 1590 to Patrick Gordon of Auchindoun. This Andrew is still unexplained, but he is certainly the man mentioned in the will of Alexander of Torriesoul 1566 (q.v.), and may be identified with the Andrew who witnessed a charter for John, eighth of Muldavit, in 1563 (see page 18), the same John witnessing one for him. He was probably brother of John the eighth.

'Aug. 28, 1581. Rex confirmavit cartam dicti Adami Gordoun di Auchindoun (qua vendidit Patricis Gordoun fratri suo, heredibus ejus et assignatis masculis quibus cunque) dictus terras tenend de rege cum precepto sasine directo Andrae Duff in Clunybeg.

> Test. Joanni Duff de Connes (Conage in Rannes).
> Alexandro Duff de Torriesoull.
> Jac. Gordon filio Johan G. di Carnburro.

'Apud Huntlie, 10 April 1573 ' (*Reg. Mag. Sig. Scot.*).

These witnesses are interesting as showing at least a juxtaposition of the then Clunybeg, Muldavit, and Torriesoull [4]

---

[1] See Preface   [2] Cramond's *Church of Cullen*

[3] It was in 1612 that these lands were finally sold to James Lawtie, by Patrick Duff of Darbrinch, ' with the consent of Walter Duff, son of John Duff of Muldavit (and therefore nephew to Patrick), present prebendary of Cullen, and with the consent of Adam Duff, brother-german to Patrick Duff

[4] In the same year we find Alexander Duff of Corsindae appointed Deputy-Sheriff of Aberdeen Who he was we cannot ascertain

As already stated, it is now quite certain that, although Adam Duff in Clunybeg, who married Beatrix Gordon of Birkenburn (she unfortunately is not mentioned in the Balbithan MS. history of the Gordons), and had the large family of sons known to us, was *not* descended from the family of Muldavit in the way stated by Baird, yet his connection with the family is undoubted, and the present Duchess of Fife may, as Mr. Bulloch says in his *Free Press* article of May 17, 1912, trace her descent, on the Duff side, back at least to 1404.

Adam Duff, then, youngest, or youngest but one, of the sons of John Duff of Muldavit and Margaret Gordon his second wife, was born, as has been seen, in 1590. At his death, in April 1674, he was aged eighty-four, and it is certain that he was twenty-one when he executed the deed to his elder brother Patrick, quoted on page 19, otherwise the consent of his mother or curator would have been necessary, and this was in 1611. It was in that year also that he was 'placed in Ardione.' (Baird, as already mentioned, places his birth in 1598, while making him the *younger* son of John Duff and Isabel Allan, this John Duff being in reality Adam's nephew, son of his half-brother, and probably born a few years after him.) Baird calls Adam 'the Restorer of his family, for he was the father of a numerous offspring to whom he gave a good education and good provisions, whose male descendants have most of them flourished ever since, both the stock and the branches. Several old men who lived within these forty years (written about 1770), and knew Clunybeg well, spoke of him with great regard as a man of strong natural sense, perfect integrity and indefatigable industry. He was a zealous Loyalist and Anti-covenanter, and was fined by the ruling party (in October 1646) 500 merks either as a malignant or for the malignancy of his two elder sons (who served with Montrose).'

In the Rose MS., Advocates' Library, frequent reference to him is found: 'Margaret Gordon, 2nd dau. of Carnburrow, gave to Adam her youngest son, the farm of Ardrone in 1611. He was a very honest man. He lived in Ardrone till about 1623. About 1657 he was not in affluent circumstances, as he was "taken" for £100 Scots, when his son Alexander was his cautioner to Andrew Hay of Darbruich. At that date he was also tenant of the Mill of Auchindoun.' [1]

In the Rose MS. there is a copy of a deed signed by Adam Duff at Keithmore on June 5, 1662, binding himself to deliver certain papers to his son Alexander or his heirs : 'Adam Duff in Clunybeg writes a paper

[1] Thus Adam Duff was a Gordon vassal, and W. Rose notes: 'Let it be remembered with truth, that industry, care, and attention has brought this family equal to any peer—owing their original credit to the Marquises of Huntly, who protected the Duffs who transacted their business.'

granting himself to have received from Alex. Duff of Lettach, his son, the papers aftermentioned, to Witt ane discharge from John Miln to him, out of Horn and Caption raised on Horning, Miln contra Duff of dait 1655: Miln contra Duff and Gordon 1644 or 1654: Contra Ogilvie and his cautioners: Doubles letters of horning, etc., sie scrib. Adam Duff.' William Rose saw this paper, and notes that he 'delivered it to Mr. Cranston, January 31, 1801.' The present writers have not been able to trace it.

Innumerable notes in the Rose MS. show Adam Duff of Clunybeg as a 'younger son of Mr. John Duff who died April 23, 1593, and Margaret Gordon, second daughter of Gordon of Cairnburrow, by Bessie Gordon, Buckie's daughter,' but, unfortunately, authorities are not always given. 'Adam Duff lived in Ardrone in 1611; he married, first, a daughter of Murray of Milegan, and then a daughter of Gordon of Birkenburn, of whom Keithmore, Corsindae, and William, Provost of Inverness. Adam was a burgess of Banff (his ticket dated 1662).'

Part of his history is to be found in the public records.[1] In the *Acts of the Scottish Parliament*, Adam Duff appears several times. In 1644 he, with his two elder sons, Alexander and John, aided in the plundering of the house of Alexander Strachan of Glenkindie. Glenkindie's complaint states that these several persons (of whom seven were Gordons and three other relations of Clunybeg's) [2] 'in contempt of the lawis of the kingdome, haveing no reason but onlie because the said supplicant was ane Covenanter, had violentlie broken up with soir hamers the utter and inner Yettis, doores, kistis, coffers, lockfast places and plundered the haill moveables,' and prays to have these things restored to him.

Full details of this 'spulzing of the House of Auchagatt' are to be found in the Book of Hornings, now in Banff. The date of the original raid was April 15, 1644, and the account states that 'these persons, with their complices as common and notorious thiefes, came bodily in forse with swords, durks, bands, staves, hagbuts,[3] pistolles and other invasive weapons, to the said Alexander Strachan of Glenkindy his dwelling-place of Auchagatt and violently, with forse and instruments of hammers and others brought be them to the said place of Auchagatt, break up the yeattis and

---

[1] 1646   Ane Act of the Committee of Parliament whereby 400 merks to support the army were levied on Adam Duff in Clunybeg

1648   Adam Duff in Clunebeg and his sons John and William are found in the records of Horn, at the instance of John Lesly in Buchromb

[2] John Ogilvie of Auchoynany, his half-brother; George Geddes of Auchinhoof, his son-in-law; George Adamson in Floors, whose mother was a Duff of Drummuir

[3] Crooked fire-arms, anciently used.

doors thereof and having taken entry within the samen, broke up the haill
kists, coffers and other lock-fast Lumies,[1] and theftously by way of master-
ful sleuth[2] and theft, reif, staw,[3] and away-took furth the said Complainers
haill silver work to the availl[4] of an thousand pounds, as also the sum of an
thousand merks of lying money, breaking his Charter kist and staw and
away-took furth his haill evidents of his lands together with dwene bonds,
Obligations and other securities containing great sums of money addebted
to him be his Debtors extending to the sum of twenty thousand
merks together also with the haill guids, gear, insight, plenishing of the
said place, and victuals being within his girnals[5] to the avail of 2000
merks, and transported away the samen and other guids at their pleasure
and sich like, being fortified by the said Walter Ogilvie of Milltoun of
Keith.'[6]

In the following year, there would seem to have been a fresh offence,
for the same indictment, bearing the seal of Charles I., goes on to state that
' under cloud of night in Aug. 1645, these persons came to the Complainer's
place of Annochie and theftously broke up gates, etc. and staw [stole]
fourtie nolt [i e. cattle] and guids to the availl of a thousand merks . . .
and in the month of Dec. came and away-took a black hackney horse worth
a hundred pounds.   For the which theiftous crimes as well of stealing, as
of receipting the foresaid stolen guids the forenamed persons, committers
thereof ought and should be punished in terms of law and to make re-
stitution, etc.'   Precept of horning signeted February 24, 1648.

They were accordingly cited upon the 11th day of March 1648 ; ' James
Leslie, Messenger, past and chargit Adam Duff in Clunybeg, and Alexander
Duff, his eldest lawful son, at his dwelling-house in Clunybeg where Adam
and his wife lived and where the said Alexander his eldest son last resided,
and copies left with Adam's wife as they were from home, personally to
compeir within the Tollbooth of Edinburgh the 12th of April then next' ;
but in 1649 Strachan was still clamouring for redress.

In 1651, Adam Duff in Mylnetown of Auchindoune, with James Ogilvie
of Raggall and others, are cited at the instance of Robert Sanders in
Ardincidle in the parish of Keith.   The complaint being that ' these persones
in the month of October came to the lands of Dallochie and rancounterct
with nyne of the said complenar his servants going to the Knok of Strylay
to sheir their master's coines growing thereupon and forced and compelled
them to go to James Ogilvie's place of Raggall and sheir his coine all that
day.'

---

[1] Utensils	[2] Tracking.	[3] Robbed, stole
[4] Worth	[5] Granaries	[6] Stepfather of Adam Duff.

For this, and for a cruel assault upon Sanders and his wife, in December of the same year, Adam Duff was 'personeallie apprehended' on April 23, 1655. On November 30, 1657, Robert Sanders, messenger, notes that 'after sex knockes upon ilk ane of their most patent doores, he affixed and left authentik copies of the letters of horning (because he could not find them personallie), before witnesses, George Gordon, sone to George Gordon of Lickestoune, George Duff, sone to the said Adam, and lykways arrestit twa thousand merks in the hands of Mr. Andro Hay at the Nether Mylne of Strylay, belonging to the said Adam Duff.'

Horning was not a very serious matter in those days, and very shortly afterwards the offenders made their peace with the authorities, and Adam appears in a year or two as a respectable citizen and a witness before the Presbytery.

He seems, however, to have been a somewhat turbulent person, for, on April 14, 1663, in the *Register of Privy Council of Scotland* is found a record of a 'complaint by John Lyon, elder of Muiresk, and others against the Earl of Aboyne, Alexander Duff of Keithmore, Adam Duff in Clunybeg, and divers others their accomplices, to the number of fifteen persons, all boddin in feir of weir,[1] aimed with swords, pistolls, gunnes and other weapones invasive, contrar to diverse Acts of Parliament made against bearing and wearing of hagbutts and pistolls and convocation of the leiges, did by way of bangstry [2] and oppression, without any warrand or order of law in ane military manner come to the ground of that foresaid lands, and affixt and held ane pretendit court, did unlaw and amerciat [3] the absent tenants and decerned those that were present to receive tacks for him of the said lands,' etc.

When this case came on for trial, only Alexander Duff of Keithmore appeared as a defender, and was 'assoilzied.' It is possible that the Adam Duff of Clunybeg of this incident may be, not Alexander's father, who would have been seventy-three years of age, but Alexander's younger brother Adam, who also appears in the Horn Register, 'Adam and James Duff sonnes to Adam Duff in Clunicbeg.' [4]

Adam Duff had, by his first wife, one daughter, Margaret, married in 1641

---

[1] Prepared for a warlike expedition.   [2] Strength of hand, violence   [3] Fine

[4] This reference was first printed by Cramond in the *Genealogist* in 1887 'Adam and James Duff sones lawful to unqll Adam Duff in Clunicbeg,' and he gave to it the date 1649, as coming after an entry of that date, and before one of 1652, but it has been pointed out by Mr. Ree that the entry (which has been verified in the original Book of Hornings, now in Banff) is *valueless* legally and historically, as it bears no date of issue at Edinburgh, receipt at Banff, or of execution, and in the light of subsequent entries in the *same* book, duly dated, showing Adam of Clunybeg and Milntoun of Auchindoun as alive in much later years, it is obvious that this entry must be an error of name, of place, or of position in the Book of Hornings.

to George Geddes of Auchinhoof; by his second wife, Beatrix Gordon, he had a large family. To quote again from the Rose MS.: 'The sons of Adam Duff of Clunybeg, son of "Mr." John Duff (who died April 23, 1593), who was born 1590, and died by an accident at the Miln of Auchindoun 1675,[1] are Alexander, John, William, Adam, James, George, Andrew, and Thomas. Mr. Lawtie knew all the young men of the family of Adam Duff in Clunybeg, well known, too, in the farm of Ardione in the parish of Keith. He lived there and at Miln of Auchindoun with several of his sons in 1649.' The three elder sons, Alexander, John, and William, will be treated of in separate chapters; George, of whom nothing personal is known, is spoken of with severity by Baird as 'an idle, lazy, stupid fellow, very different from his three elder brothers.'

George Duff witnesses his father's signature on more than one occasion (Rose MS.), and he may possibly be identified with George Duff, servitor to Gordon of Edinglassie in 1680 (*Aberdeen Sheriff Court Records*). It was he who gave up his father's will in 1674, presumably as being the eldest son at home. George Duff was in Clunybeg in 1665, and gives an assignment to Alexander Duff his brother. (Adam their father was then alive.)

1712. The same George, writing from Burnend, grants a discharge to Braco for his annuity, and mentions his deceased brother Keithmore. Witness, Thomas Duff, servitor to Braco.

Not much is known of the others. Adam and James, as we have seen, were called at the instance of Thomas Spence (Horn Register), and in 1667 James Duff, lawful son of Adam Duff of Cluniebeg, grants an obligation to one Meldrum, which is witnessed by the said Adam Duff and George Duff, brother of granter (*Aberdeen Sheriff Court Records*).

James is said to have succeeded to Auchindoun, and James Duff, Milntoun of Auchindoun, occurs more than once as a witness.

John and Andrew are witnesses in Banff 1650 (Rose MS.).

Thomas appears in the Horn Register of 1653 as son to Adam Duff of Clunybeg. According to Rose, he was a skipper in Banff, and his children had property there.

John of Bowmakellach afterwards held Milntoun of Balvenie, as he renounced the same to his brother Alexander at Keithmore, April 21, 1674. John Duff signs it, Isabel Pringle, his wife, initials it 'I. P.,' and Alexander Duff, writer in Edinburgh (Braco) witnesses. Keithmore paid £60 Scots for the goodwill.

Two of Clunybeg's sons were dead when Baird wrote in 1773 or there-

---

[1] Really 1674.

abouts. One ' went south and never returned to the north country again,'
and one was ' drowned when crossing the water of Fiddich in a Spate,'
but no Christian name is given to either. The former was probably the
progenitor of a family of Duff which settled in Durham county, now represented by Mr. Edward J. Duff of Holly Lodge, Cressington Park, Liverpool.
Family tradition states that his ancestor, who belonged to the Clunybeg
and Keithmore family, left Scotland in connection with the political
troubles of the seventeenth century, but the intervening links have unfortunately been lost.

It is also stated that Adam of Clunybeg had another son named
Patrick or Peter, who would make the ninth, and was possibly the one
who ' went south.'

Besides the numerous sons, Adam Duff had by his second wife, Beatrix
Gordon, two daughters :

' Jean, married to John Muiren of Mather Cluny, and Helen, married to
—— Taylor in Ardgaithnay ' (Baird).

Baird seems, with his usual carelessness, to have transposed the
Christian names of the two daughters, for in the Botriphnic Kirk-Session
Records we find under date ' 1657. Compeared Patrick Taylor and Jean
Duff, before the Presbytery.' Ardgaithney is situated close to the station
of Drummuir.

Mether or Nether Cluny afterwards passed into the hands of the
descendants of Adam's son George, whose son was Adam.[1]

There is another side to the biography of Adam Duff of Clunybeg,
in which he appears as a pious elder of the Kirk-Session of Mortlach, some
extracts from the minutes of which may be given :

In 1623, among the elders in ' the Parochin of Mortlach,' we find Adam
Duff in Auchindoun.

In 1627, Adam Duff is appointed to be the keeper of the box containing
the ' commone guid,' to be distributed ' be the advice of the Sessions.'

From 1627 to 1647 (at which latter date there is a gap in the minutes),
Adam Duff of Clunebeg appears frequently as cautioner and suretie for
various persons, which shows him to have been a man of substance. In
1641 he is surety at the marriage of his own daughter Margaret to George
Geddes of Auchinhoof.[2]

In the same year he is appointed one of the elders, ' for the ingathering
of the penalties,' Auchindoun being his particular district.[3]

---

[1] Adam Duff in Mether Cluny, elder of Mortlach, 1711
[2] He therefore probably married his first wife about 1620
[3] For the above extracts we are indebted to Mr Ree of Boharm

' PRESBYTERY OF FORDYCE

' 26 July 1655   Visitation of Mortlach

' Adam Duff parishoner ther regrated that being ane elder, the minister had removed him off the Sessione w.out ordei, be sending to him ane man desiring him to byd fiom the Sessone, and 2dly that he had compared him to Elimas, the sorcerer.   The minister answered to 1, that he desired him to byd fiom the Session, be reasone of ane Act of the Generall Assemblie, as being accessorie to the lait unlawfull ingagementes, and to the second he answeied that he did but utter the apostles words and did not apply them to any.   The said Adam Duff stood to his assertiones and immediately departed saying that in tyme and place convenient he had moi to say, which he was to mak out quhen he was put to it.'

Notes of Clunybeg's death and funeral are thus given in William Rose's papers :

' Adam Duff of Clunybeg, whose Father was John Duff of Muldavit and Mothei, Margaret Goidon, must have been 84 years old at his death. Lord Braceo said George Duke of Goidon was at this burriall and Ogilvie of Ardo and Lord Findlater who died 1730.   Ogilvie of Ardo told Mr. Lawtie at Fordyce that he was at school at Deskford when the Corps passed to the Isle of Cullen,[1] from Clunybeg and Milntoun of Auchindoun.'   'All this I hold true, for George Duke of Gordon married and came north in Oct. 1676 '

(Adam Duff's funeral was therefore befoie the Duke's marriage.   He was not, of course, created Duke of Gordon until 1684, but he married Lady Elizabeth Howaid, daughter of the Duke of Noifolk and Earl of Norwich, in 1676).

There is, unfortunately, no monument to Adam of Clunybeg in Cullen or elsewheie.

There is a very powerful portrait of him by Honthorst in the possession of the Duchess of Fife, which is reproduced as a frontispiece to the present volume.[2]   An inferior painting of Beatrix Gordon is now at Montcoffer.

Adam Duff's will, which is very brief, is amongst the Duff House papeis. This fixes his death as having occurred in 1674 :

[1] The family burying-place of the Duffs of Muldavit   See chapter II

[2] The date, of course, is a later addition, and is recognisable as being in the same hand as other inscriptions on pictures in the Duff House collection, which later reseaiches have shown to be incorrect   See John Duff and Agnes Gordon in chapter II.   As Adam appears to be about fifty years old, the date should probably be about 1640 to 1645   The picture was formerly ascribed to Jamesone, but the name G Honthorst has been found upon it

' The Testament of the deceased Adam Duff in Clunicbeg, who died upon the — day of April 1674. The will given up by George Duff, lawful son to the deceased.' [1]

---

[1] Dr Charles Henry Duff, of East Bridgeford, Nottinghamshire, traces his descent from one of the younger sons of Adam Duff of Clunybeg, most probably James of Milntown in Auchindown, who is conjectured to have had a son James, who resided in Inverness

The first ancestor of whom Dr Duff has authentic record is Robert Duff, born 1711, whom he believes to have been great-grandson of Adam Duff of Clunybeg, and therefore second cousin to and contemporary of William, first Lord Fife   Thereafter the family is as follows.

Robert Duff, born 1711, had a brother Thomas, born 1713, died 1801 ;
he m Barbara Gordon, and had fourteen children   He is buried in Inverness

John Alexander, 1759-1829, m Catherine Lucy Maudsley.

Thomas William Duff, 1789 1856, lived in Southwark, and was a clerk in the Bank of England   Was married three times   By his first wife, Utricia Goodman, had two sons and one daughter

John, o s p

William Henry, 1815-1883, m Charlotte Burton

George, killed by Kaffirs in South Africa, 1860

Fanny, o s p

Charles Henry, born 1861, m Edith M Baily in 1909

Thomas William, died in Australia

Fanny Louisa, m Captain Horatio Bland

Barbara Gordon, born 1910.

David Shere, born 1912

Horatio, R N , died 1901

Charles E W , born 1881

ALEXANDER DUFF OF KEITHMORE   HELEN GRANT, HIS WIFE

From their tombstones in Mortlach

CHAPTER V

ALEXANDER DUFF OF KEITHMORE

THE history of Alexander of Keithmore, eldest son of Adam of Clunybeg, is thus given by Baird : ' He was the heir and worthy successor of Adam Duff of Clunybeg, and was an officer under Montrose in all his campaigns of 1644, '45, and '46, and when the Marquis went beyond sea in consequence of his capitulation with Midleton in September 1646, he went over to the Continent likewise, but to what country I do not know. He came home in a year after, when the violent prosecutions of the Loyalists were over. But it is affirmed, he was then taken up by the Covenanters and thrown into prison, where he lay a long time. However, he got his liberty at last.' Among the Duff House papers the following records of his military career are preserved :

'George, marquesse of Huntly, his Majesty's Lieutenant of and in the northern partes of this his Majesty's Kingdome of Scotland. . . . Be vertue of his Majestie's Commission Granted to us, we doe by these presents appoynt you, Alexander Duff captain of ane troup to consist of fiftae horses with their Ryders sufficiently armed, to be within the regiment of our sonne the Lord Gordon,

Giveing you full power to exercise all the functions and ducties belonging to ane captain of horses and to command all your inferior officers and souldiers, as they are to be obedient to you. Provyding alwayes, you be accountable to us for deschargeing the said office and obedient to the command of your superior officers. Given under our hand and seale at Huntly the 23rd of October 1645.'

'Captain Alexander Duffe is heerby ordained to passe into the lands of Mulben, Strayla, Grange, Rothemay and Tordewhill, and to levie from thence ane horseman for his Majesty's service sufficiently armed out of euerie daugh [1] of the said lands excepting only such lands as pertaine in proper possession without being wadset to Glengarrioche, Burkenburn, Miltoun, Carestown, Achaynochie, Brako, and Floores, And to conduct the said horseman to ane rendewoues appoynted at Huntly upon Monday next, the last of this month, be ten houres in the fore-noon, for which these shall be unto the said Captain Duffe ane sufficient warrant. Signed at Huntly the twentie-fourth day of November 1646.'

'By Major-General Middletone. These graunts protection to Alexander Duff, sone to Adam Duff of Clunybeg, from all violence and wrong to be done to him in his person, estate, goods or geir by any whosever, hee alwayes behaveing himself deutifullie not joyneing wt. the enemie, and being answerable to Church and state for his varriage [2] whensoever he shall be called. Given at Strathbogie the 7th day of May 1647. Jo. MIDDLETONE.'

'June 1647. Mr. Walter Day, minister of Deskfoord, Wm. Leslie of Milton of Balvenie and Walter Leslie of Tullich, testify that they, conform to the ordinance of the Church holden at Aberdeen in May last, received Alexander Duff, son to Adam Duff of Clunebeg, this day after divine worship, and after his public and solemn humiliation in presence of the Congregation of church of Mortlch, have absolved him of all censure for his dehquenere.'

'By General Major Middletone. These are requiring all officers and souldiers or any whomsoever nott to trouble or molest the persone or goods off Alexander Duff seeing he hath satisfie both Kirk and estautt. Given at Pitluig the eight day off February 1648. Jo. MIDDLETONE.'

'Pass by Major General Middletone, Commander of the Forces. . . . I doe hereby graunt unto Alexander Duff sonne to Adam Duff of Clunybeg full assurance of his life and fortune to be unquestioned in either of them, for any deed done by him in the late course of rebellion hee hath formerlie bene in, or in relation theirto, Provided hee behave himself dutifully in time comeing, otherwise this favour to be voyd. Given at Petlug the 26th day of March 1648. Jo. MIDDLETONE.'

'These are requyring the comander of party, lying upon Alex. Duffe off Sichache, uponne sight heirof to remove to his truppe wt. his party, as lykwais requiring all officiers under my comande not till trubill nor mollest the said Alex. Duffe untill suche tyme that the business betwixt him and Captaine Dauisone or his father be discussit farther before the Comitty off Estaits or Lords

---

[1] Four hundred and sixteen acres.   [2] Feudal service

of Sessione. Given at Leith the twenty-seuinthe day of Dec 1649 yens. DAVID
LESLIE.'

Keithmore was a little man, according to Baird, and ' in the deeline
of life beeame very eoipulent, which was probably owing to the fatiguing
eampaigns he had with Montrose. This made his friends call him Croihe [1]
Duff,' and under that title a ballad was written about him, whieh must be
given here :

'CREELY DUFF

(ALEXANDER DUFF OF KEITHMORE AND BRACO, 1623-1696)

1. Oh, heard ye e'er o' Creely Duff
   Wha lived intill Keithmore ?
   My troth he was a comely wight,
   The gudeman o' Keithmoie.

2. Creely had neither chaise nor coach
   For him to ride in state,
   But a puir yad (hoise) was never shod,
   Though Braco noo rides great

3. His saddle was o' gude sheep's skin,
   Weel covered wi' the wool,
   And it wad never change its hue
   For weathei fair or fool.

4. His stirrups was the thiawin' wands,[2]
   His bridle was the hair,
   And oh, he was a comely knight,
   Wi' a' his ridin' gear

5. He had a creel upon his back,
   Made o' guid foreign segs,[3]
   It was to carry his maiket waies—
   His chickens and his eggs

6. On ilka scoie he gained a plack,[4]
   And laid it up in store.
   This is the verra way that he
   Got wadset of Keithmore.

---

[1] ' Croil,' a distorted person, a dwarf (Jamieson) It has sometimes been said that the
name Creely Duff was derived from the fact that he did at one time go about the country with
a creel, as in the ballad, but this is unlikely
[2] Weaving wands.   [3] Rushes
[4] A small copper coin equal to the third part of an English penny

7   There dwelt a witch wife in the land,
       Wha mony an ane did wrong—
     Both lairds and knights and gentlemen
       O' jolly and high renown.

8   She pit a red cow till his fauld
       Wha ever heard her cries,
     Wadset their lands in Braco's hands,
       And this made Braco rise.'

In the year 1650, Alexander Duff married Helen, daughter of Alexander Grant of Allachie, brother of Archibald Grant of Ballintomb, and Baird's further account of this notable couple is so delightful that it must be given in full :

'Keithmoir was a judicious, frugal, honest man ; and, tho' abundantly active and diligent, a great share of his success in acquiring money is ascribed to his wife, one of the most industrious, painstaking women of the age in which she lived, or perhaps of any other. She was a sturdy, big-boned woman, and at last became so fat and bulky that it is said it required an eln of plaiding to make her a pair of hose, and that one time when she threw herself hastily into her chair, without taking notice that the house cat was lying squat upon the seat, she prest puss so effectually to death with the weight of her body, that it never wagged a foot more, and she was so broad that no armed chair of the common size could admit of her sitting in it. [1]

'Helen Grant was a most hospitable kind housekeeper, while at the same time she neglected no commendable and virtuous method of thriving.

'It is said of Keithmoir's lady, Helen Grant, that she would have gone to market with 1000 elns of plaiding, all made of the wool of her own sheep, and riden on the horse crupper behind one of the loads herself, and brought home 1000 mks. as the price of her plaiding.

'It's said she had alwise great plenty of gold and silver specie. In those troublesome times people were afraid to lend out their money, or even to be let it known that they had any, for fear of being robbed, and therefore hid it in holes and bores for this purpose. I heard lately one of her grandchildren tell the following story : During the Usurpation of Oliver Cromwell she had concealed a great leather bag full of ducatons in the ceiling of the Hall at Keithmoir and the rats had just finished gnawing a chasm in the bottom of the bag, when a large company was at dinner, a shower of dollars fell on the floor, everybody rose to give their assistance

---

[1] The portrait of Helen Duff, by a Venetian artist, is in the possession of the present writers The proportions of the lady fully justify the above story.

HELEN GRANT

in gathering, but the Lady entreated them all in a very peremptory tone of voice to keep their seats, for she did not want anybody to gather but herself!

'And in the beginning of King William's reign, about 1689, being informed one day that a party of military was in the neighbourhood, and afraid lest they should come to Keithmoir and take her money, she delivered a sealed bag of gold and silver coin to her grandchild, old Lesmurdy, a boy then seventeen or eighteen years of age, and desired him to hide it somewhere in the ground and to set a mark at the place that he might find it again, but to be sure to hide it well, because she would rather wish it was lost than that King William's Dragoons should get it The boy dig'd a hole at the side of a strype of water which runs alongst the Green of Keithmoir, in which he laid the bag and covered it with earth, and when the party was gone he took it out and delivered it to his grandmother.

'Keithmoir got a good portion with this honest worthy lady, and afterwards by the death of her brother, Patrick Grant of Allachie, succeeded to 100,000 merks more, including the Wadset of Allachie itself and Belcherie which was most profitable, and not long ago redeemed from the last Lord Fife, by Sir Lodvick Grant and sold to James Grant of Cairon; for tho' there were three or four sisters all married, Keithmoir and his wife were greater favorites of the brother than any of the rest. And by a proper improvement of this and his own original stock, he died possest of 24,000 merks of land rent, and this besides large purchases which his eldest son Braco made in his father's lifetime, for he was near fifty years old when Keithmoir died. He got the Wadset of Keithmoir from the Marquis of Huntly sometime between 1640 and 1646, and very probably exchanged it with Clunybeg (his father) on such terms as they could agree on

'In 1676, he got his armorial bearings matriculated, and the following certification from the Lord Lion:

' " I certifie and make known that the coat armorial appertaining and belonging to Alexr. Duff of Keithmoir, lineally descended from the family of Moldavid and Craighead, and approved of and confirmed by me, Sir Charles Erskine of Cambo, Lord Lyon King-at-Arms, to him of this date, is matriculated in my public register, etc., viz., a fesse danizette ermine, between a Buck's head caboshed in chieff, and two escallops in base, or," ' etc.[1]

---

[1] To the statement above made, a different but apparently contemporary hand adds ' There is good reason to believe that he is not the representer of Craighead ' This note may still be seen at the Lyon Office, but, pace Dr Cramond, it does not throw any doubt upon Alexander's descent through his father, Adam of Clunybeg, from 'Mr.' John Duff of Muldavit, who died in 1593, but merely indicates what we already know, that some descendants of some of Adam's ten or eleven elder brothers were still living at that period, especially John Duff,

William Duff, Inverness, to William Duff of Dipple

'INVERNESS, 27th Febry. 1691.

'D: NEPHEW,—I receeaved my joint letter with your postscript theron giveing me the sadd newes of your mother's death [*Helen Grant of Allachie*]. I pray God grant all concerned grace to submitt humbly and patiently to the good hand off God who corrects us in measure and less than we deserve. I pray Dear Nephew give your old father your best and most Christiane advise for his comfortable subsistance in the world for I only pittie him in this juncture. I mett with my Lord Lovat the day at the burriall and xcused yow to him. I receeaved Mortomer's lyne to you—but I am firmly resolved not to ingage in wictuall this year the two half anchors are filled with sack from Bailie McIntosh which holds just two ye can make sure and pay him att your return. I expect to see yowe very sone the next week and till y^n I remaine your affectionat Uncle,

WM. DUFF.

'ffor William Duff off Dypill ffor the present at Keithmore, there.'

'Keithmoir and his lady are interred in the Church of Mortlach, under a stately monument of cut stone. And above then grave both their statues stand, very well chiselled, and extremely like. As I was informed, they are placed on a stone bench, and make a comely graceful appearance, both jolly figures and looking like peace and plenty.[1] The following inscription is engraven above them.

'"Within this tomb are deposited the remains of Alexr. Duff of Keithmoir, and Helen Grant, his spouse, the lineal and lawfull heir to the ancient family of Craighead, lately in possession of that estate, and originally

burgess of Aberdeen, and his son John Duff who went to Rotterdam and died in 1718, and was always known as 'the heir' It apparently escaped Cramond that, on the same page of the Lyon Register, but above his brother, William Duff (afterwards Provost of Inverness), matriculated the *same* arms with the difference of a mullet, in right of his being 'a 3rd son of the family of Craighead, which is the same as Muldavit,' and that the contemporary commentator, whoever he may have been, in this case made no objection.

[1] Alexander paid the bill for this monument at the time of his wife's death, and sketches for the figures are preserved with the receipt Owing to its position in Mortlach church this monument cannot now be photographed, but the sketch at the head of chapter was done some years ago by Constance Tayler, sister of the writers, and gives an excellent idea of it

descended, he from the most notable Thanes, Earls of Fife, and she of the most illustrious and powerfull Clan of the Grants." [1]

' Tho' this inscription is no proof of the Duffs being of the same stock with the old Thanes of Fife, it shows that the story is not newly trumped up, but that it was supported a hundred years ago by an old and invariable tradition ' (Baird)

Keithmore left three sons: ALEXANDER DUFF of Braco, born 1652; WILLIAM DUFF of Dipple, born 1653; and PATRICK DUFF of Craigston; and four daughters: 1. MARGARET, married to James Stewart of Lesmurdy, and had one son. 2. JEAN, married in 1680 to Mr. George Meldrum, minister of Glass (see chapter xxvi.)—she died 1725. 3. MARY, ' married in 1684, 1st to Dr. Andrew Fraser, Physician at Inverness, to whom she bore one daughter, Helen, married to Charles Hay of Rannes, and by him mother of a numerous issue. And after Doctor Fraser's death she married, in 1710, Thomas Tulloch of Tannachy,[2] one of the oldest families in Murray, to whom she had one son Alexander, the present Tannachy, and two daughters, the younger of the two, Elizabeth, married to Alexander Cuming of Craigmiln, who was engaged with Prince Charles in 1745, taken prisoner at Culloden, and died in jail at Carlisle in 1746, leaving, by her, five daughters and two sons, one an officer in France and married to a Frenchwoman, and the other a Miln-wright in Jamaica ' (Baird).

4. ELIZABETH, in 1685, married to a son of Thomas and a brother of Sir James Calder, but he died ' within the year,' and there was no family.

The three following letters from Alexander (of which the originals, very difficult to decipher, are preserved amongst the Drummuir papers), are interesting :

Alexander of Keithmore to his nephew Alexander Duff of Drummuir

' KEITHMORE, *Dec*. 21, 1685.

' AFFECTIONATE DEAR NEPHEW,—You will perceive by my son's line to you and by his line to me which he desired me to send along to you, wherein falsely

---

[1] Hoc conduntur tumulo reliquiae Alexandri Duff de Keithmore et Helenae Grant uxoris suae charissimae qui quadraginta annos et ultra felici et faecundo connubio juncti vixerunt uterque quidem ingenue natus Ille ex nobilissimis Fifae Thanis per vetustam familiam de Craighead paulo ab hinc superstitem proxime et legitime oriundus Illa ex splendida et potenti Grantorum familia eodem quoque modo originem trahens ortu non obscuri suis tamen virtutibus illustriores opibus affluxerunt et liberis ingenue educatis floruere pie juste et sobrie vixerunt et sic in Domino mortem obiere, Illa anno Domini 1694 aetatis suae sexagesimo—(unfinished).

[2] Tannachy is now Invererne, near Forres Thomas Tulloch was grandson to the man mentioned in the deeds of Montrose as 'Tannachy Tulloch,' one of the 'loyal gentlemen ' who came to greet Montrose when led a prisoner through Inverness, May 6, 1650.

malitiously and unjustly we are troubled by Arthur Forbes under treaty which occasions us to put you to this trouble to look upon the copies of the charges offering, and to raise a suspension for us with all the haste you can and to get the Will of the date Dec. 17 and to cause intimate it to Arthur however soon you can and to advise letters of loosing of arrestment conform to the copies sent herewith. There are many more laid upon our tenants which we could not get up so speedily. I have according as you will see by this line, written a line to Mr. Thomas Gordon and sent 6 dollars which you may deliver or not as you think expedient. If you cannot get this business done yourself with as much diligence as Mr. Thomas Gordon can, I have sent a precept to raise Horning against some of my Lord Gordon's tenants, which he did put a factory upon me to collect some bonds which you will have cause raise and then by adducement contained in the horning. If you think it needful and deliver the letter to Mr. Thomas Gordon, what more monies he calls for be pleased to advance it and it shall be sent you very thankfully. We have written likewise a line to Mr. William Gordon, Lesmoir's son, to be assisting in the affairs if you should require him. My son will see you when needful.

' I pray you take so much time as to writ howe your own affairs are going on and what Dorothy [1] is doing. You will receive the 6 dollars with this letter and do as you think best, before I cast the stress of the affair upon you. Pray you despatch the monies to your cousin Brikenburn and despatch the bearer how soon you can.—Your loving uncle,   ALEXANDER DUFF.

'To Alex. Duff of Drummuir.'

The same to the same

'KEITHMORE, 4th Feb 1686.

' AFFECTIONATE DEAR NEPHEW,—Having occasion to send this south to my son, I could not omit the occasion to salute you and to let you know that, blessed be God, all friends and relations are in good health, and wish to hear the like of you and wish to be refreshed with good news of your affairs. Please know the bargain anent my Lord Airlie's salmon fishing is closed. Westerton, your father, Provost Stewart, Bailie, my son William and William Calder partners. They advance £14,000 Scots for the 10 years tack, my lord keeps the creels to himself. I entreat you acquaint me how the prices of Westhall are like to be and how the affair of Auchflunkart goes, and with Dorothy, and how my sone's affairs goes with Arthur Forbes and what Crombie is doing and what counter occurrence is passing. With greetings from my bedfellow and my own humble service is all at present, from your loving uncle,   ALEXANDER DUFF.'

---

[1] Dorothy Lawson, stepmother of Drummuir's wife. See chapter xxii.

Alexander Duff of Keithmore to his hon. brother William, Provost of Inverness

'KEITHMORE, *Mar.* 6, 1693.

'AFFEC. DEAR BROTHER,—I received yours as to the land of Bellyhack, which truly if it were not agrassed with my other land and conformed I could easily be persuaded to obtemper your desire, but I am only an [*illegible*] and my sone have been at paynes in purchasing the right and are more loth to break the interest being out confirmed, but if you and my son can fall upon any terms of satisfaction, I shall be a good instrument thereanent, though wist you whatt of shall be acceptable for truly I am very tender (*i e.* infirm), and my wife also. We both tender our kindly respects to you and your bedfellow and children and other friends and relations with you and remain, your affectionate and heartie,   ALLXANDER DUFF.'

The writer was then over seventy years of age, and died three years later; his wife in 1694 (eleven months later).

The much honoured Laird of Braco from Jean Duff, daughter of Alexander Duff of Keithmore and wife of the Rev. George Meldrum

'AFFECTIONATE BROTHER,—Receive enclosed, one double of Ardmeallic's libel with one letter from Tarlair, who it seems received not your letter timeously, but I 'll show you it was none of my default, for James Lumsden was sent with it to Banff on Wednesday after you went from this place, but not finding Tarlair in the town entrusted the delivering of it to one other who, it seems, has neglected it.

'They came here by Mr. Francis Grant of Cullen his brother this forenoon, and the bearer is sent express to know your thoughts of it and to advertyse you timeously that you may take your own methods thereon, and this with my love and respects to yourself, and lady, is all at the time from your affectionate sister and servant,   JEAN DUFF.

'My son-in-law,[1] his wife and sisters remember you kindly.

'CROMBIE, *June* 27, 1699.'

A bill follows, 'Fully paid and done,' for sums paid to Daniel Simpson for the advice at the instance of the Lady Crombie and John Ramsay against Isabel Meldrum and Gordon of Ardmeallic her husband. The other items are of no interest.

Various conflicts with the authorities on the part of Alexander of Keithmore have already been noted in the chapter on his father. Two later episodes must here be mentioned.

---

[1] James Duff, afterwards of Crombie. See chapter xxvii.

In 1662 Alexander Duff of Keithmore was charged with 'defrauding the customs.' The complainers, Thomas Fraser and Alexander Burnet, younger, burgesses in Aberdeen, went to St. Rufus fair, held at Keith, and bought from James Grant (at Keithlich in Auchindoun) a web of linen cloth, measured to 70 ells.

'But Jas. Grant, with Alex. Duff in Keithmore and others of sett purpose to affront and abuse the merchants and burgesses of Aberdeen upon pretence that the said cloath was not rightly measured, did insted of performing their bargan for delyverie of the same, calumniate and abuse them, threathen and menace them and in the oppen mercat did draw furth durkes of purpose to have murthered them—which abuse was powerfully occasioned by the ignorance of James Barclay, dean of gild of Banff who pretendit to have the rule and government of the said mercat, and most illegalli caused one George Mintie, indweller in Banff, measure the said web—who caused the same to be holden and drawne be thrie severall persons and thereby rent and racked the same to two elnes more nor the said Jas. Grant had caused Alex. Duff to measure the same, and 4 elnes more than the 70 elnes which was the number at which the same was bought and measured, and by force, bangstry [1] and oppression of James Grant and Alex. Duff, and throw the malice and ignorance of the Dean of Gild, forced the compleaners to make payment of four elnes more of the said plyding cloath than was the true and just measure of the same as it was first measured upon the place be the saids complianers and afterwards by honest merchants in Aberdeen—Lykas the said Jas. Grant did openly confess that the said web was only 70 elnes truly and that he had cutted off 4 elnes therefore before he had come from home.

'Defenders having been charged did not appear. The Lords ordain them to be put to the horn and escheated' (*Register of Privy Council*).

'1664. Complaint by Alex. Kemp in Auchindoun against Alex. Duff of Keithmore, and John Duff in Milntoun his brother, for assault and illegal warding.

'Alexander and John Duffs, having conceaved ane deadly malice against the said complainer, without any just cause or provocation on his part, did upon the —— day of May 1661 come to his house of Tanon, accompanied with diverse persons armed in ane hostile manner, and apprehend his person, and band his hands behind his back and most cruellie gave him several most dangerous and deadly wounds, and thereafter patt him in a pair of stockes, where they keepit him be the span of 8 days and above, in ane dungeon in the house of Auchindoun, while the whole blood of his body ran out at his finger ends and by that and by famen within and rattones and other vermin without, he was lyke to be destroyed' (*Register of Privy Council*).

James Duff in Milntown was called as a witness, but the result of the trial is not given.

-----

[1] Violence

ALEXANDER DUFF OF KEITHMORE.

In spite of this, in the year 1666 Alexander Duff of Keithmore was granted ' a commission to apprehend rebels.'

In 1695, Alexander of Braco, Keithmore's son, complains that in the year 1689, by General Mackay's order, troops were quartered at Balvenie under Captain Gordon and Captain Grant. At that time there were 500 bolls of meal in the castle—part of which was used by the soldiers; after the battle of Killiecrankie the rebels came to the castle and took away the rest of the meal. He prays for payment for his meal ' as he himself was attending the meeting of the estates.' He adds that his ' father, an old man of seventy years of age, was taken by the rebells out of his own house (of Keithmore), which was plundered and destroyed by them, and he himself keeped in a starving condition untill he was necessitat to pay a ransom for his relieffe.' Compensation for the meal was granted to Braco (*Acts of the Scottish Parliament*).

In the *Seafield Correspondence* there is a letter from George Ogilvie to the Earl of Findlater, in which he says: ' Keithmore Duff has dealt very treacherously, which he is like to suffer for by the Highlanders.'

He had apparently been ' holding' the castle of Balvenie (which was later fortified by his great-nephew William of Braco in 1715), in the interests of King William and General Mackay, and after Killiecrankie he had retired to his own house of Keithmore.[1]

There is a very beautiful portrait of Alexander Duff of Keithmore, as a young man (painted, apparently, by a Venetian artist), in the possession of the Duchess of Fife, here reproduced.

Alexander of Keithmore, eldest son of Adam of Clunybeg, obtained from the Marquis of Huntly a wadset of Keithmore, Mortlach, which long continued to be his residence. The old house, of which little is left, is now turned into a cow-byre, and a new house has been built, but in the old walls can still be seen the loopholes for defence; also the arms, on a stone in the dyke. Clunybeg is to the north of the old house of Keithmore.

Alexander Duff added greatly to the estates held by his father. His name occurs frequently in the list of Banffshire sasines.

In 1646 he got a wadset of Keithmore.
In 1650 of Succoth.
In 1657 ' Alex. Duff of Soccoth and Helen Grant his spouse took saisine of the lands of Lettach and old Auchlaggan.'

[1] It seems somewhat hard upon Alexander Duff that he should have suffered in his youth from *having joined* the Royalist party, *i.e.* his father was fined for his ' malignancy ' and he himself forced to fly the country, and again in his old age should have been maltreated for *not having joined* the same party.

In 1660 of the town and lands of Pittyvaich and Fittie.

In 1666 of the town and lands of Clunybeg.

In 1673 of Bellyhack and Towie.

In 1677 of Towiemore and Delchan.

In 1678 of the towne and lands of Farmtoune and oythers.

In 1678 All the lands of Medder Clunybeg and 8 oxgates of Milntoun of Balvenie.

In 1679 Miln of Auchindoun. Another wadset of Keithmore, August 16, 1679.

In 1683 the dauch lands of Turtorie with lands of Coldhome and Idmitter, with the lands and lordship of Balvenic.

In 1688 ane yearly arent of 300 merks out of the lands of Edinglassie.

And finally, in 1692, 'the renunciation of Alexander Duff of Keithmore in favours of his grace the Duke of Gordon of the lands of Keithmore and Mylne and mylnetoun of Auchindoun and lands of Clunybeg and Shenwall wt. yr pertinents.' He had Braco in the year 1678 and in 1681 made it over to his son.

After he acquired part of the lordship of Balvenie, he was 'Baron Baillie' for the Duke of Gordon in Auchindoun. He first appears in the suite roll of Barons and Freeholders of Banffshire in the Midsummer Court, 1675, where he is entered 'for the lands of Lettach and Auchlaggan.' In the Pasch Court of 1678 he also appears as superior of Buchromb and Milntown of Balvenie, formerly held by his father-in-law, Grant of Allachie.

BRACO HOUSE (REBUILT AND MODERNISED)

CHAPTER VI

ALEXANDER DUFF OF BRACO

1652-1705

'ALEXANDER DUFF OF BRACO was born in 1652. After his education at school and college was over[1] he attended a Writer to the Signet's (A. Boyd's) chambers at Edinburgh some years, and came into employment himself as an agent, but retired to the country in 1675. He married early to Margaret Gordon, daughter of Sir James Gordon of Lesmore, who outlived him many years; he sat long in the Scotch Parliament, as one of the representatives of the county of Banff; he took the oath of allegiance in 1689 and sat again in 1693-1701, and was alwise for what he thought the interest of his country. In the beginning of the eighteenth century it was the general opinion of the Scotch nation that an incorporating union with England would be very detrimental to the interest and honour of their country. Braco, being of this opinion, opposed the union strenuously, and was on that account much regarded by the Duke of Hamilton and all the leading men of that side. Mr. Gordon of Pitlurg, who was then one of the representatives for the county of Aberdeen, used to tell that when Braco went north on account of his private affairs, the duke always stipulated with him that he should return against a day appointed. (He likewise

---

[1] He was at Marischal College, Aberdeen, in 1664.

said that though Braco went very plain and even coarse at home, he was still extremely well drest at Edinburgh.) He lost all patience if he suspected that any of his friends was like to desert and join the court side, and would threaten them bloodily. Being informed that one gentleman,[1] a near ally of his, was wavering, he came into the room where he was, drew his shable, and drove him into a corner, alwise shaking it over his head in great passion and saying, "Ha, man, ha, man, are you going to vote against the good of your country? Deil ha' me, I'll head you like a Sybow" (*i.e.* a spring onion).

'At another time, being told that several of the Peers were gained by the Ministry, he swore he would buy a whole bench of them out of the ground.

'He was certainly a good countryman in all national concerns, and a very useful member of society in the north of Scotland, by the care he took to have all the Highland robbers and thieves who pestered the low country at that time apprehended and brought to justice, on which occasions he frequently exposed his own life to very great danger, but at the same time gave good proof of his courage and conduct. One instance which made a great deal of noise at the time, was the seizing of James Macpherson and Peter Brown at Summerrive's fair[2] at Keith, September 1700. These were two notorious villains, breakers of the peace in all sorts of villainy, whom Braco had made several attempts to catch, but as they were protected by the Laird of Grant, he was still disappointed. As soon as he spied them in the market, he desired his brother-in-law, Lesmurdy, to bring him a dozen of stout able men which he did; they all attackt the villains, who, having several of their accomplices with them, made a desperate resistance. One of them made a pass at Braco, intending to run him through the heart, but the dirk slanted alongst the outside of his ribs, without cutting the skin, and one of Braco's men stabb'd the fellow dead. They carried Macpherson and Brown to a house in Keith, where Braco and Lesmurdy left them with a guard, not expecting any more opposition. But when they were in an upper room with two or three of their acquaintances concerting the committment of their prisoners, the Laird of Grant, with thirty armed men, came to the door calling for them, and swearing that no Duff in Scotland should keep them from him. Braco, hearing the noise of the Grants, came downstairs and said, with seeming unconcern and good-humour, that he intended to have sent them to prison, but he saw they were protected by too strong a party for him to contend with, and he must give them up; but without losing a moment he took a turn through the market, found other two Justices of the Peace, held a court, and assembled sixty

---

[1] James Abercromby   [2] A corruption of St Malrubius' fair

bold men who retook the criminals. They were sent to prison, carried to Edinburgh and tried; they were both condemned to be hanged. Macpherson's sentence was executed,[1] but by Grant's interest Brown's was changed into banishment.

'I have heard likewise, that to all his relations and allies, Alex. Duff of Braco was a faithful firm friend, and would have gone any length to serve them. In a word, he was a very significant man in his time, and bore great weight in the public and private transactions of the Shire of Banff while he lived. One trifling anecdote, which I heard from his nephew, old Hatton, shews his acuteness and the quickness of his reflection to that point which he seems to have had alwise in view. A sturdy Beggar, having heard that he had pickt up a halfpenny from the street of Banff, came up to him craving an alms and saying, "God bless ye, Braco. Gi's a babee, and if ye winna gi's a babee of your awen, gi's the babee that ye fand." "Find a babee to yourself," says Braco.

'He made a great many additions to the Family estate in his father's time, whom he only survived five or six years;[2] they both joined in bringing about the Purchase of the noble estate of Balvenie, which they had in view from about the year 1675, and completed in 1687' (Baird).

This castle is one of the finest ruins in the north of Scotland, and contained the magnificent room known as the Dane's hall. 'The building bears traces of occupation by the Stewarts, Earls of Athol, who built it, and the national arms occupy a niche over the entrance door. The strong gate is still in position. In its palmy days the castle consisted of a large square occupying about a Scotch acre in extent, with a lofty tower at the gateway and turrets at the four angles. Since 1720 it has been roofless, and is now a complete ruin.'[3]

Cordiner says: 'Through all the periods to which our more authentic histories extend, the possession of this fortress was an object of ambition to the most noble and powerful families of the kingdom. There is a large circular tower at the S.E. corner and small towers on the other angles.'[4] In the book of the Barons and Freeholders of the Sheriffdom of Banff, 1664-1722, the Master of Saltoune is entered in 1685 for Balvenie; in 1696, Alexander Duff of Braco for the lordship of Balvenie.

He purchased many other estates in Banffshire. In 1684 there is an order by the Marquis of Huntly to the tenants of Grange to 'grind out' their corn at the Nether Mills of Strathyla possessed by Alexander Duff of Braco.

---

[1] At Banff on the Gallowhill
[2] It was in reality nine years
[3] Shaw's *History of Moray*
[4] Cordiner's *Remarkable Ruins*

As appears from the description of the lands comprised in the Braco entail (File Estates Improvement Act, 1858, 21 and 22 Vic cap. 4), 'the lordship of Balvenie comprehends the tower, fortalice, mains, and manor place of Balvenie, with yeards, orchyeards, miln, milnlands, multures,[1] sequells,[2] woods, fishings, parts, pendicles and pertinents thereof, advocation, donation and rights of patronage of the parish kirks of Keith and Grange and the whole teinds, as well great as small parsonage and vicarage of the said parishes. Also the lands of Middle and West Bochromes, half davoch[3] lands of Lettervandich, and half davoch lands of Braigach, Cluniebeg, Medder Cluny, the eight oxgate of land of Milntoun of Balvenie, Lynemore, Dellachame and Succoth, half davoch lands of Bellyhack, davoch lands of Rudderie and Lyne, Parkmore, Little Tullich, Lettoch, Auldachlaggan, lands and barony of Edinglassie, with castle tower, fortalice, etc., Meikle Dummeath, Lesser Dummeath, Succoth, Pittavaich, Laighie, Tomnamuid, Parkbegg, etc., etc. The aforesaid lands lie in the parishes of Mortlach, Aberlour, and Glass.'

The castle of Balvenie, built by the Earls of Athol, came next into the possession of Abernethy of Saltoun and then into that of the family of Innes. Arthur Forbes of Blacktown attempted to purchase it about 1668, but he had neither the capital nor the business capacity to carry through such a transaction. He, however, assumed the title of Balvenie in 1670-1671, but a few years later Alexander Duff of Braco and his father began to lend Forbes small sums of money and afterwards bought up a great many of his debts, amounting in all to £21,000 Scots. In 1687 Alexander Duff of Drummuir, who seems to have been acting for Braco against the unfortunate Arthur Forbes, obtained 'a decreet of removing' to turn him out, and so got possession of the estate. An action was raised against Braco before the Privy Council for some acts of violence committed upon Forbes and his tenants, but, as Baird sagely observes, 'Braco being in possession of all the rents, the process went heavily on, and Arthur died himself in 1694 or '95.' After this, Braco redeemed the wadsets upon that estate as soon as they expired. 'There were likewise at that time, a great many of small owners of parcels of the Lordship of Balvenie, mostly in the Parish of Mortlach.'

---

[1] *Multure*, the fee for grinding grain

[2] *Sequels*, small parcels of corn or meal given as a fee to the servants, over and above what is paid to the multurer, and they pass by the name of knaveship, and of bannock and lock or gowpen (Jamieson's *Scots Dictionary*).

[3] *Davoch* or *Dwach* is explained by Mr. Cosmo Innes, in his work entitled *Scotch Legal Antiquities*, thus—an *oxgate*, or 'what effeired to the cultivation of one ox, where pleuch and scythe may gang,' was 13 acres. *Husband-land*, 2 oxgates, 26 acres *Plough-gate*, the quantity of land tilled by 8 oxen, 104 acres *Davach*, equal to four ploughs, 416 acres

A story is told of him, that gazing one day upon the number of little homesteads lying in this valley he remarked, ' I 'll gar a' that reek gae thro' ae lum yet.' For the English reader, we may explain that it was his intention to cause all the smoke from the various family hearths to pass up one chimney, presumably his own. To continue from Baird :

' All these Braco deprived of their heritage at as little expense as he could. And it is too well known and much to be regretted that he was not very ceremonious either as to the Legality or Equity of the method ; and I really believe his severe and oppressing treatment of these little Proprietors who were not able to defend themselves brought a great deal of Odium upon his name, and made John, Earl of Kintore, add a new petition to his Prayers, " Lord, keep the Hill of Foudlin between me and Braco." [1]

' William Duff of Braco and the late Lord Fife purchast several parts of the Lordship of Balvenie which came in the market in their time in a fair and candid manner, and most of them at high prices, so that the present Lord Fife now possesses a very great part of that Estate , and I believe he and his predecessors have, considering everything, paid an adequate price for the Whole.'

There was a curious incident connected with the estate of Balvenie, when it was in the hands of the Abernethys of Saltoun. ' One James Abernethy (grand-uncle to the last Mayen, who married Jean Duff of Hatton), a near relation of Lord Saltoun, an advocate and manager of cause against Stewart of Blackhall, a sly fellow, went to London in 1657 and, being properly recommended to Oliver Cromwell, got an order from him to Lenthall, then Master of the Rolls, to allow him to inspect the Records and other writs from Scotland, which were lodged in the Tower, upon pretence that some personal papers belonging to Alexr. Lord Saltoun had been carried up in mistake, and there he tore out three leaves from the records of the Court of Session of the year 1605 which contained the Decreet loosing the voluntary Interdiction of John, Lord Saltoun, in 1600, and brought them with him to Scotland, without communicating what he had done to any person. His villainy was not discovered till Martinmas 1691. His brother Alexander found the three leaves among James' papers after his death, but concealed the thing to save his brother's memory, and enclosed them in a box of wood which he fixt under a couple in a new house which he was then building ; [2] but at his own death he imparted the whole, under promise of secrecy, to one James Ogilvie his nephew ; and he, when on his

---

[1] Another version of this story gives the phrase as being ' between me and that damned Duff '

[2] Now the farm of Mains of Mayen

own deathbed, touched with remorse of conscience and under great agony of mind for having concealed it so long, acknowledged the whole and signed a declaration of all the circumstances which was sent to Edinburgh. A search was then made, the box found and sent to Edinburgh. The three leaves tallyed exactly with the place from which they had been torn, and were writ on paper of the same stamp. The Lords ordered them to be replaced and accounted as part of the record in all time coming. But this replacement was of no great consequence at that time ; for the family of Saltoun and their trustees had, several years before, surrendered all their rights upon Balvenic ' (Baird)

The wadset of Bellyhack, in the same district, was obtained by Alexander of Braco from Adam of Drummuir in 1681. The subsequent history of that transaction will be found in chapter xxiv. The ' Disposition ' by John Abercromby of the lands of Drummuir to Duff of Braco 1682 ; the ' Decreet of Adjudication,' Alexander Duff of Braco against the representatives of the late Adam Duff of Drummuir 1685, and the ' Disposition ' of whole estate of Drummuir by Alexander of Braco to Alexander Duff, merchant in Inverness, September 1688, are also fully explained in the chapter on Drummuir.

From 1677, Alexander Duff was ' of Braco,' for in that year there is a sasine to Alexander Duff of Lettach (and Keithmore) and Alexander Duff his son, writer, of the lands of Braco, Nethermill of Strathisle, etc. In 1696, after his father's death, there was a disposition by William Cumming of Auchen of the lands of Letervandich and Braccach in favour of Alexander Duff of Braco

' Besides the fishings on Devern from Lords Anly and Cullen, and Doune from Lord Cullen and other lands near Banff, Braco bought a great deal in the Strathisle and about Keith.

' There was then a number of small Heretors in that country, most of whom ran in debt ; all their estates he pickt up, some from the proprietors but acquired many of them by buying up their debts and adjudications, comprysings, or other shimp or imperfect rights on their land, as with the lands of Balvenie. And if he only got possession he was not very scrupulous about the security more than about the Justice of his title, by which means these Gentlemen or their heirs had many of them Claims and Complaints too well founded for the most part ; in all these his son, one of the most upright worthy men alive, did everybody Justice by entering into a fair compt and reckoning, and paying them the ballance which appeared to be due, and the last Lord Fife told me that all these clearances cost his cousin above a hundred thousand pound Scots, and there was two or three which, by minority of the Claimants or other accidents were left for him to

transact,' and added to the numerous lawsuits which kept him busy (Baird). See chapter ix.

ALEXANDER DUFF of Braco, born 1652, died in December 1705; he married, in 1678, Margaret Gordon of Lesmoir, who died 1721. Their children were:

1. MARGARET, born 1679, and married, in 1694, Charles Gordon of Glengerack.

2. HELEN, born *circa* 1681, married about 1700 William Gordon of Farskane, whence the Grant Duff family.

3. MARY, born *circa* 1683, married Alexander Abercromby of Tillie-body, co Clackmannan

4. WILLIAM, born *circa* 1685 (he was apparently not 'of age' at his father's death), died 1718.

5 ANNA, born 1689, died unmarried.

William will be treated of in the next chapter. The daughters in chapter xxxii

Later on in his book, garrulous old William Baird, in dealing with the rise in fame and fortune of ' the lucky Duffs,' adds : ' Those of this name in this country owed their success in their private affairs merely to their bestowing more attention upon the management of them than many others did.   Mr. Hay of Delgaty, who was an exceeding good judge of men and things, used to say that he thought the Duffs were rather well managers of their own money than covetous of other people's.   I am afraid (*and this is the significant passage in the present connection*) Alex. Duff of Braco was an exception to this rule ; but there is an old and musty maxim " Exceptio firmat regulam ! " '

He goes on to say : ' Most of the fortunes of the Duffs have been acquired by Husbandry or Trade, joined with good economy, both innocent and commendable callings, and two principal Sources of the population, Prosperity and wealth of a nation ; and I do not remember that any of the name ever held a lucrative post under the Government.

' It is also to be noted that the family of Duff, that is Keithmore and his three sons, Braco, Dipple, and Craigston, his grandson William Duff of Braco, and his brother Provost Duff, and his son, all abounded in money at a period of time in the first part of which money was scarce, Land cheap, Interest high, and Rents low, and all the noble Familys about them, Gordon, Finlatyr, Duffus, etc., with most of the Landed Gentlemen of large fortunes, sunk in debt by means of the Civil wars and other public commotions, wherein they had almost all been involved on one side or the other at vast expense and but lately come out of.   And in the last part of this time the Tenantry in many parts of the country were left in a miserable condition

by the seven years of Famine preceding 1700, which had made land of very little value by laying it waste in many places, and making a great scarcity of Farmers; for all these concurring circumstances were favourable to purchasers and gave these gentlemen the command of the Market' (Baird).

At one period, indeed, a great part of Banffshire, Morayshire, and Aberdeenshire was in the hands of members of the Duff family, with out-lying estates in Kincardine and Forfar. Vast estates were owned by the head of the family, and the numerous cadet branches, many of which have since died out, owned smaller properties. Titles to farms, single houses, or what would now be called crofts, were granted by the head of the family to all those relatives who would accept them, for political purposes. See chapter XI.

The two following letters from Alexander of Braco to his father, and to his cousin of Drummuir, are interesting as showing his anxiety to keep always within the letter of the law and to make profit out of all transactions. In the account of the family of Drummuir the part he played in connection with the bankruptcy of Adam, the troubles with his widow, and the re-demption of the estates, will be duly noted. His name occurs in dozens of lawsuits and other disputes with all the parties concerned.

Alexander Duff of Braco to his father

'BRACO, Dec. 18, 1685

'LOVING FATHER,—I received yours but yesterday in the afternoon, and I think strange you were so long in advertising me and in taking some course against that charge of horning, for the other charges are of less moment, but the charge of horning may lead to demur and to putting your single escheat in hazard. They inform me you received the charge on Saturday and this is the 6th day and the charge is within six days so that it is no remedye but to post a bearer presently south and write, with this line, one line to Drummuir and desire him give in ane bill of suspension both for you and me, for it is prob-able I may receive the like by fees and shall oblige ourselves to warrant him of his reward, for it is fit he be cautioner. And send four or five dollars and if it be any more, order Drummuir to advance it. Send immediately forward this line of mine to Mr. Thos. Gordon and Mr A Gordon and to Drummuir. I will trouble you no more at present, but if you can come here on Monday at night I shall go with you to your place, because I sent all the letters from Crombie.— I am, your loving son,   ALEX. DUFF.'

Alexander of Braco to Alexander of Drummuir

'Dec. 28, 1685.

'HONOURED AND LOVING COUSIN,—I writ to you the other day in reference to that affair of Horning of my father's and mine. . . .

'Mr. William Gordon saith he hath not my charter under the great seal of the Lands of Balvenie, or Arthur Forbes adjudication which I judged in my best memory, I sent south with you to town   I perceive the man is turned altogether lax and debauched and I am in a panic fear that he has either losed my papers or consigned of some for his debts, and I could be gladly quit of him and have my papers out of his hands.   But this will be gone about wisely and in a fair manner and without letting him know anything of my suspicions and jealousy, and if so, you must carry his own letters to him, but keep them up until you try his pulse and tell him that you and he must consult some law in my affairs against Stewart and against Arthur Forbes, and for that effect pray him to take out all my papers which you will find written, with any parts under my hand written upon the end of one of his own letters.   ALEX. DUFF.' [1]

In the *Seafield Correspondence*, edited by James Grant, LL.B., there are various letters to and from Alexander of Braco, and references to him.

On October 29, 1697, Sir Patrick Ogilvie writes to the Earl of Findlater : ' I have given your Ldp: the trouble of this letter to let you know that I can get Braco's son [2] to my daughter, and he is to give him twanty thousand marks a year free of any burden, and all the rest he hath after his death, and he will have from me with my dauchter all the land I have, but I am to get ten thousands marks and all the muabils, so I would have your Ldp.'s opinion in it, for I think it is a good bargain '

The marriage, however, did not take place, for William Duff married Helen Taylor ten years later.

In 1699, Alexander of Braco writes to the Earl of Findlater ' anent rogues guilty of many crimes who are by the court ordained to be carryed to Cullen and yr: to be putt to death.'

In that same year he announces his purchase of Doune (afterwards Macduff).

In January 1702, he writes again to Lord Findlater, being apparently extremely anxious to recover a sum of money lent by him to Findlater's son, Lord Seafield, as he has ' a considerable soume to pay against the terme of Witsunday.'   The editor of this *Correspondence* adds a note to the effect that nothing was scarcer in Scotland at that time than money.[3]

In a postscript to a letter from Anna, Lady Seafield to Lord Findlater, of date December 21, 1705, it is stated ' Brachy dayed on Wadsenday last.'

Braco was buried in the old church of Grange ; but his body was after-

---

[1] Drummuir papers   [2] Then aged twelve!

[3] Letter from John Abercromby, at Birkenbog, to the Laird of Drummuir at Inverness, November 25, 1701 ' Davitston is in danger of being imprisoned for debt   Send him drafts payable by Braco We are all straightit for want of money at this term, for there is no money among the country peoples at this term.'

wards removed to the mausoleum at Duff House, when the following
inscription was placed on his monument :

'Frigido sub hoc marmore jacet
Alexander Duff de Braceo
ex antiqua familia D. D. Joannis de Craighead et D. Helenorae Hay ejus conjugis
filiae legitimae comitis de Enzie ab avo ejusdem familiae filio necnon ex prae-
claro McDuffo Fifae Thano ejusdem nominis coryphaei avita oriundus stirpe
Qui
ope et opera, virtute ac frugalitate, alto consilio et intrepido corde paternos
limites haud paulo amphavit ob incorruptam mentem, inviolatam fidem in justo
proposito constantiam in eodem prosequendo audaciam ac omnia optimi civis
judicia omnibus probis luctuosum sui desiderium reliquit.
Obiit 19 Die Decem. A.D. 1705.
Aetatis 53.'

Translation :

' Under this cold marble lies Alexander Duff of Braco of the old family of
John Duff of Craighead and Lady Eleanor Hay, lawful daughter of the Lord
of Enzie, descended from the family through his grandfather, as well as from
Macduff, the celebrated Thane of Fife, who was chief of his race. By energy,
activity, perseverance and economy, profound sagacity and undaunted courage,
he greatly extended the boundaries of his paternal estate and died 19th Dec.
1705, in the 53rd year of his age, deeply regretted by all good men for the sound-
ness of his principles, for his high sense of honour, for his firmness in a just purpose and his boldness in carrying out the same, as well as for all the sentiments
which characterise a good citizen.'

There is a portrait of Alexander Duff by Richardson in the Duff House
collection, here reproduced by permission of the Princess Royal.

As so many hard things have been said about Alexander Duff of Braco,
the following extract may here fitly find a place.

From The Parish of Spynie, by Robert Young :

' The rise of the family of Duff is owing to various reasons.   In the first
place, for five or six generations it was, without exception, composed of the
most shrewd, calculating, long-headed men, who turned everything to the
greatest advantage, and lost no opportunity of improving their position.
They turned their attention to merchandising and trading at a very event-
ful period in the history of the country, and had the command of ready
money when very few in the north had it.   The country was exhausted by
the long civil wars of the seventeenth century.   The nobility and gentry
were generally poor, were anxious to get loans, and to mortgage their lands.
The long succession of bad harvests, in the end of seventeenth and begin-

ALEXANDER DUFF OF BRACO.

By Jonathan Richardson.

ning of the eighteenth century, also depreciated the value of land, and the unfortunate Darien scheme (1695-99) nearly ruined Scotland. In these various depressing circumstances there was a fine opportunity for acquiring land, and the Duffs did not lose the chance. They dealt largely in wadsets and other mortgages, which were never redeemed, and they readily foreclosed them, or purchased up the rights of reversion for very small sums, and entered into absolute possession. Much of their lands were acquired by wadset rights. There was nothing unfair in this. It was the order and practice of the day. The Duffs made their money by merchandise, agriculture, private banking, money-lending, and other arts of industry and peace, pursued for a long period of time, and with every favourable advantage, and thus acquired an enormous estate by fair trade. They offer a favourable contrast to most of the ancient families in the north, who gained their estates generally by war and bloodshed, and preying on their weaker neighbours. The rise of most of the old families of Scotland is a painful history, and the Duffs need not fear to contrast their actings and acquisitions with any others, for they will bear a close inspection. They were men of good conduct, just in their dealings, honourable, some of them religious, and strictly fulfilled all their engagements.'

BALVENIE CASTLE

CHAPTER VII

WILLIAM DUFF OF BRACO

William Duff of Braco,[1] only son of Alexander of Braco and Margaret Gordon, is thus described by Baird :

' William Duff of Braco got a very competent education at school and college with a good private Tutor, then studied the civil law at Leyden, and there acquired an excellent taste for all polite literature. He made abroad, at London, and at Edinburgh, a large collection of books, in Latin, French, Italian, and English, of Classic Learning, civil law, History, and all the branches of the Belles-Lettres.

' He married, about 1706, Helen Taylor, a woman of much inferior rank to him, tho' come of very honest parents. It is affirmed by his friends that his penitence and anger at himself for making so low a match was the cause of his unhappy death.[2]

' But, to do his widow Justice, who has now outlived him about sixty years, she has, by her virtuous behaviour, charity to the poor, hospitality and good offices to all her Husband's Relations, Allys and friends, to whose

---

[1] Born *circa* 1685.
[2] He committed suicide at Balvenie Castle in January 1718.

memory she has still shown a most grateful regard and attachment, gained the esteem of all who know her.'

Her husband had a great opinion of her business capacity, and left his affairs largely in her hands. Margaret Gordon, widow of Alexander Duff of Braco, writing in 1718, refers to ' the deceast William Duff of Braceo my son, and the charges I was at on his account in repairing the Miln barn of Braco, victual houses of Nether milln of Strathisla and house of Eden, conform to an order drawn by him upon Helen Duff his spouse, as factor for him.'

The order is also in existence, and must have been written only a few days before his death.

William Duff of Braco to his wife Helen Taylor

'BALVENIE, 15*th Januarie* 1718.

' DEAREST,—Thes are ordering you to pay to my Mother on sight hereof one Thousand merks as what I am to allow her ffor reppairing the Victuel house of Neither Mill of Stryla and on the dwelling House of Eden and gett up my letter to her theranent and ane letter ffrom her that I have ordered you to allow her the same and that you done it acordingly ffor doeing wherof this is warand from and shall be allowed in your ffactory accompts by WILLIAM DUFF.

' All former warrands to my Mother or you ffor this purpose, tho in her or your hands included. WILLIAM DUFF.

' ffor Helen Duff my Spouse.' [1] (*D*)

' Braco was a most benevolent, generous man, adored by his servants and farmers, who all lamented his death as if they had lost their father. Several of the old people at Balveny told me that the winter before his death he offered all his Tenants long leases at the present rent, and gave them to such as were willing to accept.

' When Lord Marishall was attainted in 1715, Braco told Mr. Keith his Doer at Aberdeen, and to whom Peter Duff, Braco's cousin, was then bound apprentice, that if £10,000 Stl. would procure his pardon, he was willing to pay the money, and there was found in his Cabinet, after his death, an order to Mr. Duff, who did all his term affairs at Aberdeen, to pay Mr. Keith £500, to be sent as he had conceited with that gentleman before, which was to remit it to Lord Marishall. This order was dated a few days before

---

[1] *Cf* ' James Duff in Mains of Ardbrack grants me to have received in friendly borrowing from Helen Duff, spouse to Wm Duff of Braco, the sum of ten shillings sterling, 1711 The same James Duff grants discharge of legacy 20 merks Scots left by his brother Alex.' This James Duff has not been identified.

Braco died, and never given to Mr. Duff. Both these particulars Mr. Keith told me, and Braco was no Shuffler.

'He went over to Holland in the end of 1716, and after staying in that Country till next Spring he proceeded to Prince Eugene's Camp in Hungary, and was at the Siege of Belgrade ; he returned to Scotland in the beginning of winter, 1717, and died at Balveny in the month of January 1718. He left only one daughter,[1] MARGARET, who was married in June 1721, when but eleven years of age, to her cousin Peter Duff ; he died in December 1763, without issue, and in 1768 she married Alexander Udny ' (Baird).

That Peter or Patrick Duff, son of Patrick of Craigston (*q.v.*) thought he was doing a somewhat odd thing, which required justification, in marrying this child-heiress, whose affairs he was managing, is evident from the following letter, which he wrote to his cousin, Alexander Duff of Drummuir :

Patrick Duff of Premnay to the Laird of Drummuir at Inverness

' MUCH HON'D SIR,—I had the pleasure of yours, I am very fond to have your approbation of my marriage, you may believe, if tyme had allowed, I had writt you of it before, if it puts it in my power to be so much the more useful to my friend, I 'll reckon myself very happy. . . .

' My Moyr. in Law and my Wife offer you, your Lady and family their very kind service, and I shall be alwise very heartily and with all respect, Sir, Your affect. cousin and most obedt. servt., PATT. DUFF.

' ABERDEEN, *Aug. 8th,* 1721 '[2]

There are three letters from this William Duff to Alexander of Drummuir among the Drummuir papers :

'To the Much honoured, the Laird of Drummuir, These.

' MUCH HONOURED,—I have yours and was come from Edinburgh or it came to hand. I shall gladly waite on you any time after Candlemas att Elgin or any place you appoint. In the meen time, I give my humble and kind respects to your self, your father, Ladie and family and to all Friends, and I ever am, Much honoured, Your most affectionate cusin and most humble servant,

' WILLIAM DUFF.

' BALVENIE, *2nd Januarie* 1712.'

The same to the same

' MUCH HONOURED,—I have gone South, most part on account to be in a condition to perform my father's obligation to you, which tho' it were to the

---

[1] There were four children, but three died young.
[2] Drummuir papers.

greatest stranger I would do to the utmost of my power. Mr. Boyds tells me he was still ready to have waited upon you at Edinburgh and Tillybody writes the same. Mr. Boyds sayes many of these papers ye took up from me are ranked in your own name, and my ffather's obligation presented by you to make up your right thereto. If there be anything wanting to perform the said obligation to the full on either side, if ye be not coming up your Self, write to your Lawiers your Demands, and I shall consider them and perform them, in so far as concerns the said obligation. Mr. Boyds has some thoughts of going your length, ye may send an exact double as I have oft demanded of the said obligation to him and an order to your agents to make forthcoming what papers they have relative to the performance thereof, as I wiote fully to you in my last, I shall never think that since I am so willing to perform my part, that one of your prudence especially considering our relation, would propose any thing beyond the terms of your obligation. I have since I began to write, got yours with the Inclosed for John Stewart. I give my service to your ffayther, your self, your lady and all of your friends and believe me still to be, much hond: Your aff: cousin and most humble Servt: WILLIAM DUFF.

'ABDN , 27 *April* 1714.

' I have communicat to Mr. Boyds my thoughts pretty fully anent what the differences are or may happen twixt you and me and if ye please to do the same and consider what proper methods can be taken for performing what I am bound to do, with the terms of my father's obligation to you, then I will conform to it.'

Another letter from the same to the same

'MUCH HONOURED,—I am favoured with yours dated the fourteenth of this month and besides our Relation, I shall always reckon my Self very much bound to you for your many favours, particularly for your Care of my affairs During my minority and your Discretion and kindness to me all along. I intreat if you intend south this Summer on your pose to end that obligation you have from my Father, you would be pleased to send south the Double of it ten or twelve Days before you come your Self that I may consider with friends and be the more capable to perform it. This is all the business I know is betwixt us. I expect Diple also here, for I intend to expede a Charter upon my lands in favors of my self and heirs male upon my Tailzie. I desire to deal frankly with you. I reed. once ane unsign'd memoiandum weh Diple told me he had from you, in weh there was some proposals for dismembring my superioritys and the lands of Balvenie, which I neither can nor will grant to any man, or I had done it to you, therefore I earnestly beseech you to consider seriously and to ask nothing of me weh is extraneous and impossible, for in all other things there shall be none more willing to testify themselves.—Much Honoured Cusine, Your most humble Servt.,   WILLIAM DUFF.

'EDINBURGH, *May* 21*st*, 1717.'

A letter from his brother-in-law Alexander Abercromby of Tillicbody, who married Mary, his third sister, explaining a claim he had against deceased Braco, says :

' 4th July 1717. £60 was for business, in sending £200 stg. to Vienna, Braco having wrote me that he designed to go to the Imperial Camp.

' December 1717. Braco having wrote me from the Imperial Camp a letter that Colonel Gibson, Durie's brother, was so kind to him that he desired me to give Durie and the rest of his brethren at Edinburgh a handsome entertainment and got letters of recommendation from them in favour of Braco to the Colonel, desiring him to take care of Braco, because he was a stranger and not well in his health, which I did, and had all Braco's friends, with Durie and his friends in town. It was in Don's house, cost £48.'

There are also, still existing, bills drawn by William Duff on Patrick Duff his cousin and factor (afterwards his son-in-law), dated Rotterdam, May 12, 1717, and Vienna, June 12, 1717, and September 1, 1717. The battle of Belgrade, which resulted in the brilliant victory of Prince Eugene and the Austrians over the Turks, took place on August 16, 1717, and after this date William Duff seems to have returned to Scotland. The two following letters refer to this period :

William Duff to Patrick Duff of Premnay

'CAMP BEFORE BELGRADE, 13th August 1717.

' SIR,—Ive no doubt but you will be surprysed that I draw so much money but this is ane good distance and costs more money as I thought of. The Hunder Ducats were honestly payd me and they cost Mr. Taylor of Amsterdam ffive hunder and sixty dutch gilders curtt, who bought up ane Bill and endorsd it to me in reckoning, if Mr. Auchterlony offer the sd hunder Ducats so you will order the payment of the same and gett the necessaire aquitances of that and my Bills ffrom this and Vienna both on you and my Mother. If you or any other ffreind have sent orders to London ffor any more credit on my accompt cause recall them because I am to come down soon to fflanders and will not write more from this now draw ffor any mony if it be not some small thing perhaps on Mr. Gordon and then I shall acquaint you and you shall be honestly relieved and payed of all my Bills and my wife will give you mony as it can be gott and always as she pays you give her the necesarie discharged Bills I avised.—Your affect. cusine and Servant,　　　　　　　　　　　　　　　　　WILLIAM DUFF.'

Lady Braco to Patrick Duff, Writer in Aberdeen

' SIR,—I hae yours with Mr. Archibald Grants to you inclosed. I am very glad my Lord Cullen has consented to take his mony pleasantly. I shall (God

willing) do all I can to gett it ready and how much he takes at Aberdeen so much the better. I have not been able to go to Rothiemay [1] since your last, but how soon I shall be able to go I shall wait upon him and send you his answer by post or express. I have gott no mony from John, William, James nor Robert Duff but I am hopefull to gett quit the midle of the next month. I cannot be sure before that time how much I will have occasion to Borrow from Diple. Let Robert Moors mony be apart of the thing thats payed at Aburdeen and what mony you have of Braccos beside you, you may bring it out in Gold and gett ane account, if you can, how much Lord Cullen will have payd at Aberdeen if Diple call for the factory I will let him see it but will not registratt it till I see further. Let me hear from you when you gett Mr. Hordgies return, and I am, Sir, Your humble servant, HELEN DUFF.

'BALVENY, *Sept* 23*rd*, 1717.

' To Mr. Patrick Duff, Writter in Aberdeen.'

William Duff committed suicide at Balvenie Castle early in 1718 ; [2] the castle has never since been inhabited.[3] That it was, at one time, used as a fortress appears from the memorial by William Duff's uncle and successor (William of Dipple) to Walpole :

'Memorial of William Duff of Braco to the Hon. Sir Robert Walpole, Chancellor of the Exchequer.

' Wm. Duff of Braceo, his predecessor during the Rebellion (1715), garrisoned the Castle of Ballveny, in Banffshire, and defended it against the rebels until it was delivered into the hands of Col. William Grant's lieutenant. Gave a general bond to the defenders, securing pensions, etc. Prays to be discharged of about £200 for non-entry dues, for which his predecessors were indebted to the Crown ' (*Calendar of State Papers*, Record Office).

Simon Fraser, Lord Lovat, to Sir James Grant of Grant

'BEAUFORT, *Feb.* 9*th*, 1739.

' MY DEAR SIR JAMES,—Tho' the officers att Fort Augustus pretend without grounds that Major White dyed lunatick, yet it is nothing as to the laws and customs of our country if it had been so ; for the Laird of Bracco, who murder'd himself, was believ'd to be for severall years before, lunatick and mad, and

---

[1] William of Braco advanced money on this estate, which was afterwards bought by his cousin Lord Braco See chapter IX.

[2] There was one portrait of William Duff of Braco in the Duff House collection and another at Rothiemay Both show an expression at once melancholy and discontented

[3] His cousin, William Duff, afterwards Lord Braco, built the new house of Balvenie in the square French style This was only inhabited for a short time, and stood empty for over a century. It is now used as a granary for a distillery.

There is a receipted bill, dated March 1726, marked 'Accompt of the Horse hyres paid for carrying stones to the Boat of Fiddich for the House of Balvenie.'

attempted to kill himself severall times, abroad and at home, before he gave the fatal stroke at Balveny. Yet his escheat fell to the King, and the late King gave the gift of it to Brigadier Ker, the Duke of Roxburgh's brother. I went in to the King's closet and half hour after he got it, and his Majesty was so kind as to tell me that if I hade ask'd that gift one hour sooner I would have got it, but that he gave it to Mr. Ker, the Duke of Roxburgh's brother, who was then groom of the bedchamber in waiting, and he sold it for several thousand pounds to this Lord Bracco's father. So you see that pretended lunacy, even tho' believ'd to be reall, does not save escheats in Scotland ' (Fraser's *Chiefs of Grants*).

The estate of Braco, which escheated to the Crown, was afterwards recovered by Braco's uncle, William Duff of Dipple, his heir-male, the estate of Eden only going to Margaret Duff, his daughter. Baird thus describes the subsequent proceedings :

' When Dipple succeeded to his nephew as heir of entail, he granted to Margaret Duff (that nephew's daughter) a bond of provision for £3000 sterling, which was much about a year's rent of the Braco estate. But Premnay (her husband) being advised that her father's Entail was liable to several objections, served his lady Heir of Line to him, and got her infeft in every part of the estate. But in 1724 matters were compromised, and he accepted of £10,000 sterling from William Duff, afterwards first Lord Fife, and he and his lady discharged all further pretension.'

Patrick Duff of Culter died in 1763, and his wife afterwards (1768) married Alexander Udny of Udny, he and she being subsequently known as Mr. and Mrs. Udny-Duff ; he died 1789, and she in 1793, without issue.

She left all her personal property to her cousin James, second Earl Fife, grandson of her adversary Dipple, when fresh lawsuits followed between him and her late husband's heirs.

Eden passed to Margaret's great-nephew William Gordon, the heir of entail, who assumed the name of Duff, and subsequently to his niece, Margaret Milne Duff, and the Grant Duff family (*q.v.*).

William's wife, Helen Taylor, as already stated, survived him and drew her jointure for sixty-two years, being over one hundred years old when she died.

A portrait of her in middle life is at Rothiemay House, and one in extreme old age was in the Duff House collection. Her tombstone in St. Nicholas Churchyard, Aberdeen, bears the following inscription :

' HELEN DUFF,
relict of William Duff of Braco,
who died (at Forrester hall) 20 Nov. 1780.'

This lady, on January 30, 1734, forty-six years before her death, intimated her desire that at her decease the Town Council would accept the

sum of 2000 merks (£111 2s. 2d.) as a mortification for the purpose that the annual rent or interest might be paid to a young woman. The qualifications of the damsel were that she should be sober, virtuous and poor, the daughter of a burgess of guild, a Protestant, and under the age of thirteen years. The rent of the mortification was to be applied for her education and maintenance in 'Learning Sueing and all Millinaris work, Pastrie and other such useful Education, fit for a Gentlewoman, within the town of Aberdeen, that may enable her to gain her bread honestly and in a lawful way.'

The Town Council were to become patrons after the decease of Patrick of Premnay and Margaret Duff, his spouse.

There are two notes regarding Helen Taylor from the Rose MSS., printed in the *Aberdeen Notes and Queries* The information given is somewhat contradictory.

'I. Genealogy of Helen Taylor, Lady Braco (taken July 1784 by Mr. Stewart of Edinglassie and given in before his death in Sept. 1786). She was daughter of Robert Taylor who resided at the place of Fintry in Fintry parish. He was the representative and grandchild of Taylor of Whitemires, who sold the lands of Whitemires in Newhills near Aberdeen, now an estate of about 3000 merks of rent and the property of the town of Aberdeen. Helen Taylor's mother was daughter to Rev. M. Cheyne, parson of Kinoull, brother to the Laird of Esslemont. Her grandmother, Mr. Cheyne's wife, was daughter to Sir John Jonston of Caskieben, and Sir John Gordon of Haddo, afterwards Earl of Aberdeen and Chancellor of Scotland, was married to Mr. Cheyne's sister Sir John Johnston's wife was daughter to the Laird of Drum, and Drum's lady was daughter to the Earl of Marischal.'

'II. Lady Braco, Helen Taylor, was married in London about 1706. Her daughter Margaret, Lady Premnay, born 1710. Lady Braco was born in Fintray. She keepit the sheep at Cook in the Parish of King Edward. Before her marriage she wrought a harvest with John Durno at Mill of Likliehead, in Premnay, for which she got 4 merks and a pair of shoes. She served John Hay, sacrist at King's College and Margaret Tarnell his wife, where her acquaintance with Braco begun. Braco went to Prussia after the marriage, and exposed himself on the walls of Belgrade. He had four children by her. Braco died in the old castle of Balvenie by suicide January 1718. Her husband insisted on her wearing plain and low mutches. She lay not on feathers, but on a hard bed of Baken hair called a pallet. She ate oat buttered bannocks. She was about thirty when she married. If so, and if she married in 1706, and died after 11th and before 22nd November 1780, she must have been over one hundred years old. It is certain she died November 1780, for Lord Fife contended her half-year's annuity.

'Margaret Duff, Lady Premnay, married June 27, 1721, when scarcely twelve years old. It was well known she had an attachment to Major

L

Home, Prince Rupert's grandson' (Rose MSS., *Aberdeen Notes and Queries*, August 1892).

Prince Rupert had a daughter Ruperta, by Margaret Hughes, an actress. Ruperta married, about 1696, Brigadier-General Emanuel Scrope Howe, envoy-extraordinary from William III. to the Most Serene House of Brunswick-Luneberg. It must have been Ruperta's son who is alluded to above, but it is not stated when and where he met Margaret Duff.

There is one letter from her :

Mrs. Udny-Duff to Lord Fife

'My Lord,—It will give me great pleasure to learn you have enjoyed good health and passed your time agreeably att Marr Lodge about this time you may probably be thinking of leaving that place and may make a visit at House-dale. It would give Mr. Udny and I great pleasure to have the honour of seeing you at Culter, which would be easy from thence. We know how much your engaged but to give a day and a night which robs no time I really expect it, and you know I wish you well and if I did not sincerely desire the one and ardently wish you every felcity belive I would not trouble you with Compts en Passant.

'We I thinke can now depend on being here till first or second week of October.

'I had good accounts from Logie yesterday.—Belive I, My Good Lord, I 'm with Particular Esteem your Lops. most obedient humble Servt.,

'M. UDNY-DUFF.

'CULTER, 5 *of Spt.*'

And in a letter to Lord Fife from his sister Sophia, dated November 1774, shortly after her marriage to Thomas Wharton, occurs the following : 'Did your Lordship write to Mrs. Udny ? I wish you would do so, as she is very much interested in your family. She is a most formal being. I expect we shall have a dinner from her one of these days. I would rather go without one for a week ! '

There are portraits of Margaret Duff, when Mrs Udny, and her second husband, Alexander Udny, at Rothiemay.

CHAPTER VIII

WILLIAM DUFF OF DIPPLE

The second son of Alexander of Keithmore was born 1653 and died 1722. We cannot do better than begin our account of him with another extract from Baird's book:

'Dipple was a middle-sized, well-made man, of a fair, ruddy complexion, and very good features, of solid sense, an active lively spirit, and a most facetious agreeable companion. His sister, Lady Tannachy, a very sensible well-bred woman, used to tell the following story, which she said had often been attested to her by her father and mother.

'It was Keithmore's custom to sit beside his Lady the first night after she was delivered; the night succeeding Dipple's birth, Keithmore was placed near the fire with a candle before him, reading the Bible; about midnight, a tall big woman, clad in a green gown, appeared upon the floor and walkt up to the cradle in which the child was laid, and stretched out her hand over it, upon which Keithmore rose, ran to the bedside, and made the sign of the Cross, first on his Lady and then on the Infant, saying: "In the name of the Father and of the Son and of the Holy Ghost, may my Wife and child be preserved from all evil." Upon which the Apparition immediately vanisht.'

After Dipple's education at school and college was over (he was at King's College, Aberdeen, in 1666, aged thirteen), he was bound apprentice and afterwards became partner in trade to his uncle, Provost William Duff of Inverness (who traded as early as 1662), and Sir James Calder, and continued at Inverness till about 1703,[1] when he married his second lady, and they came to Elgin where he lived until his death.' It is believed that he lived for a short time at Dipple.[2]

The 'trade' which he carried on with his uncle, the Provost, provides the foundation for the ridiculous story which appeared in *Truth* at the time

---

[1] He was Treasurer of Inverness, 1682

[2] *Dipple*, an ancient parish in Morayshire, on the left bank of the Spey, opposite Fochabers. The church was formerly dedicated to the Holy Ghost, and at the lych gate stood a small building known as the House of the Holy Ghost, round which funeral parties carried the corpse There is no mansion-house now remaining, the present farmhouse being quite modern

of the Duke of Fife's death to the effect that his great-great-grandfather (should have been great-great-great-) came from Ireland, and kept a general merchant's shop in Inverness

The following letters are interesting in this connection :

William Duff of Dipple to his cousin, John Duff, Messenger, Aberdeen

'Sir,—At five days sight of this my onlie 2 Bills, paye to James Dunbar y^r Merchant in Inverness or order the somme of ane hundred and twenty punds scots moe[1] for the value due to him for some salmond off that price sold by me to Alex^r fforbes and John Leslie, merchants in Aberdeen. Make good thereof and it shall be allowed by me in part off the [*two words illegible*] sterling executed by you from them on my account which will be all from Your affect. cosine to serve you,   Wm. Duff.

'Innes, 3 *Ap.* 1703 '

Laird of Innes to William Duff of Dipple, 1685

		Scots.
To 3 pints of Wine to the Publie House	. . .	£2 0 0
To 8 pints of ale to the Publie House	. . . .	0 10 0
To an pint of Brandy . . .	. . .	0 5 0
To Tobaco and sending therefor to Cullen .	. . .	0 8 0
To a mutchen of Tai	. .	0 2 6
To a pint of Vinegar	. . .	0 8 0
To half anckei of whyte wine .	. . .	1 10 0
To two dozen tobaco pypes	. . . .	0 4 0
To sending twice from Garmouth to Inverness	. . .	3 0 0

Nota—3½ computed miles.

To four pints of Sack Wine at 16 sh. p. pint—not charged for.		
A peck of Whyte Salt . . .	. . .	0 4 6
A haill Boll of Gray Salt .	. . .	5 0 0
Two stone of Butter at £3 is	. . .	6 0 0
Two stone of Tallow at 3 meiks is	. . .	4 0 0

Scots money, £23 12 0[2]

*Sir Hugh Campbell of Cawdor to William Duff of Dipple, Merchant
in Inverness*

'Cawdor Castle, *July* 19, 1677.

' Lo. Friend,—Pray be pleased with your first occasion to cause bring the goods under wrytin from Holland or quhairever ellis ye came most readily, to me

---

[1] Money.   [2] Drummuir papers.

to Inverness or Findhorn, and the price of them shall be readily allowed you in your accompt.

' Imprimis, as much lead (not to be casten in casks, till it come hom) as can be bought for £200 Scots at Holland or England.

' Item, 3 or 4 duzzon of big glass botellis, holding twixt a pint and a quart and als many lesser botellis holding pyntes or chapynis.

' Item, 50 or threescor hansom light muskett barrelis, wluich I mynt[1] to stock and furniss at hom, for weapon gunnes to our watch or militia ; let them not be too long, nor too havy for a man to travell with his other wapons, and bee of ordinar muskett bor or rather less, but the ordinar bor will be good.

' One hundreth or two weight of gune powder, very good for the militia, the watch and my foulleries use, and one hundreth weight of small shott, the one half for mysell and the other halff of two sorts in equall pairt, one very great for veild geisse and roe and such lyk, and the other pairt pretty small, for pluveries and leisser foullis.

' Item, als much fyn diaper or dornich[2] cloth as will make 3 or 4 tabel cloths of 4 eln long a pere and a dusson napkins to each tabel cloth.

' Item, some capers and olives and a little quantite of anchoves. Upon these three exceed not the value of £20 Scots.

' Item, a dusson of the botells with very good watter, iff they be deirer than brandy, use the least bottell and quhen off the brandie . . . tak the biggest botell.

' I expect ye will cause follow and answer this my commission exactly and place it to my accompt, quho are still, Your real friend to my power,
                                        ' SIR H. C. CAWDOR.'

This letter is endorsed :

' Andrew Cunninghame, chamberlane to the Laird of Calder, acknowledges receipt from William Duffs, elder and younger, merchants in Inverness, of 20 barnes of lead, 100 lbs. schot, 200 lbs. powder, 1 double anker sack, one quarter cask brandie, sixtie muskett barrelhs, 20 fouling pieces, 2 hampers with 6 dozen botell glasses, 17 Dutch eln off Dornich ; 9th Dec. 1677.'

Another letter from the same to the same

' ARDERSIER, 16 April 1679.

' MUCH RESPECTED,—You will be pleased to get two terces[3] of your best wine aboard of Thomas Couper in Findhorn his boate, quho will carry it this length and give him lykways six or eight bolls of salt, but let your wine be verie good, otherwayes send it not. And if ye please to come out yourself, I long to see you, quhich is all at present, from your verie loving friend to my power,
                                        ' SIR H. C. CALDER.'[4]

---

[1] Intend.   [2] Fine linen from Tournai   [3] Ter, a barrel, i e casks
[4] Letters communicated by Miss J C. Duff

'But many years before his death, William Duff had given over merchandizing and made large purchases of land in Moray. He bought the Estate of Dipple from Sir Robert Innes [1] in 1684 and paid £70,000,[2] and he would often say that he "likt very well to see a merchant turn Laird, but he did not like so well to see a Laird turn a merchant"' (Baird).

To continue from Baird :

'Dipple was a conscientious, honest man in all his dealing, and indeed I never heard that any unfair thing was ever laid to his charge. He was the easiest creditor in the world, and it was said in Moray that he never did diligence but against one person who had attempted to impose upon him ; and if he saw an industrious honest man, opprest with difficulty and endeavouring to extricate himself by his diligence, he was alwise willing to give him time to pay and even to advance him money. This acquired him a great deal of public love and had a very good effect among the Commonalty while he merchandized, in so much that a man who had not paid his accompt when it fell due, was disgraced, and lost all credit among his equals, and they used to tell one another in a bragging way, after their turn was over : " God be thanked, I have paid the Laird and William Duff," for so he was called before he got any land estate of his own. For being a second brother, he got only 10,000 mks. of Patrimony from his father, and by his mother's influence the wadset of Keithmore, for which his brother Braco paid him afterwards 6000 marks.

'He was extremely fitted for business, and to this, one particular felicity of Constitution contributed greatly, viz., that the longer he sat at his bottle, he became still more cautious and secure, so that if at the beginning of a Sederunt, we might get a tolerable bargain of him, after he was a little in liquor it was impossible to overreach him.' [3]

Two other quotations from letters to him may be given. One from Lord Huntly, beginning :

'HONEST DIPPLE,—I am glad to give you ashurances, all the nois about yr being summons to this place will prove little or no consequence, therefore I

---

[1] There is a memorandum, of date January 14, 1686, which shows that Innes was in pecuniary difficulties even after the date of sale of Dipple ·

' Wm Duff To offer to lend the other £4000 provided that the Laird of Innes near relations, and who knows the condition of his estate and fortune will bind cautioners for the whole £10,000 and the payment of principal sum ' (Rose MSS)

[2] Scots

[3] In this connection must also be added the story of his going down the great stair at Gordon Castle before it had got the ravelne (i e the balustrade), upon which he said to the Duchess that it was a good ' forenoon ' stair

ashure you, you need be in no pain about it, when I see you I shall give you some accounts of it, which will be agreeable.—Your affec. good friend to serv,

'HUNTLY.' (O.)

The other from Lord Findlater about some dispute :

'CULLEN HOUSE, *Dec.* 22*nd*, 1718.

' MUCH HONOURED,—It shall be much against my inclinations if ther be any stop putt to your Signature on my account, for I am a sincere well wisher to you and your family and shal take all opportunitys of doing you what Service is in my power. I attribute it to the mistake of the late Braccoes writters that ther is any clause in that Signature which gives me just ground of complaint and had he Lived, he was to have given me a Declaration for Saving of my right in ample forme, and he and I were to have mett, in a very few days about that matter, if it hade not been prevented by whatt happened. Your Sone and your doers at Edinburgh have mett with John Philp who has sent me north a draught of a letter to be signed by you, which draught I send you by the bearer. All I desire is that it may be by way of obligation, otherwayes it cannot be effectual for my Security. I do not question but you will Signe it and in that case that you may meet with no delay, I have sent with William Lorimer a letter to John Philp, desiring that ther may be no further opposition made on my account, to the passing of your Signature. He will deliver it to you, upon the signing of the obligation.

' I heartily wish to hear of your being in perfect health ; and on all occasions you shall find me with the greatest sincerity —Much honoured, Your most faithfull and most humble Servant, FINDLATER.' (O.)

WILLIAM DUFF of Dipple married, firstly, in 1681, Jean Gordon of Edinglassie, and through her obtained sasine in the lands of Bukenburn ; they had nine children ·

1. HELEN, born 1682, afterwards Lady Roscommon.
2. CATHERINE, born 1683, married Alexander Duff of Hatton.
3 MARY, born 1684, died young.
4. ISABEL, born 1688, married Alexander Mackintosh of Blervie.
5. ALEXANDER, born 1690, died young.
6 ELIZABETH, married Thomas Donaldson of Kinnairdy.
7. JEAN, born 1694, died young.
8. WILLIAM, born 1697, afterwards Lord Braco.
9. LUDOVICK, born 1698, died young.

After the death of Jean Gordon, William Duff married again, in 1703, Jean Dunbar of Durn, sister of Anne, Countess of Findlater, and by her, who lived until 1750, had one son and four daughters :

10. ANNE, born 1705, married William Baird of Auchmedden.
11. JANET, born 1710, married Sir James Kinloch of Kinloch.

12. MARY, born 1714, married General J. Abercromby of Glassaugh.
13. ALEXANDER, born 1715, died at the age of six.
14. HENRIETTA, died unmarried.

There are two letters from Dipple's first wife:

'INVERNESS, 16 *April*

'MY DEAR SIR,—I received your last the 2 of this instant. With the help of God I shall strive to give you no occasion of offence. All that you wrote of your affairs or myself I shall observe it well. Your Uncle nor Drumminuir is not come home as yet so that I can give you no account of the quarrel but the fringe I had from London is too short and will not serve any purpose. I shall take nothing for myself but what you please but the head dresses for children, for I have sent Helen to School Mind Magdalen's [1] gown and petticoat. Recommending you to the Lord in all your affairs.—I am, your obedient wife,

'JEAN GORDONN.'

'MY DEAR,—I received your letter which is great contentment to me to hear that ye ar weall, your daughter is beter now, as for heaving a ear of any thing I shall doe the best way I can under God to giv you content. I intreat you heast you as son hom as your conveniency can permitt I think much long for you not being abell to writt at length I shall forbear to trubell you at present wishing the Lord to preserve you, I continue, Your loving and obident wieff,

'JEAN GORDON.

'ffor William Duff yre Merchand in Inverness for the present att Elgine, Thesse.'   (*D*)

Baird, in enumerating Dipple's seven married daughters adds, 'I believe it is doubtful if there has been in our days a dozen of Gentlemen in Brittain that had seven daughters who were all so virtuous women and so good wives.'

Dipple was a cautious man, and kept himself free from taking sides in the civil wars of his time, though undoubtedly his sympathies were with the Stewart cause. When the Elgin troop went out to the rebellion of 1715, 'which I have heard,' says Baird, 'was a very handsome and well equipped body of men, Dipple said, "William Duff would have gone with them, but Dipple would behold the event"' (being unwilling to imperil his newly acquired estates).

He, nevertheless, did not entirely escape, as seen by the following letter 'from the Earl of Sutherland to the Laird of Dipple':

[1] It is probable this was another child, whose birth has not been recorded, who died young

' Whereas for the mantainance of the forces now under our Command for His Majesties services, a Loan was directed to be leveyed out of this country in money and meall and whereas by the parcelling out the payments into small moyeties, the levying the said loan has not proved any way effectuall and seeing a speedy advance of money is absolutely necessary for the King's service, Therefore we, pursuant to the powers and Instructiones to us given, require you, Wm. Duff of Dipple, forthwith to pay unto Hector Monro of Navar our Comissary for that effect the sum of two hundred pound sterling, we hereby oblige our selves shall be repayed to you by the Treasury.   SUTHERLAND.

' Given at Elgin the 7th of December 1715.'   (D)

And a week later, from Lord Lovat :

' AT FIORRAS, *ye* 14 *of Dec* 1715.

' DEAR SIR,—I was surprised to receave here positiv orders from ye Earle of Sutherland to secure you and cary you prisoner wt. me, since you did not pay ye two hunder pd. of a loan yt he desired of you in ye Kings name and for ye Kings service. So Dr. Sir I beg you may come imediatly to Inverness sinc I am bail for you or take a speedy way to satisfy my Ld Sutherland. Yt I may not get a reprimand for not seizing of you and yt another may do it who will not be so much yr ffid as I am and will be on all occasions.—Dr. Sir, your most oblidged Servant,   LOVAT.

' To the Much Honoured Mr. William Duff of Dipple, at Elgin.'   (D.)

In 1714 he bought the estate of Coxton from Sir George Innes at what was, by outsiders, considered a very high price, but hearing that the late owner was rejoicing uproariously at the amount he had got, Dipple sagely observed, ' Poor fellow, he is as well pleased at parting with his inheritance as I at getting it.' He also took over all the debts of the Laird of Coxton, who, being an indolent man and much given to his bottle, gave in and signed a list of these debts, which was £20,000 Scots short of the full amount. Dipple paid, at once, all the creditors in the list given to him, but after Sir George's death the other creditors appeared and sued Dipple in the Edinburgh Court of Session, which awarded them their claims. Dipple carried the matter to the House of Lords, and they reversed the decree, finding him only liable for Sir George's signed list.

' It was lucky for Dipple, as well as for his father and uncle and both his brothers, that all of them were possessed of ready money at a time when interest was high and land cheap, owing to a variety of causes, including the seven years scarcity and the political troubles. They were thus enabled to lay the foundations of the family prosperity as Lairds ' (Baird).

' When a great barony was to be bought and no ready money forthcoming, the Duffs found the money for the purchase, taking a mortgage or wadset over the land, together with the security of the borrowers. In

truth, before banks were established, or insurance companies dreamed of, the Duffs dealt largely in money. They were the bankers of the North, and carried on the business much as we read of its being managed in Florence and Genoa and other free cities of Italy in the olden time' (Shaw's *History of Moray*).

Dipple died in 1722 at the College in Elgin, and with his first wife, Jean Gordon, was buried in the Duke of Gordon's aisle in Elgin Cathedral, 'at the desire of the first Duke of Gordon (who died in 1728), on account of the intimacy which existed between them.'

On December 22, 1711, William Duff of Dipple and William of Braco, his nephew, were cautioners for Alexander, Marquis of Huntly, son of George, Duke of Gordon, 'as a singular mark and testimony of their friendship for the family.'

There is a portrait of him by Wessing, which was in the Duff House collection, and shows him as a good-looking young man.

By his will he left to ' Jean Dunbar my spouse for all the dayes of her life, the lands of Quarrelwood and Dykeside in the parish of Spynie with the Mills of Mosstowie and other farms, as holden by me of our Sovereign Lord the King and that there be given to her therefrom fuel, faill (*i.e.* clods) and divots, as by the law and practice of this kingdom, conform to the contract of marriage between her and me of March 5, 1703. These lands were formerly granted by me in favour of my son Alexander.[1] Should she remarry, this provision shall be null and void, and all the lands above mentioned shall belong to my other heirs.'

She survived till 1750, and did not marry again.

He also left to his daughter Anne, 20,000 merks.

To Janet, 15,000 merks.

To Mary and Henrietta, 12,000 merks each

To Alexander of Hatton, 4000 merks.

To the eldest son of Alexander MacIntosh of Blervie and his daughter Isabel Duff, 2000 merks; to their eldest daughter, 1000 merks.

To William Donaldson, eldest son of Thomas Donaldson and Elizabeth Duff, 3000. And 1000 to Alexander Tulloch, son to Thomas Tulloch and Mary Duff.

One thousand merks to Patrick Duff, writer, Premnay (his nephew). He also ' mortified' £1000 Scots to the poor of each of the following parishes, Glass, Mortlach, Dipple and Longbride,[2] and the same sum to the minister of Elgin for the use of the poor in Pluscarden, Quarreywood and Dykeside in Spynie. Will dated May 7, 1720.

---

[1] Born 1715, died 1721.　　　　[2] Now Llanbryde.

WILLIAM DUFF OF DIPPLE

By Wessing

To return to Dipple's daughters :

The eldest daughter, HELEN, married, in 1702, the Hon William Suther-land of Roscommon, third brother of Kenneth the third Lord, and son of James, second Lord Duffus.[1] He also owned Mosstowie and Aldroughty. William Sutherland was Member of Parliament from 1703 to 1706, and Provost of Elgin ; he was ' out ' in the '15, his estates were forfeited, and he died abroad, although he returned to Scotland in 1729. (See the letter below.) He had previously borrowed £20,000 Scots from his father-in-law Dipple, who drew the rents of Roscommon for the years 1713 and 1714.

There is one letter from Helen to her brother :

Helen Sutherland to the Laird of Braco

' DEAR BROTHER,—I ame well pleased to know of your being att Balvenie since your being ther givs mee the satisfaction to believ that my sister youe and the children are in health. Mr. Innes is att last goot free of this place hee hase bein forced in to some measure that he would not hav inclyned but that it was thought better to give a hungrie dog a bone then leav a business of such import-ance unfinished · the stones shal bee sent the begining of the week. John Duff wil bee with you att that tyme. Ime not sure but your humble servtt may giv youe the trouble of a short visit but Ime some frighted for Mr. Hunters seatt. I ever continue, Dear Brother, Your most affect. sister and humble Sertt.,

'HELLEN SUTHERLAND.

' ELGIN, *19th March* 1726.

' To the Laird of Bracoe known to be att Balvenie.'

And one from Lady Braco to Lady Roscommon :

' DEAR SISTER,—The Tweedlin came safe here and is very good of the kinde for which I return you thanks. I hope now that the marketts are over you 'll be so kinde as let your freinds see you. Since you may easiely judge it is impos-sible for me to travel any where otherways you would have a good title to a visit Youn Brother and Sophia gives you their humble service and I assure you I always desire to be very sincerely, Dear Sister, Yours, JEAN DUFF.

' BALVENIE, *Jully* 26th, 1732

' To the Ladie Roscommon at Elgin.'

Duncan Forbes of Culloden, Lord President, to the Duke of Newcastle

EDINBURGH, *31st Oct.* 1729.

' In the whole course of my enquiries I have heard of but one attainted person that came into Scotland since the first letter on this subject which I had the

---

[1] Roscommon being part of Lord Duffus' Morayshire estate; the name has now dis-appeared.

honour to receive from your Grace, and that is Mr. William Sutherland, brother to the late Lord Duffus. He landed sometime in September in the neighbourhood of Banff in the Moray firth. His errand, as my informer, who is a man of understanding, told me, was to draw some money from his wife, who lives at home and is in good circumstances, but he managed that design, it seems, so imprudently, that his wife and her friends declared war against him, and he finds it necessary to lurk as well to avoid them as the officers of justice, which is the reason that my informer could not tell me where he now is. That this account of Sutherland's expedition is true, I verily believe, partly as I know the circumstances of his family, which makes it probable, partly as I know the character of the man, which is so low that the Pretender and his advisers, fools as they are, could scarce be so simple as to employ him, and partly because the Jacobites here whom I have sifted since my arrival know nothing of his coming to Scotland, though he is now more than a month in it '[1]

After Sutherland's death, Dipple allowed his daughter to live in the old castle of Quarrelwood, afterwards called Quarreywood (long since disappeared), and made her an allowance, which was continued by William of Braco, her brother. She died in 1747 or 1748, and had no issue. There is a portrait of her, by Kneller, as a pretty child, with her mother, in the Duff House collection.

The second daughter, CATHERINE, married her first cousin, Alexander Duff of Hatton, the eldest son of Patrick of Craigston, and her history belongs to that of the Hatton family.

Alexander Duff, writing from Craigston to the Laird of Dipple, February 13, 1710, about William of Braco's business, adds, ' Your daughter [*Alexander's wife*] and all the rest of your ffreinds heir are (blessed be God) well and have ther haintie respects to you—your lady and ffamalie—and long to heir the like accompt ffrom you—expecting to see you att the Lady Marchioness of Huntleys buriall which is the 22nd instant.—Your affectionat son,[2] to serve you.'

The third daughter was ISABEL, married in 1706 to Alexander MacIntosh of Blervie, and the mother of twenty-two children, whose names and dates of birth have all been preserved.

William,	born	1707	Mary,	born	1715	Alexander (2nd),	born	1723
John,	,,	1708	Elizabeth,	,,	1716	John (2nd),	,,	1724
Jean,	,,	1709	Lachlan,	,,	1717	Isabel,	,,	1725
Helen,	,,	1710	Magdalen,	,,	1718	Rachel,	,,	1726
Alexander,	,,	1711	Ludovick,	,,	1719	George,	,,	1727
Catherine,	,,	1712	Janet,	,,	1720	Charles,	,,	1729
James,	,,	1713	Anne,	,,	1721	Christina,	,,	1730
						Mary,	,,	1731

---

[1] From the *Scottish Papers*, Record Office.   [2] Son-in-law.

We only have records of the ninth and twelfth and sixteenth children.[1]

Elizabeth, when residing with her aunt, Lady Roscommon, at Milton Duff, was courted by a young man named Anderson, who did not meet with the approval of her aunt, and whose visits were therefore forbidden. He, however, persuaded Elizabeth to elope with him one evening, when Lady Roscommon was engaged at her devotions. They had reached the river Lossie, through which he was in the act of carrying her, when Elizabeth suddenly remembered that she owed half a crown to the laundress and must return to pay her debt. Young Anderson succeeded, however, in persuading her to defer this, and they safely reached Elgin and his brother's house, where Elizabeth was locked into a cupboard for safety until a parson could be procured to marry them. After the ceremony, the youthful bridegroom had to return to Aberdeen to complete his education, while Elizabeth, though offered a free home by her brother-in-law and his wife, elected to earn her living by working as a clerk in the former's office (Cramond's *Milnes in Banff*).

Ludovick is known to us by a letter he wrote to his uncle Lord Braco, in 1747, pathetically asking for five guineas to pay a bill for lodgings and medicines while ill in Shields : [2]

'SHIELS, *25th December* 1747

'MY LORD,—I humbly beg you 'l excuse the Trouble, which only necessity should occasion.

'Haveing wrote your Lordship some time ago, representing my being sick of an ague, without money, and at the mercy of Strangers, who wou'd affoord me Relief, only for mercenary ends ; and had no Return, I 'm forc'd again to entreat the Favour of Leave to draw on your Lordship for five Guineas, without which, although my Distemper is less violent and may let me sail in ten days, I cant proceed to Sea being indebted for medecines and otherwise.

'It were with utmost Concern I did any Thing might have the least Tendency to give your Lordship a bad Impression of me, whose Friendship (next Providence) is my chief Dependance ; and hope you will not let me loose Time, now more than ever precious, by delaying an Answer. I am, as in Duty bound, with all Honour and Esteem for you, your Lady and Family, My Lord, Your Lordships most aff: hum: Sertt., LODOVICK MACKINTOSH.

'*P.S.*—Least my former Letter should have miscarried, I think proper to acquaint your Lordship that I wait your orders at Mr Jolly's in North Shiels.' (*O.*)

---

[1] After her death Alexander MacIntosh married again and had ten more children

[2] He seems to have been in the Navy, for the Master of Braco, writing to his father, says that ' Lodic MacIntosh is entitled to £800 of prize money, which would be very agreeable news to him if he knew of it.'

John MaeIntosh, another of Blervie's sons, applied to Lord Fife for
help in apprenticing him to a Physician or Apothecary. January 30, 1760.

Alexander MacIntosh, father of this large family, in 1724 sold his estate
of Blervie to Lord Braco, who left it to his son Lewis.

Dipple's fourth daughter, ELIZABETH, married Thomas Donaldson of
Kinnairdy. She and her husband rebuilt the old eastle, and their names
may still be seen carved above the door. A portrait of her, and her Family
Bible, are still preserved at Kinnivie Castle by the Leslie family. The
Donaldsons claimed descent from the Macdonalds of Gleneoe. Elizabeth
had, at least, five children · Katherine, who married Lauchlan Mackintosh,
whose mother was a Duff of Corsindae ; Alexander, referred to in the
following delightful letter ; Elizabeth,[1] who married Nicolas Dunbar of
Tillienaught ; and another daughter ; also William, the eldest.[2]

Elizabeth Donaldson writes thus to her brother :

'KINNAIRDY, 1st Nov. 1743.

'MY LORD : DEAR BROTHER,—As my son Sandie was speaking to me that
your Lordship was pleased to say that you would give him a letter to Captin
Gedes [3] I entreat your Lordship to dow it. I have spoken scariously to him
that if he did not setell now better than formarly that non of his frinds would
take any concern in him and I swore to him that I would never see his feas again
if he did not take your advice, and I gave him my advice as I was capable.
So he did give me his hand and his promiss that he would folow your Lordship
advice upon your countinanceing him is all that I shall truble with att present.—
My Lord, Dear Brother, Your most affect. Sister and most humble Servant,

'ELIZABETH DUFF.' (O.)

And again about her daughter :

'BANFF, July 27, 1751

'MY LORD, DEAR BROTHER,—I shall be very glad that this find my Lady
Braco and your Lordship and all the rest of your family in good health which
will give me great pleasure to see the same from you. The reason I have troubled
you with this is my daughter Mrs. Lowson told me the last night that she had
some thoughts of maring Docter Irvin I told hir that I should giv hii noe answer
but think of it and will giv hir my opinion within this two days. Dear Brother
I thought most proper to leat your Lordship know of this and would not give
my consent till I had your opinion this she dows not know that I hav written
to you, but I want your advice how I should dow as I know Jeams Hay has been

---

[1] A son of this Elizabeth Dunbar afterwards applied to the second Lord Fife for financial
assistance. Lord Fife notes ' An industrious poor man, with five children '
[2] See page 90
[3] This Captain Geddes had also at one time been in charge of William, Master of Braco
See letter from Lord Braco, chapter x.

seeking hir but in my small opinion I think Docter Irvin is before him for Jeams Ilay he is young but the Docter is doucer I know not the Docter scarcumstance but that he is coming in to good business, I will expect your answer. Mak my compliments to my Lady Braco, and I am with great regaird and estim, My Lord, Dear Brother, Your most affectt. Sister and most humbell servant,

' ELIZABETH DUFF.'   (D.)

Thomas Donaldson appears to have been in constant financial diffi- culties, which preyed upon his mind. His brother-in-law, William Duff (before he was Lord Braco), writes : ' I would be glad some way were fallen on to serve Kinnairdie, at least not to determine himself.'   Elizabeth died in 1761.

ANNE, the eldest daughter of the second family, was married in 1721 to William Baird of Auchmedden, the delightful author of the frequently quoted *Memoirs of the Duffs*.   He 'went out' with the Jacobites in 1745, and consequently had to remain in hiding afterwards, first at his brother- in-law's house of Echt, and afterwards at St. Andrews [1]

But William Baird seems to have been in difficulties before this date, as William Duff writes, before 1735, ' I have Auchmedden's son now on my hands and shall get part of his entry bond to pay,' and several other re- ferences occur to help asked and given ; thus, like almost all the brothers- in-law of William, Lord Braco, Baird of Auchmedden seems to have come to Braco for financial assistance.   The following letters from Anne to her brother show that he did not come in vain :

' *Nov 29th (no year)*

' MY LORD,—I was honoured with your Lordship's two Letters, one from Rothiemay the other from Old Meldrum, and as I ever said, so I 'm resolv'd to doo as your Ldp. bids me, had Auch. taken my advice, he would have sold his estate some years agoe, when he would have had a good deall more reversion, but that is what he must own he would never doo.   I have for some years past expostulate with him in the strongest terms, against his answering his Eldest son's demands, to the ruine of both, but so far in vain, that I have found out within some days, that his son has in a manner bully'd him in to answer some new demands.   Your Ldp. will own it is haird for me to have spent my time, my fortune, and all in my power for the good of a family, and to see him and his son, goe on spite of my teeth to ruine us all, God knows that is the case.   The Enclos'd will tell your Ldp. a little more of this, if you will be so good as to take the trouble to read it, wich if you are pleased to doo, I must humbly beg you will Let no other

---

[1] In a letter to Ludovick Grant of Grant, May 25, 1746, William Duff, Lord Braco, says ·

' You 'l doe me a great favour if you 'l apply to the General for a protection for my poor sister Lady Auchmedden, and a protection to John Forbes for Carnousie's house, who was verie friendly to me before he entered into this unhappie rebellion.'   (O.)

see it, but burn it emediately. I only want your Ldp. to believe what is true that if Auch: had done his part as I bless God I have done mine, his son might have succeeded him, in the small fortune has been in the family for some generations. Your Ldp.'s goodness and charity will Lead you to think my condition very trying, and I hope will plead for me the blessing of your continuance, and my Ladys to me and mine. I really wish your Ldp. or my Lady had time to caution him as to his Eldest son, no mother can Love a son more than I do him, but I ever thought his father has taken the way to ruine both, it is with great fear and concern I have presum'd to trouble your Ldp. with writting so much. You may depend on it I will not attempt it again, but will ever be as I ought,— Your Ldp. most aft: sister and obed: faithfull servant,　　　ANNE DUFF.

' Your Ldp. and my Lady are the only friends I have now my Dearest sister Jessie [1] is gone, if I or mine have any good offices from my mother it will be owing to your Ldp.'　　　　　　　　　　　　　　　　　　　　　　　　　　　(O.)

Anne Duff, Auchmedden, to the Lord Braco

'AUCHMEDDEN, Sept. 15, 1750.

' MY LORD,—It is with very great reluctancy I trouble your Lordship with my letters for I must know your time is taken up many ways but as your Lop. promised to me that how soon Mr. Pat: Duff came to Rothemay you would cause him settle the Legacys my Dearest sister Henie [2] left my children, so I hope your Lop. will not be offended at my putting you in mind of it, as it is now full time and Sr. Ja: Kinloch seems inclend to have it finished if your Lop. please to order my part of the Interest to be payd me at Mart: next I would then have occasion for it but whatever you think fit in this and every other thing concerning me I am willing to submit. It is now time for Mr. Band to know where he and family are to goe at Whit next, if you can give us the house of Echt he seems much inclined for it, tho' I own I had much rather goe to a toun on accompt of my daughters education if this is not thought proper I must be advised and will ever be gratefull when your Lop and my Lady are so good as take that trouble with me.

' May God bless you and yours and preserve you long for a blessing to your family and friends.—I am, with the utmost respect, My Lord, Your Lordships most affectionate Sister and obliged obedient Servant,　　　ANNE DUFF.'　(D.)

Anne Duff, Echt, to the Earl Fife

'ECHT, Dec. 23, 1760.

' MY LORD,—Your Lordships compliance with my reasonable demand, gives me more relief than I can express ! I was sensible of the impropriety of sending an express to your Lop. on this affair but as I had, without efect wrot your Lop.

---

[1] Janet, Lady Kinloch　　　　　　　[2] Henrietta, died unmarried 1748

by post again and again representing in as strong terms as I was able the distress of my condition I resolved to take this last method in hope it would have the necessary influence. The old fellow I sent is famous for going erriands, of a much longer journey than to Ed. but, I own, I neglected to acquaint your Lop. that he is a notorious knave in many respects, he was not rob^d by the way—this I made him confess and I thank your Lop. for paying the half of his hire.

' I assure your Lop I will live frugaly, while I live at all, but cannot live as a scoundrel and I shal be sure to let you see every aiticle of the accompts you have Inabled me to pay with our own money, then you will be convinc'd that no part has faln to my share, nor any one article contracted that it was possible for me to prevent but mournings for my mother. There is one Resollution I have taken which I must beg leave to tell your Lop., it is that I 'm determin'd to spend the remainder of my days in some toun where we can have a house and other conveniencys cheapest, the small farm here, the garden, etc. occasions us to have duble the number of servants here that we wou'd need there, this with the aditional rent of window tax, provisions of every sort as dear here as at Abd. makes the place not cheap to us.

' I beg leave to offer the Compliments of the Season to your Lordship the Countess and to all your family. I have the honour to be with the utmost respect, My Lord, Your Lordship's most obedient faithful humble servant,

'ANNE BAIRD.' (D.)

William Baird of Auchmedden to Lord Fife

'BALVENIE, *July* 30, 1772.

'MY LORD,—I take this opportunity of giving your Lordship hearty thanks for our good Lodging these *five* weeks past, which I am afraid will make us take the worse with our pigeon holes at Aberdeen. We have been likewise much obliged to the civilities of all the neighbourhood, in your interest, and most of them my wife's relations. She finds now by experience that the country air and travelling is rather of more use to her than the goat milk and we proposed to have gone as far as Inverness and returned by the Boat to Duff House, Hatton, etc., but without regard to my own health which would not make travelling my choice, my wife is become so lean and her health and strength so much faild [1] that the easiest carriage now fatigues her and she is obliged to go home the nearest road and try what short airings will do.

' We made only one trip last week to Elgin and saw Innes in our return where I observd with pleasure at every step the effects of your elegant taste, within doors and without. We happened to breakfast at the Sheriff Clerk when the new claims and new objections were given him and I am extremely glad to see that in all probabihty you will stand your ground both in that country and this.

---

[1] She died in the following year

N

'Mr. Duff, Schoolmaster here, is a most obliging, friendly lad and most sensible of your goodness. He is just now at a loss for want of some books of Divinity which his Professor has recommended. His father's[1] conduct has been very blameable and I hear he is conscious and ashamd of it himself but the story of his going with an ax to attack another man, was a malicious calumny for he was only carrying it home from one to whom he had lent it. I knew John's time of his cutter was out the 22 of last month but I wanted to know if he had any chance for promotion. I know he has made several applications by your advice, But its on your open friendship he principally depends. My wife and I join in our kindest compliments to our good friends and I am with the most sincere esteem and gratitude, My Lord, Your Lop. most obliged and most obedient humble Servant,   WILL: BAIRD.' (D.)

Baird's brother-in-law, Alexander of Hatton, writes to Lord Fife:

'I believe Auchmedden does not want funds if he could apply ym to the Business he was then engaged in—and I really think the man as honest as any merchant can be that wants money, and had it been convenient would have runn some risk with him myself; so far I sympathise with an old Brother tradesman. I have heard nothing since I wrote but what Achmeden mentions and I hope, wont.

'Achmeden's conduct in his own affairs publick an private has been most inconsistent and ungratefull to your Lordship, but friends must overloock and forgive.'   (D)

William and Anne Baird had a family of six sons and four daughters,[2] but all died without issue except the youngest daughter, who married Francis Fraser of Findrach, Lumphanan, and preserved the portrait of her father, by James Ferguson the astronomer.

The death of the daughter Anne is chronicled in the *Aberdeen Journal* of November 4, 1756, and a long laudatory notice concludes with the words ' she never willingly committed a fault nor neglected a duty.'

Anne Baird died in 1773, and her husband in 1775

Braco's second half-sister JANET married Sir James Kinloch, who appears to have been on very friendly terms with his brother-in-law, as Braco writes from Nevay in 1745 about the letter from Hatton with proposals for the hand of his eldest daughter. They had thirteen children : William, the eldest son, and five others, David, James, Joseph, Francis Peregrine,

---

[1] Peter Duff of Mather Cluny   See chapter xxviii

[2] William, the eldest, ' an advocate, died of a pestilent fever caught when listening to cases at the Old Bailey, and of the same fever died the then Lord Mayor of London and divers other gentlemen '   John, a sailor, was drowned , James and Alexander died in the East Indies, and Charles and George in the West Indies, all without issue   A daughter Katherine died young. Helen and Henrietta married, but the latter alone left children

and another ; and seven daughters, Jean, who married Robert MacLean ; Mary, married John Rankine ; Henrietta, Anne, and three others died unmarried.

The son James was first in the Navy, and afterwards traded in Cochin China with his mother's first cousin, Archibald Duff of Craigston. Another son, David, is only known to us from the record of his having ' fallen in the mesels ' occurring in a letter from his aunt. There are several letters from Janet and her husband.

Sir James Kinloch was ' out' in the ''45,' being a colonel in Lord Ogilvy's regiment, and, like his brothers-in-law, had to claim the protection and assistance of Lord Braco. His wife was taken prisoner after Culloden at the same time as her niece Janet, Lady Gordon. In the *Stamford Mercury*, May 1, 1746, there is a London letter, of date April 26, announcing letters from Cumberland, from Inverness, date April 18. Amongst other items of news, it says, 'Four of their (the rebels') Ladies are in Custody, viz. Lady Ogilvy, Lady Kinloch, Lady Gordon, and the Laird of Mac Intoshe's wife.'

Among the Rose papers (Mr. E. G. Duff) there is ' an Inventory of the Writes produced for Dame Janet Duff for instructing her claim upon the estate of "the late " Sir James Kinloch, Nevay, attainted.' These are the ' Contract of Marriage dated 3rd and 15th January 1730, and Instrument of Seasine following thereon in ffavours of the said Dame Janet Duff dated 27th Jan. 1730, and registered in the Particular Register of Seasines of the Shyre of Fforfar upon the 3rd July thereafter.' Sir James only possessed the estates for one year, but was, of course, not dead in 1747 when these writs were produced, but being attainted, was described as ' late.' He was tried and condemned to death, and the estates forfeited, but he was afterwards pardoned and the estates and barony purchased by his friends and restored to him, with reversion to his son William. He was the third baronet of Kinloch, Fifeshire, and of Nevay, Forfarshire (his mother having been Elizabeth Nevay of that ilk). The present representative of the family is General Kinloch of Kilvie and Logie. The old creation of baronet ended with Sir James. There is a new creation in the same family of which the present Sir George is the third baronet.

Janet Duff, wife of Sir James Kinloch, to Lord Braco

'Ed., July 7, 1746.

' My Lord,—I receved by the express your most kind and oblidging latter with the bill and the rest of the letters. Your good and jenerous behever at this time to me and my helpless children, I hop God Almight will rewerd and

bliss you and your fine yong famelay I am not abel to put in words my thank-fulness. The sume you have aloued me is more then I did expet I have sent two expresses to his oun frindes writen by himself and can not bring the lenth of your favers amongst them all, which gives me not a littel unesnes and con-firmes my opinion of them. I beg your Lordship to honour me whin at London with your good and frindly adviss. Mr. Phargewson has been most kind to me and has don everything in his pour to asist me and by no mines would tuch my monny he said it was shur annf whin I was in a better way but the othr advocat did it. I am disiared with out loss of time to git tistifactes (*sic*) from all minesters of Sir James milde and diseret behaviour the time he had any comand in the Rebchon. I dou not think if they dou him justes that they will lay harship to his charg during the time of his unhapy command in the Rebel's servess.

'My Lord you will blive me to be with all due regard and estime your most aff. Sister and oblidged obedent humbel Servent, JANNET DUFF.' (*D.*)

Sir James Kinloch, Nevay, to Lord Braco

'BARNSTAPLE, 12 *July* 1751

'MY LORD,—The reading of this I'm sensible must needs give your Lop. a great deal of grief and concern as I know the great regard you had for your Sister and the friendship you have on many occasions showen to me and poor family. I had the honour frequently to inform Lady Braco of the indifferent sense of health my poor wife had been in for some time past for the recovering of which she was advised by Physitions at London to drink the waters of Bristol hot wells. With that Intention she set out from this place to a little seaport about ten miles distance in order to take shipping to carry her to Bristol. But unfortunately just as she was upon the Quay going aboard she was suddenly most violently scised with a strong convulsion, on thursday last about eight at night. We had all the proper applications made and everything by the advice of a skillfull physition done that could be done but all in vain. She languished from that time till Sunday morning about seven when pleased God to deliver her from her pains and take her to himself. I had her buried as privately and decently on tuesday as possible and indeed all the Gentlemen in the Country showed the greatest politeness and regard that was possible to be showen, meeting the Body on the road and unasked attending it to the place of Interrment.

'I shall not trouble your Lop. longer upon this melancholy subject indeed to moveing for me to insist upon and shall only beg the continuance of your Lop.'s freindship and Countenance and that I may possess the same share in your esteem as formerly. I am now to begin the world anew which at my time of life is no easy matter and my great family craves for freindship and assistance of all their dear mothers freinds and well wishers. It shall be utmost endeavour to show my regard for the mother by the most tender care that is in the compass of my power over the children and my respect for your Lop. and others my dear wifes relations by the greatest gratitude for the many great and undeserved

favours they have showen me. In a particular manner my best wishes shall always attend all your Lordship's concerns and that God Almight may long continue your Lop. and my Lady a blessing to your fine family is the earnest wish and prayer of, My Lord, Your Lordships most oblidged and most affe. faithfull Brother and servant,   JAS. KINLOCH NEVAY.' (*D*)

Sir James Kinloch, Nevay, to Alexander Duff of Hatton

'BARNSTAPLE, 12 *June* 1752.

' DR. SIR,—I hope this shall find you, Lady Hatton and ffamily in very good health of which none more heartily wishes the continuance tho' I have not heard anything from you this long while. I thought it my duty to acquaint you that I have received by the Ship Lord Anson Capt. Touls Commander in which my eldest son went over to China about two years and a half ago, a most kind and oblidging letter from your brother the Doctor,[1] dated Canton in China 12 Novr. 1751. He hearing by being evidently at Canton at the same time with Capt. Touls of my son's being aboard enquired after him and has perswaded James to remain with him in that Country to try his fortune which he says if it please God to favour their industry he doubts not but it may turn out to his great advantage. Your Brother wits me that his success in that Country has been very various having lately mett with great losses at sea and having in August last his houses and all belonging to him burnt down by a most dreadfull fire which in two hours time consumed above four hundered great houses on the other side. Happening to put into Cochin China about 3 years and an half ago he had the good fortune to cure the Emperor of a festula, after he had been treated for two years for it and was despaired of by his own Phisitions, two Chinese and one Roman Missionary, ffor which peac of good service he has severall great and extraordinary Privi-ledges in Trade granted to him so that by the means of these and assistance of ffriends he is better enabled than ever to carry on a trade to China which he says is a most Beneficiall one and is glad to have a relation to be partner with him and he offers his services and compliments to such of his ffriends and relations as I 'm acquainted with and desires they may be informed of his wellfare. Wee must hope the best and leave the event to God Almighty.

' I offer my sincere Best wishes to my Sister and all your ffamily within and without doors, and I ever am with sincere regards, Dr. Sir, Your oblidged humble Servant and affect. brother,[2]   JAS. KINLOCH NEVAY.' (*D*.)

MARY, the seventh surviving daughter of Dipple, born 1714, died 1786, married James Abercromby of Glassaugh, afterwards General.[3]

James Abercromby's sister married James Duff of Craigston. His mother was the granddaughter of the sister of Adam Duff of Clunybeg,

---

[1] Archibald Duff. See chapter xix   [2] Brother-in-law
[3] In the Royal Regiment of Foot, now 1st Royal Scots, and Deputy Governor of Stirling Castle in 1775

and sister-in-law of James Duff of Crombie, and his father's aunt married
Adam Duff of Drummuir. The fortunes of Duffs and Abercrombys have
always been inextricably mixed.

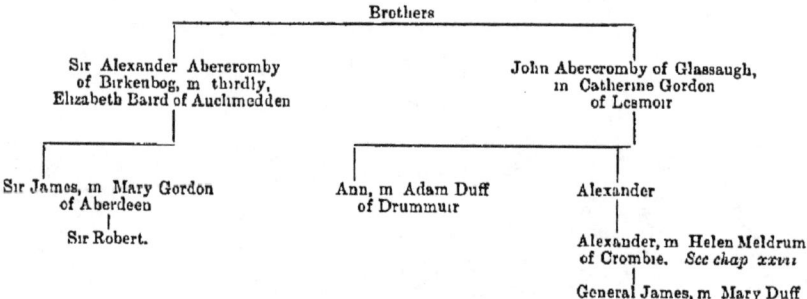

General James Abercromby seems to have been the favourite brother-
in-law of Braco, and great friendship existed between them. Allusions to
'Glassa'' are frequent in William's letters, and he appears to have valued
Abercromby's advice on many matters, including the management of his
unsatisfactory eldest son. Abercromby also succeeded him in his seat in
Parliament, and represented Banffshire for many years. But, like all the
others, except Hatton, he came to his brother-in-law for financial help.

James and Mary Abercromby had three sons and two daughters :

Captain William, who married his cousin Mary Abercromby of Birkenbog, went bankrupt 1799.

Colonel James, married Charlotte Gordon.

The Rev. Thomas St. Clair Abercromby (bishop) and King's Painter for
Scotland.

Jean, married, in 1767, George Morison of Haddo, second son of Morison
of Bognie, and, secondly, in 1781, Admiral Robert Duff of Logie.

Keith Margaret, died unmarried.

The sons all died without issue, and Glassaugh eventually passed to the
descendants of Jean, her daughter by her first husband marrying her stepson by her second, and thus further complicating the relationship of the
families of Duffs and Abercrombys. The further fortunes of the family
of Glassaugh are to be found under the heading of Fetteresso, chapter xx.

There is one letter from General Abercromby among the Rose papers :

'London, 15th March 1747/8.

'My Lord,—We are preparing to set out for Holland in pursuance of orders
issued yesterday. I hope to set out in eight or ten days at farthest, tho' I am not

HENRIETTA DUFF
in a very good condition to undergo much fatigue besides other inconveniences
I cannot draw on a boot and my surgeon tells me it will be the middle of Summer
before I am quite sound. This hurt with the Consequences attending it has
impaired my finances so much that I shall leave Mrs. Abercrombie very little to
support her and her family I hope their for it will be no inconveniency to your
Lordship to pay two years rent at Whitsunday next either unto Mr. Philip or
remit it to Mrs. Abercromby as is most convenient to your Lop. her discharge
is good by the factory I granted some time agoe and before I leave this I shall
send a State of the account. We have a great fall of snow and very cold frosty
wheather if this lasts it will mend the prices of corn.

'Sr. Robert and Mrs. Abercrombie joyn with me in our humble Duty to your
Lop. and my Lady and Jane and I am, my Lord, your Lordships most obedt. and
obliged humble servant, JAMES ABERCROMBY.' (R.)[1]

Dipple's tenth daughter, HENRIETTA, is thus described by Baird: 'She
died at Edinburgh, Aug. 8, 1748, unmarried, having declined several good
matches She was one of the most accomplished young women of her
time, being endowed with every virtue that can adorn the sex, and the
numberless offices of Charity, Generosity and Friendship which she bestowed to a surprising extent, for her fortune will long be remembered by
many.' She seems to have been a godsend to all her young nephews and
nieces (she had over fifty !), and the house in Edinburgh in which she lived
with her mother, old Lady Dipple (who survived her until 1750), was a
happy home for them all. Her fortune she left to her nephew James
Kinloch, who seems to have been unlucky. The following delightful letter
from her fitly closes the account of William of Dipple's family :

Henrietta Duff to Lady Braco, her sister-in-law

'EDINBURGH, 16th Julhe 1746.

'MY DEAR MADAM,—I had the pleasure of your Laps. by my sisters express
and forwarded Sir James Grant's letter next day. It would be very ungratefull
in me to neglect anie thing that you recomended to me. I onlie wish it were
in my poor to show the sence I have of my Lds. goodness and yours to my
unhappie sister[2] at thiss time not to mention your former feavours to my self.
Your Ldp. will finde put up in the box Lady G.'s[3] robe I could not get a rose
couler Damask under the price I write you of but as thiss is a full pink I hope it
will pleasse it is a verie good silk and I could get it nothing down of eleven and
sixpence ye yeard, in the band box is the mob handkerchief and ruffles. I hope
your Ldp. will like the lace and think it reasonable. I am sure I did all in my

---

[1] In *Old Quebec*, by Parker and Bryan, General James Abercromby is described as 'a vain
and obtuse military martinet' He was present at Ticonderoga in 1758.
[2] Lady Kinloch   [3] Lady Gordon

poor to get a good penieworth of it, but after searching at the shoppes in town I cannot finde a bit of your swatch [1] which I am much vexed at, they say the coulur is not faysion and they have not had anc for some years. I have scant your Ldp. two swatches but they weare so different from the other that I could not venture to take the silk. I am afraid I cannot depeand on the distant prospect you give of your being in town nixt winter; I have been so often dispointed in thiss that I dare secree flatter myself it will happen; all I shall say is that your being in town will be the onlic attachment I will have to it for tho' I am in never so gay a houmer which God knows I am the wearie of at present I have now got so " large a fammche " as will confine me prittie much at home for we have persuaded my sister to leave Davie here, who she proposed to carrie up to London with her which to be sure would have been most wronge and a trouble. Mrs. A. would not been fond to have him! we likeways expect Jeanie Baird in a month or two. Youn Ldp. will wish me joy of "my sons and daughters" when I have the happiness to see you nixt. My sister K.[2] gets out thiss week in a coach with Lady Murray and some other comp: she could get none before now which detained her here so long and I wish to God her going may be of anic use but as he desired it no bodie could take it upon them to dissuad her from it. He write me also to come up, but I thought ye monie I behooved to speand on the journie would doe him more service in another way, so I have given over al thoughts of it and remited ye sum to Lon she has left her two Eldest with Lady Dinm. R: till she returns I wish she would take your Ldp.'s advice as to Jamie which would surelie have much more wight with her than mine, I shall end thiss longe scrall with my aff: humble complements to my Lord in which my mother joins to your Ldp: and him, I beg you will be so good as write me soon and beleve me to be, Dear madam, with great Esteem and aff: Your Ldp.'s much obliged faithfull servt: HENRIETTA DUFF.' (O.)

A further account of William Duff of Dipple, taken verbatim from the Rose MS., may be appended :

' William Duff of Dipple, second son of Alex. Duff of Keithmore, born in 1653, died 1st May 1722. He got 4000 merks of portion. Learned as apprentice to Wm. Duff Provost of Inverness, his uncle in 1671 for 7 year. Began business in the 1678. Acquired a fortune 1686, to buy Dipple, with his industry from Holland, France and Spain, dealing in wine, hemp, iron, gin and brandy, Tallow and butter. He was a very honest, and likewise a very industrous man. He told his nephew Alex. Tulloch of Tannachy to be of caution. Gave him 1000 merks to go to Holland and purchase goods, saying, "If you are as luckie, civil and honest as I was, you can triple it." Mr. Tulloch went accordingly, but was unluckie and dissipated his time agt. Dipple's advice, who never had confidence of him as a merchant and had no intercourse with him in business, tho' kind to him otherwise.

---

[1] Pattern [2] Lady Kinloch

'When Dipple died, he had of land 30,000 mks. yearly and £80,000 Scots of money of his own acquiring. He was not above his business in all its denominations. His accompts show it in various instances, with the Laird of Innes, Laird of Grant, Ld. Duffus, Grangehill, Muirtown, Coxtown, Laird of Grant, Duke of Gordon, Findlater, etc. He always pretended that he knew nothing but plain simplicity. He attended at Old Miln all night and day whyle his melder of Corn was in the miln, slept on a rack and shared a pint of ale with his own and other Tenants. He dealed also in salmon, meale and grain and greatly in malt. In short his progress and success were miraculous. For five years preceding his death, he drank a pint of claret, or two bottles every day.'

'Discharge Wm. Duff to Alexr. Duff, 1678.' 'I, Wm. Duff merchant in Inverness (afterwards of Dipple) second son to Alex. Duff of Letach Grant me to have received from Alex. Duff of Letach my father 5000 merks Set. in part payment of my portion natural bairns pairtt of gear,' etc. 'Subscribed at Keithmore, 30 Mar. 1678.'

'And the said Wm. Duff Grant me to have received from said Alex. Duff of Letlach now of Keithmor full payment of all portion natural bairns pairt of gear Subscrid. at Keithmore, 27 Nov: 1687.'

'Accompt of money due to Wm Duff of Dipple for his share of the African Company "The Company of Scotland trading to Africa and the Indies."—1707.'

'Mr. Dunbar of Thunderton, Provost of Elgin, fell under the displeasure of the Earl of Sutherland, the King's Lieutenant in the North. He was seized by the Earl's orders and incarcerated in Elgin Jail, but was eventually liberated on a bail bond, Sir Harie Innes and William Duff of Dipple were cautioners '

James Duff to the Laird of Dipple

'HONRD. SIR,—Conform to your desire I went and saw the wrack of your Barque and took Peter Baird alongs and we called for John Ross who had offered for it befor, we are feared of fire here and they are dayly taking from it and will do : he offers now only fifty merks without the boat-mast, rudder and iron work, I spoke to Durn about it, who said he wondred he would give so much. You will do well either to send ane express or commission to sell it, for the longer it lyes it will be the less worth. I give my best wishes to your self Lady and family and continue, Honrd. Sir, Your obliged cousine humble servant,

'JAMES DUFF. [1]

'PORTSOY, *July* 7, 1715

'ffor the much Honrd. The Laird of Diple.'   (*D.*)

---

[1] It has not been found possible to identify the writer of this letter. He was probably a son or grandson of one of Keithmore's brothers Possibly the same James Duff who writes from Findhorn to Dipple when at Rotterdam, and signs ' your affectionate cousin.'

Three further letters to William Duff of Dipple may be added – two from his sister Mary, and one from his sister-in-law:

'TANACHIF, *Aug* 13, 1716.

' BROTHER,—I receved a lyne from you with one from my housband under John Robartson his cover of deat July 11th and spock to him to pack the fish when others packed, which no doubt he will not faill to dow, as for bills there is non I can promis on : the tenantts bills for rents I was not free to meadell with and grantt discharg to them, not knowing what might hapin and the bear I wrott of, a good part of it givin to credtors for payments of presing onual rents which these reselts will show. There is on hand in the straw and threshen, I belive, fortie Bolls yit undisposed on which is the most of what will be had of the last crop. My husband wrott by his last the Bond and disposishon he gave my daughter Lisie was not good, and there was a claus in my contrack for macking up that disapoynttment which if he was spared he would mack effectuall. I am persuaded you and he both was not egnorantte tho we had not fallne in his misfortons that my childring was not secqured as they might be and the Lasie not to have right to a farding is hard indid, but who can shun misfortons. I thought yee had takine advyss as to what conscins my young ons and lett me been esie what ever should be in the mater, but I believe the thrang of your own affairs puts such trifils as my all out of your mynd, I did expect yee would had that regeard to me and your own condock to have bean att sume peans to preventt my own and childrings misrie if posabill for I most say I did not first or last move in conscrning this bargan without your advyss soo ye may think if I be mead misrabell and triublsume to ame frind, it most be you and that is what yee will not allow, soo look to it. My husband wrot me he was to dispose his movabells to sume credatour. I wish he may considere howe his famallie is to be subsisted, and wher the monie will be had to defray his and his sons charg. I shall give you no furdare fash at presentt, but I expeck your adwyss in the worst of eneuff how to behave, and I am your affeconatt sister,   MARY DUFF.

'My husband wrott for his first and second Contracks of marriage which I have sent by this berar.'   (D.)

Mary Duff, to her brother

'TANACHIF, *August* 20th, 1716

' BROTHER,—Have yours of deat the 9 instantt with the bond I spock Johnathan Alnass to back the sesing who hath three othere to tack on the Land of Tanachie and promised to done what I proposed with the samme breth and told me it would be allamorouss if it ware understood here and that I should prosede befor other credators would lock lyck conivance this mead me dellay tho perhapss it be not for the chyld's intrest ye will advyss me if ther be hasard in this as I hope ye will tack kear of whatt conscrnss me I wrot you the 13 at lenth I am dauly discovring mor of my scrcomstancess which is not esie tho the govern-

mentt never had a farding of us soo I am in pean till I hir from you as I beag ye spair not expence I am told the greatest loss will be myne. If I loss him self and I and myne be mead begers it is no small misfortoun. The fish shall be packed and keried as ye propose, the tenantes will exceppe of none of my dischergs nor grant bills, there will be non but Tanachie there is Dischargess sent to be syned by my husband as yee may adwyss John Robertson see them dissured and receve there bills if ye adwyss I shall deliver them with his oversight. I wrott of the bear in my last if it is not threshen " of the growth of the means " it may be disposed of tho' not delivered till there be youss for the strawe there. An I hold bee fore upwards of 40 Bolls in the tenants hands and about the toun as if yee apriehend dengare lest it be disposed of and delivered when threshed I expect ye will give me cunsell as to the movabills and domishalls [domiciles] if ye apriehend dengare aboutt them and abow all when yee understand the Govermentt's disyns as to my husband there is geniall chargs of horning with iniebishons. I shall not fash you furdar at presentt, for I expeck to her from you how shoun yee can, for I am Your affexonatt sister,   MARY DUFF.' (D.)

Margaret Gordon (widow of Alexander of Braco) to the Laird of Dipple

'HONORED AND DEAR BROTHER,—I receaved a letter from the Duke of Gordon desiring the money due to him at Martimasse from my husband and offering to give Tillibodie such obligations therfor as he shall think necessary for him to give, this I could not neglect to show you and to get your advise and concurance therein for now since it hath pleased the Lord to remove your brother ther is none that I will confide in so much as you and expect that you will order and advise in my sons affairs as ye wold doe for your selfe and what lyes in my power I shall God willing show to the world and to you that I shall never forget so worthee a husband. I think it necessar ye writt to Tillibodie and acquaint him with what the Duke writs and ye know that the Duke performing his part he will still make your brothers aires lyable to performe ther part and it is much better to doe it in lym now when he hath use for the monie then be forst to it and dissoblidge him, never the lesse therfor with all conveniency writ to Tillibodie and desire him to give you a free and full anseer and that ye wold not wish your nephew to live otherways with the Duke then his father hath done and that he may put the Duke to it to performe his part and that theirupon show that ye and he and I are willing to performe your brothers part for I am affraid that some way or other things may be negleekted and goe wrong ye may remember what ye did see in the Duke's letter to your brother il ye wold be pleased to writ to the Duke it wold clear al doubts how soon ye canc put this affair to a close do it for I should not wish any thing your brother did put his face to for to goe wrong. I wroat to you concerning the selling of the vittuall, let me have your answer therin, so wishing to hear of your weullfaire, I am, Your affectionat sister and humble servant,   MARGARET GORDON

(After 1705.)

'For the Laird of Dippell this.'   (D.)

DUFF HOUSE

CHAPTER IX

WILLIAM DUFF, LORD BRACO AND FIRST EARL FIFE

1697-1763

' WILLIAM, the first Lord Fife, Dipple's only son who survived him, was born in Autumn 1697. He got a very compleat education, and was a better scholar than most gentlemen commonly are, who have not been bred to any of the learned Professions. For he was master of the Latin, French and Italian languages, with some tincture of the Mathematics, and was very well acquainted with ancient and modern history.

' He was a member of the British Parliament for the County of Banff from 1727 to 1734 and alwise joined the country party. He was one of the Bedford hand Club, kept by Sir William Wyndham, Sir John Rushout, Mr. Shippan, etc., about thirty in all, worthy gentlemen and true patriots.

' I am informed that he spoke a few words in some particular occasions in the House of Commons—once in 1730 when a debate came on whether to continue the Hessian troops in British pay ; he stood up in his place and said, that the affection of the people was the best security of the Government, and if they possest that, there would be no occasion for hiring mercenary Forces from any foreign country in time of peace ; and besides

it was reasonable to give our own Fish-guts to our own Sea-maws (*i.e.* Gulls). The English members did not understand this phrase, but when explained to them, said it was a most significant and judicious expression.

' He was created Lord Braco by King George the 2nd in 1735, and Viscount Macduff and Earl Fife in 1759—(Irish honours).

' He was a man of extraordinary good sense, which, improved by his stock of acquired knowledge, seven years sitting in the British Parliament, and an intimate acquaintance with the best company in Britain, made him a polite well-bred man, and an agreeable, entertaining, and instructive companion.

' In his private character he was a most indulgent Parent and husband ; and the kindest and easiest master to his Tenants and servants.

' He had inflexible principles of honour and justice from which nothing could make him depart but misinformation or prejudice, which last, if once he had contracted it against any person, it was not easy to remove, especially if he thought he had met with any Disingenuity, or been in the least imposed upon. However, this went no further than to make him less sanguine in doing that person any good offices afterwards ; for I never could observe anything of vindictiveness in his nature, and upon a proper acknowledgment, he was most ready to forgive a fault.

' He had an anxious concern for the welfare of all relations and friends, and he was a friend to merit wherever he found it.

' He was naturally very ingenuous and had no reserve when he believed his confidence would not be abused ; he did many generous, humane things, gave a good deal in Charity to the poor and in a very private way, and tho' I don't pretend to say his liberality was very extensive, yet it was equal to that of any of his great neighbours.   For I have known him several times give 50 and 100 guineas not only to relations, but to others, merely on account of their merit   In Aprile 1746, when the Duke of Cumberland was at Banff before the battle of Culloden, he gave £250 of drink-money to the common soldiers of his army, merely that he might with more freedom ask protection for the Houses, Cattle, Horses and other effects of any of his friends and relations who had the misfortune of being engaged.   And indeed, at that time both he and his Lady exerted their utmost efforts to save all that they could from being plundered or otherwise harrassed.[1]

' Everybody has their foibles and perhaps he discovered too great an ambition of ruling the elections and other political disputes in those counties where his Estates principally lay.   And I believe this disgusted a great many who had no connexion with or dependance upon his family

---

[1] There are many allusions to this in their letters.

and looked upon themselves as his equals in every respect but that of
fortune, and that this was the mainspring of that opposition which he some
times encountered, and of that implacable envy and detractions which on
some occasions attempted to run him down ; and besides those who had
served him in politics might some times think he had not made them such
returns as they expected !   After all, it must be acknowledged that, considering his large property and numerous connections in the County of
Banff, he was extremely well entitled to the greatest political interest in
it, and that in Moray, where his estate paid a third part of the Land Tax of
the whole shire, it was unreasonable in any other great Family to propose
to make a Cypher of him '

In 1735, he purchased the superiority of the estates of Mar, for
£10,000 sterling, and in 1737 the estate of Glenbucket from John Gordon
the famous Jacobite.

He expended vast sums of money in building.   He built the new house
of Balvenie in 1724-1725, and resided there for a time.[1]   In 1730, he began
to build Duff House, but, owing to a dispute with Adam the architect,
which engaged him for many years, he never occupied the house, and
when obliged to drive past it on his way to Banff, always drew down the
blinds of his coach.

' He also spent much in Lawsuits and in political disputes, for when he
once took a cause in hand he spared no cost to carry it through.   Yet, being
an excellent economist, he made many valuable additions to the Family
estate, and most of them at very good prices.   Upon the whole I am persuaded that he will be always allowed by those who knew him well to have
been an honest, valuable, and worthy man.'

(This is the account given of William, Lord Braco, by his brother-in-
law, William Baird, the first historian of the Duffs, who had himself
doubtless benefited by the patronage of this successful member of the
family)

The following is an early letter from William Duff, afterwards Lord
Braco (who in his young days was also in the family business), to Robert
Grant of Tamore .

' SIR,—I have given the Bearer 12 pounds good English hopps, old weight,
which I hope will please.   Have likeways given him a bottle wine the best I
have gott.   I shall be glad if it please the Collonell, in case he be for it I can give
half a hogshead at 4 pounds ten shillings and shall wait your answer for five
or six days.

---

[1] It is now part of the distillery, having been last used as a private house on the occasion
of the ball given by Lord Macduff (the late Duke) in 1878.

LADY JANET OGILVIE.
FIRST WIFE OF THE FIRST EARL ...

'I offer my dutifull respects to Ballindalloch and Mrs. Grant and am, Sir, Your oblidged humble servant, WM. DUFF.

'BANFF, 28 *Sept.* 1727.

'Please do me the favour to forward the enclosed letter to my friend Craigenach' (see chapter xxx.).[1]

William Duff married, in 1719, Lady Janet Ogilvie, daughter of the Earl of Findlater and Seafield, late Chancellor of Scotland, and widow of Hugh Forbes of Craigievar, but she died without issue on Christmas Day 1720, in the twenty-fifth year of her age.

He married, secondly, in 1723, Jean Grant, eldest daughter of Sir James Grant of Grant, M.P., and for some years resided at Braco and Balvenie, and several of their fourteen children[2] were born at each place. That the family of Lord Braco lived at one time in the mansion-house of Balvenie is proved by many letters to and from that place and by an inventory of furniture there, dated 1764, and another list of articles broken during the family's stay.

During his frequent absences from home he was a most industrious and affectionate correspondent, and hundreds of his letters to his wife are still preserved (in the possession of Mrs Chancellor alone there are more than eighty), mostly addressed to 'My dearest life and best of Daties,[3] and signed 'yours for ever, yours while B. your loveing houseband,' etc. Some are mere scraps · 'This letter will be short, but I cannot miss writing with this post,' and others concerned only with business.

His business affairs kept him a great deal in Edinburgh, and his parliamentary duties, for the first seven years of his married life, took him to London. In 1733, while still William Duff, he writes to his wife, dating from 'Chorlton, within a myle of Greenwich,' 'Your father, Sir James Grant and other two friends are here with me spending a pairt of the holidays.' In the same year: 'I missed letters from the north last post, which they say is occasioned by the waters being out beyond York. (It was indeed a fearful distance in those days for a man to have between himself and his wife and babies!) Direct to me at my house in Conduit St. since I have got a good house there opposite your father's. You see I have been

---

[1] MS British Museum.

[2] William, 1724-1753. Anne, 1725-1805, Janet, 1727-1758, James, 1729-1809, Alexander, 1731-1811; Jane, 1732-1776, George, 1736-1818; Ludovic, 1737-1811, Patrick, 1738-1738, Helen, 1739-1778; Sophia, 1740-1826; Catherine, 1741-1765, Arthur, 1743-1805; Margaret, 1745-1786

[3] Daty, darling

led into a fine dance by being in Parliament, however with the assistance of God I 'll doe the best I can.'

In 1710, when he had the two girls with him in Edinburgh, he writes : ' I have engaged an Italian master who undertakes to finish your daughters in the spinet in less than 5 months.' On another occasion he writes from Dundee that he has ' been obliged to send back the footman with the horse, as it could not make out the journey,' and once he had to leave behind some friend who was travelling with him, and a servant to take care of him, the hardships of the journey had been so great. During this period he also writes to his wife about his proposed purchases of Rothiemay (1741), on which his cousin William of Braco had already lent money,[1] and Echt.

Quite early during his stay in London he seems to have made himself felt in legal and political circles. He writes : ' I find the Dutchess (of Gordon) has writ Sir Robert Walpole, rateing me in a high manner, and desyring a gift of the feu-duties of the Estate of Dumfermling. However, I hope I have closed that door upon them.' And at the same period : ' God give us a happy meeting for long doe I think to see you. I know not how it is with you, but I assure you I find it very cold to be here without a bedfellow.'

In 1733, William, the eldest boy (there were already six children, and the mother was only twenty-eight) broke his arm, and the father writes many anxious letters : ' I am exceeding glade that your boy is out of hazard. I beg you will take the best care of yourself and be heartie and cheerful wh: is the greatest favour you can do me.' At this time, Jane was the baby, and he writes hoping that the next child will be a son. There followed three in succession. After 1734 he no longer went to London, but his absences in Edinburgh were longer and more frequent, as he got involved in many lawsuits. He had disputes with Lord Findlater as to fishing ; also with the town of Banff and with Lord Banff, and the Duke of Gordon and various other members of the family of Gordon. ' I hope care will be taken that James Duff (of Corsindae who acted as his factor) and

---

[1] On February 9, 1716, Alexander Abercromby and William Gordon wrote from Banff to the Lord Advocate, 'asking the pardon of Archibald Ogilvie, son to Sir Patrick of the Boyn, he having been concerned in the late unnatural rebellion. The prosecuting of him will bring little or nothing to the Government, the purchase he made of Rothiemay in the county being by money borrowed from Duff of Braco, as will appear by the registered disposition in anno 1712, of the lands, with ane assignation of the rents and profits in Braco's favour' (*Scottish History Papers*, Record Office).

In the previous century the House of Rothiemay had been a stronghold of ' the rebels,' as James Baird in 1635 petitioned for repayment of his expenses in ' taking the House of Rothiemay out of the hands of the rebels' (*History of the Bairds* —Ed W Fraser)

Adam Panton keep possession of Lord Banff's fishings, since now that Rothiemay is in the north, all measures will be taken to brangle me out of them.'

'Braco, *Monday forenoon*, 1736

'My dearest Dr. Dr. dearest Datie,—I have sent you this express to tell you that Mountblene and I have been here since Saturday and are in good health but the weather has been soe bade that we were stormstead here yesterday and are like to be soe this day soe I hope you 'l not be uneasie for we 'l be with you God willing how soon the weather breaks up and it will be best to keep Delmoor and the other Gentlemen.

'We were heartily fatigued last week for from Moonday to Satiday we were 10 hours Closs amongs old papers evene day, and it was Thursday befor I found all the papers I wanted as to the Duke, but the discovring them must be keept a Secret for some time for reasons that I 'll tell you at meeting. I have likewise got papers that will be of great use to me with respect to Arthur fforbes, soe that the time for the Search was weal Imploy'd.

'Noe doubt you have heard that Johnstons ship and all his cargoe was lost and your Shangai and some other things from London was on board Thomas Duff, with my great timber was load Thursday last and if he came out of Aberdeen on Satrday his ship and cargoe will have the same fate, for there never was more stormic weather than since I left Balvenie. We had closs rain and wind on Saturday all the way from Banff till we come here. I have been in great concern about you and your health ever since I left you and there is nothing can give me greater satysfaction than to find you in perfect health chearfull and casie upon which the greatest part of my happiness depends, may God's blessing and myne always attend you. Pray make my Complements to Mrs. Grant and your companie 'I am with the utmost affection whyle I breathe. My Dearest Dr. Dr. Dr. and best of Daties, yours for ever. B.

'I desired James Duff [1] to tell you that we could not get thro' our papers soe soon as we Intended and sure I am you would wish us to doe something before we left them. Adieu my Dr. Dr. Dr. life.' (O.)

'Aberdeen, *20th August* 1736.

'My dearest Dr. Dr. Datie,—I have at last agreed with Echt and our papers will be ready for signing this night and as to the bargain I can only tell you just now in Generall that it will not be near soe dear as I did apprehend. I hope to get from this the morrow in the day soe as to be at Aboyn Sundays night, but I don't expect great success from that expedition only I 'm resolved not to let my wood goe so far under the value as people would be at.

'I was sorrie to hear the Dissaster that happened to poor Thomas Duff [2] and the loss of his Ship. I hope all is weal with you since I left Banff and I doubt not of your keeping sight of my work that it goe forward in all the particulars.

---

[1] Corsindao.   [2] Craigston's son

P

I cannot yet fix on a precise day for being at home, but you may be sure it will be as soon as I can. Echt has some thoughts of leaving that place even before a term which will oblidge me in that case to return that way, soe as care may be taken of everie thing till I get ane other tennent ffor his ffriends will not let him keep it and this will perhaps occasion my staying a day or 2 longer. It will give me the greatest pleasure that Datie has got the better of her fall and I beg you 'l take the best care of yourself till I have the happeness of seeing you. I am always with the greatest sincierity and affection, My Dearest Dr. Dr. Datie and Life, yours till death,   Braco. (O.)

'I have been in perfect good health since I came from Banff and rather the better of my journie.'

'My dearest best and bonie Datie,—Your last brought me a bill of leave for altring your blew ring which shal be obey'd and I hope your best ring wont Set you the worse that it has Attie's hair and yours within it, till I can get a better one for you. The inclos'd is from Mr. Sellers anent your Son. I find that notwithstand all the strong letters that I 've wrote to your son and all the trouble and great expenses that I 've been put to on his acct, yet he has not mended one bit, soe that now I quite dispair of any reformation However I have yet told Mr. Sellers that I 'll take a little tryal and if matters are not better I must quite alter my plan for I think it 's a hard case when I have soe much to doe and soe many other children to take care of to be throughing soe much money upon one abanden'd wreach that will never mend or give any satysfaction but will rather be a disgrace to his parents and friends. I have with the assistance of the Almighty conquer'd myself soe as to make this mysfortune as easie as possible and I hope and wish you may doe the same. The dissapointment, God knows, is great to me for at this time of day considring the perplexed affairs of one kind or other that I have on hand, I have great need of help and if he had turn'd out as I wish'd considring his age, in a some little time he would have rekeiv'd me of a good deal of my burden beside the advantage that my famile and children would have. But we ought chearfully to Submite to what providence has alloted for us.

'We are now setting about our arbitration. Since what 's above I have called the Goold Smith about your blew ring But there is a bit of the stone cracked which would fly out if it was streached and if it was set again the Place behoved to be taken down after loseing that bit soe that tis best to let it be as it is rather than spoyle the Stone. Fareweal my bonie Datie.—Yours whyle,
                                                                    'Braco.' (O)

The three topics which occur most frequently in these letters are his long disputes with Adam over the accounts for the building of Duff House, a suit with Keith of Bruxie (which 'came to a head' in 1739),[1] and another

---

[1] There is a MS account of this case, covering a roll of forty feet long. It was a dispute about the lordship and estate of Balvenie which Alexander Duff of Braco had obtained in 1687 from Arthur Forbes, who owed him a large sum of money In 1732 Miss Mally Seton claimed a right

WILLIAM DUFF, LORD BRACO
AND FIRST EARL FIFE

By William Smith.

connected with some kind of wall he wished to build on Speyside, frequently alluded to as ' the Bulwark,' also the wadset of ' Meyan ' (*sic*). At times he seems to have felt depressed at the amount of time he spent on these matters. ' Coll: Abercromby proposes to set out to-morrow, your brother goes to Hopetown, everybodie gets their feet loose except me, who have been so inborrowed with my own blunder of having to do with Adam. My father could have prevented all this trouble and hazard to me if he had taken the advice of any person of skill. However, he did many good things, and I ought not to complain of this oversight I don't blame myself for anything that has happened, except that I was so unluckie as to put trust in a fellow that has turned out as great a rogue as ever was on earth. Who indeed had supporters as void of conscience as himself.' From Edinburgh also he writes : ' The want of you makes me much paine, my dear Datie, my absence soe long from you is not the least of my trouble, and the more soe that I have been the sole cause of it. But I am like all Scotsmen (*i e.* litigious). However, I hope after all this, God will grant us happier days together, and it may happen that the trouble and expenses that I meet with may make them that come after me the more easy. May God bless you and the poor little bairns.'

And again : ' God bless my Datie and send us a more settled and peaceful living, for people's wicked designs has hitherto given me a most troublesome life and has put me to great expenses.'

About another suit which he had pending he writes : ' The lawyers have a good opinion of my cause relating to Moyness. The only loss that I'm at is that it depends altogether on writing, and there are few of the judges there that understand writing.' On looking at some of the legal MSS. of a previous century, on which presumably the case depended, one can perhaps understand the difficulty. This letter appears to have been written about 1740. Braco does not always remember to add the year.

Re an election then pending : ' I have made only two new barons—to wit Muriefold and John Duff in Elgin, neither doe I propose that either of them should be enrolled or vote except in the event that Rothiemay or the family of Gordon make new barons, and in that case all the world will approve of what I have done.'

Of his eldest son he never has anything pleasant to say ; doubtless he was a trial. ' I have this day paid a bill of £100 for bringing William out

---

to Arthur Forbes' estate by a disposition from him, and before this case between her and Lord Fife, Braco's nephew and heir, could be determined, Arthur's nephew and heir granted a bond of the whole estate to William Keith of Bruxie, who in consequence brought an action of reduction and improbation against Lord Fife, and the process lasted twenty-two sessions before the Court of Session, but at last was settled amicably in 1743

of Captain Geddes' ship and sending him abroad with his tutor. I wish to God that our honest intentions may have the desired effect in recovering him, for you see what fatigue I have at home and abroad in keeping matters right, and in bringing myself out of one scrape bequeathed by my predecessor and another occasioned by myself.'

After Lady Fife and family had removed to Rothiemay, and the family grew larger and his means greater, he seems to have been called upon to execute numerous commissions for her. He goes to Leith to choose carpets in 1739. He buys silk, tea, dates and other confections, and in one letter laments the length of time they will be on the way ' even though the French do not get the Kinghorn boat ! ' In 1742, he remarks that the Kinghorn boat, which presumably made a slow voyage from thence to Leith, is too rough for ' his old age,' and he prefers to make the longer journey round by land. He was then forty-five. ' Farewell my bonnie Datie, you and your old and young companions have my dayly prayers.' And in 1741, ' I intend God willing to goe north by way of Aberdeen for the Cairn Road [i.e. *over the mountains by Braemar*] is vastly fatiguing '

From Aberdeen, December 31, 1732 : ' I thank God for it, I came safe here by night. The weather was favourable and I hope to get to Montrose the morrow. Mr. Donaldson (his brother-in-law) took me up on the road, but was obliged to ly at the old Town this night to be free of arrest. Send along with bearer a bit of the silk to show the exact wideness you would have it of, and at the same time I beg you will send a bit of your hair that I may have it set in a ring. I was dreaming about you three times last night. However, I hope all is well.' (This last is a curious and unusual touch of sentiment and superstition)

In 1741, he mentions that he has not sent the rapee snuff, as he finds it would not keep, and in another letter he says, ' a little glass with hartshorn drops goes with this.' As the sons and daughters grew a little older, he was also commissioned to buy clothes for them. ' I will cause send cloaks with capuchin hoods for your daughters,' he writes to his wife, ' they are worn by all the fashionable folk. Stays for the lasses. Laces for your daughters, and a pretty mob for my Datie. I propose to have your mantle made of red velvet. Small cloath is too much upon the common ' ' It were best that you send the measure for coats for James and Sandy, since I would have them made here as well as the vests. I think improper to get swords for the lads, but if they please mama and Mr. Abel and mind their book I will bring them each a pair of buckles to their shoes ' And again : ' I am glade of the news that you give me of your children and their progress with their book. It is very agreeable to me. I have bought the

frocks and cloaths and breeches for your boys. There was only three hats commissioned for, but if Lewis [*aged six*] keeps his head even, I'll send a pretty little hat with a silver lace.'

He also interested himself greatly in the affairs of his household, and sends to his wife a bale of stuff 'that will make proper frocks for your servants, that will weare some time, viz., for the porter, the boy who attends the tea table and the coachman.' In 1743, he took upon himself to engage a cook. He says, 'I have two cooks in my offer; one of them came from the Earl of Kintore last term, and the other from the Earl of Glasgow; they are both well recommended.' He doubts if she would like one of them, as 'he has a wife and three bairns.' In the next letter he says: 'I have engaged the cook Thompson. I am persuaded he'll please you, for he understands his business and is well recommended. If you want any kitchen furniture it will be best they be bought while the cook's here.'

There are frequent references to contemporary events:

'I have sent you that pairt of Col. Abercrombie's letter which gives information of the French fleet being seen upon the British coasts, which is the best account that is come here of it.' With true Scottish economy he adds: 'I thought it needless to swell the postage with the rest of the letter.' 'There is uncertain accounts of the battle in Germany, but the French is beat off the field with great loss, and several circumstances told to the honour of the British troops' (Dettingen, June 27, 1743). 'A bloodie battle has happened in the Mediterranean' (off Toulon, 1744). 'The Earl of Aberdeen died and was found stiff.' 'We had the account yesterday of Edinburgh being taken' (by Prince Charles; September 1745). 'I have three sisters and two of their husbands now in Edinburgh. Long, long doe I think to be with Datie, which, God willing, shall be soon.' 'It is here talked of that there is a peace, but it must be such an unglorious one that the King or his ministers have not yet ventured to make it public, and I'm afraid that the parliament will not bring us out of our difficulties Poor Admiral Haddock killed himself because his hands were tyed up from attacking the Spanish fleet going to Italie' (1746).

The letters after 1743 are filled with allusions to his youngest son Arthur, 'my bonnie Attie,' who would appear to have been, from his birth, the favourite of both parents. When the child could not have been more than a few months old, he adds as a postscript to his letter: 'I have sent with Duncan a cheeping bird for Attie.

'I am having my Datie's hair and my little lad's set in a diamond ring.—May every good thing attend you and Attie and all the rest of the

young folks.—Were I at home, we would place Attie betwixt us and sport with him by turns.—I send some toys which you may distribute as you please, for you'll soon found out what's for Attie. Take care of yourself, Attie, Clossie (Sophia), and the rest.

'Pray take the best care of yourself, for I don't fear your caring for Attie. Long, long do I think to be north with my Datie and her Attie, which I hope and wish for, since I will be all the days of my life my dearest and best Datie, Your with the utmost affection, BRACO.'

And in 1745 he writes : ' I envie Arthur for he has mama to himself, and mama has Arthur, and Papa has neither.'

' I am glad you have weaned my little boy, and that he is none the worse.' In a previous letter he had hoped she would not do this until he came home, ' unless the child should suffer.' All his thought was for this youngest son, born when he was forty-six, and only twenty at the father's death.

In one very short letter he writes, ' I have this moment the opportunity to tell you that I am in perfect health. I only want you and Attie. May all good attend my dearest Datie and my Arthur.'

' I congratulate you, my dr. Datie, upon my bonnie little lad's getting out three chaft teeth, by which I hope the hazard of teething is over with him.'

He begins to yearn much to be at home again : ' If I were free of Calder and Adam, I would be quite easy, for I'm not much afraid of what Drummuir can do. If I get a good luck of Mr. Adam as well as of Bruxie I daresay you'll be pleased.' ' If I were free of that villain Adam, I should have little to doe here.' ' Tho' I have missed being at an end with Adam through the Justice Clerk's default, yet I must do something in other matters and stay here a short time, which is most undesirable, and disagreeable to me.'

' There never was a judge did show more partiality than the Justice Clerk, nor a party more barefaced villainy than Adam.' ' We have now Adam, Drummuir and Calder on hand.'

He sends her many directions as to the management of affairs at home . ' Mind David Stronach to take care not to take in mixed meal.' ' I think it will be best you cause block up any fireplace about the barnyards except in the henwife's house.' ' The looms in the summer house . cannot be better employed than in holding my oats.'

In November 1743 he sent her an account of all sums to be paid out in Banffshire ; and other directions for farm work and buying and selling operations are frequent.

In 1749 he took the waters at Bridge of Earn. ' I have drunk the

waters two days since I got the doctor's directions. I propose to make use of the ' Hot bath ' the day after to-morrow, and hope to be the better of both.'

He is most anxious that she should keep up her dignity in his absence, and writes urging her never to drive out without four riding servants. ' I think indeed when you make the visits you mention that you should have four riding servants with you, for it looks very bad to have a coach and four and only one servant or two, and I am sure your neighbour Abachie will not scruple to go with you.'

' EDINBURGH, 1st March (circa) 1745.

' MY DEAREST BONIL AND BEST DATIE,—I have the satysfaction of your last, coving the Historie of the McDuffs and am exceeding glad that you and your young people were soe weal diverted on the occasion of the old Datie's birthday. I think you have done verie right in diverting yourself in making the visits you propose. But am afraid that the weather has not been favourable to my Datie. We have been attending Wardhouse's tryall who with the other two panells will not only be acquite but I believe Blackhall will be soused in damages and expenses.

' I shal mind the Commission in your last with respect to the confections wanting. I have sent for your diversion some copies of Wardhouse's Information which will Intertain you and which you may disperse among your ffriends. Ther are toys sent for Attic and the other young children with the boxes that are sent to Aberdeen which you may distribute when you please for you 'l soon find out whats design'd for Attic.—Fareweal my bonie and best Datie ffor I am for ever Yours most faithfully, B.' (O.)

After he became Lord Fife, in 1759, he was seldom away from home, and there are comparatively few letters of his after that date. He died in 1763 at Rothiemay House, and was buried at Grange, his body, and those of his wife and his granddaughter Frances (see next chapter), being subsequently removed to the mausoleum at Duff House.

Two years before his death he acquired the mansion in Edinburgh known as Fife House. A contemporary account says ' Lord Fife had a good house, outside the city wall '

' Fife House.—This mansion stood on ground now occupied by the north-east portion of Lothian Street, near the north end of Potter Row. It seems to have been entered from a road which skirted the outside of the town wall. In Edgar's plan of 1742, published in Maitland's *History of Edinburgh*, it is designated "Duke of Douglas's." That nobleman died in 1761, and, according to Chambers's *Traditions of Edinburgh*, the house was then acquired by the Earl of Fife. In the map of the city in Arnot's *History of Edinburgh* it appears as " Fife House." '

Some of Lady Braco's letters to her husband show a certain resentment at his long absences, and one which has not been preserved was sent back by him that she might revise the undeserved expressions. But very little ever occurs to mar the perfect understanding and tender feeling that existed between them. ' Never man had a better wife.'

She writes to her husband from Banff, December 17, 1739 :

' MY DEARLST DR. LIFE AND BEST OF DATIES,—May God bless you for the two last kind letters you write me, they are the greatest and best present you can make me and what I hope I never shall be ungratefull for ; our town is turned exceeding gay. I have gote a german here that plays finely upon a sorte of instrument : I was fryday last at his concert ; and am to be there this night again, he has gote the town house for entertaining his company in. We have allways a ball after the musick is over, and you 'll be surprised to hear that I am so well and cliver at present as to be able to dance minuets and country dances ; but I will take care not to venture over far. The younge Andrew [1] be one of the best natured boys I ever had and this I hope you 'll not faill to tell Montbleanc off as I am perfectly persuaded he takes this strain of goodness from him. The Knight of Durn [2] is in perfect rapture with our german musick he stayed in town these ten days attending it : and likewayes brought his lady here friday last, but sometimes we have enough adoe to drive the spleen from him upon account of his lossing his wager with me. I am very well pleased that both my daughters have the musick master once a week, I notice what you write as to the term matters and will not faile to keep Duncan in mind of it ; and he and I shall take an opportunity to speak to Charles Buit as you recommend. I was obliged to Robie Moor for sending me Plays, what I had was just done when his supply came. I beg you 'll take care for it and tell him and Corvichen that I will write them both very soon ; but I am in a hurry to-day to get dressed for the Ball ; Rothiemay and Lord Maitland came not to town the Lady Betty wrote Doctor Fother [3] of their dyet, great bodye moves slowly. My kind compliments to Corvichen and all that 's best to you ; for God's sake take care of yourself and doe not drinke too much, intertaining the Lords or other friends for your health is precious to me above all thinges being my happiness depends upon it for I am unalterably in my affection, but not in my faults, my dearest Dr. dr. Dearest life, yours while breathing.   J. B.'

' Dec 17th, 1739.

' MY DEAREST LIFE AND ONLY DATIE,—This letter was gone to the post house when your express arrived so I called it back that it might goe the length of Abdn. with him. Duncan is busie looking out for your papers and I am just going to the Concert : I heartily wish if it had been possible for you that you

---

[1] Andrew Hay.   [2] Sir James Dunbar
[3] Dr Fotheringham, a well-known physician in Banff.

JANE GRANT,
SECOND WIFE OF THE FIRST EARL FIFF

had given Melross what he wanted. They are so obligeing in every thinge and if it had not been for them I believe your plummers had been idle for want of Scots coal before Mr. Abernethie's shipe arrived , I was quite overjoyed when I saw the express from Abd. believing to have heard by him of Bruxies defeat, but I hope that will come afterwards, you shall hear from me again by the Wedensdays post, and in the mean time I beg that you 'll believe that I am with all possible esteem while I breath my dearest Dr. Dr. Datie, Yours faithfully,

'J. B.'[1]

And six years later from Rothiemay :

'*January 30th,* 1745.

'MY DEAREST DR. DR. DATIE,—I had the pleasure of yours from Edinʳ, and it is a vast sattisfaction to me to know that you gote safe there, and in good health. Mr. Sellers letter is what I regrete, but is no surprise to me, indeed I joine him in oppinion that it is a pittie to throw away so much money, since there appears to be but small hopes of reclaiming my son from his folly in that ways and I dare say you 'll now thinke of putting him upon a quit different plan, as I am persueded a governor can be of no further service to him and is only an additional expence to you, Mr. Abell tells me that your sones here are doeing wonderfully well, which is one great comfort to ballance a Cross, as too their Lessons their Master must be left judge, but as too their behaviour otherways I can with truth affirme it, that it must please everybody, they and all the rest of Dada's Daties are in perfect health, only longs for my Dearest Datie, and Arthur is no less mindefull of you than of us. Sanders Stronach tells me that the Cook would not allow the frock to be made, that I order'd for him, since he said he would not wear it, for that you had promised him one at a guinie and £10 ster. of wages besides other perquisites, I thought it best to mention this to you, in case you had judged it proper to speck to Monblearie on any other at Edinʳ that might have been present when he was ingaged ; so as we may have no disputes about the matter, indeed I imagined that he had only been upon the same footing with Andrew Phillip, however as the Cook has never yet said any thinge of this to me, so I am to take no notice of what passed between Sanders and him till you return home ; God preserve you and give you success in your affaires ; and believe me to be with outmost affection and esteem, My Dearest Dr. life, Yours very faithfully, while   J. B.' (*O.*)

A year before her death she writes thus to her second son :

'11ᴮ HOUSEDALL, *June 29th,* 1787.

'MY DEAR FIFE,—Much do I regrete the troublesom journey you are obliged to take, considering the short time since you came to the country, and that it deprives your friends from the pleasure to see you—last week I imageined that I never would have had the satisfaction for indeed I was very ill of an intermit-

---

[1] Rothiemay papers

Q

ting fever and nigh unto Death, but by the great care of my son and Mrs. Duff I have got better but not so well as to be able to leave Housedall. When will this horrid mallicious association end. Your opponents had nothing but to occasion trouble and expence which appears to be their motive, it is a true proverb and holds so in the present case—that one cannot live in peace beside litigious neighbours. God preserve you at all times and give you success to defeate their wicked schemes and give you a speedy and safe return to the Country.—I remain, as I ever was, my Dear son, Your very affectionate mother,   J. Fife.' (O)

Two early letters from her father are of historical interest :

James Grant to his daughter, Lady Braco, at Rothiemay, written from the Speaker's Chamber

'London, 24 *Aprile* 1746

'Dr. Jeanie,—The Express came this morning from his Royall Highness the Duke makes me hope that this letter will come safe to you. I heartily congratulate you on the good account of the entyr defeat of the Rebells, I hope this will finde my Lord Braco you and the young ffamily well. If once all were quite settled I have some thoughts of being in the North if it were but for twenty dayes time. The Plundering and barbanity committed by the Rebells must noe doubt make the country look generally very miserable and I am much affrayed that the destruction of the corn and grain will produce bad effects. I saw Mrs. Abercromby to-day, she with Sir Robert and Lady Abercrombie are well. I can offer noe other news from this, compliments in the kindest manner to Lord Braco and ffamily, and I am, Dr. Jeanie, your very affect. ffather,

'Ja. Grant.

' This is written in the Speaker's chamber ; where his Majesty affords us noe better paper (tho' great plenty of it) than this.'   (O.)

The same to the same

'London, 7 June 1746.

'Dr. Jeany,—I have yours of the 20th of May, and as you say that it is a longe time since you ore Lord Braco had any letter from me, it seem that letters does miscarry for it is not longe since I wrote to you both, and had noe answere from my Lord to it, but as you are all well, I doe the more easily excuse it. I doe most sincerely lament the miserable situation of some of our country men and particularly some of them we are more nearly concerned with, but as they have brought ruine upon themselves by their own doeings, all we can doe, is to be most heartily sorry for, and commiserat there condition. It is a sadd view the outter ruine of themselves and innocent Posterity. I much commend what

you have done as to your daughter Jesssy (Jessie).[1] God help and comfort her. I am told the Lords Prisoners in the Tower will be tryed in Westminster Hall, and all think they can't escape suffering as I doubt not severall taken Prisoners will in other parts. God be thanked that now that cursed design of the Rebellion seems to be at ane end, I hope the like shall never be attempted for the future, I am sorry to see that Carnousy and Abbachy[2] had concern in it. Gen.ll St. Clare I hear is not yet sailed on the expedition. Pray where is Sophie, some say she is with you, but as you make no mention of her, and that she dont write me, I know little about her, I hope the Rebels have not made seizour of her. I offer my kinde compliments to Lord Braco and your young ffamily and continew, Dr. Jeanie, your very affect. ffather,   JA GRANT.' (O.)

She was a most affectionate wife and mother, and a kind and indulgent grandmother. When she had her house full of grandchildren in 1775, she writes humorously: 'I am so plagued and hurried that I can scarce turn me!' In January 1773, ten years after her husband's death, she gave a ball for them. 'The Countess Dowager of Fife held at her house in Edinburgh the first masked ball seen in Scotland.'

In the *Scots Magazine* we read. 'On Jan. 16, 1788, died at Rothiemay the Countess Dowager of Fife, aged eighty-three. She retained all her senses and her usual cheerfulness to the last. Having married young, she saw and lived with her descendants to the fifth generation.' This presumably refers to the family of Jean Gordon, who married Urquhart of Burdsyeard, and died in 1767, twenty-one years before her grandmother, and whose own daughter was very likely a mother before 1788. She also left one son, Robert Urquhart.

Jane Grant, born 1705; her daughter Janet, born 1727; and *her* daughter Jean, 1746. Three generations in forty-one years. There were possibly three more in the remaining forty-two years of Lady Fife's life.

In 1776 she had written to her son Arthur : 'My health is now very precarious and my days cannot be long in this world,' but she lived for twelve years longer. In June 1786, Alexander Duff of Mayen writes to William Rose from Rothiemay : 'Mrs. Duff was to have dined here this day to meet Sir Robert, Lady and Miss Bess Abercromby, but was prevented by a slight cold and the warm day. Lady Fife was in the Kirk, which I hope will be agreeable information to all friends.' She was then eighty-one. Her portrait and that of her husband, done by Alan Ramsay,[3] for which twenty guineas each was paid, were in the Duff House collection.

---

[1] Lady Gordon   See next chapter   [2] Avochie
[3] Alan Ramsay was King's Painter, in which office he was succeeded in 1784 by Reynolds, who describes it as 'a place of not so much profit and of near equal dignity with his Majesty's Rat-catcher.' The salary was then £50.

Major the Honourable Lewis Duff of Blervie to William Rose

'ROTHIEMAY, *Jan* 17*th*, 1788.

'SIR,—Jean Countess Dowager of Fife my Mother died yesterday. The favour of your Company here on Munday the twenty-first instant by eleven o'clock before noon to attend her funerall from this house to the ffamily Buriall place at the Church of Grange is requested by Sir, Your mo: obdt. Hum. Ser.,

'LEWIS DUFF.

'William Rose, Mountcoffer.'

There is one letter to Lord Braco from his mother, written towards the end of her life :

'MY LORD,—I am just now favoured with your Lordships letter and have receaved from the berer fiftie two pounds fiftion shillings six pencons and two thirds woth your not—one Mount Blerie for fiftie pounds stirling more which pys my anniuty to witsonday fortie foive and I send your Lordship inclosed my Discharg ther is no ocasion for making any apoligie for not sending the monie sooner it hes come in good time and I returne my herty thanks for your punctuall payment and beg you will believ I shall whill I breath have a most gratfull senee of the many favours you have confered on me and my cheldren.

'I wish your Lordship and my Lady mouch joy of Mistress Duffs maraig [1] and everything that is happy to you and your familie my daughter hade a letter of the saim deat with your Lordships from Mester Abercromby she offers her affaxnot humbal duty to you and my Lady bracco my best wishes and blising shall ever atend you and your family, for I am with the greatest regaid and esteem, My Diei Lord, Your Lordships most affaxnot mother and much obliged faithful humble servant,   JEAN DUNBAR. (D.)

'GLASSA, *Jun* 7 *day*, 1745'

And one from Lady Braco to her sister-in-law, Lady Roscommon :

'DR. LADY,—I will be glade to hear you got safe to Blearvie and was in time enough to the Roup as I hope all has been gott to your advantage. I am much in the same case with the cold when you left this but I hope it will wear of in a short time as you desired have send my measure for Bodies and you may please buy at the Marcat 50 elns of tweedlin and 2½ ditto of tykin. Billy hopes youll mind to send Willie Duff in case his health will permitt of itt and I sepose youll take care to be here before he goes south to give him your blissing and bid farewell to a younge friend. Mr. Duff and Sophia joine in Compliments to you, and I ever am very sincerely, Dr. Lady, Your most affectionat sister and faithfull servant,   JEAN DUFF.

'*Jully* 21*st*, 1735

---

[1] Janet's marriage to Sir William Gordon of Park

' Mr. Duff has gote a call just now to Edr. about privat business and he talks of taking Billy with him but I own I am against it till his health be better established. Adieu.

' To the Lady Roscommon to the care of Provost Robertson at Elgin.'

One further letter to Lord Braco may be added :

Helen Fraser, his first cousin, to Lord Braco

' My Lord,—I am just now favour'd with your Lordships of this Date and am glad to hear that your Lop., Lady Braco and all the family att Rothiemay are all well to whom I make offer of my kind complints. As for Adam Duff of Clunebegs being second or fourth son of John Duff of Muldavat I really cannot acquaint your Lordship neither do I remember to have ever heard my mother talk on that subject. I 'm convinced if any person in this country can inform your Lordship about this affair James Duff, Cushenday, will do it.—I am sincerely, My Lord, Your Lordships most obedt. obliged humble Servt.,

' HELEN FFRASER.[1]

' Rannes, 20*th Octr.* 1757.

' To the Right Honourable My Lord Braco att Rothiemay.'   (*D.*)

This letter from Alexander, second Duke of Gordon, to the Laird of Grant shows that the successful rise of the Duff family was not received with unmixed satisfaction by the neighbouring lairds. Envy was doubtless the principal ingredient in this dissatisfaction :

' Gordon Castle, 6 *July* 1724

' Sir,—I hav some reason to beleev Braco is in barguen with yow about Allanbuy, if so, I hope yow will giv it in such a manner as that he may bee no trubilsom nabhor to mee about the mosses which probable he intends, if Aldchach is to bee dispos'd off. I wish yow would not prefer those who by ritches support themselves and valu no man's freindship, and doe unnabhorly and unfreindly offices to most people to mee in particular. I refer to this honest bearer, to both our good freind Bucke who will talke to yow of other particulars I was inform'd of, but I am shure without good grounds, thought I doubt not of the Dufs giving hints of theire good intentions wer it in their powr, but I hope to bee free of them ere long. They may then find I am as ease in wanting their freindship as they undervalw mine ! Yow, I know, hav some gues of their manner of doing, and as I am tould, is to be free of them accordingly ere long. I wish yow and family all happiness and am your most affectionat cousin and humble servant,   Gordon.' [2]

---

[1] Daughter of Mary Duff, Keithmore's daughter   [2] Fraser's *Chiefs of Grant.*

William Duff, Lord Braco, to Ludovick Grant, his brother-in-law

'Banff, *March* 1*st*, 1736.

'Dear Sir,—I have your last of the 23rd past, and I am soe far satisfy'd with what you say, that I think grudges ought not to be keept up on either syde, but rather that the same friendship that was betwixt our predicessors long before our days should be intertained with us; and though your connection and myne is much nearer than thers was, yet its impossible that ther can be a stronger or more heartie friendship than was amongs them on all occasions.

' I have it to say for myself that I made your cause and your quarrell always myne; and for my pairt, I 'm for passing over everie thing that has hapen'd lately, and that bygones may be bygones, and fair play in time to come on both sydes.

' Your sister has given me a fourth son and the mother and child are in as good a way as can be wish'd. . . . Braco.' [1]

' 5 March 1747. Memorial for the Lord Braco to the Lord Advocate.

' Upon the 12 and 13 dayes of Aprile 1746 the King's Army under the Command of his royall Highness the Duke of Cumberland was quartered on Lord Braco's lands on the west side of Spey and his other adjacent grounds, the tenants of those lands were during that time so vexed by the depredations of the Army that scarce any of them was able to toill or sow their gardens. His Royall Highness was so sensible of the losses the poor men had sustained that he gave fyfty guineas to the Minister to be distributed amongst them and desired that a particular account of those losses might be made out.

' Accordingly the whole tennants compeared before three of the Justices of Peace of the County of Murray and deponed upon the particular losses sustained by each of them and the Judiciall procedure whereof with a particular account of saide losses in a peaper apairt are herewith sent to Justice their claim and the fyfty guineas given by his Royall highess is deducted from the claim.

' Its therefore hoped that the Lord Advocate will make proper application to the Secretary at war or otherwayes for giving the poor people some pairt of the losses sustained by them.'

William Lord Braco's large family is treated of in the next chapter.

---

[1] Fraser's *Chiefs of Grant.*

ROTHIEMAY HOUSE
(MARY QUEEN OF SCOTS SLEPT A NIGHT HERE IN 1562)

CHAPTER X

CHILDREN OF WILLIAM DUFF, LORD BRACO AND FIRST EARL FIFE

William,	born 1724	Jane,	born 1732	Sophia,	born 1740
Anne,	,, 1725	George,	,, 1736	Catherine,	,, 1741
Janet,	,, 1727	Lewis,	,, 1737	Arthur,	,, 1743
James,	,, 1729	Patrick,	,, 1738	Margaret,	,, 1745
Alexander,	,, 1731	Helen,	,, 1739		

OF the family of William, Lord Braco and first Earl Fife, a good many details can be gathered from a large collection of letters preserved in the different branches of the family, a few of which have already appeared in print. With three members of the family at different times in the House of Commons, and one in the House of Lords, franks were, of course, plentiful, and for some considerable time Jane, Lady Fife, and her youngest and favourite son Arthur corresponded almost daily—a rare thing in those days, and one which affords a wonderful storehouse of information on both contemporary and family politics.

The eldest of the family was WILLIAM, born when his mother was nineteen and his father twenty-seven. From his earliest years he would

seem to have been unsatisfactory; neither mother nor father had probably much time to attend to his early training and education, as she must have been entirely occupied with the management of her nursery, and he with the business of money-making (to be followed later by a plentiful crop of lawsuits), as well as with his duties in Parliament, both of which kept him much away from home. William was sent to school at Dalkeith, but did not get on very well, and was afterwards privately educated by tutors, who travelled with him all over England and part of France. No expense seems to have been spared. Indeed the father, in a letter to the mother, complains bitterly of the amount that ' your son has cost,' and elsewhere describes him as ' an abandoned wretch, nothing can ever be expected from him,' ' his drinking and idleness still continue,' ' I can do no more, I have done my pairt.' ' I found the enclosed from " Glassa' " (Gen. Abercromby) anent your unhappy son. It is a bad omen that he has not mended anything under Capt. Geddes.' ' The unhappy creature, your son, and Mr. Sellars are at Berwick. I have no word from them yet, only Lt. Dunbar who had seen them, sent me a note of it. He says that your son has a shaking of the hand, like one that has the palsie, and that his head is not right, which is no wonder.' ' Sellars has gone to London for your son. I have desired that their stay there may be as short as possible, and they are to go on to Boulogne and Rheims ' (1742). ' Mr. Sellars gives up all hope of doing him service, or doing any good with him ' (January 1745).

James Duff, Beaufront, writes to Lord Braco on August 6, 1746 :

' It gives me great pleasure to have your Lordships approbation for removing your son from Bishop Aukland which is very much augmented by its having so good ane effect. But as I wrote My Lady Bracco the 6th curiant which comes by this post I shall refer you to that where youll see a just and true account of Mr. Duffs present situation. Your orders shall be obeyed as to his pocket-money and my best advice shall not be wanting in perswading him to make his expenses as moderate as possible and he agrees with your Lordship in thinking his signing the Bond of Interdiction one of the best things ever he did. But as Mr. Sellers after his return from Rothiemay last year told several people that he had had great offers from you to induce your son to sign the Bond of Inter-diction and condescended on sums that I would be ashamed to mention. It was no wonder a young gentleman was very much startled who was living in a very idle and unhappy way and was intirely ignorant of the nature of the write and could not but think it a write design'd to cut him of from the Estate than any other thing when you would have offered such large bribes to anyone to get it execute. But on my representing to him the true design of the bond and that it was not agreeable to common sense you could have made any such offer he was quite of another mind. I am satisfied Sellers will make loud complaints on me

for setting this obligation in such a strong light to your Lordship which I do not in the least value since I should have thought myself a very great villain had I keept silence in ane affair of this kind wherein your interest was concerned. I shall write Montblairy anend the perce of linnen. I shall write you as oft as I see occasion anent your son and you may beleive Ill do every thing in my power to render my self worthy of the confidence you have reposed in me and continue with the greatest respect, My Lord, Your Lordships most obligded humble servt.,   JAMES DUFF.'[1] (D.)

According to family tradition, the unfortunate young man had strong sympathies with the Jacobite cause, and would have gone out with his brother-in-law, Sir William Gordon, but was driven back by force. He seems to have had no profession, nor taken any part in public life, though he went up to London with good introductions, and writes from there in 1749 :

William Duff, eldest son of Lord Braco, to his father

'LONDON, 31st January 1749.

'MY LORD,—I arrived here safly the twinty fift of this mounth and loges in Pal Mell. I have viseted Sr Lodwick Grant and Coll. Abercrombie who are both extreemly sivel to me and has a general invitation to there houses, as soon as my cloaths are ready Sr Lodwick is to introduce me to the Duck of Newcastle and Mr. Pelham as he thinks it proper I should pay my levay. The Duck of Gordon has several times desiered Major Grant to bring me along with him to spend the eivning which I intend to do as soon as my cloaths are ready. I supt at Sr Lodwicks last night and there was an officer inquering about Lodie Mc intosh[2] but could get no account of him. The officer told me that Lodie was intitled to eight hundred pounds str as his shear of prise money which would be very agreeable news to him if he knew of it. Sr Lodwick Grant and Coll. Aberciombie have there compliments to you. Please make offer of my duty to my Lady and behve me to be with great sincerity, My Lord, Your Lordships most Dutfull and affectionate Son,   WILLIAM DUFF.' (O)

William Duff never married, and died in London in 1753. Of his last days we have the following accounts ·

Colonel James Abercromby to Alexander Stuart of Edinglassie

'CRAVEN STREET, 3d March 1753

'DR. SIR,—This day sevennight I informed you of the state of Mr. Duff's health who the day thereafter pressed much to have the famous Mr. Ward's advice being greatly possessed in favours of him from the accts he had from

---

¹ See chapter xxix.   ² See chapter viii

severals who had been cured by him in similar cases upon which I went immediately to Dr. Pringle who most readily approved because he knew where Ward had had remarkable success in such cases where all the skill of regular Physicians had failed. Upon this Ward was called the 25th in afternoon and that night Mr. Duff took his powder and has since followed his prescription which have had little other effect than to reduce the swelling in his ancles. Both Dr. Pringle and Mr. Ward are of opinion that his lungs are affected, in which case they despair of accomplishing a cure, in the mean time all possible care shall be taken. You will take the proper way to communicate this to My Lord Braco and if any extraordinary change happens I shall not fail to write to you by next post.—I am, Dr Sir, Your most obedt humble servant,

'JAMES ABERCROMBY.' (*D.*)

G. Grant to Lord Braco

'LOND., 27 *March* 1753.

'MY DEAR LORD,—Last night poor Mr. Duff paid his last debt to nature which I forsaw for some time tho' others were of a contrary opinion. I have Coll. Aberciombie with me to Breakfast this morning and we have agreed to bury the poor youth in a frugal but decent and genteel manner in St Margets Church, Westminster, in a Vault where his Grand Father Sr. James and several of his cousines lie, we propose to do this on friday next in the evening [1]—there are some debts due to tradesmen for necessarys supplied your son which it will be worthy of your Loidships honour to pay of, these cann amount to no greate sum, . . . what was necessary for Doctis, Nurses, Lodging necessarys when languishing under sickness were it my case, I would pay these as well as his funeral charges. I beg pardon for offering unasked advice on this occasion—I have no view but regard for your Familys Honour. I shall allways be glade to do everything you cann expect from a friend to convince you that I am most truly, Your Lops. Mst. faithfull and Obedt. Sert., G. GRANT.' (*D.*)

The two eldest daughters, ANNE, born 1725, and JANET, 1727, seem, unlike their eldest brother, to have had greater educational advantages than the younger ones. In the winter of 1739-1740, when they were fourteen and twelve, their father was passing the season in Edinburgh and took these two children with him, presumably leaving the six younger ones at Rothiemay with their mother. They had lessons in writing, dancing, music, etc., and their father seems to have taken great interest in their progress, and writes that he is 'to give all their masters a bottle of wine, to prompt them to be at pains in teaching them.' Later in the winter he writes that the 'fever of cold from which Anne was suffering has turned to a fever of small-pox'; both girls seem to have had the disease rather badly, and Anne at least was in great danger and was marked for life. They were

---

[1] To avoid the arresting of the body for debt.

nursed by the landlady ' with great attention,' but with apparently no
thought of isolation. During the crisis, her father writes that he has
been ' brought in to promise a watch to Anne, on condition that she doe
everything that 's advized for contributing to her recoverie, and that she
don't touch her face or hurt her eyes. This being the 11th day she fell
into the small-pox, they are blackening very well, but she has had a good
load of them,' and later, ' She will be prettie much pittied, but we should
be thankful when life and sight are preserved. She has plucked up a good
deal of spirit since she got her sight again. She was uneasie with the
diffluxion in them Janet these two days past has a gentle fever. I shall
be well pleased if prove the small-pox, because they are yet favourable.
If there is anything worth while I 'll write you by the post, but I hope this
will make you easier '

Again : ' I much approve your calmness and good disposition on that
head, which is worthy of you To tell you the truth, Anne was in great
danger, and therefore we have the greater reason to be thankful to Almighty
God for her recoverie. Janet is now in perfect health ' But Janet was
a delicate girl, and some time afterwards was threatened with consumption ;
lists of curious medicaments supplied for her use still exist, and the universal panacea, asses' milk, sometimes also ' goots' milk,' was prescribed,
and ' tar water for the spitting of blood,' of which her father writes that
' since it is ane innocent thing, I see noe harm tho' Jessie try it ' It is
strange to remember this in view of the hardships she went through in
her later life, but she died at thirty-one. Her father also describes her as
' a very thoughtless and imprudent girl.' Anne was evidently the favourite.

Anne married, at twenty, her cousin, Alexander Duff of Hatton, and
her subsequent history with that of her daughter is treated of under the
Hatton family. She lived to be eighty.

Janet married at eighteen, in 1745, Sir William Gordon of Park, who
had already identified himself with the Jacobite cause. He was described
by an official of the Commissioners of Excise as ' A rebel Collonel, and very
actif in distressing the country by levying money, using very violent
measures.' Her father alludes to ' the young Knight of Park,' in connection with some fishing dispute in 1733, so he was considerably his wife's
senior. She is said to have eloped with him from Rothiemay, leaping from
a window for the purpose, and when, in the same year, Alexander Duff
made proposals for the hand of Anne, the father writes to his wife that he
strongly disapproves, and warns her to allow no correspondence and to
guard Anne carefully, ' in view of what happened lately ' Apparently
the veto was shortly after removed in the case of Anne, and Janet was
forgiven, for when her husband was proscribed after Culloden, and remained

some time in hiding on his own estates, she was with her mother at Rothie-may, and her daughter Jean was born there. Sir William escaped to Douai, where his brave wife followed him with her baby, somewhat against her father's wishes, and they lived there until William's death, June 5, 1751. The following letters give a pathetic picture of Janet's state of mind and of her life in exile :

Janet Gordon, Park, to her father, Lord Braco

'*Aug* 26, 1747.

' My Lord,—Nothing can give me more conscarn then my being obliged to write your Lordship of my resolutions of going abroad a thing that must be against what you would wish me to doe. God knows what sorrow it gives me the thoughts of disobliging you but then I know my own weakness so well that tho the many good reasons you would may be give me for my staying might get the better of me so far as I would yeald to your advice and promise to stay but I know I am quit uncapable of keeping to that resolution so I think it best to dell honestly and tell you my weakness. I hope in God as a kind parent you 'll forgive me for this step when you see its not in my power to get the better of it, in the first pleace were I to stay it would make a breach between my husband and me, as he has layd his positive comands on me to come over to him, and after what past between him and me at Edin' I know it would break his peace and mine for ever if I disobey'd him. My dear Lord, you know I have mate with many missfortunes but the lose of my husband's affection would be heavier as all I have mate with and you may be assured that would be the consequence were I to stay after so many absolute orders he 's given me. I most earnestly beg of you that you 'll forgive me doing this and dont add your angie to my miseries as it would give me the utmost truble and uneasiness to offend my Lady or you, if you think it any way needfull for me to be in this country in the spring or at any time, I will most willingly come back as all I want is to see my husband and to show him that Ill obey him, but as I said befor whatever time you desire me to come back you may depend on my obeying you, when I see my husband Ill endeavour to show him that his sitcation of his affairs is not in such a bad way as he imagions and show him at the same time that his friends is doing all that lys in there power to bring things to a happy conclustion. I shall add no more to this but beg your Lordship will continue your friendship to my husband and me and be assured that we will never fell in our dutifull regard what ever be our fates.—I ever am, My Dear Lord, Your most affectionate Daughter and Faith-full servant,   JANET GORDON.' (*D.*)

The next is to her mother two and a half years later :

'Douai, *May* 19, 1750.

' My dear Madam,—As I have the opportunity of Mr. Smith going to Scotland I can't deny myself the happeness of writting your ladyship and to

asure your ladyship of the satisfaction it gives me to hear you and all your familie being well, which I have thee pleasure to hear pretty often, as there is alwise people coming to this from Britton, which I think is a great advantage to this pleace our hearing often of our friends.   We would live pretty reasonable hear, if it were not for some English families that has come heai to settle, I dont mean merchants but people of condition, some upon accounts of there health and others for reasons that they choose to keep to thereselves, there is only some of them that I choose to be acquainted with, but not to be intimet with eithere of them, for its not for compinie that we stay hear, its to leave as cheap and private as possible and even if I could affoid it I have no inclination, for the tender state of health I 'm in, the only devertion I take is any day that I 'm cable to go out, which is not many, to goe a little aning in the chaise, as Mr. Johnston [1] is obliged to keep a chaise and horse upon the account of his traivling sometimes upon his bussiness and its cheaper as hyering hoises, he leaves me to-morrow, and is oblidged to stay theie till the fiist of November with his bussi-ness, I would gladly hope he will get back for a few days when I am brought to bed, as at that time you may be sure it will be a great comfort to me, his being in the same place, whatever be my fate, considering the tender state I am always in, it is no great suiprisse if the worst should happen me at such a time, but as I came thiow last in the same tender state of health, it ought to encourage me now.

' We was a good deal alarmed hear with a feavour that they say was raging in Aberdeenshire, it gives me pleasure to hear no more of it.   I was afraid it would come to Banffshire, I 'll asure you my dear Madam, that my thoughts is oftenest there and many an anxious wish have I for all your health and happe-ness.   I think oftener on my friends as I ought to doe, as it can be of no use to them and it only serves to disturb my mind, and can never bring me neaier them. Tho Mr. Johnston is as often with me as possible, yet its impossible for me when I think of being absent from all the friends I have, but it must make a very depth impration on me.   I 'll asure your ladyship all the other unconveniences I have is not near so hard upon me as being banished fiom you and my dearest friends and not to think I have paients, but must be denyed the blessing of seeing them for even to have the happeness to be in the same country with you, its impossible that ever that can happen.   Eveiybody els has a chance, but we have none, ever to be so happy, you may be sure that the same thought is hard upon my friend and gives him more uneasiness as he cares to show, for my part I never speak to him on the subject, as my sorrow and grief is more touching to him as his own, for my melancholic may be casilie read in my face.   You never saw such a chainge upon a person as there is on me every day and I am afraid instead of time making it the more easy to people in our way, it will iatheie make it the worse, I am afraid the maladic du Pais will kill the most of us in spite of all the spirits the best of us have, the only happeness we can have is to hear some-times from our fiiends.   I beg my dear Madam, if you will make me happy to let me have but a line from you now and then to keep up my spirits.

---

[1] This name was used by Sir William Gordon for purposes of concealment.

'I beg you would cause my brothers write me, they blame me for not writting them oftener its impossible to them to think how hard it is on me to write or hold my head down to anything, I am so tormented with a violent trouble in my head which I am convinced is something of the ague, as it comes on alwise at a set time. I have neaver been altogether free of it since I come to this country, they say the bark is the only cure I can have.

'My dear Madam, I hope your goodness will excuse this long scrawl and be so good as to make offer of my affect. humble duty to my lord and my affect. best wishes to my young friends. Mr. Johnston is writting your ladyship so I shall only add that I am with the greatest respect and regard your ladyship most faithful and duttyfull humble servant, JANET JOHNSTON.

'I return your ladyship many thanks for the dryed fish they came very soft here and is very good. I wrote my sester to see if possible there could be a cook-maid sent me to dress our meat and help to wash our linnings, the man servant I got over is learning to market for me and seems to be very honest, as he does for that part. I want to keep no servant in a better way as a cookmaid. For a gentlewoman I am not such a fool as to set upon that footing, and I have been at a great loss with a drunken creator I have had for some time by past.—My dear Madam, Adieu.' (O.)

Her son John was born at Boulogne in 1749, William in 1750, and a second daughter, who did not long survive, in 1751, after her father's death. The name of Johnston was adopted, even in letters to her parents, as a disguise for the attainted Jacobite, who still seems to have been very busy in his master's affairs. After his death, Janet writes that her mother may now address her as Duff or Gordon, since there are 'others taking the name of Johnston.'

George Forbes to Lord Braco

'DOUAI, 9 *Aug.* 1751.

'MY LORD,—If I had not reason to belive you was acquainted some time agoe of Sr. William Gordon's Death, I would have wrot you sooner on that subject and informed you fully of his Lady's melancholy and even destitute situation. She is not as yet brought to bed, as I was perswaded that Lady Braco was wrot to on that head I never doubted but some reasonable suplay would have been remitted to her, altho I have not talked to Lady Gordon about her situation as it would surely renew her grief, yet I find she would be intirely destitute in this country were it not for a very good firm in this place, the regard I have for your Lordship and Familie obldges me use this freedom which I hope youll be so good as excuse to inform you that if you doe not order her money without delay she and her Family will be reduced to the greatest straits, for altho I and severall oyrs in this country have all the Inclination in earth to doe her all

the service we are capable of, yet as to money matters which is what she needs most its entirely out of our power and I can assure that had she been in any oyr town but this she had been badly off longe befor this time, but here she luckely found a friend who hath supplied her hitherto, but as his funds are not very considerable it will not be in his power to continue the same favour much longer so for Godsake My Lord take this affair into your serious consideration and doe not delay sending her a speedie relief. As your Lop. may perhaps be at a loss to know what remittance she would presently need as not knowing the state of Sr. Wms. affairs here I shall take the liberty to tell you that Sr. Wm. had some few debts which he was necessarly oblidged to contract for the support of his Family and if these are not speedily paid all the little effects he had and even his and his Ladys body cloaths will be sold for the payment of them which surly you would be vext at besides as he was not in a way to have any Ready money she hath been living on credit and therefor I believe you will need to remitt her betwixt 3 and 400 £ over otherwise she will be surly reduced to the greatest want. This goeth under cover to Mr. James Petrie advocat in Aberdeen. Ill bege your Lop. will be so good is make my Compliments to Lady Braeoe and worthie Familie and belive that I am, with the greatest truth and esteem, My Lord, Your Lops. most obed. and faithfull Hum. Sert.,

'GEO. FORBES.' (*D.*)

Janet Gordon to her mother

'DOUAY, 24*th Jan.* 1752

'MY DEAR MADAM,—I delay'd answering your Layship's kind letter till I should write to my Lord Clare and have his answer. He thinks I will know something of the Court's determination as to my Pension by the Month of Aprile, Tho' may be will not have it intyerlie Settled, and possibly it may be sooner, but that's what we cannot know till we see what time they bring all the affairs of Gratifications, and of Pensions before them. Mine will only be determined when those affairs comes in.

'But as your Layship observes it will be the Month of Aprile befor I could take such a jurnie with my familie. I think it's best for me not to give over thoughts of it till I see what is to be done. At any rate I could wish it were not dissagreeable to my frends and not prejudutiall to my affairs in this Country, I would be glaid to come over to see my friends as I believe being amongst my friends and my own Country air will be the first thing that will ever bring me health ore spirits.

'I will have some Guess against Summer, if what will be granted me be worth my while to stay in this country ore not, if I find its any thing considerable, I can Leave my Children hear, as I am sure they will be taken care of, and there being hear will make my Going out of the country for some time not taken notice off. If it is considerable ore a triffle that they Grant me I will write you Lay-

ship as soon as I can have my knowledge of it, and your Layship will give me your opinions if you think it worth my while of Robing myself for the rest of my days of the happeness being amongst my Friends.

'As I see things turn out, I can have your Layships advice if I should bring over my familie or not, I am pretty sure I'll get it so managed that I may come over for a few months and see my friends without being of any prejudice or hinderance to what Settlement they make for me, which will at least be Pleasure to me in the meantime, if I be so unhappy as to Leave absent from them afterwards to tell your Layship my true Sentiments, the thoughts of it, is very unsuportable, to me, and had I none but my Self to provide for I would rather choise to Leave in the narrowest Circumstances at home, then I would be oblidged to Stay in this country. It was hard upon me befor I lost all that was dear to me in it, but God knows it's Doubly so now Since He is Gone, if it be my fate I must Submite to it, as I have done to all my former missfortunes however hard it be upon me. Its one thing quit ceartain that I can never be a year out of thess country without the resk of lossing any Penssion that is Settled on me and living in this country may be my interest, but will never be my inclenations let things be never so advantageous for me. But I shall be intycily derected by my Papa and you, and is determined what ever you think will be best for the interest of my familie I shall follow, I will Live hear as frugally as possible, till Summer that we know a little more what will be done.

'I have got a promise of a first Leutt Commession to my Eldest Son which is about five and theirty pound a year, if they make out these promise I will soon know, as that Commession is just now vacant. It will at lest educate him, and if he be spared till he come of age and nothing better turn out for him at home it will give him a good rank for a better Commession

'As near as I can tell you of my Suttuation in this Country is ; the Hunder Pound your Layship was so good as give me, cleared all the Debts we were owing, such as house Rents, familie accounts, and the Expeneess of my familie at Boulogne when I was absent and the Physicians account at Boulogne for attending my Eldest son when he was bad, and the rest of the children, The Physicians and Apothecary's accounts hear, and all the other Extraordinary Expeneess that the unhappy accident of Sir Wm.'s Death brought me, pay'd all the Chairges of my lying in and cleered all I was due till that time.

'Since I was brought to Bed you may believe I have not brought my Self in to great Difficultys as I have lived quit retyered, and at the easyest way possible, However my Sister's Bill of forty Pound was a very Seasonable relief to clear bygones and provide some little necessaries I stood in need of.

'My familie consists of tow maid servants, three children and my Self ; my youngest Child I have out at nurse, She stands me about eighteen shillings per months.[1]

'My Health is rathere better than when I wrote your Layship last, but I am still very weak and tender and has violent headachs ; I beheve I shall never be

---

[1] This child died young.

well till I have the happiness of seeing my friends, I thank God my young folks is pretty well save Willie that is a little tender with Teathing.

'I beg my most affectionate Humble Dutty to my Lord and my sincier good wishes to my Brothers and Sisters and sincierly wish every thing that's good to you and them, I ever am, with the greatest regard and Respect, My dear Madam, your Layship Dutifull Daughter and most humble Servant,

'JANET GORDON.' (O.)

Apparently it was arranged that all should return, and in 1753 she married again, George Hay, younger of Mountblairy, and had a happy married life with him at Carnousie (which he had purchased from the trustees of Arthur Gordon), and she died there March 3, 1758. She had several Hay children, but only one daughter, born 1754, survived her.

There are many happy letters from her to her parents from Carnousie— Janet was always an excellent correspondent,—and the following from her husband about the children of her first marriage is interesting :

'I am very Happy to hear that your Lordp. has brought Mrs. Hays affair and Captain Gordons to such a bearing and must confess if your Lordp. had not the interest of these Children more at heart then other people, it had never come such a length. I hope the children will be gratefull, which is all I believe your Lordp. espects for your great Expense and trouble. Thank God they are all weel and want no thing so much now as a proper Plan of their education, which can be concerted by your Lordp. and then other friends. Wee have a surmise that Capt. Gordon hourly expects a call but in any event I dare say he will wait of your Lordp. Lady Cubbin [his sister] and him dine here this day. Lord Banff and I have been pritty oft together since he came to the Country and joking about the Sale of his Estate and I am not shure but if he finds a hearty merchant will dispose of it, this I only mention to your Lordp as he does not want any person should suspect his selling, but if anything further occurs shall acquaint your Lordp. but should incline this letter should be burnt and not seen to any.

'If your Lordp. and family will honour us with a visite in your way home it will make us all very happy, and should be glade to know when you intend to sett out from Edinr. All this family in the sincerest manner joins me in good wishes and respectfull compliments to your Lordp. Lady Braco and Family, and I always am with the greatest respect and esteem, My Lord, Your Lordships most obedient and most obliged humble servant,   GEO: HAY.

'CARNOUSIE, 3d Aprile 1755.

'To the Lord Braco at Rothiemay.

'P.S.—Mrs. Hay would have wrote Lady Braco but is just now most violently taken ill of one of her Collecks which wee are afraid may prove

s

dangerous in her present situation Laudonum is the only thing she expects ease from.'   (D.)

Jean Gordon, elder daughter of Janet and Sir William Gordon, married Duncan Urquhart of Burdsyards and had issue, and died 1767,[1] twenty-one years before her grandmother.   It is conjectured that it was to *her* grand-children that allusion is made in saying that old Lady Fife 'saw her descendants to the fifth generation.'   Janet's two sons were both soldiers. John, the elder, had in his infancy a commission in the French army.[2] In his early manhood he became a great thorn in the side of his family, both Duffs and Gordons.   Having been born abroad, after his father's attainder, he had, of course, no legal right to the baronetcy or the estate of Park.   Eventually he obtained the baronetcy, but the entailed property went to his uncle, Captain John Gordon of the Marines.   He came to Scot-land in 1775 to claim both, and demanded money from his relatives.   There are many allusions to him in Arthur's letters, who says in one place : ' Although Park makes him welcome to the title, I believe he will not have the complaisance to part with the acres.'

His uncle, James, Lord Fife, writes to Arthur : ' He is a terrible boy, John Gordon ; keep clear of him, my dear Arthur, as much as you can. He has come to the country to lay his relations under a contribution of a trifle of £3000.   Do you think he will find it easy ? '

Arthur, the bachelor uncle, did offer money to send him back to France, but, at first, John would not go, and when he did, returned in the following year.   ' Gordon is to sail in two days ; Lord Fife will not see him, but says if his behaviour merit it, he will serve him ' (March 14, 1775).   ' He wants £3000 to purchase a colonelship in the French service.'   Arthur then describes him as ' an eyesore to all the connection, a worthless, desperate, mean-spirited, lying, dishonest wretch.'   All money advanced to him, even that obtained with great difficulty by his hard-working younger brother, was spent in gaming and dissipation.

' Poor Will Gordon, I am sorry for him, his horrid brother hath hurt him in more ways than in the purse.'   ' His advance to his brother makes him live the life of a hermit.'

His grandmother, Lady Fife, was at one time favourably disposed towards him, and even mildly scolded her favourite son Arthur for hard-ness of heart in the matter, but she could take no pleasure in his society. ' I am informed,' she says, in the whimsical manner which makes her

---

[1] September 7, 1767, ' Died about ten days ago, some weeks after childbirth, Lady Burds-yards, at the family seat near Forres ' (*Aberdeen Journal*).   Burdsyards is now Sanquhar
[2] For longer account see chapter xxxii on Gordons of Park

letters such delightful reading, ' that Sir John is coming north next month, and is to take up his quarters with me all winter. I have had more agreeable company, but, poor man, he is to be pitied. I think his head is wrong.' At length, even she decides that his father's people ought to provide for him, and that ' the Captain [1] will have to draw his purse to him.' James Duff of Banff also refers in one letter to ' poor Johnny Gordon,' and intercedes for him.

He was finally despatched to India, with some difficulty. Arthur writes to his mother : ' We had a very disagreeable interview with Sir John Gordon yesterday. He had outrun the constable at Portsmouth, and without a fresh supply must have been arrested and lost his passage. Colonel B. Gordon and James Duff and I advanced twenty guineas to relieve him, with positive assurance we would not give one penny more, or ever again see him until he returned from India.'

His wife, Hannah Corner, the daughter of a baker in St. Martin's Street, London, had a sister married to a man in some position of authority in India. Arthur remarks, ' The connexion *there* might be useful. Here it is surely neither very honourable nor advantageous.' There were three children of the marriage : John Benjamin, died young ; Sir John Bury Gordon, and Jessie, who married Richard Creed of Hans Place. Sir John died in 1781, killed at the siege of Bassein.

William, who was born at Douai, a year before his father's death, was a much more reputable personage, but unfortunately cursed with epilepsy. He got a commission in the 52nd Regiment, and became a lieutenant, but was unable to purchase a company. He served in America, and was on particularly friendly terms with his uncle Lewis, who was there at the same time. He died at Mountblairy in 1776, aged twenty-five, being at that time engaged in recruiting in the north.

Arthur writes : ' I cannot tell you how much affected I am at poor Will Gordon's death. I could not sleep last night with concern. Thank God, it did not happen at Rothiemay. I am told he had a fit when upon foraging duty in America, and was very near taken prisoner, being carried off the Field by five soldiers or it must have happened. This was, it seems, the reason, altho' unknown to him, that he was sent upon the recruiting duty.'

His grandmother also felt his death very much, and comments thus on the want of feeling shown by his aunt . ' I have had a letter from Lady Anne on the subject of poor Willie's death She writes with as much indifference as if it had been her Catt that was dead ! '

---

[1] His uncle and the then possessor of Park

*William Braco Gordon, son of Sir William Gordon of Park, to
his grandmother, Jane, Lady Fife*

'LONDON, 16*th March* 1775

' MY DEAR MADAM,—I certainly would have done myself the honor to have
wrote your Ladyship on my arrivel delayed from day to day in expectation to
have had the pleasure of acquainting you that a reconciliation had taken place
betwixt Lord Fife and I. I made use of every means possible to bring it about.
I'm exceeding sorry to say that I have found his Lordship quite obdurate, and
consequently must have recourse to other friends for their assistance as I cannot
depend nor build upon the smallest aid from that Quarter, which you may believe
me, my dear Madam, gives me real Concern. I have wrote Gight requesting
the lend of two hundred pounds. I never mentioned the subject to him before,
notwithstanding I'm pretty confident the favor will be granted. I have wrote
Cpt. Lewis Duff on the same subject for one hundred pounds, Mr. Hay, Rannes
one hundred pounds, Mr. James Duff of Banff one hundred pounds and the two
hundred pounds which your Ladyship had the goodness to promise me together
with my little capital will amount to the sum totale for ascertaining the purchase of a Company when a Vacancy offers, which I'm certain cannot possibly
happen before the Regt. returns to Great Britain, when I make no doubt their
will be toe three for sell. I intend restricting myself to Lieut.'s pay after I
arrive at the Company and to allow the difference together with my annuity
which will amount in all to about £150 per annum and in less than six years will
repay my friends, while I shall always retain a proper sensibility of the obligation. Nothing but absolute necessity and ambition to get on in the World
could have enduced me to follow this plan. I have been extremely punctual
in attending the plays and other publick amusements every night since I came to
Town and propose persisting during my residence, which will be but short. We
embark Wednesday for certain and proceed strait for Boston, there are only
8 officers aboard the Transport I sail in. It will be doing me a particular favor
to write me as often as convenient. My direction, Lt. Gordon, 52nd Regt.,
Boston. The American affairs are the chief topic here, every Coff. House and
every different company you go into that subject is always brought upon the
Carpet that you neither know which party to credit. When I get to Boston I
shall endeavour to give your Ldp. the most authentic accounts I possible can.
I don't despair of being able to eat a Christmas goose with your Ladyship at
Rothiemay.

' I was exceeding sorry to hear from an officer yesterday of the Eighth
Regt. that all the absent officers were order'd to join immediately which I'm
realy sorry for on account of my friend the Capt.[1] as I'm persuaded returning
a second time to America will be perfectly disagreeable to him. I have the

---

[1] His uncle, Lewis Duff.

honor to be, with the greatest gratitude and sincerity, my Dear Madam, Your most obedient and very Humble Servant,

'WILLIAM BRACO GORDON.

'Lady Fife.'   (O.)

The fourth child of William, Lord Braco, and his second wife Jean Grant was JAMES, his successor in the titles. His character and career are described in chapter xi. He was born in 1729 at Rothiemay. In his early years he and his brother Alexander were instructed by the tutor, Mr. Abel, and afterwards he was presumably at St. Andrews University, as were his four younger brothers (but the roll of alumni, as published, only begins just early enough to include Alexander, who entered in 1748). On the death of his elder brother he became his father's heir, at the age of twenty-four, and in 1759, as the eldest son of the Irish peer, he became Viscount Macduff. He seems to have had rather an overweening sense of his own importance, and quarrels between him and various members of his family were of frequent occurrence. His youngest brother Arthur says 'he volunteered in his quarrels with his friends'; but during the latter part of his own residence in London appears to have been on most friendly terms. His mother writes of one of these occasions: 'Your noble brother is just as was expected. I would let him enjoy his good friendly temper at Whitehall by himself.' Lewis also writes: 'I received a very polite epistle from his Majesty of Fife in answer to one I wrote him about Billy Gordon.' But that his family affections were strong many of his letters to his favourite sister Anne, and to his youngest brother will show. Anne writes to her mother about some appointment which her husband was endeavouring to obtain: 'Macduff has really by his activity and friendship upon this occasion bound Mr. Duff to perpetual obligation. Lord Adam writes that the Viscount is immensely active, and I assure you Mr. Duff is very grateful.'

In 1760 Lord Macduff begs leave to recommend to the Duke of Newcastle, his brother-in-law, Mr. Duff, as candidate at next election for the county of Aberdeen, at present represented by Lord Adam Gordon. This must have been Alexander Duff of Hatton. Nothing seems to have come of the idea.

The fifth child and third son was ALEXANDER, afterwards third Earl Fife, whose career will also be found in the chapters on the Earls of Fife. His early education was the same as that of his brother James, two years older, and he afterwards went to the University of St. Andrews. He seems to have given no trouble to his parents in his youth, either as regards his health or his character. He was always an extremely correct person, and anxious to stand well 'with the powers that be.' His younger brother

Lewis writes in 1767 : ' I have seen honest Arthur twice since he came to town, but Sandie, for fear of disobliding his brother Fife, will not pay me a visit, and I am glad to see Sandie act so much like a politician, and as he thinks it will put him in the Court's good opinion, I shall most certainly excuse his visits.'

The sixth child was JANE, born 1732.[1] She married at twenty-one, in 1753, Keith Urquhart of Bethelnie, and is described in the *Aberdeen Journal* of the day as ' an agreable young lady, with a handsome fortune.' He was son of William Urquhart of Meldrum, who wrote thus to her father about her :

'MELDRUM, *October 10th*, 1753.

' My LORD,—Having lately understood that my son has a very great regard and affection for your Daughter Miss Duff and intends to offer his Service to her : I think it my duty to acquaint your Lordship, that it is a thing extremely agreeable to me, providing it be so to you and my Lady Braco ; and I will reckon it a great happiness to him as well as an advantage to my family, to have the honour of so near a connexion with your Lordships. I 'm sorry that I can't make his fortune so great as she deserves, but you may believe that I will go all reasonable lengths that my circumstances can allow ; and I will be very glad to know your Lordships Inclinations.

' I beg leave to offer my respectfull compliments to my Lady and all your Family and am with great respect, My Lord, Your Lordships most obedient and most faithfull humble servant,   W. URQUHART.' (*D.*)

They had four sons : James, who succeeded, born 1754 ;[2] Lewis, a captain in the Army, who died 1790 ; two others died in infancy ; and two daughters, Jane and Mary, both unmarried. Shortly after the birth of her youngest child Jane left her husband and resided in London. All that is known subsequently is contained in the following letters from Arthur to his mother, and from her husband to Lord Fife of the same date. None of her own letters have been preserved, and her name rarely occurs in the family correspondence.

Arthur, as usual, interested himself in the career of these nephews. He took a great deal of trouble to obtain a commission in the 58th Regiment and a lieutenancy for Lewis, and helped him to raise the necessary men.

The two daughters were a good deal with their aunt, Lady Anne. One died in 1804.

---

[1] 'November 16, 1732. Jean, lawful daughter of William Duff of Braco, was baptised Named after Dipple's first and second Lady and Lady Braco ' (*Banff Registers*).

[2] 'On December 8, 1754, the Lady of Keith Urquhart of Bethelnie of a son and heir, at their house of Meldrum, to the great joy of this ancient family.'

Hon. Arthur Duff of Orton to his mother

'SUFFOLK STREET,
LONDON, March 19th, 1770

'MY DEAR MADAM,—I was happy to understand by yours of yesterday that you was in good Health, altho almost buried with Snow. I met Lord Fife this Day at the House of Commons, who gave me a Piece of Intelligence and desired me to communicate it to your Ladyship. For this five years past it seems Lady Jeane Urquhart has lived at Mile End, unknown to any Friend. She Died last night, and is to be privately entered Tomorrow Evening, McKey the grocer and His Servant only to be present. I beg'd He wd. not put Her Death in the Papers, but cannot tell you whether He will comply or not, I leave this place on Saturday or Sunday morning and will hardly write again until I get to Edinboro, as I will be much hurried getting all my things put up, and attending the Militia Ball, and our appeal, which comes on Tomorrow and Thursday. Lewis and Mrs. Duff are very well, they go to live at Hampstead on Monday and will remain there a month. George and Mrs. Duff were well when I saw them last, which was a few days ago. The Admiral is much better and I am with great Truth, Dear Madam, most affectionately yrs.   ARTHUR DUFF.' (O.)

Keith Urquhart to Lord Fife

'MY LORD,—I received yours yesterday with the accounts of Poor Lady Jean's death. Several circumstances mentioned by your Lordship have very sensibly and tenderly affected me—I have to thank you for the melancholy trouble you have taken upon the Occasion. I yesterday sent an express to Rothiemay to acquaint my Lady Dowager of this event and have delayed informing my daughters of it until I shall have her Ladyship's answer. I must acknowledge that I have some doubts of the Propriety of publishing her Death in the Newspapers and of my Familys' going into mourning. It will again set the talkative tongues of the world agoing and revive a Topic of conversation which seemed to have been for several years exhausted. However if your Lordship still continues of the same mind I shall most certainly think it my Duty to comply. The delay will not be much as the event is known to none in this country except to Mr. Duff and Capt. Abercrombie to whom I communicated it and who both seem to be of the same opinion with me. They and all your Lordships relations as well as mine will immediately go into mourning. I believe I need hardly ask if Lady Jean has made any savings or if she has thought of her children in the disposal of such. I much approve of your Lordship's disposal of the few things in the House with the exceptions you mention—I intended this summer to have given a commission to Mr. Muir the Agent to buy watches for each of my daughters. May I presume to beg of your Lordship to take that trouble. I will not speak of a price nor of the kind of watches as I am sure you will do what is decent without being extravagant for my circumstances. I would suggest to sell their mothers watch and her few trinkets for what they may bring, and the overplus

shall be most thankfully paid to your Lordships order. I wait with some impatience for your answer and have the honour to be, My Lord, Your Lordship's much obliged and most obedient humble servant,   KEITH URQUHART. (*D.*)

'BANFF, *March 27th*, 1776.'

The Urquharts of Meldrum of the nineteenth century are descended from the brother of Keith Urquhart.

GEORGE, the fourth son, was born in 1736, and with his next brother Lewis went in charge of a tutor to St. Andrews in 1751. Previous to that date, these two were in Edinburgh. William, Lord Braco, writes to Archibald of Drummuir, April 1747, ' I have been here since the mid. of Nov. and must remain here until the end of the month, chiefly on account of my two younger sons, who are at the Colleges in this place and whom I do not think it convenient to leav.' The tutor, A. Morton, writes in 1753 that he is ' endeavouring to make George acquire a good hand of write, arithmetick, and book keeping and the French tongue, so necessary in the way of trade.' So he was apparently designed for a mercantile career, but at the age of nineteen was gazetted a cornet in the 10th Regiment of Dragoons, and was two years in the Army. In the end of 1756 he contracted a hasty marriage with Frances, granddaughter of General Dalzell, and kept it secret for some months. He left the Army and settled in London in Burlington Street, as his wife, who brought him some money, refused to go to Scotland.[1] It is not known exactly what he did in London, but he resided for many years in Clarges Street, and Queen Street, Mayfair, and subsequently at Putney (then a very remote country place). His brothers James, Lewis, and Arthur all complain of his want of friendliness and sociability, but he was a most devoted father. He had four children : JAMES, the eldest, born 1758, unfortunately, a lunatic from birth ; GEORGE, born 1760 ; JANE, 1765 ; and FRANCES, June 26, 1766, in Elgin. His wife died in 1778, and after her death and that of his daughters, he returned to Scotland and resided at Milton Duff, near Elgin, and latterly at the 5th College in Elgin, which he purchased in 1768. He took some share in public affairs, and became Convener of the county. He died in 1818, aged eighty-two, and intestate, leaving considerable landed property. In 1755 Lord Braco had disponed to his son George the lands of Straloch ; in 1756 the lands of Dunnideer—this for political purposes only.

By his testament-dative, issued by the Court after his death, all his lands including Bilbohall (*vide infra*), went to his second son GEORGE.

The eldest son JAMES is referred to occasionally in the family letters,

---

[1] At least for the first ten years of their married life

'George's son returns on Monday to school, and he is to go with him in the coach,' and in the following from his mother :

Frances Duff to Lady Fife

'Dec 31st . . .

'DEAR MADAM,—I was honor'd with your Ladyship's favor, and shall take as much care of Fanny as possible, the giving her brimstone is thought to be unneccessary.

'The children are well, and they give us many agreable hours, indeed in this place their company makes us very happy, as we should be often at a loss for want of amusements.

'Denton is very alert, she is here and there, up stairs and down stairs, unfortunately, in the midst of a contest with the cook, she fell and maim'd her leg, which has confined her some days to her bed, she thinks that it is a judgment on her for the altercation she had with the cook. I am frequently in amazement

'Mr. Duff observing that I am at a loss for subject to write to your Ladyship in this retirement, desires me to apologise for his not being a better correspondent, I answer that he has so often practis'd that part of epistolary writing, that he can do it infinitely better than I can.

'Jem just now read to me, good gods ! how he does read. He is a riddle, I hope some sensible man will expound him.

'Mr. Duff joins with me in desiring our affectionate compliments to all friends round your fire side.—I am, with great respect, Dear Madam, Your ladyship's Most Dutifull and Obedient Serv: FRANCES DUFF.' (O.)

This James Duff long remained a mystery, as he was known by the following letter (from the grandfather of the present writers to his sister) to have been alive in 1828, but the mystery was solved by the discovery that he had been placed at a private asylum named Beaufort House, North End Road, S.W., under the name of James Thompson.

'ABERDEEN, 31 May 1828

'MY DEAR BESSIE,—I have deferred for some time writing, wishing to give you the issue of my endeavours to establish myself, as far as could be done, in the property, intended for me by Lady Jane's late cousin Major George Duff. The other properties of which he died possessed were left to the second son of General Duff and to Mr. Wharton respectively, but owing to the state of the titles of the property of Bilbohall which he intended for me, being incomplete, the Disposition in my favour was not made out at the time of his death. Lord Fife, however, and the others nearest in succession, have, as far as in their power, endeavoured to carry into execution the Major's recorded intentions in my favour. But as he left a brother who has been insane from early life and is now towards

T

seventy years of age, full possession cannot at present be given, that brother, notwithstanding his state, being Heir at law, and steps are taken in the meantime to give me control of the property by having me made Curator Bonis.

'ALEXANDER FRANCIS TAYLER.'

Two months after the death of George, in July 1828, a certificate was obtained from the surgeon of Beaufort House, Mr. Maule (whose private residence was in Piccadilly), who writes thus :

'I hereby certify that the person designated as Mr. James Thompson and alluded to in the accompanying certificates, is in reality James Duff the eldest son of the Honourable George Duff of Elgin ; that fifty-seven years ago he was placed in the establishment called Beaufort House where he still is, under the superintendence and management of my late father, who as an intimate friend of the late Hon. George Duff undertook the guardianship of his idiot son, that as a matter of delicacy and family feeling, or from other motives the origin of which I am not acquainted with, he was nominated James Thompson, under which name he has ever since been known ; that since the death of my father, thirty years ago, I have executed the same office of friendship by watching over the well-doing and proper treatment of the said James Duff, otherwise Thompson, and that I have regularly paid for his support, maintenance and clothing, such sums as his late father appropriated and were found sufficient for that purpose. Finally, I certify that I saw him a few days ago (June 29), when he was still in the same hopeless state of fatuity in which I have seen him for the last forty years upwards, that his infirmity is irremediable, and that he is in every way incapable of managing the most ordinary affairs.   WM. MAULE.'

James died in Beaufort House, March 29, 1832, after nearly sixty years residence there, aged seventy-four.

George, born 1760, is frequently referred to in the family correspondence as 'the Ensign.' He was at school at the 'Kensington Gravel Pits,' [1] where his uncle Arthur visited him. While at another school, he was sent home ill, 'in a raging fever, speechless, delirious with quinsy. All his skin came off, and every servant who attended him was in some degree effected in like manner.' Nowadays little George would probably have been isolated for scarlet fever. Lady Fife writes of his parting with his sister Fan : 'The ensign left me Monday last. He went to Houseday (Housedale) that night. It was a terrible "greeting" [2] morning here, but I hope we will get over his absence.' His uncle James obtained a commission for him in the Guards in 1781. He was given to gambling

---

[1] Now Orme Square, Bayswater   The gravel was sold to contractors and laid down on the Nevsky Prospect in St Petersburg   A Russian eagle in stone now adorns the centre of Orme Square in commemoration of this fact

[2] Crying.

and bad company, as shown in the following letter from James, second Earl Fife, to his brother Arthur :

'*Feb* 15*th*.

'MY DEAR ARTHUR,—I have wrote my mind fully to Brother George about his Son, to which I refer you, there is an absolute necessity for doing some thing directly. I hear that George is going to shops and taking up goods in order to raise money, that he has taken into Company with a Valet du Chamber who is out of Place and some Adventurer in Gambling, you must see where this must end and that directly, I did not say this to his Father as it is so very disagreeable, he must not be deceived, and yet one would not like to inform him of more than is absolutely necessary, you may easily figur how much pain this gives to me. I have fairly offered my Brother my opinion and sent the Stile of letters I think necessary for him to write.

' I am really quite weary with this horrid weather, worse this day almost than ever, I think above they are all mad. Duty to my Mother.—Yours, etc., etc.,
' FIFE.

' After full consideration I think it best to send my letter to George oppen that you may deliver it in a proper time but for God sake delay not for I am in terror I cannot describe, for fear of some thing horrid '   (*O.*)

On February 10, 1784, Lord Fife writes to his brother George from London :

' Since my letter of the 7th Instant, I have had several conversations with your son and have got him to give me a state of the money he owes, but I will not answer for the authenticity of it. From the information I have, I find it absolutely necessary to get him out of this town and for that purpose I have been obliged to make application to the commanding officer for leave of absence which with great difficulty I have obtained for two months My principal reasons for so doing were that applications for the payment of most of the money would soon come upon him, particularly the Jeweller the nature of which transaction being exposed might bring disagreeable consequences upon himself besides injuring him greatly in the opinion of the Regiment ; added to the above, I must likewise observe to you that the manner of his living in this place could not fail, by his continuing, to involve you much deeper in expense. I have therefore advised him to set off immediately for Scotland and himself lay the situation of his affairs before you. In this my Dr. Sir I have acted to the best of my Judgment for your Interests. You will have time to determine what steps are best to be taken as I mentioned in my last, if I can be of the least service in extricating you out of this disagreeable situation or assisting you in getting an Exchange for him with some other regiment, I shall be happy in doing everything in my power. As little time as possible should be lost in forming some resolution and acquainting me therewith, as it will be impossible to get his present leave of absence extended.'   (*R.*)

In 1786 it is reported that his conduct was ' better ' He was promoted as Lieutenant and Captain, April 7, 1784, and exchanged as Captain to the 58th Foot, April 6, 1785. He went on half-pay in 1791, and was then transferred to the Irish half-pay list. He was mixed up in a disgraceful scandal in Ireland in October 1792. ' Henry Arthur Herbert has obtained in Ireland a verdict of £15,000 against Major Duff of the 38th Regt: (58th) for " criminal conversation " with his wife.' There are allusions to the case in his uncle's letters, and also in one from Miss Jean Duff.[1]

Jean Duff, Scarborough, to William Rose

'*May* 18, 1791

' I was sorry to hear of the conduct of Major G. Duff. I fancy from all I have heard of him, he has been extremely giddy and thoughtless and has given much trouble to his Father in the former part of his life. This affair he has been engaged in will in all probability prove a serious business. I am afraid the Father will be the greatest sufferer as the consequences must fall upon him, if there is damages procured.'   (*R.*)

James, Lord Fife, to his brother Arthur

' INNES HOUSE, *June* 17th, 1796.

' DEAR BROTHER,—I wished to have breakfast at Orton this morning, but I take it for granted you staed at Elgin. I am so harryd with different things that I cannot make longer stay here just now, but hope to be able to return soon. I freely felt for poor Major Duff, I got the letter I put in your hands just a little before. I have writ to him this morning to make him easy, the delay is owing to Mr. Herbert's Militia situation. I had a letter on the subject from Mr. Chas. Herbert last week ; they are anxious to bring it to conclusion, so of course will push it, and poor George Duff has only to be as much at ease as possible, with the full assurance of being free of every apprehention of danger from any trouble, for that I get quick settled. I realy hope from his letter that he will from Youth and a resolute life recover health and strength.'

After this, little is heard of George. He never married, and died in 1828, leaving the bulk of his estates to his first cousin General Alexander Duff's second son, George Skene Duff, then a minor, as the elder son James, heir to the earldom, was already sufficiently provided for. (According to old Scottish custom, his will directs that earth, water and coin from the estate, and the clapper of the mill be handed to G. S. Duff as a sign of possession.) Some other portions had been previously made over to Richard Wharton Duff, another first cousin, and the small estate of Bilbo-

---

[1] See chapter xxxiv.

hall, near Elgin, he had intended, as previously seen, to give to the husband of his cousin Jane, Major Alexander Francis Tayler.

'Bilbohall came into the Duff family in 1724, being conveyed to William Duff of Braco by John Dunbar. In 1751 Lord Braco conveyed the property to his son Alexander, and the latter in 1755, with the consent of his father, conveyed it back to Lord Braco in liferent, and to the Hon. George Duff in fee. George and his son George both appear to have held the property, but no title was made up in their names. Major George, the son, died in 1828, having by will disposed of all his properties except Bilbohall, which accordingly fell into intestacy, his heir-at-law being his brother, Mr. James, who was "fatuous." But owing to the papers conveying this estate to Major Tayler having been duly prepared although not executed, the relatives of Mr Duff applied for the appointment of Major Tayler as his Curator Bonis, and at the same time granted a deed conveying to him all right and title which they, as heirs of Mr. James Duff, might have to the Estate at his death, and binding themselves to grant any further deeds which might be necessary for completing the major's title.' Four years later, at the death of James, the major's title was made absolute, and his son, William James, had a formal conveyance from the Earl of Fife, dated 1863. Bilbohall is now in the possession of the present writer, and the facts in connection with it have an additional interest from the circumstance that the Mr. Duff who, in 1912, considered himself to have a claim to the Fife title, believed himself to be descended from the above Major George Duff, whose name he stated to have been Daniel George.[1] His own grandfather, whose name was Daniel only, was an entirely different person, and will be noted in the proper place.

George's elder daughter, Jane Dorothea, was chiefly brought up by her mother in London, but in 1776 was at Rothiemay, as her grandmother writes accounts to the parents of her progress under an 'epidemical distemper,' and in 1780, after her mother's death, she was living at Rothiemay, as her father writes to enjoin her to conform in all things to her grandmother's directions. She seems afterwards to have returned to London and kept house for her father. In 1792 her death is recorded 'while on a journey in the north of England for the recovery of her health.' It is not known where she is buried.

Frances, or 'little Fan,' the youngest child, seems to have been the universal family pet. She was brought up at Rothiemay by her adoring grandmother, and constant allusions are made to her in the letters of all the family. She seems to have been very delicate, and at one time fell a

---

[1] Or from a younger brother of George, named Daniel.

victim to the scourge of smallpox, and later would seem also to have been consumptive, while in 1777 she had jaundice. Constant references occur to her small appetite. Her little cousin James, son of the Admiral, had been ill, ' but the little fellow is now fine and well and sends his love to his cousin Fan, with orders for her to eat hot meat '; and James's elder brother (afterwards Colonel Robert William of Fetteresso) is thus alluded to : ' Bob sends his love to Fanny, she has his whole heart.'   Both children were then about nine.

In 1775 Lady Fife describes how she and Fan play ' catch honour ' every evening, and how her small companion ' diverts her more than any other company.' She was the greatest favourite of her uncle Arthur, who sends constant messages to ' Miss Monkey,' to ' Lady Fan,' and to his ' little wife,' also packs of cards, books, ' provision for her birds,' and other gifts. At one period he is moved to compare her attainments unfavourably with those of her sister Jane in London. (Jane at this period was ten and Fan eight) :

' Pray make my most respectful compliments to Miss Fanny and inform her that she will be much affronted if she does not give very great attention to her new master, as I do assure you she is at present far, nay, partial as I am to her I must say, *very far*, behind her sister, who reads English and French extremely well, speaks both languages very easily, writes and counts to admiration, and is I am told very good at her needle, and as to her carriage it is quite elegant. Much would she be ashamed to have any occasion for a bridle, and I am in hopes, against we meet, Fan will have as little, or she will not be able to hide herself in any corner, but I shall find her and send her in a ship to Mrs. Denton's care, but if she is a good girll, I will get liberty for her to stay with you and will bring her some prettie things beside.' [1]   (O.)

Affectionate letters to her from all her aunts are to be found, almost always inquiring after her health, and there is also an invitation, dated 1783, from Mary Morison, stepdaughter of her uncle Robert (and future wife of the ' Bob ' who had given her ' all his heart ') to pay a visit at Haddo. She died suddenly at Rothiemay in 1787, at the age of twenty, and was buried at Grange, the body being subsequently moved to the mausoleum at Duff House.

' ROTHIEMAY, *8th March* 1787.

' DEAR SIR,—Miss Frances Duff my niece died Here Tuesday last and is to be Interred at Grange upon Monday next the 12th inst.

' The Honor of your Company Here by Eleven of the Clock that day, to

---

[1] In 1779 a servant named Grizel Crow writes to ask for news of ' Miss Fanny, charming young creature,' and signs herself, ' The humble handmaid of the good old Countess.'

attend Her Funeral to the Place of Interment, will confer a singular obligation
upon, Dear Sir, your most obed^t Humble Servant,   ARTHUR DUFF.
      ' To William Rose, Montcoifer.'   (*R.*)

From a letter written by Keith Urquhart to his mother-in-law, Lady
Fife, of approximate date 1785, it appears that his eldest son James had
fallen in love with one of the daughters of his uncle George, presumably
Fan, who must have been a most attractive person.   Keith Urquhart's
letter is so characteristic of the tyrannical father of the period that it must
be given in full .

'MELDRUM, *circa* 1785

' MADAM,—As my Son has been twice at Rothiemay within this short time,
and for a good while together, your Ladyship and Mr. Duff, I presume, cannot
be ignorant of his Errand.   You are both likewise so far acquainted with the
Circumstances of my Family as to comprehend thoroughly that any marriage
which does not bring money along with it, must end in *his* Destruction, and put
an End to our Family with Regard to its Station among the landed Gentry of
this Country.   I have always loved my Children, and have ever had it in view
not only to save, but, if possible, to build up my Family.   For this Reason I
have abstained from re-Marriage myself, at a time of Life when many a Man
would have thought himself well intitled to please his Fancy, and to embrace
any Condition of Life which he might think would most tend to his satisfaction.
What Steps I have taken to procure an advantageous marriage for my son, it
is not now the Time to declare, nor am I altogether at Liberty to do so, yet I
will go the Length to say, that a full Consent was obtained from two of the nearest
of kin (one of them the Parent) and nothing remained to be done, but that he
should endeavour to recommend himself to the good opinion of the young Lady.
That is now over, which is Disappointment enough to me, and though I never
thought myself intitled to force a Marriage upon him, yet I think myself perfectly
well intitled to put a negative upon any marriage which I may judge to be improper for him.   That negative I *have* put upon the present occassion, and will
steadily adhere to it, and have little Doubt but that your Ladyship, who are the
common Parent of both the young Folks, will concur and co-operate with me.
Give me leave, therefore, to expect, as I believe the World will, that your Ladyship and Mr. Duff will forbid my Son the House of Rothiemay for the present
I have let him know roundly what he was to expect at my Hands, have forbid
him this House and the Prohibition shall not be taken off until he returns to a
sound mind   Your Ladyship knows that by my Contract of Marriage, I can settle
my Estate upon any Son of the marriage.   You know that I am the unlimited
Proprietor of the Estate, insomuch that I can sell it, or I can contract Debt
to the Value of it, and convey the money by Bonds to the Children I may have
by any subsequent marriage, or to whomsoever I please.   My Son was yesterday
at Hatton Lodge, from which Place he wrote a long Letter to me, full of crackt
brained Extravagance, and the most Childish Impertinence.   I believe no Father

before ever received a Letter in such a Stile from a Son. I am sorry for the Pain which this subject must give your Ladyship, and I have no Doubt but I have your Sympathy in Return. I desire to offer my best Respects to Mr. Duff, and have the Honour to be, very respectfully, Madam, Your Ladyship's most obedient and most humble Servant,   KEITH URQUHART.

'He has exposed his whole story to Dr. and Mrs. Abernethie.'   (O.)

The Mr. Duff referred to is Arthur, now retired from Parliament and settled at Rothiemay. James Urquhart seems to have submitted to the parental decree and subsequently (in 1788) married Miss Forbes,[1] but had no children, and the estates passed to a cousin. He and his father were never on very good terms. Keith Urquhart and *his* father had lived together in the same house for some years without speaking.

Next to George in the family came LEWIS, originally called LUDOVIC, born in 1737. The name occurs in both forms, but that he himself preferred the English form is shown by the following note to his brother, Lord Fife, when his signature was required for the (proposed) sale of Braco :

'KILVEDON, *Mar* 18, 1772

'MY LORD,—I remit the paper signed, agreeable to the Directions received —I have always signed Lewis, In the paper I am designed Ludovick. I have adhered to my usual subscription, thinking there might be an Impropriety in deviating from the established custom. I suppose this difference of Signature can be of no material consequence, as they are confessedly the same name. Mrs. Duff joins in affect. Respect.—I am, my Lord, Your affect. Brother and obedient Servant,   LEWIS DUFF '[2]

Lady Fife records that George, Lewis, and Helen all had ' the good kind of pox ' together. Whether this refers to chicken-pox or to a mild attack of smallpox, is not explained. Lewis was educated with George until 1754, when he presumably showed greater aptitude for learning, and was sent from St. Andrews first to Leyden and then to St John's College, Cambridge, where he is entered as 'the Hon. Lewis Duff, born in Banff, Banffshire.'

His elder brother Alexander writes shortly afterwards that ' Lewis' studies goe on but slowly, and the company he keeps is none of the best.' There is no record of what line of study he pursued, nor of his success or

[1] Miss Forbes, daughter of William Forbes of Skellater and Balbithan, niece of Mrs Abernethy, wife of Dr. Abernethy, a physician in Banff It was in honour of this lady that Isaac Cooper wrote his famous melody, ' Miss Forbes' Farewell to Banff '

[2] Lyon Office That he was wrong in so signing, his baptismal certificate proves 'On June 13, 1737, LUDOVICK, fifth son of William, Lord Bracco, was born and baptized and so named after Ludovick, Laird of Grant and Major Lewis Grant ' (*Banff Registers*)

otherwise in the schools, but if he were destined for a learned career some other influence would seem to have stepped in, and in 1757 he appears as a Cornet in the 1st Royal Dragoons. In 1762 he was transferred as Captain to the 8th Regiment, and in that he remained, serving in Germany in 1767, and in America 1775, and retiring in 1777. He seems to have been blessed with fair health, but an incurably melancholy disposition. Even from Cambridge, in writing to his mother for money, he complains that the climate does not suit him, and that everything is against him. After entering the Army his grumbles are perpetual, as to how hard it is to live on his pay, the small chances of promotion to one without great interest, the uncertainty of a soldier's life, and the frequent changes of abode. He seems to have been stationed in various parts of Essex for some time, and in 1767 he married Deborah, daughter of Griffith Davies of Harwich. She does not appear to have brought him any fortune, but for nearly thirty years she was a devoted wife, putting up with his misanthropic humours. She writes to his parents at frequent intervals :

Deborah Duff, wife of the Hon. Lewis Duff, to Lord Fife

'QUEBEC, *August 2th,* 1770

'MY LORD,—At this time of year we have frequent opportunities of sending letters to England which makes me be rather a troublesome correspondent to you but as you have often expressd a desire of hearing from us induces me to write often to inquire how your Lordship and Lady Fife is. I hope both well, and likewise hope next summer to find you so on our return home. A great many people goes from this in a day or two. Amongst which is Col. Carlton, Mr. Obrian and Lady Susan, a number more but those are unknown to your Lordship so it would be needless to mention them. This country at this season is very pleasant but the weather by far too hot in the day for which the evening rewards us by being delightfully cool and you may walk very late by moonlight and not be a sufferer by the dew which in great Britain falls after sunset and is very dangerous ; but here I have never felt the least dampness in the air at that time and have often wished your Lordship was here for a week to enjoy the sweet rural rides through the most romantic agreeable woods that can be imagined, as I am sure you, for that time, would like this country. Longer than that might tire you.

'I suppose your Lordship is now enjoying yourself in the sweet walks at Duff House, it was a most beautifull spot when I was there, but the improvements you are always making must have rendered it still more so. The 52nd Regiment are all here but W. Gordon is not yet come, having got the Major's leave to go and see a little of the upper Country and does not return till November. We have made every inquiry and find he turns out very well and is much liked, by the best part of the Officers. I hope soon to be favord with a letter from your

v

Lordship in which I hope to here good news of all my friends health. My
Dearest friend joyns in wishing your Lordship and Lady Fife every happiness
and I remain, My Lord, your Lordships most obliged Humble Servant,

'D. Duff.' (D.)

To his mother from Harwich : ' Do try to persuade him to come to
you as soon as our time is out here. His health is better, and I am sure
if once he could get the better of his whims, that the journey would make
him still better.' And later, from Scotland : ' The Major is not so well
nor so contented as I could wish, but I hope time will make him so.'
They had no children.

Nine years after his marriage, Lewis left the Army, apparently entirely
by his own wish, because he saw no chance of advancing beyond the rank
of Major,[1] and was moreover unwilling to go a second time to America.
But no sooner was the step accomplished than he began to regret it, took
various unavailing measures to recall it, and lamented it for the rest of
his life. Seemingly, had he not retired just at that juncture, he might have
had the chance of commanding his regiment, and the brothers on hearing
of this unanimously exclaim that they are ' sorry for his wife.' ' The
Lt.-Colonel of Lewis' regiment is dead, and promotion open without
purchase. What an unfortunate man he will be ' (December 20, 1776).
A year later Arthur writes, in December 1777 : ' I had a letter from Lewis
last night. He seems, poor man, still in very low spirits and repines at
being forced out of the Army. Had he continued he must have been this
day still more unhappy, as he would have been a prisoner with Burgoyne.
It indeed he had survived the fatigues of the campaign.' So sure was
his family that in whatever situation Lewis found himself, it would be
matter of complaint. About this time, Deborah writes again . ' My dear
Major has been a good while and greatly distressed with his bilious complaint. My stomach much about the same. Both I fear are too deep-
rooted ever to be cured, patience is the only doctor.'

And later to her mother-in-law :

' Birnie, Forres, 27th Dec 1776

' My dear Madm ,—Most sincerely do I wish that this letter may find you
and all friends in that good health that the major and I so ardently hopes will

---

[1] He wrote to his brother on the occasion .

' Forres, Septr 14th, 1776.

' Major Duff presents his compliments to Lord Fife. He takes the Liberty of informing
his Lordship that He is obliged to quit the army, that notwithstanding his very severe Service
he has met with peculiar ill usage, indignity and oppression to which as he had no interest to
support him he has been forced to submit The Major returns Thanks to his Brother for his
generous Protection and kind countenance from his first entering into his Profession to the
present Period when every object of ambition is terminated '

ever attend you all. This season of the year is generally observed by all ranks and degrees of people and employed by social meetings of friends and Relations together the time passes in scenes of Mirth and Jollity. Give me leave my Dear Mad^m to express My Wish that you may injoy a Merry Cheerfull X'times and many returns. The Major and me rec^d a great shock from the Accounts of poor Billy Gordons Death tho the manner of it was no more then from the nature of his melancholy complaint might have been dailly expected yet when Accidents Like that happens the shock must be great to all Friends concerned. I should think if sir John has any feelings of nature about him he must upon the present occasion be miserable. I hope it may have a good effect and bring him to some sense and consideration. He has lost a good friend and a truly affectionate Brother, it is not a month ago since poor William sent an express from Rothiemay to the Major for £30 to make up the sum wanted to send sir John out of the country, expressing at the same time his regret at not being able to give it himself. Poor Lad, I fear he gave too much. Do not, My Dear Mad^m, let his Death hurt your Spirits, he is at rest and no doubt happy. While he was alive he was in constant danger and his friends in constant terror.

'I have not seen any of the Brodie family since I wrote last, having been confined with a swelled face and tooth ach, but hear Lady M is much as usual Brodie fine and hearty. I will go as soon as I am able after which I will acquaint you how I find things. Mr. and Mrs. Cumming with some more Acquaintance Passed the X'mas day here they are both well. The new years day We are to be at Altyr with the same party The Delvey family and Altyr are at present quite out. The wheel of time will turn them in again. They each think themselves in the right and I think them both in the wrong, for so few neighbours as we have here about it is nonsense to quarrell. I beg my kindest good wishes to Mr. Wharton Lady S· Fanny and little Arthur,[1] being ever Dr Mad^m with sincere respect, Your most Affect. and obed^t,   D. Duff.' (O.)

After his retirement, Lewis and his wife lived for some time in Craven Street, and the three younger brothers saw a good deal of one another in London. Subsequently he adjourned to the small property left him by his father, Blervie, near Forres, and built a mansion-house there.

'The estate of Blervie, situated 2½ miles S -E of Forres, was purchased by William, Earl of Fife, in 1724, from Alex. MacIntosh, his brother-in-law. The Hon. Major Lewis Duff, quitting the ancient castled seat of the Dunbars on the summit of the hill, built a handsome modern seat, snugly sheltered.' The estate was later in the possession of the Grant Duffs of Eden and Ainslie Douglas Ainslie, who sold it to Captain Galloway.

According to Lewis' own and Deborah's letters, never had man been so deceived or ill served by workmen. Deborah writes : 'The meest part of the house is now "going about," and if the workmen are not watched

---

[1] Wharton.

narrowly they will do nothing aright.' 'They served us ill with timber for the roofs.'

And when once they were settled in their own house, never was neighbourhood so unwholesome or so dull. He writes to his mother of his toothache as if it were a national calamity, and seems uncertain whether he is more injured by attentions or by neglect from the despised neighbours. Even his sister Margaret at Brodie he seldom saw, as he was not on friendly terms with her husband, and declined a visit to Hatton and another to Rothiemay, owing to some fancied slight in the manner of conveying the invitations. After Deborah's death in 1796 he did not live much at Blervie, but took up his residence at No 13 Margate,[1] from whence he writes: 'Health is now my sole speculation. I pass my time very agreeably with reading, walking, and conversation '

He writes to his brother-in-law, Thomas Wharton :

'13 MARGATE, *July* 1, 1798.

' DEAR SIR,—Altho' there is nothing in this Place, that can possibly interest or amuse you, yet I think it my Duty to inquire after you, Lady S. and Family—and it will make me very happy to learn that every thing is in the State I wish. I am settled in the comfortable House where I lodged last year. Our Society is small but select. There is an ease and tranquillity which is pleasing to one long satiated with the Bustle, Dissipation and Folly of the World. It is indeed a perfect Contrast to the Scenes passing around which are in a stile of Whim and Eccentricity beyond Description. We have a very sensible, agreeable old Lady who dines occasionally with us, she is a Sister of the celebrated Wilks, she has seen a Variety of Life, is full of anecdote and makes proper and just observations on every subject that occurs in the course of Conversation. She is indeed a Character, but there is a general Humanity and Philanthropy which throws a pleasant Vail over her Peculiarities. Nothing so forcibly evinces her oddness, altho' she has taken a large house, with a full establishment of Servants, who live in the greatest luxury, yet she dines with us every Day in order to enjoy a Dish of Chat without Ceremony. I left the young Consul Brodie[2] in Town, He is entirely out of employment, which at his period of life is rather awkward and dangerous. He seems prudent and rational. I hope by the aid of his Uncle the Nabob, He may strike out some Line in India, which will be a more brilliant speculation than a return to Spain. I have thoughts of remaining here till October. I contrive to pass my Time tolerably in Reading, Walking, tea Parties, Excursions to the different Villages in the Vicinity which are peculiarly beautiful and picturesque. As to the Diversions of the place I am a mere Spectator. It will give me great Pleasure to hear from you. A letter will find me at No. 13 Margate. I beg my best Wishes and remain with real Regard your affect.   LEWIS DUFF.' (*O.*)

---

[1] It is interesting to note that at that period this address was sufficient
[2] His nephew, William Brodie.

He lived to the age of seventy-four, dying in Craven Street, London, in the same year as his brother Alexander, 1811, and is buried under the monument at Blervie which he had erected to his wife. Portraits of George with his father and Lewis with his mother exist at Rothiemay House, both by Mossman. In the pencil miniatures on chicken skin, now in the possession of Mrs. Chancellor, Woodhall, Juniper Green (great-granddaughter of Lady Sophia), Lewis appears as a rather depressed little boy. The six other portraits, which are all that remain, are of both parents, of Anne and Janet, very charming and almost exactly alike; Alexander, very solemn; and Arthur, the universal favourite, with his sweet smile.

The ninth child and sixth son was PATRICK, born and died 1738.

The tenth child and fourth daughter of this large family was HELEN, born in 1739, and married in 1764 to her father's first cousin, Admiral Robert Duff. Her history and that of her children properly belong to the family of Fetteresso, and will be found in that chapter. She died in 1778.

The eleventh child and fifth daughter was SOPHIA, born 1740, during the trying winter when her two eldest sisters were lying dangerously ill two hundred miles from home, and the patient mother was complimented upon her calmness. She was thirty-four when, July 13, 1774, she became the third wife of Thomas Wharton, Commissioner of Excise, a man five years her senior, with three sons. They resided chiefly at Lauriston, near Edinburgh, and four sons and three daughters were born to her. Of the first, her mother writes to Arthur, November 19, 1776 : ' Sophia has brought Mr. Wharton a charming stout boy. You would be diverted to see the Commissioner gazing so fondly on the boy, as he had had never a child before.' Mr. Wharton suffered at times from painful illnesses which sound remarkably like attacks of gout, during which ' neither sick nurse, servant nor wife can please him, and poor Sophia is almost worn to a shadow.' ' Mr. Wharton has so many whims of his own, without considering Sophia.' She lived till 1826, dying at the age of eighty-six. This family will appear again under the heading of Orton.

Of CATHERINE, twelfth child and sixth daughter, very little is known. She was the only unmarried daughter, and there is but one letter of hers among the family MSS :

Lady Catherine Duff to Earl Fife

' ENR., *April the* 2, 1765

' MY DEAR LORD,—I wrote you a very long letter which should have gone by Mr. Dunbar and after keeping it a few days it shared the same fate of many

of my other letters to you hath done, the flames; the thought of your not coming down this summer grieves Meg and me much, but there is nothing but disappointments in this life. Rose [1] came here a few days ago and called for us, he apear'd to be in low spirits and told us he was afraid you would not come North but for a month or two. I begine to think you in earnest and I am much sunk by it. I had a letter from Lady Fife which both grieved and surprised me. I wrote Lady Fife an answer which I am afraid she would scarce read; I have a good deal of little chat to write but will not trouble you as I shall write Lady Fife to-morrow. We are to go from this in three weeks the highland road. Lewes left us some weeks ago and Arthur is to go this. I have never heard of Sandy since we seed him at Aberdeen. We are at present a very grave family. My love and best wishes attend you and Lady Fife and in very low spirits I ever am, My Dear Lord, your very affectionet friend and obliged humble Servant,

'CATH. DUFF.' (*D.*)

It is probable that she scarcely ever left her mother and her home. She was born in 1741, and died in Edinburgh in 1765, aged twenty-four. A portrait of her exists at Montcoffer House, Banff. The only mention of her in the family correspondence is in a letter from the husband of her sister Anne (her elder by sixteen years), with whom apparently two of the children (Catherine and Arthur) were spending a winter in 1752. Alexander Duff of Hatton, husband of Anne, writes to his father-in-law : ' The young folk with me are in very good health and applying very close, Arthur in particular (aged nine). If I had been at home I would have sent you a sample of Arthur and Katty's (aged eleven) writes. They expect they will be remembered in some playthings about the Christmas time.'

After the birth of three daughters in succession, it may be supposed that Lord Braco, now getting on for fifty, must have welcomed with joy the arrival of his youngest son ARTHUR in 1740. At all events, from the moment of his birth and throughout his life, Arthur was every one's favourite, and must have had an exceptionally sweet nature not to have been spoilt by so much petting and praise. All the letters of William, Lord Braco, to his wife contain constant references to ' my Attie ' and ' my little lad,' who seems to have been a perpetual source of joy His early education is not mentioned, except during the winter of 1752, which he spent at Hatton, but at the age of fifteen he went, like his brothers, to St. Andrews University, and subsequently to Glasgow University. Later, his name is found among the English-speaking students at Leyden, 1769, ' Arthur Duff, Scoto-Britannicus,' and he subsequently became an advocate. He was very tender-hearted, and writes to his mother from college : ' Forgive me for not coming to bid you adieu, as I have an utter aversion to

---

[1] The factor

these formalities at any time, more especially in such a distressed time as
when I left Rothiemay.' It was apparently during his father's last illness.
In 1774 he was elected member for Morayshire, his brother's interest being
strong in that county, as well as in Banffshire. The number of electors
in those days was very small, and an election was frequently swayed by
one person.

There is a curious schedule of the proposed procedure in the Michaelmas
Head Court at Elgin, October 2, 1772, ' upon Supposition that Lord Fife's
party has the Majority.' 'The "Preces" and Clerk, Mr. Arthur Duff and
Patrick Copland being chosen, the meeting is to proceed to consider the
objection lodged against those standing in the roll in the following order ·
(1) Sir Lud. Grant ; (2) Capt. Thos. Dundas ; (3) Mr. Tulloch of Tannachie ;
(4) Lord Fife. The next step is to take up the claims of the following
Gentlemen who are to be admitted to the Roll in the following order ·
(1) Lord Fife ; (2) Mr. Patt. Duff, minister of Old Aberdeen ; (3) Lachlan
Duff, W.S. ; (4) Lt. A Stuart of Parkbeg ; (5) William Duff of Corsindae ,
(6) Capt. John Urquhart.

' These claims being separately read and admitted, the following eleven
claims are to be taken up (here follows a list of persons not Duffs, nor in
any way connected with the family). But if it shall, in point of time, be
found that it will be three of the Clock before the claimants formerly
mentioned can be taken, the eleven claims immediately above mentioned
are to be rejected before the other claimants are admitted.

' Then the following claims to be taken up · (1) A. Stuart of Edinglassie ;
(2) Dr. Chas. McIntosh ; (3) A. Donaldson of Kinnairdy ; (4) Adam Duff
in Aberdeen, merchant ; (5) Dr. Arthur Duff, Corsindae ; (6) Governor
Grant ; (7) James Grant, Corriemonie ; (8) L. Grant, W S.'

When it is remembered that Lord Fife's mother was a Grant, that
two of his aunts had married respectively Donaldson and McIntosh, while
Urquhart and Tulloch were also related to him, it seems probable that he
would have a majority in the electorate of seventy-seven persons, which
is the number of electors of Morayshire given in the *Political State of
Scotland*, 1778.[1]

Arthur Duff of Orton writes to his brother James about his candi-
dature :

' ROTHIEMAY, 27th August.

' MY LORD,—As Lewis has no thoughts of standing as Candidate at the next
Genᵉˡ Election for Murray and as George, from any thing I have heard, will

---

[1] On April 10, 1773, Admiral Robert writes to Lord Fife to congratulate him on ' having, at
a late political gathering, defeated the combination of Gordons, Grants, and Gardens, with all
their following Truly a great victory '

take no concern for himself, if your Lop. approves I shall be very willing to try
my Fate against the Common Enemy, more especially as I have reason to think
it would be agreable to Lady Fife, Lewis and other friends at this place, at the
same time if your Lop. has other views I shall not be much disappointed, remaining with regard, your affect. Brother and very Humb. Sent,   A. D ' (O.)

Arthur's election was a matter of great rejoicing to all his family, and
from 1774 begins that charming series of letters to his mother of which
several of her descendants kept portions, and which reveal to us his most
attractive personality. He seems to have resided in London even before
he became a Member of Parliament, for he writes to his mother from Suffolk
Street in 1772, ' Yesterday we were blessed with the first good news we
have of a long time got to comfort us for the many misfortunes we have
met with. Governor Grant in conjunction with Admiral Barrington,
have taken the French Island of St. Lucia. D'Estaing landed and
attempted to retake it, but was beat off with the loss of 1600 men killed,
wounded, and Prisoners Upon our part there was about 30 killed, and 100
wounded, among the latter General Meadows.' Some of the letters are
very short, mere notes, but he seems unwilling to let more than two days
go by without sending something, and he and his mother at times reproach
one another for slackness in writing with a great deal of humour and
tenderness. A postscript to one of her letters says, ' Lady Fife has writ
to Mr. Arthur Duff Monday, Tuesday and Thursday of this week,' and in
1779 he can say, ' I have never missed one post in writing to your Layp
since I came from Scotland.' On December 23, 1775, ' We adjourned
to-day for the holidays—until January 25, and indeed I do not know when
at school I felt more joy at getting the Play.' The weather, however,
became so severe that he was unable to leave London even to get as far
as Bath. It seems to have been a record winter both in England and
Scotland.

Two days later he writes . ' Quebec has been relieved, but Montreal
must I fear surrender to the rebels'; and in January 1776 following· ' The
rebels have taken the island of St. John's—the loss will be felt by our army
in Boston, as from that quarter they derived much of their fresh provisions.'
In the same winter he expects ' some fun from Wilkes, Hopkins and the
Liberty boys in the streets.'

On January 23 he writes : ' We ought to meet on Thursday first, but
as the roads are in many parts impervious, I dare say there will be another
adjournment for want of members, for which I am very sorry.' (The thaw
came in February.) On one occasion he tells her that he has met with an
accident on the ice and has scarred his face, which prevents him ' from
going abroad for some days ' She replies in great anxiety lest his appear-

ance should be spoiled, but characteristically adds, ' But you will aye be bonnie enough to them that love you.' He inquires perpetually for her health and sends careful directions as to her diet, exercise, and general mode of life. In 1775 he says he has been made very happy by hearing from Mr. Stronach that she was looking so well, ' she might pass for forty ' (she being then seventy). At one time he seems to have been haunted by unreasoning fears as to her being ill, but chides himself by saying, ' Thank God, although as a seventh son I may be born a doctor, I have not got the second sight, with all my Highland blood.' In 1781 he writes that he is glad she has not gone to Banff, *i.e.* Duff House, from Rothiemay. ' I dread your changing your bed.' In 1777 she writes to him · ' My dearest Arthur, take care of yourself and want for nothing that can give you pleasure, since if you are well nothing can come amiss to me, being unalterably your very affectionate mother,—J. FIFE.' And again, in answer to some tender reproach : ' I never meant an unkind thing to you all my days.'   (O.)

Hon. Arthur Duff to his mother

' SUFFOLK STREET, 19*th Feb.* 1778.

' MY DEAREST MADAM,—I did not expect when I concluded my Letter to Mr. Wharton, that I should have been able to write your Lap. by this Post, as I expected a very late night in the House. However Tis waiting us To-morrow or next week, for this Day we had only Four Hours. I had it from pretty good authority this Day in the House that Government has now got certain Information of the Treaty betwixt France and America which will probably be productive of a French War ; and a Change in administration Tis said would be the consequence. I have so good an opinion of Lord North's Integrity that I should most sincerely regret his Loss. But I will not allow myself to believe it, altho I confess my Spirits are a few *Pegs* down upon the occasion. I need not Caution your Lap. not to mention me as the author of any news of this kind to others than my Sister and Mr. Wharton. I have this Day the pleasure of a letter from The admiral,[1] which I enclose for your Ladyship's Satisfaction, I wrote him a Long Letter by the Last Packet and made all your Compliments which I knew I might with great Safety without a mandate take upon me to deliver. We are now beginning to feel Winter when we had reason to expect Spring ; since Sunday a great deal of Snow has fallen, and in the Country I dare say it is pretty deep, but have not, since that Day, been further than betwixt this St. and the House of Commons, and as I begin to feel the want of Exercise am determined to pay a visit to-morrow forenoon to Kensington Gardens. Your Lap. says you hope I attended Service upon the 30th Jan[y].[2] I confess I did not neither am I

---

[1] Robert of Logie.   [2] Anniversary of the death of Charles I.

X

by principle a great admirer of that Days Ceremony, but there is none of the Two Hundred and 56 Members a more Constant Attender upon Prayers which once a week is equal to one of the honest Parsons longest Sermons. You never say whether you go regularly out in the Chaise. I am sure you are much to blame if you neglect it ; 'Tis really impossible you can take in this Weather the necessary Exercise to make the Blood circulate on foot.—Believe me ever most sincerely, My Dearest Madam, Your most affectionate and Dutiful Son, etc., etc.,   ARTHUR DUFF.' (O.)

The same to the same

'SUFFOLK STREET, 16th Jan. 1779.

' MY DEAREST MADAM,—I apprehend as I have not had a letter from your Ladyship since Monday, that the Snow in Scotland has considerably encreased, and indeed we had this morning a smart shower, but it has gone off, and did not prevent me from taking a round of Kensington Gardens, which I do almost every Day, and find the good effects of it at Four o'Clock, but I believe I must discontinue the Practice after Tuesday, as late nights are expected, and I would not be able to hold out without a dinner, which now the Coffee House is burnt down, could not easily be obtained consistent with attendance—Mortimer writes me the Gardener feeds the Partridges, I wish you would desire Him to count them and let me know their number, which should I think be pretty considerable, as I only killed Eleven last Season, I wish you would desire Him to lay some Corn about the Manoch Hill, as it will draw those at a distance into the Park, and tis there I wish them to breed next year as the Grass below it will be the last out. . . . Mr. Leslie had a letter from the Admiral this week,[1] He and the Children continue in good Health, I understand His Prize Money amounts to several Thousands. I have nothing more to add this Post, but best wishes to my Brother, Mrs. Duff and Fanny, remaining always Most affectionately, etc.,
'A. D.' (O.)

He seems to have taken his duties very seriously, as he frequently alludes to the long sittings and late nights, also to his long walks in search of fresh air, and when on one occasion he took out his kinsman, Lachlan Duff, and was obliged to leave him, he wondered if he would ever find his way home again. He lived in Suffolk Street, apparently in rooms, and had with him a manservant from Rothiemay who had a ' sleeping place under the stairs, without a fire or a window,' and when the unfortunate youth fell ill, 1777, of a ' putrid fever,' presumably typhus, some surprise is expressed by his master that the ' people of the house ' insisted upon his removal for fear of infection, but ' no doubt he will get better air and attendance elsewhere.' Lady Fife is, of course, in an agony of appre-

---

[1] Lady Helen had recently died.

hension lest her darling should catch the infection, but this apparently was avoided.

He sends her frequent comments on the news of the day, the progress of the American War and Lord North's attempts to govern the country, and the intractability of the opposition. In December 1778 : 'The present minority would be in every sense contemptible, but that their abandoned principles rouses other emotions, many of them do not scruple to avow that they wish to see the country a province to France to mark the imbecility of the present Administration and make the Nation repent when too late that they had not been called into Power. From such patriots, Good Lord, deliver us ! '

In April 1777 he tells his mother, 'We have now paid his Majesty's debts, at the expense of a very severe cold to your humble servant, for I could get no carriage home this morning when I left the House.' 'The weather of London would kill the Devil could we get him here.'

'A late night at the House—I did not dine till between 12 and 1 at night. Fine hours for a poor farmer ! ' He also sends her notes of matters literary and dramatic. 'When Mrs. Siddons performs the whole town crowds and with good reason, for she is a most capital performer, greater by much than any I have ever seen, not excepting Garrick.' He frequently sends her plays to read and daily or weekly newspapers. She has to confess that she does not read much. Doubtless she was too notable a housekeeper, and also was much occupied with the care of the various married daughters who lived in the neighbourhood, and of the grandchildren consigned to her care.

Arthur is consulted in all family difficulties and is applied to for news of his brothers, George and Lewis, both poor correspondents. In January 1779 he writes : ' I have not seen George this some days, but we have been taken for other several times since we met. A lady the other day inquired at me after Mrs. Duff, and my children and if they were yet gone to school, and an old friend of mine made up to him at the Smyrna and by that means found me out here.' In the same letter, ' When next I goe to the city I will buy Miss Monkey a pretty pack of cards.'

When George had an accident and broke his leg, he removed to Putney and then to Hanwell Heath for the sake of his health ; Arthur complains of its being too far for a morning's call, and moreover a fifteen shillings coach hire.

When Arthur at length retired from Parliament, on being appointed Comptroller of Excise in Scotland, April 4, 1779, his resignation· was placed in the hands of his brother, Lord Fife, that the seat might be instantly filled by another member of his lordship's clan or circle of friends,

and thus the balance of parties might be preserved. Arthur then went
to live at Rothiemay with his mother, until her death, subsequently dividing
his time between that and his own estate of Orton in Morayshire He
never married. The following letter was written a few months before
his death, which occurred at Orton on June 2, 1805. He is buried in the
mausoleum at Duff House.

Arthur Duff of Orton to Lord Fife

'ORTON, 19th Jany 1805

' MY LORD,—I hoped to have been able as usual to have addressed your
Lop. with the compliments of the Season ; but these days were long past before
I had the ability. My usual Xmas Party was so obliging as come here but I
was obliged to name a Landlord and go to bed after drinking the Health of the
Company in a single glass of Madeira nor have I yet exceeded Three or tasted
Port but a single glass to success to my Fishing Bargain. . . . I have now
had a very tedious confinement not being once over the door since the 6th of
December: I have however never lost hope nor spirits.

' With every good wish to your Lordship I remain, with great truth and
regard, Your Lordships very affectionate Brother and much obliged Humble
Servt.,   ARTHUR DUFF.' (D.)

There is a charming portrait of him in the possession of Mrs. Chancellor.

George Duff, Elgin, to Lord Fife

'ELGIN, 12th June 1805.

' MY LORD,—I had the honor of your letter of the 10th of this month by
yesterday's post which gave me great pleasure to hear that you had arrived safe
and in good health at Duff House : I have not been well for sometime or would
have attended the funeral on Tuesday. Arthur's death has hurt me much, in
him I lost not only a Brother but a sincere and affectionate friend. This has
been a very disagreeable year to me, God grant that it may end better . wishing
your Lordship Health and all happiness, I always with great regard, My Lord,
Your affectionate Brother,   GEO. DUFF.' (D.)

The youngest daughter, LADY MARGARET, born in 1745, when her mother
was forty, seems to have been the most unlucky of the whole family.
At twenty-two, in 1767, she made a runaway match with Brodie of Brodie,
but was unhappy in her married life, and suffered from constant ill-health.
In 1773 her mother writes, ' Margaret's days will not be long.' Her name
never occurs in the family letters except in connection with some trouble
or other.   At the time of her marriage her brother, Lord Fife, writes with
a curious air of detachment : ' I am informed Mr. Brodie and Lady Mar-

ARTHUR DUFF OF ORTON

By George Watson

garet have stole a marriage—I wonder neither the one nor the other chose
to drop me a little civil note. However, their want of discretion gives me
no pain. I wish they may pass a happy life together.' She had five
children, from whom, however, she does not seem to have derived much
happiness, and the financial state of the family was pitiable. Margaret
writes a long letter to her brother James from Newcastle, undated, stating
that they are unable even to keep a servant. She does not mention what
they were doing in that locality, but goes on to explain that Brodie's affairs
are in a very bad way, but he ' hopes to save something for the children.'
They had hired a ship to convey them home, ' but the press gang was so
hot upon the river that the crew were obliged to come ashore and take
shelter in the houses.'   (D.)

    The children were :

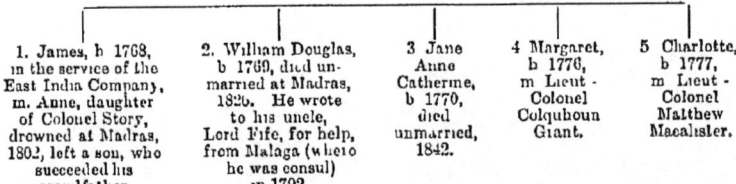

| 1. James, b 1768, in the service of the East India Company, m. Anne, daughter of Colonel Story, drowned at Madras, 1802, left a son, who succeeded his grandfather. | 2. William Douglas, b 1769, died unmarried at Madras, 1826. He wrote to his uncle, Lord Fife, for help, from Malaga (where he was consul) in 1792 | 3 Jane Anne Catherine, b 1770, died unmarried, 1842. | 4 Margaret, b 1776, m Lieut - Colonel Colquhoun Grant. | 5 Charlotte, b 1777, m Lieut - Colonel Matthew Macalister. |

She made frequent long visits to Rothiemay, where her mother tried
to nurse her back to health, but the rest of the family found these visits
extremely trying, and avoided the house during their duration. Lewis
writes that she has no visible appetite, and recommends the procuring of
ass's milk for her. He laments that he and his wife can see her so seldom
when she is at home, though such near neighbours, they not being on good
terms with her husband, while James, Lord Fife, frankly announces that
he will not go home while she is there (in 1775). ' Her temper and health
by indulgence in caprice is brought into a terrible state. She eats nothing
but a little bread and Sallery, and that little at every time requires an
hour's coaxing I think she must soon succeed in putting her period to
her day.' In the following year she nearly died at Rothiemay of ' strong
fainting fits and vomiting of blood,' and in 1777 Lady Fife writes : ' She
is just in the same situation that she was in last year at Rothiemay, and
a horrid one it was.'

Lady Margaret Brodie to her mother, Jane, Lady Fife

'BRODIE HOUSE, 11th *January* 1777

  ' MY DEAR MADAM,—I am very sorry to hear by your letter that you have
been so ill since you went to Ed^r I sincerely wish to hear that you may now begin .

getting the Better of your Complaints. Altho this is a very Bad time for one that is ailing, but your Ladyship is in a Place where you can have Proper assistance. I am very Glad to hear that Poor Fanny is Better, as Your Ladyship does not mention Lady Sophia I am in hopes she is well, I am anxious to hear how the nurseing agrees with her, I hope it does not fatigue her too much, a great deal depends upon The Way that the Child is in, I beg my Best Respects to Mr. Wharton and Lady Sophia. Wishing your Ladyship and them many Happy Returns of the Season, and shall only add that I hope soon to hear that your Ladyship is Better, being with Great Respect your most affect. Daughter and oblig^d humble Servant, MARGARET BRODIE.' (R.)

In the year 1787 she met her death by an unfortunate accident, being burnt to death in her own bedroom. Her youngest child, aged nine, who was with her, escaped from the room, and Brodie himself, who slept in the room above, rushed to her assistance, but was too late to save her. He wrote next day to Major the Hon. Lewis Duff at Rothiemay, per express :

'Brodie House, five o'clock Saturday morning.—My dear sir, what language shall I use to tell you that my dear Lady Margaret was alive and well four hours ago, but is now upon eternity. Her death was occasioned by her cloathes taking fire as she was going into bed. I can dictate no more—but I am sure you will not only sympathise with me, but you or my dear Arthur will hurry immediately to your truly afflicted and miserable
J. BRODIE.'

A letter written by Arthur Duff to Lord Fife gives further details : ' She had the whole day been remarkably cheerful and particularly funny and droll, as you know she could be at times. She played at cards till supper, and sat up with the gentlemen till eleven, when they all parted being to hunt next morning near Nairn. She had custom of reading at night after going to her own room and had once before set fire to her cloths, which made Brodie order her maid never to leave her till the candle was extinguished. Unfortunately the girl was that night ill, and having been ten years in her service Lady Margaret's humanity was too much interested to allow her to sit up farther. The child, Charlotte, was in bed, but declares she had not been to sleep ; that she had frequently called to her mother to come to bed, but that she always answered, ' Be quiet, ye little fool, don't disturb me. I am reading.' That at last she saw her mother all in a blaze come towards the bed, which she set in flames, and fell down at the foot of it ; that she herself flew to a closet for safety, but not being able to get the door shut, made her way through the flames to the room door, and by her shrieks she alarmed her father and two servants, who came at

the same instant. Brodie came down in his shirt and rushed into the room, sought Lady Margaret first in her bed, then in her chair at the fire, and found her at last among his feet at the foot of the bed, and brought her out in his arms all in a blaze, and had the presence of mind to roll her in the carpet of her dressing-room. But alas, too late, the soul was fled.'

The portrait of Lady Margaret, like that of her sister Catherine, was in the Duff House collection, and now hangs at Montcoffer. There is another at Brodie Castle.

Of the fourteen children of Lord Braco there were, in the next generation, forty-five descendants:

William,	born	1724, died	1753, unmarried.
Anne,	,,	1725, ,,	1805, two children.
Janet,	,,	1727, ,,	1758, eight children.
James,	,,	1729, ,,	1809, no issue.
Alexander,	,,	1731, ,,	1811, seven children.
Jane,	,,	1732, ,,	1776, six children.
George,	,,	1736, ,,	1818, four children.
Lewis,	,,	1737, ,,	1811, no issue.
Patrick,	,,	1738, ,,	1738, died young.
Helen,	,,	1739, ,,	1778, six children.
Sophia,	,,	1740, ,,	1820, seven children.
Catherine,	,,	1741, ,,	1765, unmarried.
Arthur,	,,	1743, ,,	1805, unmarried.
Margaret,	,,	1745, ,,	1787, five children.

INNES HOUSE

CHAPTER XI

JAMES DUFF, SECOND EARL FIFE

JAMES, second Earl Fife, was born on September 29, 1729, being the second son and fourth child of William, afterwards first Earl Fife. The first reference to him is in a letter from his mother to his father, dated March 1731 : ' Jamie has gone alone these two days past and has got two more teeth. It is a plague to keep him out of your room.' An anecdote is related of this same Earl James, showing the boy as father to the man. During the time that the family lived at Balvenie, he and another brother had been allowed to go to a fair at Dufftown (then known as Laighie), and each given a shilling to spend. The brother, presumably Sandie, who being two years younger, was less cautious, soon spent his fairing, but James brought the money home again, remarking that ' he had seen naething he liket better nor the shilling.' [1]

His elder brother, William Duff, sometimes styled the Master of Braco,

---

[1] *Memorials of John Geddes, being Record of life in an Upland Glen*, 1797-1881, privately printed 1899 by Sir William Duguid Geddes, Principal of Aberdeen University, son of John Geddes.

died in London in 1753, and James is also occasionally alluded to as ' the Master.' Upon his father being raised to the earldom of Fife in 1759, the eldest son assumed the courtesy title of Viscount Macduff. Little is known of his early youth, but it appears that he was educated chiefly at home by tutors, and subsequently went to the University of St. Andrews (as did all his younger brothers), and afterwards travelled abroad.

In the additional MSS. British Museum there are several letters written by James, when a young man and still Lord Macduff, addressed to the Duke of Newcastle and his secretary. In one he asks for the office of sheriff for a friend, naïvely adding that this is the first favour he has asked since he ' came into Parliament.' In 1755, on starting for a tour abroad, he asks for letters of recommendation for Brussels, Hanover, Berlin, Dresden, and Vienna, remarking that he does not like to ask for *more* at the same time, but will beg to write again, later. In 1760 he writes to bespeak the interest of the Duke to obtain for him the office of Lord of the Bedchamber to the Duke of York.

He married, in 1759, Lady Dorothea Sinclair, only child of the ninth Earl of Caithness,[1] and got with her a dowry of £40,000, but did not, as he is believed to have expected, succeed to the title and estates, which went to a younger branch. Of this union there were no children, which was a source of great disappointment, and probably led to the disagreements and unhappiness which finally culminated in 1794 in a separation, Lady Fife retiring to live at Hermitage House, Leith, where she died in 1818, nine years after her husband. One letter of hers to her husband is preserved in the family correspondence. It is brief but affectionate :

' BATH, 15th *January* 1770.

' MY DEAR LORD,—I wrote to Lord Rosebery last night, three lines, but it was too late for the post. It seems it goes away at eight o'clock on Sunday nights. I shall be very anxious to hear how you do and how you got to London.—I am, affectionately yours,   D. FIFE.

' To the Earl of Fife, Whitehall, London.'   (*R.*)

And one from her to her lawyer, Mr. Mitchelson, written only in the following year :

' EDINR., *Dec. 3rd*, 1771.

' SIR,—I shall be glad if you can send me two hundred or a hundred pounds just now to be accounted for when its convenient ; it need not be mentioned

---

[1] The ninth Earl of Caithness ' devised his own estate and that of Murkle, failing his own heirs-male, and those of his brother Francis, and the younger sons of his daughter the Countess of Fife (if she had any), to George Sinclair of Woodhall.'

or any one acquainted with it but as necessity requires, and would rather than give a receipt that you put down the date of sending me the money and I will do the same which will do as well—I hope I will get this demand that I make answered, otherwise I shall be in great streats.   I shall send a person I can trust to receive it—I have immediate occasion for the largest sum I have mentioned, and more if I could get it.—I am, Sir, etc.,   D. FIFE.'

Letter from the Countess of Caithness (Margaret, daughter of Archibald, first Earl of Rosebery and mother of the Countess) about the allowance made by Lord Fife to his wife, after the separation. It is undated :

'My lady Caithness Compliment to mr. Mitchilson beg to know if he has payed Lady Fife last quarty, whitsunday to mr. Tytler or not.   She think it is most untolerable if it not payed, but my lady is persuaded that mr. Tytler has got it long before this, but to be serton she begs mr. Mitchilson would be so good as let her know yea or no.

'my lady will be very happay to hear that mrs. Mitchelson is better as she ernestly wish her good health, booth for her owen sak and ther friends.'

A large amount of correspondence on this subject has been preserved, tending to show Lord Fife in a very amiable light. He seems to have done his best to put up with his wife's constant changes of plans and her caprices, and finally to have made her a handsome allowance.

Viscount Macduff was of great assistance to his father in the management of the latter's vast estate, and on Earl William's death in 1763 he succeeded to large tracts of land in Aberdeenshire, Banffshire, and Morayshire.   The following letter to his father from London in 1759 is interesting :

'LONDON, 1759.

'MY LORD,—I would have wrote you last post, but believ'd you to be upon the road, so I hope this will find Lady Braco and you in perfect health after an agreeable journey.   I have all the reason in the World to be satisfied with my present situation, I flatter myself that my Conduct is agreeable to my friends and I do hope they will shew some publick marks of their Esteem for me ; our Shirif I believe will be return'd and Mr. Cockburn will have no Shirfship so far, for a publick mark of disatisfaction for his Conduct and all this will be brought about without my ever having ask'd it or indeed hardly told my story, for they were all very much master of it, on my coming to town I found there was hardly a circumstance they did not know.   There has been a great desire to confer some mark of Esteem on Your Family, the day before yesterday Mr. Pit told me he intended to ask the King to creat you an Earl in the Kingdom of Ireland, this I give you my word I never suggested to him either by myself or any other, I do think it is a very great thing as it will give your Family high rank, and it is the proper step to something else if that ever should be practicable, for there is hardly an instance of an Irish Baron being created an English Peer but after

his being first rais'd to a higher rank, severals I could name you, since the little time I have been here and this things being dun without yours and my asking is certainly very handsome as it shews the County the Esteem you are in. I had no time to wait for your answer, as its probable some other may be nam'd Successor in room of the Duke of Devonshire as Lord Lieut. of Irland in a very little time, so I told Mr. Pit that I believed the tittle that would be most agreable to you would be Earl of Braco and Baron Duff, however if the thing should not be don till I can receive your answer, if there is any other tittle more agreable to you, be so good as acquaint me and it shall regulate me. You will easily judge the improprcity of mentioning this to any body till such time as his Majesty says yes to it, so——' [*The remainder of this letter is lost.*] (O.)

During his father's lifetime, James lived at Duff House, near Banff,[1] a house which his father had built from the designs of the elder Adam at the cost of £70,000, but always refused to live there, and indeed never finished it.

In 1754, Lord Fife, then James Duff, entered Parliament as M.P. for Banffshire, and continued to sit as member for that county after he succeeded his father in the title of Lord Fife, as he was, up to 1790, only a peer of Ireland. He was re-elected in 1761, 1774, and 1780. In 1784 he resigned his seat to his natural son, Sir James Duff of Kinstair, but did not abandon his parliamentary work, as in that year he was elected member for Morayshire. In a letter of the period he says his desire would be to have ' himself sitting for Morayshire and relatives for Banff and the Elgin boroughs.'

He was of immense political power, and is said to have controlled the elections in the three counties in which he had property, viz. Banffshire, Aberdeenshire, and Morayshire. That entertaining work, *The Political State of Scotland in 1788* (edited by Sir Charles Adam), states that in Banff-shire ' The Duke of Gordon and the Earl of Fife (and indeed the Earl of Fife singly) overshadow all the small and independent proprietors,' and of the 122 votes then existing in this county, gives 50 as belonging to (' votes of ') Lord Fife, *i.e.* his tenants and members of his family, and about a

---

[1] This fine mansion was presented to the town of Banff by the late Duke of Fife, and was recently, with some alterations, turned into an hotel, and later into a sanatorium (see page 225).

The Rev. Richard Pococke, D D , Lord Bishop of Meath, visited Banff during his tour in Scotland in July 1760, and mentions Lord Macduff, Lord Fife's eldest son, as inhabiting Duff House.

The following quotation from Boswell's *Johnson* is interesting in this connection: 'On Aug 25, 1773, we got at night to Banff I sent Joseph on to Duff House, but Earl Fife was not at home, which I regretted much, as we should have had a very elegant reception from his Lordship We found here but an indifferent inn '

Three years after Johnson, Wesley was in Banff, and in 1787 Burns passed through it on his northern tour, and also visited Duff House.

dozen more who are in some way or other pledged to, or connected with him, besides the so-called independent voters and partisans of Hay of Mountblairy, son of his brother-in-law and Hay of Rannes, also a connection. In Morayshire he heads the list with 27 votes to the Duke's 21, and in Aberdeenshire, out of the 178, 83 are entered as ' votes of Lord Fife,' while a great number of the 89 ' individual voters ' lean to his side.[1]

The house of Duff has provided a great many members of Parliament, covering a period of over three hundred years (1593 to 1893) :

George Duff of Cullen	Scottish Parliament,	. . .	. 1593
William Duff . . .	Scottish Parliament, for Inverness, .		1681–1682
Alexander Duff of Braco .	,, ,,	,, Banffshire, .	1689–1705
Alexander Duff of Drummuir,	,, ,,	,. Inverness, .	1702–1707
Also sat in first British Parliament for Inverness Burghs, .		.	1708–1710
William Duff of Braco (afterwards first Lord Fife)	Banffshire,	.	1727–1734
James Duff (afterwards second Lord Fife) . {	Banffshire,	.	1754–1784
	Morayshire,	.	1784–1790
Arthur Duff of Orton . . .	. .	Morayshire,	1774–1779
Sir James Duff of Kinstair . . .	. .	Banffshire,	1784–1789
Sir William Duff-Gordon .	.	Worcester,	1807–1815
James Duff (afterwards fourth Lord Fife) .	.	Banffshire,	1818–1826
Sir Alexander Duff of Delgaty	. .	Elgin Burghs, .	1826–1831
James Duff (afterwards fifth Lord Fife) .	.	Banffshire,	1837–1857
George Skene Duff	.	Elgin Burghs, .	1847–1857
Lachlan Gordon Duff . . .	.	Banffshire,	1857–1861
Sir Mountstuart Grant Duff . .	.	Elgin Burghs, .	1857–1881
Robert William Duff of Fetteresso .	.	Banffshire,	1861–1893
Colonel James Duff . . .	. .	Norfolk, .	1876–1878
Alexander William George Duff (afterwards Duke of Fife)			Moray and Nairn, 1874–1879

It will thus be seen that Banffshire was, for an aggregate of one hundred and eleven years, represented by a Duff, the county of Moray for fifteen years, and Elgin Burghs for thirty years.

Lord Fife was very active in his parliamentary duties, being a constant attendant in the House of Commons, and made many excellent and well-reasoned speeches, of which the papers of the day speak with great approval.

In a letter to his factor, William Rose, dated May 4, 1773, he writes :

---

[1] It was not always considered a compliment to receive a qualification to vote. Lord Fife wrote to Rev. William Duff, minister at Keig (a relative, see chapter on ' Ministers ') in September 1772 ' ' I propose giving you a vote in Banffshire during your life as a mark of my confidence.' Mr. Duff refused to accept. In 1807 William Rose's Morayshire vote was sold to Sir James Duff of Kinstair for £420.

'I sat next Lord Clive yesterday in the House, and heard him make a speech of two hours and twenty minutes. I have never heard so fine a one since I have sat in Parliament. I don't say there was much *matter* in it, nor perhaps was it prudent, for he sets all at defiance, but for language and composition, I never heard its equal.'

In 1763 James Duff succeeded his father as second Baron Fife, peerage of Ireland, and set about managing his large estates in the most enlightened manner. In a French biographical dictionary he is described as ' un grand agronome' (which word is further explained as meaning 'celui qui est versé dans les règles de la science agricole ; qui l'enseigne par ses paroles ou par ses écrits. Mot introduit dans la langue française à la fin du dix-huitième siècle '). He was looked upon as a most kind-hearted landlord at a time when it was not common to give much thought to the welfare of small tenants. In later years,[1] when the crops failed, and there was a great scarcity of grain and exorbitant prices ruled, so that the poor in the north were threatened with famine, he allowed his tenants a reduction of twenty per cent. on their rents, and imported cargoes of corn from England which he sold to the poor below the market price, at a loss to himself of £3000, even supplying it gratis to those who were unable to pay, and lists still exist of his poorer tenants with the numbers of children in each family, and the requisite amount of meal for each.

The two following letters give other glimpses of his relations with his tenants and dependants :

Lord Fife to W. Rose, his factor

'WHITEHALL, *Jan.* 12*th,* 1773.

' Your letter from Auchingoul dont tell me whether you are married or not, however I suppose so, as I imagine the journey in the morning ended with that at night. I write this to you both, that I very serious wish you happy, and that I do forsee you have much to combate with, which nothing but Spirit and determined resolution can get the better of. In the first place, resolve not to set yourselves up on a footing of visiting or receiving visits except to those with whom you have business and any thing thats to spear give it to your farm. Mrs. Rose must cheerfully join in the plan, and be a most notable active Housewife in the Family, and learn to ride. You must settle your own plan, and be constant to it, be in love with it and not follow other's example. An exact Economy must preside both within and without doors, you know I hate avarice, I only wish to see those I love prudent above all things, avoid a paltry affectation of finery, let your men servants continue at your farm, and dont be disgraced by having a maid servant to wait on yourself and friends at *table.* I shall be very

---

[1] 1782, 1783.

sorry if you dont gain that horrid misfortunate character of giving your visitors too little Drink. Remember your time on your estate wont permitt you to sit at dinner from 3 till morning in the Banff stile, and the *Purse* and *Constitution* will very soon be ended if dissipation takes place. I shall be wonderfully pleas'd to see you thrive and be happy, if you go on in a wrong stile you had better let me look at it rather than *hide* it, as I may give a friendly hint of amendment, and there are many that wont be sorry to see me have no credit from my *People.* You know I never scold, and that I hate Complaining, so if you are in an improper way, I have too much to do to be a Preacher—but I pray God to direct you both and make you happy which will give much pleasure to, Dear Rose, Your affectionate,   FIFE.' (*R*)

To the Same

' *March* 13*th*, 1774.

' My firm resolution is ever to stand in support of an honest, trusty servant, even should that character be attended with many faults and inconveniences. If I cannot put up with their service, I will wish to provide for them. But if one is dishonest or deceitful, I will not prosecute ; leave him to God Almighty and his own conscience ; but I will forget him and have nothing to do with him. If his dishonesty is so evident as to make it a public duty to prosecute him, I will give way to it, but if only a little picking thief, let him run off with his dirty pelf. Be rigidly economical without the least mixture of avarice. I hope I can give away money, when either my pleasure, amusement, or even disagreeable politics require it, or to promote the worthy or to relieve distress. I most anxiously wish never to be cheated or, what is worse, to permit of little smuggling unnecessary expense which neither adds to my honour nor interest. I have ever laboured to be thankful to God for the many blessings I enjoy very undeservedly, to bear with patience and resignation the disagreeable things through life, to support my spirits under their afflictions, and to avoid puffing in prosperity nor repining nor claiming pity when things are disagreeable.'   (*R*)

The town of Macduff, formerly known as Doune, owes its rise and its formation into a burgh entirely to Lord Fife. Owing to the good harbour which he built, the town has long been much more prosperous than its older neighbour, Banff.

In private life he had the reputation of being a hard man, but was merely exact and precise in his accounts. He appears to have inherited in a marked degree his father's business ability, integrity, and firmness, somewhat tempered perhaps by the softer qualities of his mother, to whom, like all her children, he was devotedly attached. A certain pride of seniority and position, of which his younger brothers complain in their early letters (see chapter on the ' Children of first Earl Fife ') seems to

have completely worn off as he grew older and wiser, and became, besides, something of a philosopher.

In an otherwise dull letter to his factor he writes : ' You know my maxim, to *make the best of what we cannot mend.*' (*R.*)

A few years after succeeding to the estates he made a tour on the Continent. In a letter to his factor he says :

' I have been making a tour for ten days over a great part of Luxembourg and the countries betwixt France and Germany on horseback. I have rode through many woods just like the woods in Mar, only this difference, that they are more extensive and fine oaks and beeches are large as any firs. They destroy and cut them pretty much in the same way, and cut them very far from the ground, by which much of the tree is lost. I desire that you will be attentive that the things are done right at Mar Lodge, as I shall certainly pass a month or two next summer in that place, and give as strict order as possible about the game everywhere. I am resting just now, the heat of the day, having rode eighteen miles before nine o'clock. I shall get to Spa to-morrow night.' (*R.*)

A little later he visited Ireland :

'DUBLIN, *June* 8, 1782.

' I have seen everything here, heard all their best speeches in both houses, seen all the Volunteers in this quarter, din'd, visit'd, and ball'd at all the great Houses. Seen everything there is at the Castle and dined with the Lieut. and his family party.' (*R.*)

Large as was the property to which he succeeded on his father's death, he, nevertheless, nearly doubled the family estates by judicious purchases in Aberdeenshire, Banffshire, and Morayshire. Among these purchases were portions of the estates of Innes, Inchbroom, Dunkinty, and Leuchars, all from the Innes family, and from the family of Brodie, Spynie, Monaughty, and Aslisk, while Leggat was taken over for a bad debt. In 1777 he acquired by excambion from the Duke of Gordon the lands of Ardgay.[1]

He was one of the pioneers of afforestation, having planted fourteen thousand acres of barren ground. He was most anxious these estates should not be divided, and in 1769 writes thus to his brother Arthur :

'DUFF HOUSE, *Nov.* 22nd, 1769.

' DEAR ARTHUR,—I have considered with great Deliberation and attention the Family Settlements, and I find that upon the failure of my Brothers and their Sons, all the Lands contain'd in the Tailie of Braco would go to a different series of Heirs, and the Lands contain'd in the Tailie of Mar would go on to my

---

[1] A later excambion between Duke of Gordon and Earl of Fife gives the Duke's lands excambed as Davoch of Grange, Kintrae, Urquhart, etc The Earl's, Garmouth, Corskie, Essle, etc. Dipple and Essle were exchanged for Grange, to suit both parties, as being contiguous to their other lands

Brothers Daughters and so on to my Sisters. Should it please God that this
event took place, the Estate would be intirely disconnected and disjoined and
all the pains taken by my Grandfather, father and self to connect the Estate,
intirely at an end, besides there would be endles Law sutes in the family about
the discription of different Lands.   I find there is a power by the Entail of
Braco that will mend this, so I want that my Brothers and I should do what
we can to prevent the Estates from separating and that in case of the failure of
my Brothers and their Sons, all the Lands in the Entail of Braco should be
settl'd in the Substitution as in the Entail of Mar, it is impossible to be more
explicate by a letter, but in case you see my Brothers before I do, from what
has past in conversation you will be able to explain the matter fully to them and
there is no time to be lost in setting about the necessary forms to get this matter
put right, as if one of us should die, the thing will not then be so easy ; in the
mean time I shall get proper advice what is the most proper way to execute it,
so as when my Brothers and I meet we may be able to do it, you will see it very
proper that this matter is keept private, as those who have very distant concern
might be allarmed, and give us trouble.—Your affec., etc.,   FIFE.' (R)

When in Scotland he resided alternately at Duff House, Banff, Mar
Lodge, Aberdeenshire, and Innes House, near Elgin.   From the latter he
writes on December 10, 1775 : ' Her Grace of Gordon was walking over
the Elgin market last Wednesday recruiting. I think no very creditable
employment for the Dutchess.' [1]

He was kind and hospitable to his neighbours, though he was always
considered to stand a good deal on his dignity with them, as well as with
the members of his family.

As there was no family mansion in London, Lord Fife bought a piece
of land in Whitehall, a part of the garden of old Whitehall Palace, and there
built a fine residence, which he called Fife House.   So true a Scot was he
that he is stated to have brought up to London, by sea, several cartloads
of Banffshire soil for the foundations of his house, as well as the stone,
timber, and shrubs for the garden, so that though he resided for a great
part of the year in England, his house stood on Scottish ground.   There
was a charming picture of Fife House in the Duff House collection   It
was built in 1772, of course before the existence of the Embankment, and
had a beautiful garden running down to the river   In May 1776 he writes
that ' the thrushes and blackbirds there make it quite cheerful. What
more could I have in the country ? ' [2]

[1] The Duchess, Jane Maxwell, was at that date raising a company for the Fraser Highlanders for her brother, Captain Maxwell

[2] The Earl of Liverpool leased it from Lord Fife's executors and lived there, and died in
the house, when Prime Minister, in 1828.   The house was pulled down in May 1869, but the
Duff arms are still to be seen over the doorway of the corner house in Whitehall Court.

In 1790 there was a robbery at Fife House. Lord Fife writes : ' The diamonds taken are worth about £100. All my coins and medals were in the same place, but very luckily they have not touched them. There are also left rings and diamonds that were in the place with the others.' Lord Fife suspected his porter of the robbery.

In the following spring his Lordship thus describes his London household : ' My Family consists at present of Rose, a colt, a new master of the household, a German footman who neither speaks English nor French, a Swiss footman, John, coachman, and his new horses, a new postilion, Thomas Reid, gardener, colt at the door, a new lady's woman, a French cook, and three housemaids. Don't you think I have much to do with the lot ? and yet I hope I shall break the whole lot in.'　　(*R.*)

He was a good deal at Court, and says in a letter, 1790, ' I am just going to the dining-room to take my leave of the King and Queen, and to see a very extraordinary thing, which is Madame d'Albany, the Pretender's widow, presented to the King and Queen.[1] It is very interesting, that if this unfortunate family had its own way this lady would have been Queen Dowager this day.'

Again he writes to his factor from Whitehall : ' I was yesterday at Court to wish their Majesties a good New Year, and kissed both their hands on being appointed (by myself !) to go to Paris for a few weeks. Put my letters under cover to Abraham, and direct " à Milord Comte de Fife." Don't put any covers on your letter but the paper you write on.' Eight days after he writes from Paris : ' There is nothing but everything gay and good-humoured. I go to the opera to-morrow to see the Queen, and shall next week go to Versailles to their Majesties.'

On January 28, Lord Fife wrote from Paris : ' There has been such a fall of snow and hard frost that there has been nothing like it since the year '40. It is still likely to continue, and freezing as hard as ever. I am vastly well amused here in a most agreeable society. You would be surprised to see the Queen here dancing our country dances better than anybody in Banffshire. She was much flattered with my praising her.'

In 1788, when nearly sixty, he writes : ' I am always at my table in the morning a little after five o'clock. Reading or writing is over before breakfast. The forenoon employed in exercise or direction out of doors. For society, if that is not always amusing, books are preferred, I state this to you to tempt you to come to me.' [2]

He was on most friendly terms with His Majesty King George III.

---

[1] Louisa de Stolberg, widow of Prince Charles Edward Stewart. He died in 1788, she in 1824

[2] From a letter written to Arthur Young, author of the famous pre-revolution *Travels in France*, with whom Lord Fife had much correspondence about agriculture and farming, in

James, Lord Fife, to William Rose, factor at Banff

'WHITEHALL, *March 10th,* 1789

' I wrote you of the two gracious messages the King sent me last week. He had a levee Saturday, and at the time he was seeing everybody, the infamous papers was allarming the country that he was ill. I went down yesterday.[1] He had most of the Privy Council with him from ten till near one o'clock. I saw the Queen, who was vastly gracious to me. I rather wished to avoid troubling the King, but only to see him ; a little before one o'clock he came out and mounted his horse, which he had not done since October. I need not hint to you how my heart warmed when I saw him. I went to the other side of the road rather to see it and not be seen. His eye catched me, and he directly called out before all the people that was there : " Lord Fife, I am glad to see you. How do you do ? Come forward. I am realy glad to see you, and I hope you are quite well." All this I bore as became me with grateful thanks. He then called out : " Lord Fife, you are no gambler. You are no rat." I then forgot all distance between King and subject, and went up and took him by the thigh on horseback, prayed the Almighty God to bliss him, and I aded : " Yes, Sir, I am a gambler at this moment ; the greatest stake I have is on that Horse, and, for God sake, take care of it, and don't ride too hard." My eyes were full of tears. He thanked me and added, " I will take care of number one. You have been good to number one." He then called for the different Park keys, and took those where he intended to ride, giving directions. All this was publick, so it did me more honor than if it had been in his closset. I saw Sir George Young, who was with him after he returned from his ride, and he was exceedingly well. Indeed his whole appearance astonished me. I never saw him look better. . . . The King has ordered all the Foreign Ministers to attend him to-morrow. You see what a share I have of the second sight by not desponding. Lord Dover is to have Lord Lothian's gold stick, and Lord Delawarr to be Lord of Bed-chamber in place of the rat Queensberry, who ran to France. This shows you that Dukedoms, great fortune, and ribbonds does not secure esteem, unless honor and virtue attends them ' (*Annals of Banff*).[2]

In 1789 Lord Fife writes : ' It is a pleasure to see the gratitude of the public to that amiable Prince, in both playhouses they every night oblige them to play and sing " God save great George our King." The galleries would pull the house down if they did not do it.' And on April 13, 1789 ·

---

the course of which he more than once apologises for the two months of autumn ' idled ' in sport (British Museum MSS.).

    [1] To Kew Palace

    [2] Banff Town Council Minutes   The Council (March 13, 1789) sent an address to the King, congratulating him on his recovery, and the Council appointed a general illumination in the whole houses within the burgh in the evening, in order to express their satisfaction upon the happy event of his Majesty's recovery

' I wish this thanksgiving at St. Paul's was over. The King is positive to go. He had, in an interval of recollections (of which he had many during the delirium), fallen on his knees and prayed to God that if ever he was returned to reason he should take the most publick manner of returning thanks to God, and this he has often repeated and now adheres to.'

May 10, 1791, London : ' I adore Burke for his pamphlet and his speech. He dined with me Sunday, and I filled a bumper to " Mr. Burke and the British Constitution." '

Being on the most intimate terms with Pitt and Pelham, as is shown by many references in his letters, and having been very assiduous in his parliamentary attendances, and faithful to the ministry throughout the King's illness, he was in 1790 raised to the peerage of England by the title of Earl Fife of the United Kingdom, and thus terminated his career as a member of the House of Commons But his activity did not abate, and he was equally constant in his attendances at the House of Lords. During the celebrated trial of Warren Hastings for malpractices in India, Lord Fife was one of the peers chosen as judges (he was junior but one), and at the conclusion of the evidence gave his opinion, with the majority, as ' Not Guilty, upon my honour.' [1]

In 1801 he made an excellent speech in the House of Lords on the conduct of the war, emphatically deploring the waste of public money, and the subsidising of foreign powers.

During the latter years of his life, having no son to succeed him, he took great interest in his nephews, James and Alexander Duff, the sons of his next brother Alexander, who succeeded as third Earl Fife. He had these boys to stay with him constantly, both at Duff House and in London, and doubtless influenced their future careers—the elder and the son of the younger eventually succeeding as fourth and fifth earls respectively.

In several early letters Lord Fife complains of east winds, etc., affecting his eyes, and as early as 1788 he writes to his factor about ' the account with Mr. Dollond, optician ' ; the affection, whatever it was, became much worse, and for the last nine years of his life he was quite blind, and had to dictate all his letters and be led about by attendants, but his faculties and activity of mind were unimpaired to the last. His blindness was the cause of an action in the Court of Session in 1816 about his will, as it was alleged that his hand was held while signing it, and that he was not fully aware of the contents, since it was only read over to him ; but the provisions contained in it were eventually allowed to stand.

---

[1] His distant relative, General Patrick Duff of Carnousie, was a warm personal friend of Warren Hastings, and wrote him a congratulatory letter upon the acquittal becoming known, dated Carnousie, April 30, 1795. See chapter xxxi.

Lord Fife died at his house in Whitehall on January 24, 1809, aged eighty, and was buried in the mausoleum at Duff House.[1] He was succeeded by his brother Alexander (two years younger), who thus became third Earl Fife in the peerage of Ireland, the peerage of Great Britain, which was to descend to heirs-male of the body only, expiring with the second Earl, to whom it was granted.[2]

The *Gentleman's Magazine* gives the following account of Lord Fife : ' He was a man of sense, sound understanding, and pleasing manners. He lived in Magnificent style, both in Scotland and at his house in the Privy Gardens, Whitehall. In his person he was of the middle size, well made, and had been when young of a very agreeable figure.'

He was a patron of art, and purchased many portraits and pictures, with which he filled Duff House, Rothiemay, Innes, and Fife House ; a number of these were sold by the late Duke of Fife in 1907. Lord Fife privately printed a catalogue of the works of art in his possession in 1808, and dedicated it to Sir Benjamin West, P.R.A. Two copies of this, in MS., are in the British Museum. His great desire was to establish by indisputable evidence the antiquity of his family, which had, without doubt, sunk somewhat into obscurity four or five generations earlier. The family of Duff of Muldavit, of which James' great-great-grandfather was a younger son, was long resident near Cullen ; of this family there are authentic documentary records from about 1400 down to 1650, after which date the last Muldavit, who had sold his lands, died. The family had a burial-place in the churchyard of Cullen, and from there in the year 1792, on the completion of the mausoleum at Duff House, Lord Fife moved two stones. One, a recumbent effigy, which had lain in Cullen church, under the arch of a recessed tomb, and the other a flat stone adorned with the incised figure of a knight in armour. Beneath the latter were found some bones, which were also taken to Duff House.[3] The inscription on the incised stone now reads : ' Hic jacet Johanes Duf de Maldavat et Baldavi obiit 7 Julii 1404,' but appears to have been tampered with, as there

---

[1] ' Funeral of the Earl of Fife   On Thursday last the remains of the late Earl of Fife passed through this place in a hearse drawn by six horses, preceded by mutes, followed by the mourners in a mourning coach with four, his lordship's carriage with six, and several other carriages, in which were the gentlemen who accompanied the funeral to the family vault at Duff House, where, we understand, the body was on Saturday deposited ' (from the *Aberdeen Journal of a hundred years ago*, 1909)

[2] The late peer had three natural children, born before his marriage, viz General Sir James Duff of Kinstair, Major William Duff, and Jane or Jean Duff, who lived long at Scarborough   They are treated of in chapter xxxiv

[3] The letter from Lord Findlater's factor, authorising this removal, is dated April 13, 1792

JAMES DUFF, SECOND EARL FIFF

By Francis Cotes

is other lettering, now illegible, and, in his zeal to identify the John Duff there buried with the one mentioned in the earliest Muldavit charter given to him in 1792 by his cousin, Lord Findlater, Lord Fife had the date recut (and presumably altered), and unfortunately allowed the cutter to make use of Arabic figures, which would not have been used in a contemporary inscription. This oversight gave a handle to the criticism and scorn poured upon his claim to descend from the Duffs of Muldavit, by the late Dr. Cramond and others. The claim in itself was perfectly genuine, though the means he took to establish it were unfortunate. The whole question has been discussed in an earlier chapter. Lord Fife also moved, as he had every right to do, the monument and the body of his great-uncle, Alexander Duff of Braco, and those of his father and mother and niece Frances, from the old church of Grange, and, with less justification, another monument from Banff old churchyard, said to be that of Provost Douglas.

Among the Rose MS., Advocates' Library, Aberdeen, is a letter to John Alexander Cameron, from George Imlach, written evidently early in the present century, in which the writer says : ' In our history we must remark the shameful spoliation, by the late Earl James, of the monument of Provost Douglas from our churchyard, and now tacked to the back of his mausoleum, where it does not willingly stick, for it is coming away from the wall of its own free will and accord. He covered the original inscription by a freestone plate, with an inscription about the place of the Carmelites, etc. . . . Old Allester will tell you all about it. It was carried off by the Earl's myrmidons, sub silentio noctis. I made Lord Fife's people believe the other day that the Provost's ghost turned the vase into the river.'

Nicol's *Banff and Neighbourhood*, 1879, states that ' over the grave of Douglas was the figure of a knight, which has now disappeared.' On another page the same writer states that ' a relic of St. Mary's Chapel is built into the back of the mausoleum, an arched vault, with the recumbent effigy of King Robert Bruce in armour. Carving round the rim of the arch, representing the vine, is in beautiful preservation, and the base stones are richly carved in panels. One bears in Latin the text, " Beati mortui qui moriuntur in Domino ; a laboribus suis requiescunt et illorum opera eos sequuntur. Apoc." Another has the St. Andrew's cross in bold relief, but, excepting one letter, the inscription that had covered the face of the cross is obliterated ; and other panels bear " Memento Mori," with sandglass, skull, crossbones, bullrushes, and other emblems of mortality.'

The supposed effigy of Robert Bruce is almost certainly that of Provost

Douglas, the monument here described having been erected probably in the Provost's lifetime.

Long before the date of setting up the Muldavit monument in the mausoleum, Lord Fife had been trying to investigate the history of his ancestors, for in 1778 he writes to his factor : ' Pray look into the family history and see who was Keithmore's mother, and what the name of his father.[1] I think Adam. I have actually found one of my family . . . the arms quite certain, and from the date I think it must have been Jamieson that painted it. The picture belonged to old Alexander the painter, and had been sold with his things. How he came by it, I cannot say.' [2]

In 1912, the vault of the mausoleum, which was full, with the exception of one space, was filled in with fine sand, and the ventilators and staircase walled up with solid masonry.

A slab in the wall of the mausoleum now commemorates the twenty-one persons whose bodies lie below. They are :

DUFF HOUSE MAUSOLEUM

Beginning at foot of stairs :

No. 1. ANNE, widow of General the Honourable Sir Alexander Duff, G.C.II., died February 14, 1859, aged 70 years.

No. 2. General the Honourable Sir ALEXANDER DUFF, G.C.II, Lord Lieutenant of the County of Moray, second son of Alexander, third Earl of Fife, died March 21, 1851, aged 73 years.

No. 3. The Right Honourable ALEXANDER, third Earl of Fife, Lord Viscount Macduff, Baron Braco, etc., etc., Born April 13 (O.S.), 1731, died at Duff House, April 17, 1811, aged 80 years. Father of General Duff.

No. 4. ALEXANDER DUFF TAYLER, died July 26, 1809, in the sixth year of his age. Son of Lady Jane Tayler.

No. 5. The Right Honourable JAMES, second Earl of Fife, Viscount Macduff, Baron Braco of the Kingdom of Ireland, Baron Fife in Great Britain, Lord Lieutenant of the County of Banff, Colonel of the Banffshire Local Militia, F.R.S. and S.A. Died January 24, 1809, in the eightieth year of his age.

No. 6. JANE, Countess of Fife, born 1704, second wife of William, first Earl of Fife. Died at Rothiemay, January 16, 1788, aged 83 years.

---

[1] His father also had been anxious to get the exact position of Adam defined   See chapter IX

[2] This probably refers to the portrait of John Duff of Bowmakellach by Jamesone, which has the arms in the corner. It was this ' Alexander ' who renovated and signed some of the Duff House pictures, and added to them unauthorised dates. See list of illustrations.

No. 7. WILLIAM, first Earl of Fife.   Died September 30, 1763, aged
     66 years.
No. 8. JAMES, fifth Earl of Fife, K.T.   Born July 6, 1814, died August
     7, 1879.
No. 9. AGNES GEORGINA ELIZABETH, wife of James, fifth Earl of Fife.
     Born May 12, 1829, died December 18, 1869.
No. 10. JAMES DUFF, fourth Earl of Fife and Viscount Macduff in the
     peerage of Ireland, Baron Braco of Kilbryde, Baron Fife of the
     United Kingdom, K.T., G.C.H., Knight of the Spanish Order of
     St. Ferdinand, and of the Swedish Order of the Sword.   Born
     October 6, 1776, died March 9, 1857.
No. 11. WATT DUFF.
No. 12. Supposed to be ALEXANDER DUFF of Braco.
No. 13. Supposed to be WILLIAM DUFF of Braco, successor of Alexander Duff
     of Braco.   Died at Balvenie, 1718.
No. 14. Supposed to be MARGARET, daughter of Sir William Gordon of Les-
     more, wife of Alexander Duff of Braco.
No. 15. Miss FRANCES DUFF.   Died at Rothiemay, March 6, 1787, aged
     20 years.   Youngest daughter of the Hon. George Duff of Milton.
No. 16. ALEXANDER FRANCIS TAYLER.   Died November 8, 1828, aged 14.
     Son of Lady Jane Tayler.
No. 17. The Honourable the Lady JANE TAYLER, eldest daughter of Alex-
     ander, third Earl of Fife.   Died at Edinburgh, May 22, 1850,
     aged 70 years.
No. 18. ALEXANDER FRANCIS TAYLER, formerly Major of the 26th Regiment
     of Foot.   Son-in-law of Alexander, third Earl of Fife.   Died at
     Rothiemay, September 1854, aged 89 years.
No. 19. Hon. ARTHUR DUFF of Orton, died 1805.
No. 20. Not known.
No. 21. Major WILLIAM DUFF, 26th Regiment, son of James, second Earl of
     Fife.   Died 1795, aged 41.

The following extracts from some of Lord Fife's letters will show that
he had much humour and family affection.   Writing from Mar Lodge in
August 1782 to his sister, Lady Anne Duff, he says :

' I have had nothing but high winds and violent rains and yet every day have
I been out, and regularly wet to the skin.   I came here last night after 10 o'clock,
after shooting two fine stags, and you never saw a duck more compleatly wet
than your brother.   I am to try to-morrow to send a side of one of the stags to
Rothiemay.   It is a wonderful trouble equiping out a poor tennents horse from
here, and another from Glenbucket, to carry this half beast, which they, I hope,
will do by Thursday night.   My dear Mother us'd to get it in dirt and stink.'
We us'd to nose it before it came to the place ; and you dare not deny that yourself and the other dear little ones us'd to get broath of vinison with hundreds of

animals! I shall niver wish to send her anything in *that* style. My rascally forrester at Glenochty gives me nothing but what he sends to Rothiemay, and all he sent last year was one lean hind, about as fat as you was when you married. Be not offended ; I speak not of you now, but only on the state of former times '[1] (Fraser's *Chiefs of Grant*).

The second is from Fife House, 1793, and is addressed to Lady Grant :[2]

' I am glad Sir James and you are safe and sound on the hill tops and the fencibles rising in number. I hope we shall have soon no use for them, that the swords will be ploughing the fertile plains of Delachaple, etc.

' I was last night at Lord Amherst's, when the good news came in of the French evacuating Ostend ; they will all soon be sent to their lawful master the D——l. God forgive you for the only sin I believe you commit ; sending us cold Strathspey wind and rain. We never smelt it till you got to Castle Grant. . . . I have been horribly distressed with inflamed eyes, by foolishly riding out in a cold easterly wind. It would have been a comfort to Sir James Grant, but I hate wind. I am however better now, and am going to dine at the Lord Mayor's feast, much against my will ; but he has behaved so honourably, that I must show him all the respect in my power ' (Fraser's *Chiefs of Grant*).

To his brother, Arthur Duff of Orton

'WHITEHALL, *May* 2nd, 1774

' DEAR ARTHUR,—I am very much fatigu'd by being in the House, till past three this morning, on the American Bills, which are now all past, one for Depriving the Town of Boston of a Port,[3] and the other two, upon the Regulations of their Civil and Military Legislation, all this, with the attendance of nine Regts. which are now order'd there, will probably bring them to Moderation, and a Dutyfull Connection to their Mother Country. I have bought a Pound of the Grass, Cabbage and Turneep Seeds for you, and shall take the first opportunity of sending them, I wish you had order'd them sooner, as I fear the Grass and Cabbage seeds will be late. We must think with Deliberation, on what is most prudent, and proper, to be done as to Brodie's affairs, the only thing I fear, is designing People doing some thing to our Prejudice, without any Benefite to him. It is better to say nothing on the Subject, and I shall do every thing I can to prevent bad People from hurting us. I hope to leave this in a fortnight and to go by Mar Lodge, to visit my farm there, and rest a few days till my Servants, etc., get to Duff House. I have wrote to Captn. Gordon lately,

---

[1] ' *Mrs. Duff is advised to drink the ass milk in the Spring have used the freedom to send for the Rothiemay ass.* She is thin but otherwise well. She joins with me in Compliments to your Lordship, Lady Bracco and our young friends —I am, My Lord, Your Lordship's most obedient and most obliged humble servt , ALEXANDER DUFF.

' BALYUCHOLLIE, 13th *Febry.* 1759 '   (D)

[2] His niece, daughter of Anne   [3] In consequence of the tea riots.

and sent him a letter from Lord Rochford, which shows I have done everything in my power for John Gordon (chapter xxxvii.) both here and with foreigners, I never had any expectations from the Captn., but I thought it right to do every thing in my power to gain his assistance, which if I do not succeed in, I think I shall then take my leave of every future Interviews with him; that from experience, I know gives no pleasure, it is a bitter Portion, and should only be taken, in Gratitude for past favers, or in hopes of those that are to come; I dont think I shall be under any obligation to test it. Adieu.—Yours affectionately,   Fife ' (R.)

To his factor, William Rose

WHITEHALL, *April 23rd*, 1776.

' I have had five days attendance from seven in the morning to seven at night on the Dutchess of Kingston, who yesterday came forth Countess of Bristol. The Lords find her guilty of fellony, but she Plead her Peerage, and therefore could not be burnt in the hand. I confess I think her Case very hard for the Duke of Kingston and she by the advice of the first Council was assured that by the Sentance of the Ecclesiastical Court she was a free Woman and could marry any body. She lived with the Duke as his Dutchess, was so Receiv'd at Court and remain'd some time as his widow. Depending on this Sentance she push'd her tryal and now the Lords set that Sentance of the Ecclesiastical Court aside; before the Licence for her marriage with the Duke was given Ld. Mansfield was consulted, the Archbishop of Canterbury keep'd her papers for a day for consideration and then gave the Licence, so on the whole I think her fate is hard, and she is now to Combat for the fortune £15,000 a year, which the Duke left her so long as she continued a Widow. So here is fine work for Lawyers and will probably involve the Remainder of her Days in Litigation [1] . . . Here is very fine hot weather, I hear you have had snow.—Yours,   FIFE.

' To Mr. Rose, Banff.'   (R.)

There is a letter from Lord Fife (at the Record Office), dated February 25, 1772, asking for the pardon of Andrew Hay of Rannes and James Gordon

---

[1] Elizabeth, Duchess of Kingston (1720-1788), sometimes called Countess of Bristol, was the daughter of Colonel Thomas Chudleigh. She was a very beautiful girl, and was appointed Maid of Honour to Augusta, Princess of Wales, in 1743. On August 4, 1744, she was privately married to Augustus John Hervey, afterwards third Earl of Bristol, but the marriage was kept secret to enable her to retain her post at Court, while Hervey returned to his naval duties The marriage was recognised later, and when she became the mistress of Evelyn Pierrepont, second Duke of Kingston, Hervey wished to divorce her. She therefore started a suit of jactitation, probably collusive, in which she declared herself unmarried, and the court in 1769 pronounced her a spinster Within a month she married Kingston, who died four years later, leaving her all his property The case referred to by Lord Fife was brought by the Meadows family, who claimed the estate She, although pronounced guilty, seems to have retained the money until her death at Paris in 1788 (The suit of jactitation could only, previous to 1857, take place in an ecclesiastical court)

of Cobairdy[1] for their share in the rebellion of 1745. In it he states that they had ever since that date behaved so as to merit the favour and protection of government, living near Lord Fife, and visiting and being visited by everybody in the country.

Lord Suffolk replies that, in view of the many forms that must be observed before obtaining a formal pardon from the King, if these gentlemen remain unmolested, it is better not to stir in the matter at all.[2]

Fifteen years later Andrew Hay seems to have been living peaceably at home, and writes:

To the Earl Fife

'My Lord,—I regret that my stupidity in not directing my last letter under your Lop.'s cover occasioned you so much trouble which I beg you'll be so good as excuse. I shall in future be more exact, as my sister is so good as Clerk for me, you'll easily read my letters which a tremor in my hand joynd to a degree of stupidity renders my letters often unintelligible. This day's post which now arrives very irregularly brought me a very friendly kind letter from Sir James Duff in which he mentions your Lop.'s good health on which my sister and I rejoices and wish long continuance of so valuable a blessing. Your Lop. is very good in attempting to regulate the conveyance of letters from Aberdeen to the North as also a releiff about the coall tax which will be very beneficiall to all the coast of Scotland especially the Engie from which your Lop. wants to take Old Moors. If I can judge from the newspapers the commerciall treaties and Mr. Hastings affair will occasion very long and fatigueing sederunts in the House. As your Lop is so kind as permit me to enclose letters I have taken the liberty to send one for Capt. Abercromby at Bath and one for my Cousin Adam Hay at Leicester. As I know your Lop. will not grudge the trouble of saveing a poor Sub Tennant a shilling.

'Nothing new in this corner but the finest weather that has been remembered which has been of great service to the country in saveing provinder and forwarding labouring. My sister and I joyn in presenting humble respects to your Lop I have the honour to be with sincere esteem and attachment.--My dear Lord, Your most affect. and obedient humble servant,   ANDREW HAY.

'RANNES, Febr 18th, 1787.'

In 1801, aged seventy-two, Lord Fife writes from Innes House: 'I dined here at three o'clock upon Sunday, rode to Rothiemay in the evening,[3] and on Monday morning rode through Auldmore and Garmouth and was at

---

[1] Half-brother to Sir William Gordon   Andrew Hay was Major in Pitsligo's Regiment

[2] *State Papers*, Domestic Series   In the same collection is a ' Permission,' dated May 31, 1760, ' For the Earl and Countess of Fife to pass, on horseback, through the Horseguards '

[3] About twenty-five miles.

Innes before nine o'clock having eat nothing, so you see what an active young fellow I am !'

But this must have been almost the last of his active days, as within the year he went blind, and eight years later he died. There is a pleasing portrait of him by Cotes, of which there are several replicas.

Some other pleasant letters of his are added, from the British Museum MSS.

To Bishop Douglas

'Duff House, *July 5th,* 1790

'My dear Lord,—I do with much pleasure congratulate your Lordship on the appointment to Salisbury, long may you live to enjoy it. I never felt more satisfaction than at the moving the late Bishop of Salisbury to Durham. I was standing by the good Bishop when the noble Marquis came forward to *praise* himself and abuse others, which is often the mode of his debate—we are often hurt by the aid of ill-judging friends, and sometimes benefited by the malevolence of a wrong-headed enemy, this reflection struck me at the time, and I could not help expressing it so to the Bishop, the present nomination is most creditable to the Bishop, and honourable to our Dear Sovereign, I wish many of his Subjects acted on the same noble principles. While I am rejoicing over your Ldp. I cannot but mourn over the misfortunate King and Queen of France, that Country must deluge in blood. I hope our meeting on the 14th of July will not be a respectable one ; I wish our mob may rise and pelt them, I dont desire a brick bat at the head of Earl Wm. Stanhop, but I do wish his Ldp. a dead cat well powdered with dust. My best Compts. to Mrs. and Miss Douglas. I am ever with much regard and respect, My dear Lord, Your most obedient humble servant,   Fife.'

To Bishop Douglas

'Mar Lodge, *June 5th,* 1791.

'My dear Lord,—Will you excuse the trouble of this letter to inquire after Mrs. Douglas and your Ldp I am keeping this day not with the Windsor magnificence, but you shall not exceed us in mirth and natural beauty. I have near two hundred at dinner ; you Lords and great ones are sure of a good dinner, but my friends would not have been in the same situation, had I been with you—they are all highlanders ; as most of them speak Gaelic, I confess I do not understand all their humer, but we have all drunk the King and Queen's health, both in English and Galic, we are above 6000 feet nearer heaven than Windsor, so we look down upon you ; they are all now dancing in the Fingal stile, and I realy wish their majestys in the *Chairs* upon the Lawn to see how happy they are, it is such a contrast to the Ball room at St. James's, that I am certain it would amuse them. I have never been here at this Season, as this is my shooting habitation, and I am certain no part of Switzerland can shew nature in greater magnificence and variety. I leave this to-morrow after having

enjoyed the heat and fine Sky of Italy, this Place lays in the very head of Aberdeenshire, the highest grounds in Scotland. My letter will be of an old date,
as it is only to go to the Post town next Tuesday. If your Ldp. directs to me,
Duff House by Banff, and convey me good accounts of your health it will much
oblige.—Your devoted, etc., etc.,   FIFE.

'I could not help observing the 21st Psalm the service of this day how
applicable : 'He asked life of Thee and Thou gavest him a long life.'

To Bishop Douglas [1]

'MAR LODGE, 3rd June 1805

'MY DEAR LORD,—I was unlucky enough to call at the Hotel in Pall Mall
and was sorry to hear you had gone out to Windsor, but it gave me pleasure to
be informed you was well. I intended to have stayed the Birthday, but received
the melancholy accounts of the Death of a favourite Brother.[2]

'I was very happy to see the King look so, and that he now attends to what
may contribute to his health and amusement which I hope will prolong his life.
I was here the first Birthday after his illness which fell on a Sunday, the Psalm
of the Service of the day particularly struck me. I wrote to your Lordship
and gave you the description of the manner I kept the Birthday next day. I
am to do the same to-morrow, and I have sent to all the Country people round
to meet on the large Lawn before the Lodge, where they shall have good Boiled
and Roast an excellent Tub of Punch a Fiddle and a Pipe it will be a very different scene from the Ball at Windsor, my Ladies will all have Petticoats, but some
of my Gentlemen will be sans coulotes, my Ball and Feast is not only Loyal but
Charitable as they probably would have got no dinner had I not been there.

'I leave this the 5th to go to Duff House. Two thirds of my Tenants in this
part of the Country are Roman Catholics, but they dont think themselves slaves,
and therefore require no *Emancipation*, I am very glade that Question was
properly disposed of ; whoever moves it, whether a Pitt or a Granville, shall
never get credit from me that they bring it forward from Religious Principles,
for I hope never to see Catholics but subservient to the Established Church,
and never have a share in the Political Government of the Country.

'If you see his Majesty will you have the goodness to say that my prayers
are put up for his health and happiness. Every good wish to your son and
Family. I remain always with much respect and regard, my dear Lord, Your
most obt. humble Servant,   FIFE.'

To Warren Hastings

'FIFE HOUSE, 28th Mar. 1804.

'DEAR SIR,—I sat yesterday to Mr. Cosway and shall sit again to him
to-morrow. It will give me great pleasure to hear that you recover your hearing

---

which I flatter myself proceeds only from cold and may be easily removed. While I live I shall never forget the impression you made on my mind from the first day you appeared at the Bar of the House of Commons till the day you was relieved from Westminster Hall. Whatever you might feel at that time for not receiving grateful returns for public services, your countenance assured me of a consolation in your own mind that your conduct had been such as to ensure the approbation of that Tribunal which is above all. Often did I wish to state my abhorrence of the illiberal persecution which came from the manager's box, so much abilities were, I believe, never directed against an object, and I do confess with all the interest I took for you, I had not the courage to draw the abuse from that box against myself.

'I am always with great respect and regard, Dear Sir, Your most obedient humble servant, FIFE.'

And one from the cousin of his brother's wife. See next chapter.

George Skene,[1] Scotland Yard, to Lord Fife

'28 *June* 1803

'MY LORD,—As your Lordship has condescended to grant me permission, I will avail myself of the opportunity of writing to your Lordship when any thing occurs which according to my apprehension can afford your Lordship the smallest amusement.

'Her Grace of Gordon[2] has made very free with your Lordsps. house, which I am afraid will bear the marks and ravages of her frequent Balls. An immense company were dancing at Fife House till six o'clock this morning, about which hour the ladies departed half stupid with fatigue and dissipation, and their naked arms dangling out of their carriage windows. The rattling of carriages all night, together with the singing, swearing and squabbling of drunken coachmen prevented any sleeping in the neighbourhood and gave us just cause to regret that we had returned from Windsor where we had seen their Majesties walking on the Terrace with most of their family behind them, forming a strange contrast to the midnight orgies of her Grace.

'The King seems in high health and spirits, and is said to be much attached to the Addington administration.

'In the House of Lords the Debate about the Clergy Residence Bill much acrimonious language passed between the Chancellor and Lord Grenville—language, which I think cannot easily be forgotten or forgiven by either of the parties.

'I have this day received a letter from my Brother Alex[r] of the Lapwing Frigate, stating that he is now at sea, bound to Newfoundland, with two men of war and a valuable Convoy under his command, and hoping for my sake and his

---

[1] See page 193   [2] Jane Maxwell.

own that he will take many prizes.—I have the honour to be, My Lord, Your Lordship's most humble and most devoted servant,   GEORGE SKENE.

' The principal supper Table used last night at the Duchess of Gordon's was forty-two feet long and eight wide ; down the center was a plateaux of flowers and framework. '   (D.)

NOTE.—From the mass of correspondence written and received by James, second Lord Fife, and preserved either by his family or by his factor, William Rose, it has been some-what difficult to select, but it is hoped that those letters printed above are interesting enough in themselves to justify their insertion, and give a fairly complete picture of a delightful personality.

SKENE HOUSE
(BROUGHT INTO THE FAMILY BY THE WIFE OF THE THIRD EARL)

CHAPTER XII

ALEXANDER DUFF, THIRD EARL FIFE

ALEXANDER, the third Earl Fife, the third son of William, first Earl Fife, was born in 1731. Being a younger son, with little likelihood of succeeding to the title, it was necessary for him to make his way in the world. He was at first educated at home with his elder brother James, by Mr. Abel, minister of Rothiemay, who acted as their private tutor. Later on, he was at St. Andrews University, and his name is to be found in the Roll of Alumni of that University in 1748. He subsequently studied law and became an advocate at Aberdeen, where most of his life was passed, though he made frequent journeys to Edinburgh on legal business But he had some experience of foreign travel, as we find him writing to his father from Brussels, in 1756, an account of an accident to his leg, which a quack doctor informed him would have to be cut off. Fortunately another doctor's advice was procured, and the threatened amputation did not take place. In 1757 he was in London, and in another letter to his father, referring to Frances Dalzell, his brother George's wife, he writes that she will not be persuaded to live in Scotland, and patriotically adds that he is sure her determination proceeded from not knowing the country, and from being misinformed with regard to it, while he concludes with the

statement that ' English ladies have unreasonable prejudices against our northern region, which they with difficulty ever get over.'

On his return to Scotland from England in 1757 Alexander was requested by his father to visit his brother Lewis at Cambridge, the latter being then in residence at St. John's College. Here, at his father's desire, Alexander administered to his brother a severe rebuke on his conduct and behaviour.

Alexander was one of the few Duffs who have been really musical, and played well. When living at Rothiemay he was devoted to the violin, and he would constantly go over to visit his musical neighbour, the Rev. Mr. Stronach. The violin which he used is now in the possession of the present writers.

Having settled in Aberdeen in practice as an advocate, Alexander Duff spent most of his life in or near that town. Amongst other cases in which he was engaged, was the action brought in 1761 by Captain John Gordon of Park against John, William, and Jean Gordon, the children of Sir William Gordon of Park, whose estate was forfeited owing to his having taken part in the Jacobite rising of 1745.

' The Hon. Alexander Duff married at Careston, 17th Aug. 1775, Mary Skene, eldest daughter of George Skene of that Ilk ' (*Aberdeen Journal*). Besides being the possessor of the Skene property, George Skene also owned the estate of Careston in Forfarshire. He had married the beautiful Mary Forbes[1] of Alford, who was deaf and dumb; she died at Careston, March 15, 1786 By her he had seven children, namely, George Skene, known as ' The Last Laird,' who died in 1825 ; James, David, and Andrew, who all died without issue before 1825 ; Alexander, who was deaf, dumb, and nearly blind, and was known as ' Dumbie Skene '—he was the nominal possessor of the estate from 1825 to 1827, when he died ; Mary, who married Alexander Duff, and Sarah, married T. Macdonald, W S. ' The Last Laird,' George Skene, erected in the grounds of Skene House[2] a monument to his dogs, with this inscription :

' Tartar, Fury, Ginger, Viper, Bess, Vixen, Muffie, etc., etc.

' My faithful dogs, by whose inviolable attachment I have been induced to banish from my mind for a time the disgust occasioned by the Vices, Follies and

---

[1] From the portrait in the possession of the present writers it appears that Mary Skene did not inherit these good looks, and she herself writes to Lord Fife about a piece of silk he was sending her for a gown, that she will need a full quantity, ' for what I have not in height I have in breadth.'

[2] It was in the library of this mansion that the original MSS were preserved *A History of the Troubles in Scotland and in England, from the year of God 1624 to the year of God 1645,* by John Spalding, clerk of the Commissary Court of Aberdeen, from which the Spalding Club edition was printed

Ingratitude of Mankind. They never anticipated Evil. A Sad Reverse is the Fate of Man.

'Cur non. G. S., 1808.'

His first cousin, also a George Skene, was executed for forgery in 1812. In the *Gentleman's Magazine*, under date March 18, 1812, occurs the following · 'This morning, Mr George Skene, late chief clerk of Queen Square Police Office, who was convicted of having forged certain receipts for the purpose of defrauding the Treasury, was executed pursuant to his sentence. Great interest had been used to pardon him, but on the Friday preceding he was informed that he had no mercy to expect. Mr. Skene was a member of a most respectable family in the north of Scotland, and was next heir to the large property of Skene of Skene ' [1]

Upon the death of Mary Skene's last surviving brother in 1827 the splendid estates of Careston and Skene came into the hands of the Fife family, in whose possession the latter remained for over fifty years. Careston was sold in 1871 for £184,000, and Skene to Mr. Hamilton in 1880, on the basis of a rental of £2000.

By Mary Skene, Alexander Duff had the following children · [2]

1. JAMES, born 1776; afterwards the fourth Earl Fife.
2. ALEXANDER, born 1777; afterwards General Sir Alexander Duff.
3. GEORGE, born 1779; died 1781.
4. JANE, born 1780; married Major A F. Tayler.
5. ANNE, born 1781; married Richard Wharton Duff.
6. MARY, born 1787; died young.
7. SARAH, born 1790; married, 1807, Daniel Collyer of Wroxham, Norfolk; died 1811.

Both the boys were brought up by their uncle, the second Earl, and the two following letters from Alexander and his wife refer to their departure from home and their early days with their uncle.

Alexander Duff to William Rose, factor, at Montcoffer House, Banff

'HOUSEDALE, *Feb.* 23rd, 1783.

'SIR,—Lord Fife proposed some time ago, that we should send our two boys to Mr. Chapman at Inchdrewer, and from what I heard of Mr. Chapman's character I thought they would be very well with him. Lord Fife writes last Post, that you have settled every thing with him, and that he only wants to know

---

[1] His four brothers all died without issue

[2] His Family Bible, giving above dates, is in the possession of the present writers.

the time that they are to be brought to him. I think that the middle of April will be as proper a time as any, as the weather then will probably be turning good, so you will be so good as acquaint Mr. Chapman of that time, and I shall be glad to hear from you as soon as convenient. Mrs. Duff joins me in her Compliments to you and Mrs. Rose, and I am, Sir, Your most humble servt.,

'ALEXR. DUFF.'

On the same sheet there is also a letter from Alexander Duff's wife, Mary :

'I have added this to Mr. Duff's letter to beg of you to let me know if Mr. Chapman would aprove of washing coats for the boys, they have red short coats for dress, but was proposing to give each two washing ones of thin cloth ; every other thing shall be provided only five of each, as they are growing. Sandy will require great attention on acct. of his [*illegible*] otherwise he is stronger than Jamie, he had a complaint too some time ago, a stress he had got crying, and the only thing I am afraid of is, their fighting with boys, which cannot always be attended to, and that I am sure would be improper for both, but Jamie could not bear it, but any body who has the care of Children will enquire into those things—knowing that boys are apt to fight, and I am sure my Lord would not propose sending them any way but where they would meet with attention—other matters can be adjusted when we carry them there—With best Compts., I am, sir, yours, etc.,   MARY DUFF.
'To William Rose, at Montcoffer, Banff.'   (O.)

Mary Skene to James, second Earl Fife

'ABERDEEN, 26th Jan. 1784.

'MY LORD,—We had the Honor of your Lordship's letters at Old Meldrum, had only got that length then and now when we have got to Aberdeen will be obliged to walk home—no Chaise can go. I am afraid I will tire—however I am to attempt it. Your letter surprised me. I am ashamed at the trouble you give yourself with the children. We need not be anxious about them when they are in so good hands. I will certainly write Mrs. Rose. I am to blame for not doing it sooner—am obliged to your Lordship giving me a hint—she was very attentive to them. My mind is quite at rest. Sandy's belt will need to remain till he be free of his Complaint. Your Lordship has power to do with them what you like. We wish much to see you—as you pass—to write a note to care of Alexr. Leslie with orders to send it to Housedale in case we should not get it in time. Mr. Duff joins me in best Compts. to your Lordship, and I am, with esteem, Your affect. and Obt. sert.,   MARY DUFF' (R)

Upon James, the elder, coming of age, his uncle allowed him £500 a year, not a very lavish provision for the heir to such vast estates. James was a great friend of the Prince Regent, and lived much at Court, where he

ALEXANDER DUFF, THIRD EARL FIFE

By Alexander Pope

early began his career of extravagance and debt. The old Earl is said to have remarked, ' Eh, but Jamie must be a very clever boy to do all that on £500 a year.'

Upon his father's death in 1763, Alexander Duff inherited the estate of Echt in Aberdeenshire, where formerly his uncle, William Baird of Auchmedden, author of *The Genealogical Memoirs of the Duffs*, had been concealed when prosecuted for his share in the rising of 1745.

Upon the estate of Echt was the dwelling of Housedale. In the *View of the Diocese of Aberdeen* we find ' Echt—Housedale, a neat little house with a good park about it, all newly raised by Forbes of Echt, younger, but sold in 1736 to Duff of Braco.'

Alexander, as we have said, lived chiefly in Aberdeen, where several of his children were born, but he also resided occasionally at Housedale, and here many of his relations came to visit him, and the place is often alluded to in the family correspondence. Subsequent to his disposal of the estate of Echt, he inhabited Kingeaussie on Deeside, and from this house his eldest daughter was married to Major A. F. Tayler in 1802. In 1801, after the sale of Echt, he had executed a bond of provision for his younger children (his eldest son James being heir-presumptive to the earldom of Fife). He left £4000 each to his second son, Alexander Duff, and to his daughters Jean and Anne Duff, and £1000 to Sarah

In 1809 his elder brother James, second Earl of Fife, died, and Alexander Duff succeeded to the title of Lord Fife in the peerage of Ireland ; the English peerage, which had been conferred on his brother and heirs-male of his body, becoming extinct. The third Earl Fife then went to live at Duff House, but he did not long enjoy his honours, for in April 1811 he was seized with a sudden illness, and ' died at Duff House after only a few days confinement,' on the 16th of the month, aged eighty. He was buried in the mausoleum at Duff House. Three portraits of him used to hang in Duff House, one as a boy, two others in later life ; there was also a portrait at Orton, and the present writers own another.

His wife predeceased him in 1790.[1]

His eldest daughter Jean, who married Major A. F. Tayler, had eight children :

1. Alexander Duff, born 1803 ; died 1809, from an accident.

2. Anne Frances, born 1804 ; died 1808, from an accident.

3. William James, born 1809 ; married, in 1864, his cousin Georgina Lucy, daughter of Admiral Norwich Duff, and was father of the present

---

[1] He left one natural son, Alexander Duff, who married, in 1783, Sophia Gill, the daughter of a merchant captain, and had issue.

writers. Mr. Tayler died in 1886, and his wife in 1896. He had purchased the estate of Glenbarry,[1] previously connected with the Duff family.

4. Jane Marion, born 1810; married Doctor Dawson; died 1869.

5. James George, born 1811; married Mary Anne Duncan; died 1875.

6. Alexander Francis, born 1814; died 1828.

7. George Skene, born 1816; Commander R.N.; married Anna Maria Scott; he died 1894.

8. Hay Utterson, born 1819; died 1903.

Three of the above children, namely, Alexander Duff, Alexander Francis, and Hay Utterson, were born deaf and dumb—a sad inheritance from their great-grandmother, Mary Forbes, wife of George Skene. The eldest Alexander Duff died at the age of six, from an accident alluded to in the following letter from his father. The unfortunate child, while pressing close to look at his new-born brother, was roughly pushed aside by the nurse, and fell into a bath of boiling water.

Major A. F. Tayler to his sister

'Duff House, 25 July 1809

'My dear Bessie,—The letter which I wrote on Saturday was too late for the post of that night I therefore sent it to Aberdeen early next morning by Dr. Skene who expected to be there before the South post went out, and if so you will have got it duly. The Doctor had been sent for express when the symptoms of Alexander's disorder from the accident assumed so dangerous an appearance and remained with him until that time. I am happy to say that things go on better. The poor little fellow is amazingly reduced in strength, but his pulse which for some time was hardly to be felt, and was afterwards for

---

[1] The Abbey of Deer was founded in 1219 by William, first Earl of Buchan (died 1233), and the lands of Barre in Strathisla were acquired by the monks by subsequent grants of their munificent founders. These lands were granted to the monks in free forest, with the right of cutting timber (for the building and repair of the monastery) in the woods, which in that age seem to have stretched around the base of the Knock-hill

In the year 1449 the lands of Barre were feued by the Abbot of Deer to the first Lord Saltoun, and were in 1557 given to John Abernethie, third son of the then Lord Saltoun, from whom the Abernethies of Mayen descended

The Abernethies 'took entries' from the Lord Marischall until October 28, 1712, when sasine was granted to 'William Duff, only son to the deceased James Duff of Cromby of the lands of Barry and the Shank of Barry with houses, biggins, yards, crofts, moss, muirs, etc, and haill universall pertinents of the samen, lying in the Parochin of Aberchirder and sheriff-dom of Banff' (Banffshire Sasines)

In 1773 Duff of Crombie sold the lands to Peter Gordon of Ardmeallie, his brother-in-law, who again sold them to John Morison of Auchintoul, son of Alexander Morison of Bognie. They then passed into the hands of Grant of Auchorachan, who sold them in 1853 to the late William James Tayler.

a length of time at one hundred and 60, is now reduced to about a hundred. The healing process seems to have commenced, and he begins to take a considerable quantity of milk which of itself must be nourishing—he latterly has now and then taken a strawberry or gooseberry, and occasionally a little morsel of bread in tea. Wine, you know, always was his aversion,[1] and to this disinclination he had nearly fallen a sacrifice. The Medical people say that nothing but the most wonderful energy of his constitution could have enabled him to undergo what he has suffered.

'Should he recover, which after so wonderful an exertion I hope he yet may, you will be happy to learn that he will be in no shape disfigured or lamed in any manner by the consequences of the scald.

'Lady Jane has recovered wonderfully from the anxiety she suffered. With much difficulty she was persuaded entirely to relinquish the nursing (she was witness to the accident), she could not have continued it without the greatest risk to the health of the infant.[2] He continues to thrive and is pretty lively and stout. Lady Jane has not been downstairs except when the accident happened, at which time she ran down in a frenzy for assistance. She however walks about the suite of apartments which are on the same floor. She has just now come into the room and joins me in kindest wishes.—Yours most affectionately,

'A. P. TAYLER.

'Half past eight o'clock. Just after I had finished my letter we were much alarmed by a discharge of blood from Alexander's mouth.'

He died the next day. The family were then staying at Duff House with Lady Jane's aged father, who had only recently succeeded to the title.

Alexander Francis was well educated, could speak after a fashion, and understood French and Latin. He died of the after effects of measles at the age of fourteen.[3]

The following letter from him is in the possession of the present writers. He was seven years old at the time of writing :

'ROTHIERMAY, 10th Sept. 1821.

'MY DEAR AUNT,—I hope you and Grandmother are very well—I hope you will be write a Letter to me very soon. Uncle George shot eleven Braces to-day.

'Papa and I went in the gig to Huntly to-day. My's wrist is better to-day. I, Papa and William will be go to see you soon. I think that you are very glad to see us. Dr. McColl got his leg broke by the kick of a horse. I think that you knew Dr. McColl

'What is the name of the boy that was nearly drowned when bathing. With kind wishes from all at Rothiemay to you and Grandmother.—I remain, Yours truly, ALEXANDER FRANCIS TAYLER.'

---

[1] Not surprising at six years of age.   [2] W J Tayler, then a fortnight old
[3] Both these children are buried in the mausoleum at Duff House

In consequence of the early deaths of her two other afflicted children, Lady Jane could not be persuaded to part with her youngest son until he had attained the age of twenty, and he therefore never learned to speak, but he talked rapidly on his fingers and carried on long conversations on paper, many of which he kept. He lived for many years in London with the family of the late Dr. Watson, who had been charged with his belated education   He was very independent in his habits until extreme old age, and was well known in old book and print shops, where he spent a good deal of money, not always wisely. He died at the age of eighty-four, and is buried at Hastings.

No other instance of deaf-mutism has occurred among the descendants of Mary Skene.[1]

A good many of Alexander Duff's letters have been preserved.

Alexander Duff to his father

'PARIS, 30th May 1755.

DR. PAPA,—I arrived at Paris upon Sunday last. I would have wrote sooner, but could not get myself settled before this time. My Brother and me left London together, he went the length of Calais with me staid there only a few hours and set out for Brusselles—I delivered my letter of credit as soon as I came here to Mr. Selwin and gave him a Bill upon you for £100. I only received 2200 livres from him, he deducted the rest which amounts to 200 livres for exchange. I thought it very high and was surprised to have my money so curtailed, but he told me it was ye common rate of Exchange betwixt this and Scotland. I shall fairly give you an account of my general and necessary expences from which you 'll be able to judge of my allowance—I lodge just now à l'Hotel de Saxe, Rue de Colombier which is reckoned one of ye cheapest lodging places in Paris. I cannot possibly have tolerable apartements for myself and servant under 8 guineas a month.   I cannot eat cheaper than 7 guineas a month. My dancing, fencing, riding, musick and French Masters will cost me about 12 guineas pr. Month and my servant's board wages at half a guinea a week amounts to 2 guineas.   Now with regard to Cloaths I have consulted and taken ye advice of people who know these things and they tell me that it will cost me 60 pound stirling at least before I can appear genteely in that article.   I 'm sure I do not exaggerate anything but candidly set down what is absolutely necessary, and I dare say from this account which I have given you you 'll perceive that my £100 especially after the deduction will be soon run out and I hope you 'll be so good either to give me a general letter of credit or if you don't incline that, I expect youll give me credit for £200 by first opportunity, for *I assure you before I can receive your answer I 'll be run near*. Once I have got well settled, and am pro-

---

[1] The children of Alexander Duff's daughter Anne will be found in the chapter entitled 'Wharton Duffs.'

vided in Cloaths and other necessaries I 'll be able to live much cheaper, but the having everything to purchase at first youll be sensible must unavoidably cost money. I shall endeavour to improve myself in everything as well as I can, and put to ye best advantage the indulgence you have been so kind as to shew me. My affectionate Duty to all ffriends and believe me to be, Dr. Papa, Your most affectionate and dutiful son while ALEXR. DUFF.' (*D.*)

To the same

'PARIS, *July 4th*, 1755

'DR. PAPA,—This is the third letter I have wrote you since I came here without any answer from you which makes me think my letters have miscarried. I design to set out from this in five or six days for Lyons. I 'm told there is a very good Academy there, and very few or none of our Countrymen in that place. I 'm advised to stay about three or four months at Lyons and return to Paris in the winter in order to compleat myself in the different exercises—besides they speak the French here with a more true and just accent than elsewhere. I will likewise have the benefit at Paris of attending the Parliament and ye pleadings in the Chatelet which is certainly a great advantage to one in my way. I have gone to these courts since I came here pretty frequently, but in the winter time they have more business and their pleadings consequently more various than in the summer. It is rather more tedious for me to attend these Courts than the Court of Session because I know but little of the French law; however I have got some books wherein the principles of the French law are laid down, and I am acquainted with a good many of the avocats who are so obliging as to instruct me in the forms. I 'll be glad to hear from you as soon as your conveniency will permit and believe me to be with all possible esteem, Dr. Papa, Your most affectionate and dutiful son, ALLXR. DUFF' (*D.*)

To the same

'LONDON, *Aprile 5th*, 1757

'MY LORD,—Upon my coming to Town, I was informed of Lewis misfortune, and of the bad state of health he was then in. I imagined that my Eldest Brother had acquainted you of his situation long ago. I never have seen him since I left Scotland, but from all accounts he was very ill, though I believe that he is at present a good deal better. The Country air would certainly be of great service to him, and I think the sooner he removes from Cambridge the better, as they tell me his studys goe on but slowly there, and the company he keeps none of the best, I 'm sure he must be strangely altered, since I had the pleasure of seeing him, for at that time I 'm certain he had not the least propensity to any kind of vice, and I 'm persuaded he 's been led into it by the wicked Company at Cambridge, and not by his own natural disposition. My brother George talks of his being in Scotland. I suppose he has wrote you of

his marriage, he has not made it publick as yet for reasons which are known to himself and his wife is still called Miss Dalzell. I drew upon you yesterday for £50, you 'll may be think the last was rather too soon spent, Lady Margaret's death put me to an extraordinary expence, as I was obliged to have a black suit of Cloaths and a grey Frock for wearing in ye morning, both which amounted to about £20 including a hat, stockings, a mourning sword, Ruffles, etc., etc.—I am with great duty and respect, Your most affectionate son,

'ALLXR. DUFF.' (*O.*)

To his mother

'ABERDEEN, *Dec 11th,* 1763

'DR. MADAM,—I had the pleasure of yours some time ago. I would have answer'd it sooner had anything entertaining occured here since your going South. If this place does not abound with publick Diversions, to make up they are the most hospitable people here I ever saw there has not a day pass'd but I have been invited to dine or sup somewhere or another, I 'm very often oblig'd to decline their kind Invitations, in order to endulge my present scheme of Regularity—the horse came back here in good health and after keeping him a day or two I dispos'd of him. I have been drinking ass milk for some time past, I was oblig'd to buy one from Lady Premnay which cost me four pound ten I find it does me much good as I am greatly better since taking it. I was out at Echt last week and din'd with Auchmeden, he tells me he intends taking a house at St. Andrew's. They had a great plot to make me stay all night in order to teize about some idle scheme or another, but I grew positive and went back here that night. I intend going to Balquholly about Christmas and after staying there some time shall come back to this place which is really more agreeable than one could imagine. We have an assembly, Concert and Card Meeting every week, so much for publick Diversions. I saw Sir Arthur Forbes here yesterday who told me he saw you at Edinr. I have nothing more to add but always am, Dr Madam, your most afft Son,   ALEXR. DUFF.' (*O.*)

To his brother James

'HOUSEDALE, *Augt 23rd,* 1775.

'MY LORD,—*I have the pleasure to inform you that I was marryd at Careston upon Thursday last.* We stayd there only Friday and we came here Saturday night. Mrs. Duff and me will be extremely happy to have the pleasure of seeing you here when convenient. I did not insist with Skene about what you mentioned we will make a shift to live upon what we have, it is only borrowing a little in the meantime till the Portion falls due. I always am, my Lord, your most affectionate Brother and humble Sert.,   ALEXR. DUFF. (*D.*)
'To the Right Honble. the Earl of Fife at Mar Lodge,
    Care of Mr. William Rose, Banff.'

Alexander Duff to his brother, Arthur Duff

'ABERDEEN, *2nd December* 1775.

'DEAR ARTHUR,—I had the pleasure of your's last post, Mrs. Duff is much obliged to you for your kind Remembrance, the Dog and Songs arrived here yesterday with the Grapes, but the Dog, poor creature was quite wore out with the fatigue at Sea, and died this morning. John Gordon is not yet come here, I heard some time ago that he was at Sunderland, it seems he wrote to Mr. Wharton for some money who I fancy has refused him by his drawing upon Mr. Mackie. I shall follow your advice in avoiding him as much as possible. I'm much oblig'd to you for the trouble you take about the Chaise which you may send when bought by any of the Aberdeen smacks, you'll send me an account of what it costs you, and I shall remit it after the Aberdeen term along with what I owe you already. We came here about 8 days ago and stay till Christmas when we intend going to Rothiemay to stay some weeks, and after that we will probably remain here all the spring. There is nothing new in this part of the Country. This town is tolerably gay just now, we have an assembly once a fortnight and a Concert once a Week, and a good deal of feasting. Lord and Lady Buchan spend the Winter here, I heard but an indifferent Character of my Lord, I have been two or three time in Company with him and really think they have done him Injustice, he seems to be intelligent in a number of things and is very affable and good humour'd, he says he was acquainted with you at Glasgow. I had a very hard Day of it yesterday at the County Club, Sir William Forbes was Preses, who is lately come home from his travels. I'll be glad to hear from you at your Convenience, as London affords more matter for a letter than almost any other place. The cold rages here most violently. Mrs. Duff has been very ill of it for these two or three days past, but is now growing better. Be so good as make my Compliments to George and Lewis and make the best apology you can for not writing them, as I cannot find one myself, I fancy it will be best to write them under your Cover. I'm afraid you will hardly get this scrawl read, my pen is so bad. Mrs. Duff joins me in kind Compliments and I always am, Dr. Arthur, Your most affectionate Brother,

'ALEXR. DUFF.

'*P.S.*—As I will probably receive ye remainder of my money from Lord Fife at ye term shall I give it him up, or keep it till you come to ye Country as you are eventually concern'd in it?' (*O.*)

Alexander Duff to his brother James

'HOUSEDALE, *April 29th*, 1777.

'MY LORD,—I had the pleasure of your's yesterday. Mrs. Duff and me are much obliged to you for the trouble you take with regard to our room, it will certainly be furnished in a better taste then we could have done it ourselves.

2 c

This is an unlucky time for laying new taxes upon us considering the low price of meal. I have not sold mine yet 8 shillings is the highest price offering here, and I think it is better to keep it awhile than to let it go so cheap. I went into Aberdeen the other day as a witness against a Mason whom I employed who stole several things from me. I wanted last year to have got him tryd before the Circuit Court, but the Advocate Depute thought proper to be of opinion that it was too trifling a cause to come before that Court, so he was tryd yesterday before the Sheriff at the instance of the Prov. Fiscal, but after the clearest proof of the theft and the unanimous verdict of the jury finding him guilty the great *punishment of banishing him the County of Aberdeen was inflicted upon him.* I think a little flogging into the Bargain would not have been improper. I own I was a good deal interested in this affair not for the value of the things stolen, but I thought that a workman employ^d about one's house acting in that manner deserv^d a greater punishment. Mrs. Duff joins me in best compliments, and I always am, My Lord, your most affectionate Brother,

'ALEXR. DUFF.' (*D.*)

To the same

'HOUSEDALE, Novr 12, 1778

'MY LORD,—I never was more affected with anything than *with the melan-cholly accounts of poor Lady Helen's death.* She certainly was one of the best creatures that ever existed and behaved in every situation in life so irreproach-ably as made it impossible for malice itself to speak ill of her. The Poor Admiral is much to be pitied, for he certainly is deprived of an affectionate agreeable companion and who was always most attentive to him. We had the honour of a visit lately from the Duke of Gordon, his Grace came here with Lord Haddo and staid a night with us, he is very easy and affable, and was remarkably kind to us at Gordon Castle. It is much easier entertaining the like of him than a number of country Lairds or Aberdeen Merchants—I 'm sorry we have not had the pleasure of seeing you since you came to ye country, we will be glad either to see you at Duff House when convenient, or if you could come here on your way to London. I did not joke in the least, when I wrote you that there would be little or nothing remaining of Mrs. Duff's portion after clearing all my debts, but however we will make a shift to live pretty comfortably as my Estate will be quite ffree ; and as none of us are of an expensive turn. Mrs. Duff and the children are in good health, she is in a fair way of producing something more—she joins me in best Comp^{ts}, and I always remain, My Lord, your most affec-tionate Brother,   ALLXR. DUFF.' (*D.*)

To the same

'HOUSEDALE, December 2^d, 1778.

'DEAR LORD,—Mrs. Duff and me intended to have gone to Duff House as we had not the pleasure of seeing you when last in Banffshire, but I believe

it will be better to defer it till next year—I am obliged to be at Abdⁿ the 21st and 22nd of this month but I will be at home any day either before or after that time that you please to appoint.   I am very anxious to get the term over too as this is the greatest one I ever had, or I hope ever shall have, about £2400 to pay off is no triffle to a man of £500 a year and I have already got £500 of Mrs. Duff's portion so you see after clearing everything there will be no great remainder, however there is a happiness in having one's Estate free and when that is the case a Person knows much better how to suit his expenses to his Income.   The Laird of *Skene must draw* his Purse at Last and I dare say the money *comes from him like Drops of Blood.*   He would have given it with a much better grace immediately after the marriage which would have prevented me from borrowing in the meantime.   There is no news here.   I am informed that the Dutchess of Gordon intends to reside at Abdⁿ some time this winter, they say she comes along with the North fencibles, who are to replace Lord McDonald's Regt. now at Abⁿ.   If that is true the town will be more gay as her Grace likes to create amusement wherever she is.   They say that the Duke goes for London this winter.   We design to go into Town about the end of January as it will be more convenient for Mrs. Duff to lye in there than in the country being nearer help.   When I saw Capt. Gordon, Park, last he told me he was informed that *John Gordon was married in India that his wife's Father was a man in office* there, that he was not rich but had a good deal of credit in the country and would be a great assistance to John in pushing him forward.   If this be true you will have probably heard of it.   Mrs. Duff joins me in best respects, and I always am, My Lord, your most affect. Brother,   ALEXR. DUFF.'   (*D.*)

The letters of his later life, down to his death in 1811, are not of any interest.   Owing to the short time during which he held the title and estates, he was not, like his brother James, the recipient of innumerable appeals from needy members of the family.

He was succeeded by his eldest son, James, at that time with the army in Spain.

CARESTON [1]
(CAME INTO LORD FIFE'S POSSESSION IN 1827 ON THE DEATH OF HIS UNCLE)

CHAPTER XIII

JAMES DUFF, FOURTH EARL FIFE

JAMES, fourth Earl Fife, eldest son of the third Earl, was born in his father's, the Laird of Echt's, town house in Aberdeen, October 6, 1776. His uncle, the second earl, having no children, took him and his brother Alexander to Duff House in order to superintend their education, and sent them both to the school kept by Dr. Chapman at Inchdrewer, near Banff. From there James Duff went to Westminster School;[2] he was afterwards at Christchurch, Oxford, and on his return to London was entered as a student at Lincoln's Inn, and appears thus in the register: ' James Duff,

---

[1] Montrose halted at Careston on his masterly retreat after the surprise at Dundee, April 4, 1645. It belonged at that time to Sir Alexander Carnegie, and is thus described by Ochterlony, a few years later: ' A great and most delicat house, well built, brave lights, and of a most excellent contrivance, without debait, the best gentleman's house in the Shyre.'

[2] *James Duff (aged fourteen) to his uncle, the Earl of Fife*

' *Friday 7th*, 1790.

' MY LORD,—I write you these few lines to inform you that the Holydays begin to-morrow, and I would be obliged to you if you would send to-morrow very soon as we come out of school at nine o'clock.—I am, Your affectionate Nephew, JAMES DUFF.' (*D.*)

fiist son of Alexander Duff of Housedale, Co. Aberdeen; enteied April 9,
1791.' At the same time he took lessons in declamation from Bannister
the comedian. In 1796 Mr. Duff left his legal studies and joined the Army
on the Continent, subsequently proceeding to the Congress at Radstadt.
He returned to England in 1798, and in September 1799 he married Maria
Caroline Manners, second daughter of Mr. John Manners and his wife,
Lady Louisa, afterwaids Countess of Dysart. He was shortly after
appointed to command the Banff and Inverness Militia, and brought the
regiment to a high state of discipline. Unfortunately his married life
was of short duration; it was duiing his residence in Edinburgh, in command of his militia, that his wife died on December 20, 1805. Her death
was caused by her being bitten or scratched on the nose by a pet Newfoundland dog; no particular notice was taken of this occurrence, although
the animal shortly afterwards became moody and ill-tempered, and bit
a groom, after which it was destroyed.

It was only when Mrs. Duff became ill that the physicians formed a
suspicion as to the probable origin of her malady. It was then too late
to save her, and the poor lady died, according to a contemporary account,[1]
of ' undoubted hydrophobia,' greatly sorrowed by all.[2]

To add to the sorrow at her death, Mrs. Duff was shortly expecting
to become a mother, the event being looked forward to with great joy by
Lord Fife's family. There is a charming portrait of this lady done by
Cosway, and engraved by John Agar, pupil of Bartolozzi, which has since
been reproduced, and many inferior copies are now to be met with.

Overwhelmed with grief at his sudden and tragic loss, James Duff went
abroad, and was for some time a prisoner in Paris, from whence he wrote
the following letter :

James Duff to Sir Joseph Banks

'Paris, July 15, 1806

' Sir,—Lord Fife having written to me a considerable time ago that you had
had the goodness to say you would make an application to the Institute in my
favour, but that at that moment you judged there was no probability of its being
attended to, and as several English prisoners have lately obtained their liberty
at the request of members of that body, may I hope you will pardon the liberty
I take in suggesting that at present there is every probability that a recommenda-

[1] See *Notes and Queries*, August 1852
[2] Tradition has it that, according to the custom of the time, she was smothered or strangled
in one of her paroxysms (Genealogical Notes in the Lyon Office, Edinburgh) But the contemporary papers say that ' the immediate cause of her death was fainting fits.' And the
Scots Magazine for December 1804 gives it as ' A fever of unexampled rapidity.'

tion such as yours would be, would be immediately attended to, should you be so good as to employ it in my favour. Mr. Hamilton who is so obliging as to charge himself with my letter has obtained permission to return to England, through the influence of some members of the Institute. I hope that Lord Fife being in Scotland, and our long and unfortunate detention in this country will plead my excuse for taking the liberty of addressing myself to you without having the honour of being personally known to you.—I have the honour to be, with the greatest respect, Sir, Your very obedient humble servant,

'J. DUFF.

'Sir Joseph Banks, Bart., etc., etc.' [1]

On obtaining his liberty he went to Vienna, and subsequently joined the Austrian army under the Archduke Charles.

On hearing of the disturbances in Spain, however, he embarked at Trieste for Cadiz, where he found his kinsman, Sir James Duff,[2] the consul, who highly applauded his resolve to assist the Spaniards. He joined the Spanish army and took part in many battles, amongst others that of Talavera (1809), where he received a sabre wound in the neck, having just saved the life of a Spanish officer. Later on, he accompanied Lord Wellesley to Badajos. On January 24, 1809, his uncle, the second Earl, died, and by his father's succession to the title, he became Lord Macduff. He continued to serve in Spain, and his next share in the fighting was at the storming of Fort Matagorda on the Isle de Leon, near Cadiz, February 10, 1810. Here he received a wound of which the effects remained with him throughout his life, and caused him ever after to limp, but by his unaided efforts he had saved the Spanish standard. While the wound was healing, he lived for some time in the house of his cousin, Sir James Duff, at Cadiz, and was carried about the town in a Sedan chair, but as soon as possible he rejoined the army. On April 17, 1811, his father, the Earl Alexander, died, but he did not go home to attend to his own affairs until 1813. His departure from Spain was much regretted. Wellington presented him with a jewelled sword which he himself had received in India, and the Spanish Cortes conferred on him the rank of General, making him at the same time a Knight of the Order of St. Ferdinand and a grandee of Spain. He was received in London with great enthusiasm, the Prince Regent appointing him a Lord of the Bedchamber, as from early life they had been on terms of great intimacy, and this lasted almost throughout the Sovereign's life. On one occasion his lordship incurred the displeasure of the King, when he opposed the Government on the question of the Malt Tax, and was summarily dismissed from his post at Court and from the

---

[1] British Museum MSS.   [2] See chapter xxvii.

JAMES DUFF, FOURTH EARL FIFE

By Sir Henry Raeburn

King's friendship. This incident was the origin of Dighton's caricature called ' The Discharged Fifer.' Subsequently the King received him back into favour and reinstated him in his office. In 1827 he was made a peer of Great Britain, as well as receiving the Order of the Thistle and the Grand Military Cross of Hanover.

When he returned to Scotland he found much to demand his attention. His uncle's extraordinary will, leaving everything possible to his natural son (James of Kinstair),[1] considerably crippled his resources and led to an action in the Court of Session in 1816, which at first involved the fourth Earl in heavy losses, but in which eventually he was successful. The legal knowledge which he displayed on this occasion was the delight of his friends, and the surprise both of his agents and opponents. Notwithstanding all his expenses, he set to work at once to make great improvements on his estates in building villages, making roads, constructing harbours, and planting great tracts of land, also in times of distress, treating his tenants with the greatest liberality and generosity. From 1818 to 1826 he was Whig Member of Parliament for the county of Banff, and on his retirement his brother, Sir Alexander, still represented the family in the House of Commons as member for the Elgin Burghs.[2] Besides being much at Duff House, he paid frequent visits to his property in Morayshire, and resided at Innes House, and it was owing to his influence that many great improvements were carried out in Elgin. He also restored part of the Abbey of Pluscarden, and was largely instrumental in preserving the ruins of Elgin Cathedral. When George IV. visited Edinburgh in 1823, both Lord Fife and his brother, Sir Alexander Duff, were in attendance on him; in the *Gentleman's Magazine* of that date Lord Fife is described as ' wearing a scarlet foreign General's uniform with Portuguese orders.' He was Grand Master Mason for Scotland, and in this capacity laid the foundation stones of the Regent Arch and the New Gaol, Calton Hill, Edinburgh, September 26, 1815.

He met many interesting people in his time and had been on terms of intimacy with some of them, amongst others the exiled Bourbons when in residence at Holyrood. He had also been acquainted with Napoleon, Talleyrand, and some of the renowned marshals of France, while a prisoner on parole in France (see above). On the death of George IV. the new King, William IV., confirmed Lord Fife's appointment as Lord of the Bedchamber. During the agitation in connection with the Reform Bill, he warmly supported that measure, and at great personal inconvenience was present to vote in the majority which ensured its passing.

---

[1] See chapter xxxiv.

[2] While Banffshire became Conservative.

To this period belongs the following letter from his father-in-law :

'PORTMAN SQUARE, 23ᵈ *Novr.* 1813

'MY DEAR LORD,—I dined with the Prince Regent on Sunday last, when His Royal Highness commanded me to say he hoped it would not be long before you returned to London, and also, not to forget the *Thousand* Westphalia Hams —So far I have executed my commission—I shall add that *Sir Carnaby* is panting for your return, and a *hundred more* who you can readily guess at—Seriously tho, we shall all be most happy to have you with us again—The Prince is in excellent spirits, so many glorious Victories as have lately occur'd, cannot fail of being most gratifying to him, and all of us—The counter Revolution in Holland, must be a dreadful blow on Bonaparte—The news arriv'd on Sunday. The Prince of Orange takes his departure immediately, two thousand of the Guards were to go to-day for Holland and twelve thousand of the Militia (who are to receive additional pay, on going abroad) will follow shortly. The Duchess joins me in love and kind regards to you, we hope your Brother and Mrs. Duff are well, pray remember us to them—I have only time to add that we hope to hear from you very soon, and Believe me, My dear Lord, Ever affectionately yours,
'JOHN MANNERS.' (D.)

In 1833 he came to live permanently at Duff House, where his arrival was hailed with delight by the poor and the workpeople, who well remembered his former kindness, and the improvement in their condition brought about by his presence. Besides the public works inaugurated by him, it was his custom to seek out persons in distress and poverty, and many were thus gladdened by his bounty. There is an old story of his carrying a sack of meal along the high road to relieve an aged woman of the burden, she being ignorant of his identity. When parting from her, he recommended her to sieve the meal well before using it; on doing so, after her return home, she was filled with joy at the discovery of several golden guineas, and her neighbour, who had watched the scene, said to her, 'Ye're up by cairts (*i.e.* up in the world) the day, to have a yearl to carry yer meal tae ye!'[1]

He was always a good landlord and let out small holdings on favourable terms, and at a time when a neighbouring proprietor was turning out his smaller tenants in order to make clearings for deer forests and sheep farms, Lord Fife wrote him a long letter begging him not to turn out his tenants

[1] On another occasion, when driving in his gig, he met an old fishwife of his acquaintance and offered her a lift into Banff On the way they encountered his brother, General Duff, who looked at the Earl's companion with haughty disapproval. On being asked the reason of his glum looks, the General replied sourly that he could not tolerate the smell of fish, to which the Earl responded that *he* 'preferred it to the smell of whisky,' in allusion to the fact that his brother had married the daughter of a distiller.

faster than the Fife estates could take them in. As has been already mentioned, he inaugurated several new villages, Aberchirder and Dufftown being amongst the number. He had extensive repairs carried out upon several of the family mansions, and employed many men in enclosing and draining waste places and marshes.

For the last twenty years of his life he lived continuously at Duff House, and as he grew older he cared less and less to go about, his old Spanish wound giving him constant trouble; but he was always glad to see his friends at Duff House, and was able to enjoy their society, as well as being a great reader. In the beginning of 1847 the town of Banff was put into a state of great excitement by the report that an attempt had been made on Lord Fife's life by a discharged servant of the name of Hammond, said to have been under the influence of drink at the time. Hammond had made an attack on his successor, and the cries of a female servant brought the master to the spot, upon which Hammond drew a knife and attacked him, but was secured before much harm was done, and in spite of his seventy years, his lordship was little the worse.

In the autumn of 1854 he began to fail somewhat, and in April 1855 had a bad illness, from which, however, he completely rallied. Two years later he caught a severe cold from which he never recovered, and died on March 9, 1857, at Duff House, aged eighty years and five months.

There is a fine portrait of him by Raeburn in the family collection, and a replica in the possession of Mrs. Chancellor, by whose permission it is reproduced.

As he left no children, he was succeeded in the title and the Irish honours by his nephew, James Duff, as fifth Earl. The peerage of Great Britain, conferred on him in 1827, being confined to heirs-male of the body only, again became extinct.

In Imlach's *History of Banff* the fourth Earl is thus described :

'He was one of the most remarkable men of our time connected with the north of Scotland, and more particularly with us, as a burgess of our royal borough; a warrior and a courtier, a nobleman and a statesman, he yet rejoiced most of all in the title of the poor man's friend. As such his name will go down to posterity, and the house of Fife as it reckons up the names on its head-roll of those who, in the spirit of their motto, *Virtute et Opera*, have achieved distinction and deserved well of their country, will not forget to render due honour to him whom it will designate " the good Earl James." '

Cramond's *Annals of Banff* thus alludes to his funeral :

'In March 1857 were deposited in the family mausoleum at Duff House, amidst general tokens of regret, the remains of one of the most notable men in

the north of Scotland. Two thousand persons followed his remains to their last resting-place, and from eight to ten thousand persons were on the ground '

Within the recollection of the present writers, old people in Banff and the neighbourhood always alluded to him as ' the good Yearl James '

A deed of entail was executed by the fourth Earl, and the list of persons mentioned in it is interesting to the family historian :

' The whole heirs of entail now alive entitled to succeed to the Fife estates under the destinations of the deed aforesaid, April 13, 1841 (printed from the copy delivered to Major Alexander Francis Tayler. See below, No 31)

Heirs-Male

1. The Honourable General Sir Alexander Duff, second son of the said Alexander Duff of Echt, afterwards Earl of Fife.
2. James Duff, Esq., M P., and
3. George Skene Duff, Esq., of Milton, sons of the said Honourable Sir Alexander Duff.
4. Garden Duff, now of Hatton, fifth lawful son of John Duff of Hatton, now deceased.
5. Benjamin Duff, eldest son of the said Garden Duff.
6. Garden Duff [aged three], son of the said Benjamin Duff, and the said Benjamin Duff as his administrator-in-law.
7. Garden William Duff.
8. Robert George Duff, now in the Mauritius, or elsewhere abroad, and
9. James Duff, sons of the said Garden Duff of Hatton.
10. Robert Duff, merchant of Glasgow, sixth lawful son of the said John Duff of Hatton.
11. Captain Norwich Duff, Royal Navy, and grandson of the deceased James Duff, Sheriff-Clerk of Banff.
12. Robert William Duff, Esq , of Fetteresso, eldest son of the said deceased Robert William Duff, Esq., of Fetteresso, who was eldest son of the deceased Admiral Robert Duff of Fetteresso, who was sixth son of the also deceased Patrick Duff of Craigston
13. Arthur Duff, now Arthur Abercromby Duff of Glasshaugh, second son of the said deceased Robert William Duff.
14. Robert William Duff Abercromby [aged six], son of the said Arthur Abercromby, and the said Arthur Abercromby as his administrator-in-law.
15. Adam Duff, late merchant in London, now of Woodcote House, Henley-on-Thames, third son of the said Robert William Duff.
16 Thomas Fraser Duff [aged eleven].
17. Robert Duff [aged ten],
18. George Graham Duff [aged six],
19 Adam Duff [aged two], and

20. Arthur Meredith Duff [*aged one*], sons of the said Adam Duff, and the said Adam Duff as their administrator-in-law

21. Thomas Abercromby Duff, Esq., of Haddo, fourth son of the said deceased Robert William Duff.

22. Robert William Duff [*aged fifteen*],

23. Alexander Gordon Duff [*aged thirteen*],

24. Thomas Abercromby Fraser Duff [*aged eight*], and

25. Adam Duff [*aged six*], sons of the said Thomas Abercromby Duff, and the said Thomas Abercromby Duff as their administrator-in-law.

26. Rear-Admiral Archibald Duff of Drummuir, immediate younger brother-german of the deceased John Duff of Drummuir, eldest son of Captain Alexander Duff of Cublin.

27. Thomas Duff, now Thomas Gordon of Park, son of the deceased Lachlan Duff, Writer to our Signet, who was lawful son of the deceased John Duff of Cublin.

28. Lachlan Duff Gordon, Captain 20th Regiment of Foot, now in Dublin or elsewhere abroad.

29. David M'Dowall Gordon, master's-mate on board of our ship *Thunderer* stationed at Malta, or elsewhere abroad, and

30. Alexander Duff Gordon, mate on board of our ship *Vesper*, sons of the said Thomas Duff, now Thomas Gordon.

31. Huntly George Gordon Duff, now of Muirtown, only son of the deceased Hugh Robert Duff of Muirtown, who was only son of Colonel Alexander Duff of Muirtown.

Heirs-Female

32. Catharine Duff, and

33. Louisa Tollemache Duff, daughters of the said Honourable Sir Alexander Duff.

34. Lady Jane Duff or Tayler, eldest daughter of the before-named Alexander Duff of Echt, afterwards Earl of Fife, and spouse of the also before-named [1] Major Alexander Francis Tayler, and the said Major Alexander Francis Tayler her husband for his interest.

35. William James Tayler,

36. James George Tayler,

37. George Skene Tayler,

38. Hay Utterson Tayler, and

39. Jane Marion Tayler, children of the said Lady Jane Duff or Tayler and Major Alexander Francis Tayler.

40. The before-named Alexander Thomas Wharton Duff,[2]

41. Anne Jane Wharton Duff, and

42. Jemima Wharton Duff, children of Lady Anne Wharton Duff, second daughter of the said Alexander Duff of Echt, afterwards Earl of Fife, and spouse of the said Richard Wharton Duff of Orton.

---

[1] As trustee.   [2] As trustee

13. Louisa Duff [*aged eight*], and

14. Helen Duff [*aged six*], daughters of the before-named Benjamin Duff, eldest son of Garden Duff of Hatton.

15. Mrs. Janet Duff or Morison, spouse of Alexander Morison, Esq., of Bognie,

16. Mrs. Helen Duff or Buchan, spouse of James Buchan, Esq., of Auchmacoy, and

17. Miss Louisa Clementina Duff, daughters of the said Garden Duff of Hatton, and the said Alexander Morison, husband of the said Janet Duff, and James Buchan, husband of the said Helen Duff, for themselves and their interests.

48. Thomas Buchan, and

49. Louisa Buchan, children of the said Helen Duff or Buchan and James Buchan, and the said James Buchan as their administrator-in-law.

50. Miss Clementina Duff, residing in Banff, daughter of the before-named John Duff of Hatton.

51. Mrs. Mary Duff or Cockburn, daughter of the deceased Alexander Duff of Hatton, and spouse of Robert Cockburn, Esq., wine merchant in London, and the said Robert Cockburn, her husband, for himself and his interest.

52. Archibald Cockburn,

53. Alexander Cockburn,

54. John Montague Cockburn, and

55. Helen Clementina Cockburn or Dunlop, spouse of Hugh Dunlop, Esq., late of Oporto, children of the said Mary Duff or Cockburn and Robert Cockburn.

56. James Dunlop, son of the said Mrs. Helen Clementina Cockburn or Dunlop and Hugh Dunlop, the said Hugh Dunlop as administrator-in-law of his said son, and also as husband of the said Helen Clementina Cockburn or Dunlop for his interest.

57. Mrs. Helen Duff or Tod, also daughter of the said deceased Alexander Duff of Hatton, and spouse of John Tod, Writer to our Signet.

58. Thomas Tod,

59. Alexander Tod,

60. John Robert Tod,

61. Helen Clementina Tod,

62. Mary Jane Tod,

63. Charlotte Joanna Tod,

64. Caroline Jane Tod,

65. Louisa Garden Tod [*aged thirteen*], and

66. Joanna Helen Tod [*aged ten*], all children of the said Mrs Helen Duff or Tod and John Tod, the said John Tod as husband of the said Mrs. Helen Duff or Tod, and for his interest, and also as administrator-in-law for such of his said children as are minors.

67. Helen Sophia Duff [*aged seven*], and

68. Georgina Lucy Duff [*aged six*], daughters of the said Captain Norwich Duff, and their said father as their administrator-in-law

69. John Bell Suttie,

70. Jane Graham Suttie,

71. Catherine Duff Suttie, children of Helen Bell or Suttie, deceased, who was spouse of George Suttie, shoemaker, and daughter of Helen Duff or Bell, also deceased, who was eldest daughter of the before-named James Duff, Sheriff-Clerk of Banff, and spouse of Thomas Bell, comedian, also deceased, the said George Suttie as administrator-in-law for his said children.

72. Elizabeth Bell, spouse of Alexander Weir, seaman in Banff, second daughter of the said Helen Duff or Bell.

73. Helen Duff Weir,

74. Anne Duff Weir, and

75. Elizabeth Weir, children of the said Elizabeth Bell or Weir, and the said Alexander Weir, as husband of the said Elizabeth Bell or Weir for his interest, and also as administrator-in-law for his children.

76. Mrs Anne Duff or Biggar, also daughter of the said deceased James Duff, Sheriff-Clerk of Banff, and spouse of Walter Biggar, Esq., merchant in Banff, and the said Walter Biggar for himself and his interest.

77. Margaret Biggar [*aged eighteen*], daughter of the said Mrs. Anne Duff or Biggar, and the said Walter Biggar, her father, as her administrator-in-law.

78 Mary Cameron Abercromby [*aged seven*], and

79. Margaret Gurney Abercromby [*aged three*], daughters of the said Arthur Abercromby of Glasshaugh, and their said father as their administrator-in-law.

80. Mary Abercromby [*aged eight*], and

81. Jane Clerk Duff [*aged seven*], daughters of the before-named Adam Duff, Esq., late merchant in London, and him as their administrator-in-law.

82 Mary Stewart Gordon,

83. Rachel Duff Gordon,

84. Eliza Georgina Graham Gordon,

85. Eleanor Frances Julien Gordon,

86. Wilhelmina M'Dowall Gordon,

87. Helen Isabella Gordon,

88. Jemima Hay Gordon, and

89. Charlotte Emilia Gordon, all daughters of the before-named Thomas Gordon of Park, and the said Thomas Gordon, their father, as their administrator-in-law.

90. Mrs. Rachel Duff or Stewart, daughter of the before-designed Lachlan Duff, W.S., and spouse of Patrick Stewart of Auchlunca, and the said Patrick Stewart, her husband, for his interest.

91. Andrew Stewart, their son.

92. Mrs. Emily Mary Davidson Duff or Warrand, residing in Inverness, daughter of the said deceased Hugh Robert Duff of Muirtown, and widow of Alexander Warrand, Esq., Assistant Surgeon in the East India Company's service.

93. Alexander John Cruickshank Warrand,
94. Catherine Munro Warrand, and
95. Louisa Sarah Georgina Warrand, children of the said Mrs. Emily Mary Davidson Duff, or Warrand, and residing with her at Muirtown, near Inverness.
96. Mrs. Jane Dorothy Stratton Duff or Shireff, daughter of the said deceased Hugh Robert Duff of Muirtown, and spouse of Captain Robert Shireff of the 2nd Madras Native Infantry, and her said husband for his interest.
97. Robert David Forbes Duff Shireff, son of the said Mrs. Shireff.
98. Catherine Dingwall or Stewart, residing at Croydon, Surrey, widow of William Stewart, Commander Royal Navy, and daughter of the late Magdalene Duff or Dingwall, who was daughter of William Duff of Corsindae, who was son of James Duff of Corsindae.
99. Patience Stewart or Reid, residing at Croydon aforesaid, daughter of the said Catherine Dingwall or Stewart, and widow of Lieutenant James Reid, Royal Navy.
100. Catherine Reid, daughter of the said Patience Stewart or Reid.'

This entail was broken in 1875, by the fifth Earl and his son the late Duke of Fife.

Six of the heirs-female are still living.

DELGATY CASTLE

CHAPTER XIV

SIR ALEXANDER DUFF OF DELGATY AND HIS SONS, THE FIFTH EARL FIFE AND HON. GEORGE DUFF

GENERAL THE HON. SIR ALEXANDER DUFF, G.C.H. (Grand Cross of Hanover), brother and heir-presumptive to the fourth Earl of Fife, was the second son of Alexander, third Earl, by his wife, Mary Skene of Skene. He was born in 1777, and when only five or six years old was sent to Duff House to the care of his uncle, the second Lord Fife, who, having no children, wished to take charge of his nephews. It must have been a little hard for their mother to part with them at this very early age. Two of her letters on the subject are to be found in chapter xii., and the letters of their father to his brother frequently end with a message or a line ' to the boys.' When they were a little older, their uncle sent them to the then well-known school kept by Dr. Chapman at Inchdrewer.[1] Alexander Duff entered the Army as Ensign in the 65th Berkshire Regiment of Foot in May 1793, being then sixteen, and joined his regiment at Gibraltar. Having been first promoted to a lieutenancy with captain's powers in

---

[1] Here it may be added that the Rev. Daniel Duff, later of Salvadore House, Tooting, for whom see chapter xxix., was also at this school, though about twenty years earlier.

an Independent Company in January 1791, he was transferred in 1795 as Captain to the 88th[1] Regiment, and in the March following appears as Major in the same regiment. The 88th was then newly raised, and family interest procured him the majority at the age of eighteen. He served in Flanders until the return of the army in the end of the same year. In April 1798 he was promoted Lieutenant-Colonel of the 88th, and went to the East Indies, where he remained until his regiment was ordered to Egypt to take part in the expedition under Sir David Baird which landed at Kosseir in June 1801, crossed the desert, and, embarking on the Nile, descended to Cairo and thence to Alexandria, which was reached a few days before its surrender to General Hutchinson. In 1806 his regiment formed part of the expedition for the reduction of La Plata, Montevideo, and other places in South America, which started February 24, 1807, and he commanded the centre column in the attack on Buenos Ayres on July 5, 1807. Here he had the misfortune to be obliged to surrender with his detachment, and appeared as a witness at the court-martial held in the following year[2] to inquire into the conduct of Brigadier-General White-locke, who was accused of ' acting contrary to instructions, of exposing his army to fire from the houses, by causing them to march through the streets without having previously reduced the town, of not being present personally at the attack, and of neglecting to keep up communications with his main body.' It was, moreover, proved that ' after concluding a shameful treaty, he went back to his headquarters without making any serious attempt to learn what had become of his column on the right.'[3] General Whitelocke was cashiered, but Lieutenant-Colonel Alexander Duff, who gave evidence as to the circumstances which led to his own surrender, was not included in the censure.[4]

General Whitelocke had made a hopeless muddle of the whole expedition.

W. F. Lord, in his *Lost Possessions of Great Britain*, says :

' Whitelocke seemed resolved on failure. Although he had made his attack at his leisure from the impregnable position of Montevideo, he had sent his troops into action so ill provided that many of them had eaten nothing for 24 hours before the fight began. He had chosen the mode of fighting in which the Spaniards excelled. . . . When his fine army (11,000 seasoned British troops) and his capable subordinates had wrested a victory in spite of the unparalleled blunders of their chief, there remained only one more step to take, and he took it. Victory being placed in his grasp, he declined to seize it. Small wonder

---

[1] The Connaught Rangers   [2] At Chelsea, January 28, 1808   [3] *Gentleman's Magazine.*
[4] It is a curious circumstance that the president of the court-martial was Sir James Duff of the Foot Guards, first cousin to Colonel Alexander   See chapter xxxiv

if the remains of his splendid force chalked up on the street walls : " General Whitelocke is a fool or a traitor, or both." '

Alexander Duff was promoted Colonel in the same year, and in 1810 went on the half-pay list of the 4th Foot. He became Major-General in June 1811, and Lieutenant-General in 1821.

In 1816 he was presented with a sword by the officers of the 88th who had served under him.

He became Colonel of the 92nd Foot in September 1823, and in the year 1828 he appears for the first time in the Army List as Honourable, his brother having in the previous year been made a peer of the United Kingdom in addition to the Irish title.[1] He was transferred to the colonelcy of the 37th Foot in July 1831.

In 1833 he received the Grand Cross of the Order of Hanover, which did not carry knighthood, but he was knighted by King William IV. in the following year. He reached the rank of full General in the third year of Queen Victoria's reign (1839).

Sir Alexander married, in March 1812, Anne, youngest daughter of James Stein of Kilbagie, and had three sons and two daughters :

1. The eldest son, born in Edinburgh 1813, died a few months later.

2. JAMES, born 1814 ; M.P. for Banff, and afterwards fifth Lord Fife.

3. GEORGE SKENE, born 1816 ; M.P. for the Elgin Burghs.

4. CATHERINE, born 1820 ; married, in 1841, John Lewis Ricardo of an old Jewish family, and had one son, Algernon Lewis, died 1871, a Captain in the Scots Guards. Catherine died 1869.

5. LOUISA TOLLEMACHE, born 1824, died 1864 ; married, 1848, Sir Richard Brooke of Norton Priory, Runcorn. She had the following children :

> Richard and Evelyn, twins, born 1850.
> Basil and Mabel, twins, born 1852.
> Jocelyn, born 1854.
> Winifred, born 1856.
> Victor, born 1857.
> Octavius, born 1859.
> Lionel, born 1860.
> Reginald, born 1861.
> Lilian, born 1864.

Sir Richard married again, after the death of Lady Louisa, and there were two more daughters.

---

[1] Though he had, since 1811, when his father succeeded to the earldom of Fife, had a right to this courtesy title.

Catherine, Louisa, and George Duff were granted the courtesy titles and the rank of earl's children on their brother's succession to the title in 1857.

Sir Alexander, having inherited no landed estate, resided for many years at Delgaty Castle, bought by Lord Fife from Garden of Troup, and sold by his eldest son, in 1863, to Mrs. Grant Duff of Eden, the purchase money being the estate of her deceased uncle, Mr. Douglas Ainslie (see chapter xxxii.). Like many others of the Duff family, Sir Alexander was anxious to attain to parliamentary honours, and represented the Elgin Burghs in the House of Commons from 1826 to 1831. He had made a previous attempt to enter Parliament, which led to the famous 'Raid of Elgin' in 1820. His opponent was Archibald Farquharson of Finzean, who was supported by Lord Seafield and all the Grant interest, while Lord Fife and the Duff interest were naturally on the side of General Duff, who was also the personal favourite of the burghers of Elgin. Lord Fife had spent enormous sums on entertainments in the town, the laws as to bribery being not then so strict as they have since become.

Lord Seafield, with his three sisters, Anne, Margaret, and Penuel,[1] were then living at their town house, Grant Lodge, Elgin.[2] The ladies, especially Lady Anne, were keen politicians, and the interest they took in the contest was strongly resented by the people of Elgin; they could scarcely appear in the streets without being annoyed by the rabble. Feeling ran high, and at length strange tactics were adopted. The Grants began by attempting, unsuccessfully, to kidnap two of General Duff's prominent supporters; whereupon the Duffs retaliated by seizing Councillor Robert Dick of the Grant faction, and transporting him across the Moray Firth to Sutherland. The Grants, not to be beaten, succeeded in getting possession of the acting chief magistrate and sent him also to Sutherland. The position was now so serious that the ladies at Grant Lodge became alarmed for their own safety, and a messenger was despatched to Strathspey to summon the clansmen. He reached Cromdale on a Sunday, just as the congregation was leaving the church, and about three hundred men immediately started for Elgin, others being instructed to follow. In all, some seven hundred reached Grant Lodge early on Monday morning, and encamped in the grounds for the protection of the chief's sister.[3] A faithful adherent of the Duffs, seeing the Grants arrive at Aberlour in the early hours of the morning, had outstripped them and

---

[1] These were the grandchildren of General Alexander's aunt, Lady Anne Duff of Hatton.

[2] Now a museum in the Cooper Park.

[3] It must have been somewhat difficult for Lady Anne, at a moment's notice, to feed such a multitude.

GENERAL SIR ALEXANDER DUFF

From the engraving by Zobel after portrait by Châtelain.

hastened to warn both Lord Fife and the people of Elgin, who were therefore ready armed, with any obsolete weapons available, when the invaders
arrived, and had taken steps to guard the safety of the remaining members
of the town council favourable to their party. Later in the day more Fife
tenants with their servants and other adherents from the fishing villages
on the coast poured into the town, which was literally in possession of two
rival armies, and a serious breach of the peace was imminent. The sheriff
of the county, Sir George Abercromby, who was fortunately in the town,
having slipped into Grant Lodge by a back entrance, made a personal
appeal to Lady Anne [1] to dismiss her turbulent bodyguard, and gave his
personal assurance for her safety and a promise that special constables
should be enrolled to keep the peace on both sides. His entreaties, which
were supported by a deputation of all the parochial clergy, were successful,
and the Highlanders were instructed to march peacefully away by a different route to that by which they had arrived. The townspeople, however,
could not be persuaded that they were not still lurking in the neighbourhood, ready to return under cover of darkness, and a general illumination
was ordered, many of the Grant faction lighting up their windows to save
them from being broken. After the election, which resulted in the return
of Mr Farquharson, the absent councillors were returned in safety to
their homes.[2]

Sir Alexander Duff died in 1851 at Percy Cross, Walham Green, London,
at that time a pretty country neighbourhood. He was seventy-three
years of age. His body was conveyed by H.M.S. *Lightning* to Banff,
where it was placed in the family mausoleum at Duff House. His wife
died eight years later, and was also buried in the mausoleum.

There were two pictures of General Duff in the Duff House collection
(one of which has been finely engraved), and another at Orton, now in
the possession of his great-niece, Mrs. Chancellor. He was a singularly
handsome man, and a fine soldier.

There are many letters from him to his uncle, Lord Fife, but they are
not of general interest.

He writes from Eastbourne on December 13, 1805 :

' MY LORD,—I returned to the Regt. yesterday Eve from Sir James Duffs.[3]
I am really much delighted with my visit. *Lady Duff is a charming woman
and the little ones interesting little creatures. The girl is very like her Father*, the
boy a fine stout fellow. I think the house extremely comfortable and a most

---

[1] Lady Anne was of great personal attractions, and George IV., who saw her in 1822, and
heard that she was the heroine of the ' last Highland raid,' is said to have remarked that she
was ' truly an object fit to raise the chivalry of a clan '

[2] See Rampini's *Moray and Nairn*, and Young's *Annals of Elgin*.   [3] Of Kinstair.

excellent garden. Sir James, Lady Duff informed me, used to take delight in feeding the poultry. His time is now intirely taken up with his children, I am happy to say my father is in good health.—Your very affectionate nephew,

'Alex. Duff.' (*D.*)

JAMES, FIFTH EARL FIFE

James, fifth Earl Fife, the eldest son of General Sir Alexander Duff of Delgaty, was born in Edinburgh in 1814

He was educated at Edinburgh Academy, and later on was in the Diplomatic Service, serving as attaché in Paris.

In 1837 he was elected Member of Parliament for Banffshire, and continued to represent this constituency for twenty years.

He married, in Paris in 1846, Lady Agnes Georgina Elizabeth Hay, second daughter of the sixteenth Earl of Erroll and his wife, Lady Elizabeth Fitzclarence, daughter of William iv. and Mrs. Jordan. He was Lord-Lieutenant of the counties of Banff and Moray.

He had the following children :

1. Anne Elizabeth Clementina, born August 16, 1847; married, in 1865, the fifth Marquis Townshend, and had one son, the sixth and present Marquis, born 1866, married Gladys Sutherst, and one daughter, Agnes E. Audrey, born 1870, married James A. Durham, son of Rev. W. Durham of Ladbroke, Warwick.

2. Ida Louisa Alice, born December 11, 1848; married, in 1867, Adrian Elias Hope,[1] which marriage was dissolved ; she married, secondly, 1880, William Wilson.

3. Alexander William George (first Duke of Fife), born May 10, 1849.

4. Alexina, born March 20, 1851; married, 1870, Henry Aubrey Coventry, third son of Hon. Henry Amilius Coventry, and died 1882, without issue.

5. Agnes Cecil Emmeline, born May 18, 1852; married, 1871, Viscount Dupplin , divorced 1876. She married, secondly, in 1876, Herbert Flower, who died 1880 ; and, thirdly, in 1882, Sir Alfred Cooper, F.R.C.S., and of this marriage there was one son and three daughters. Sir Alfred died 1911.

    (1) Stephanie Agnes, born 1883 ; married, 1903, Arthur Levita, who died 1910, and has two children, Violet and Enid.

    (2) Hermione May Louise, born 1885 ; married, 1904, Niel Arnott, and has one son, Ian Duff.

---

[1] There was one daughter, Agnes Henrietta Ida May, married Edwin Phillipps de Lisle.

JAMES DUFF, FIFTH EARL FIFE

From engraving by G R Ward

(3) Sybil Mary, born 1886; married, 1904, R. Hart Davies, and has Rupert Charles 1907, and Deidre Phyllis Ulrica.

(4) Alfred Duff, born 1890.

6. MARY HAMILTON, born February 20, 1854, died March 20, 1854.

In the year 1857 Lord Fife was made a peer of the United Kingdom under the title of Baron Skene, which was taken from the property which had come to his uncle in 1827 upon the death of his grandmother's brother, the last Skene of Skene. He died in August 1879.[1]

His funeral from Duff House to the family mausoleum was a most imposing ceremony, and had quite a feudal air. All the available members of the Duff family, all the neighbouring nobility and lairds, and friends from all parts of the country attended, as well as thousands of the tenants, so that the grass edgings of the avenues were trampled out of recognition, all testifying to his popularity. One trifling hitch occurred when on the arrival of the body at Banff Bridge Station the undertakers' men and the hearse had not yet made their appearance. The salmon fishers from their nets at the neighbouring mouth of the river were hastily summoned, and came on the scene without delay, still in their big sea-boots, but, almost unfortunately, before these picturesque henchmen had had time to shoulder the coffin the proper officials arrived.[2]

There are three good portraits of the fifth Earl, one in his youth, another, in early manhood, by Sir John Watson Gordon, and a third, by Sir Francis Grant, P.R.A., which was subscribed for by the tenantry. They are all in possession of the Duchess of Fife, but the first sketch by Watson Gordon is in the possession of the present writers.

THE HON. GEORGE SKENE DUFF

The Hon. GEORGE SKENE DUFF, only brother of the fifth Earl, and second son of Sir Alexander Duff, was born in 1816 He was educated in Edinburgh, and in November 1836 became a Cornet in the Royal Regiment of Horse Guards, but does not appear to have been a very enthusiastic soldier, as he retired from the Army in the following year and took to diplomacy, for which he was more suited, being an excellent French and German scholar. He was for some time attached to the Embassies at

---

[1] Many years before his death he had placed the management of his large estates in the hands of his cousin, W J Tayler, as commissioner, and in 1875 they were disentailed

[2] The present writer remembers the occasion as one of the most important and enjoyable (!) events of his early childhood The crowds and the pipers made a great impression on him. He had, moreover, been cautioned by his mother not to approach too near the vault when it was opened, and is told, that on being asked on his return whether he had remembered the prohibition, answered proudly ' Oh, I was one of the " men " who let him down,' having been given a cord to hold as pall-bearer.

Paris and Vienna, and became a personal friend of Heinrich Heine and Count Andrassy.[1]

In 1847 he entered Parliament as member for the Elgin Burghs, resigning his seat in 1857,[2] in failing health, though he lived for thirty-two years longer.

In the same year, his brother being raised to the rank of Baron Skene of the United Kingdom, Mr. Duff was granted the rank of an earl's son. He was appointed Lord Lieutenant of Morayshire in 1856, which office he resigned in 1871. He was also a J.P. for the shires of Banff, Aberdeen, and Kincardine.

Mr. Duff was best known as a sportsman ; he was a crack game shot and a keen fisherman, but he excelled as a deerstalker. On one occasion in August 1880, when he was sixty-four years old, he brought down in the Mar forest no fewer than eight stags, three of them royals, the fourth with eleven tines, and the other four scarcely inferior ; this is without parallel in the annals of deerstalking in Scotland.

Mr. Duff lived chiefly at Bournemouth, but he came every year to Monteoffer House, near Duff House, to enjoy the fishing, and as long as he was able he made an annual visit to Braemar for stalking. He, like his brother the Earl, was a generous and warm-hearted man, and was much regretted when he died at Bournemouth in March 1889.

There is an exquisite crayon portrait of him by George Richmond, R.A., in the possession of the present writers.

---

[1] Julius Andrassy, 1823-1890, Hungarian patriot and statesman Member of the Hungarian diet, subsequently fought against the Austrians in the successful Hungarian revolt of 1849 (only crushed by the intervention of Russia) When the thirteen Hungarian generals were hanged at Arad, Andrassy was hanged in effigy, he having escaped to France After the war of 1866, when Austria was obliged to conciliate Hungary, Andrassy was nominated Prime Minister of the autonomous Hungarian Cabinet After the Franco-German war he became Austrian Minister for Foreign Affairs, and a great favourite with the Emperor, who is said to have remarked on more than one occasion, ' I am glad I did not hang you.'

[2] Sir Mountstuart Grant Duff being elected in his place. See chapter xxii.

COAT ARMORIAL OF THE SIXTH EARL, AFTERWARDS DUKE

CHAPTER XV

THE DUKE OF FIFE

ALEXANDER WILLIAM GEORGE, the only son of the fifth Earl Fife, was born November 10, 1849, and educated at Eton from 1863 to 1866.

His first appearance in public life was on the occasion of his appointment as Lord Lieutenant of Morayshire when he was only twenty-two.

Three years later, in 1874, Viscount Macduff ' wrested the parliamentary representation of the counties of Elgin and Nairn from the Grants, who had enjoyed it in the Conservative interest for the greater part of a century.' [1]

In his first election address at Elgin, Lord Macduff made reference to the only contest in the constituency since the Reform Bill of 1832, describing it as ' the gallant attempt of his grandfather to rescue the constituency from the continuous rule of the Tories.' This was at the election which led to the ' Raid of Elgin ' (see last chapter). Lord Macduff was returned by 829 votes as against 619 cast for Colonel Grant, and the occasion was celebrated by a public dinner, at which the late Sir George Macpherson Grant took the chair.

---

[1] In a conversation about Glass and Beldorney, Earl James IV. mentioned as an interesting circumstance that his uncle for some reason neglected to secure the estate of Beldorney at the time when the old Gordons had to part with it, and it was purchased for political reasons by the famous Master of the Rolls, Sir William Grant, who was a Tory, and therefore of opposite politics to those of the Fife family. The consequence was that in the period before the Reform Bill, Banffshire was permanently harnessed under Tory régime, and bitter was the regret that the old Earl James felt at his blunder. ' Ah, many a time,' said the late Earl James, ' did I hear my uncle say, "Ah Lord, I 'll never be d———d for not buying Beldorney : I hae repentit o' it sae bitterly " ' (*Memorials of a Banffshire Glen*, Sir William Geddes).

In 1879, by the death of his father, Lord Macduff succeeded to the titles and the large estates in four counties; he took his seat in the House of Lords as Baron Skene in February 1880, and in the following May was made a Privy Councillor, and in March 1881 a Knight of the Order of the Thistle; also a Knight of the Order of St. John of Jerusalem, Captain of the Corps of Gentlemen-at-Arms in 1880, and a Member of the Council of the Duchy of Lancaster 1882.

Early in 1882 he was entrusted with the mission from Queen Victoria to invest Albert, King of Saxony, with the Order of the Garter, and in the autumn of the following year he entertained the Prince of Wales at Duff House.

During the time of agricultural depression in the early eighties he treated his tenants with every consideration, and from shortly after this period dates the commencement of his system of selling small holdings to occupying tenants. His theory, as stated by himself in a meeting at Banff in 1890, was that ' there should be a considerable number of quite small estates side by side with the larger ones, which will not only tend to create an element of greater stability in the country, but also to do away with the idea which once prevailed, that land is the peculiar appanage of one class, instead of being, as it should be, a purchasable commodity within the reach of all.' The smaller properties sold by the sixth Earl of Fife are too numerous to detail; among the larger ones may be mentioned Skene, Innes, Rothiemay, Auchintoul, Glenbucket, Eden, Glenrinnes, Aberlour, Blairmore, etc.

The Fife estates in 1883 consisted of 135,829 acres in Aberdeenshire (worth £16,240 a year); 72,432 acres in Banffshire; 40,959 acres in Morayshire (besides an unstated quantity in that county worth £1251 a year); making (with this exception) 249,220 acres, worth £72,563 a year.[1]

The Duke of Fife was one of the twenty-eight noblemen who, in 1883, possessed above 100,000 acres in the United Kingdom, and stood fifth in order of acreage, and third (in Scotland) in point of income derived therefrom, following the Duke of Buccleuch and the Marquis of Hamilton.[2]

Since 1883 a great part of the Fife estates has been sold.

---

[1] In 1879 (when the late Duke succeeded), they extended to 257,657 acres—annual rental £78,000; of these

72,432 acres in Banffshire,		rental,	£36,379
139,629 ,, ,, Aberdeenshire,		,,	£17,740
40,959 ,, ,, Morayshire, .	.	,,	£18,695
4,837 ,, ,, Forfarshire, .	.	,,	£5,768

[2] It may be remarked that the Duke of Fife had not (neither had any of his predecessors) one acre of land in the county of Fife, though the second Earl had a project of purchasing an estate there. The Duke of Devonshire and the Earl of Derby are similarly situated.

In the year 1885 Lord Fife severed his connection with Mr. Gladstone's party on the Home Rule question.

In addition to being a landed proprietor he had large financial interests, both in the London banking firm of Sir Samuel Scott and Co , and in many other important undertakings ; and at one time was actively concerned in the development of Rhodesia   He was vice-president of the Chartered Company of South Africa for nine years, but resigned the position after the Jameson Raid.

July 27, 1889, was marked by his marriage to Her Royal Highness Princess Louise Victoria Alexandra Dagmar of Wales, now Princess Royal, and elevation to the Dukedom of Fife and Marquisate of Macduff ; he had already, in 1885, been created an earl of the United Kingdom.

On April 24, 1900, he was created afresh Earl of Macduff and Duke of Fife, with special remainder, in default of male issue, to his first and other daughters.

The only son of this marriage was, unfortunately, still-born, June 16, 1890.

There are two daughters :

ALEXANDRA VICTORIA ALBERTA EDWINA LOUISE, present Duchess of Fife, born May 17, 1891.

MAUD ALEXANDRA VICTORIA GEORGINA BERTHA, born April 3, 1893.

In 1905 King Edward VII. ' was pleased to declare ' that these two granddaughters should be ' called Princesses, and bear the title of Her Highness.'

In 1898 the Duke of Fife was approached by Mr. Chamberlain with a view to his assuming the Governor-Generalship of Canada, but that and similar suggestions were declined on account of Her Royal Highness's delicate health. The Duke and the Princess resided during the summer chiefly at Mar Lodge, which was rebuilt on a new site after the fire of 1905 ; a very brief annual visit being paid to Duff House until the year 1906, when ' the mansion-house, gardens, and policies, with 140 acres of land, were presented to the towns of Banff and Macduff; the Corporations being left a free hand to put this gift to the best use in the interest of the beneficiaries.'

The Duke of Fife was Lord Lieutenant of the county of London from 1900, and Lord High Constable at the Coronation of Edward VII. and George V., on which latter occasion he was created Knight of the Garter. He was also Grand Commander of the Victorian Order.

His death at Assouan on January 29, 1912, was the unfortunate result of a chill contracted by exposure after the wreck of the ss. *Delhi* off Cape Spartel, when the Duke, the Princess Royal, and the two princesses were

on their way to Egypt. His body was brought home in H.M S. *Powerful*, and the funeral, attended by the King and the Royal Family, took place at Windsor, from whence the body was removed in the autumn of 1912 to the vault in the private chapel at Mar Lodge.

It will be recollected that in the weeks succeeding the Duke's death much discussion took place as to whether the Irish title of Earl Fife, dating from 1759, could be held independently of the dukedom, which by special remainder descended to his daughter.

One claimant to this title, now in Australia, purported to trace his descent from the Hon. George Duff of Milton,[1] son of the first, and brother of the second and third Earls, but this claim has been shown to be without foundation, there being now no living male representatives of the family of the first Earl, to whom and to his heirs-male the first titles were granted ; and all subsequent creations (except the last) having been similarly restricted, the titles to the Barony of Braco of Kilbryde 1735, Viscount of Macduff and Earldom of Fife 1759, in the peerage of Ireland, Barony Skene of Skene 1857, Earl of Fife (United Kingdom) 1885, Dukedom of Fife and Marquisate of Macduff 1889, are all extinct, while the creation of 1900 is now enjoyed by the present Duchess.

On October 15, 1913, Her Highness Princess Alexandra, Duchess of Fife, was married to H.R.H. Prince Arthur of Connaught.

---

[1] By a son named Daniel, but that George Duff had no such son is shown conclusively by the memorandum of his family left by James, the second Earl, and quoted in chapter xxix

H.H.ALEXANDRA DUCHESS OF FIFE,
PRINCESS ARTHUR OF CONNAUGHT.

CRAIGSTON CASTLE

CHAPTER XVI

DUFFS OF HATTON

PATRICK DUFF of Craigston, circa 1655, died 1731,	
m first, 1687, Anne Innes Thirteen children	m secondly, 1700, Mary Urquhart Twenty-three children

Alexander (Hatton). John (Elgin)	William (Whitehill). Patrick (Culter)	Helen Jean	James (Craigston)	Thomas, Archibald, Francis, all o.s p.	Robert (Fetteresso). Adam.	Elizabeth. Mary Margaret. Two other daughters.

THE third son of Alexander of Keithmore, Patrick Duff of Craigston, was born about 1655. Of his early history little is known, beyond what can be gathered from the following brief references:

In 1687 Patrick Duff, youngest son of Alexander Duff of Keithmore, received 6000 merks as his bairn's part. This was on the occasion of his first marriage. (Rose MS.).

In 1688 there was a sasine to Patrick Duff in Braco, formerly in Hillockhead of Balveny, youngest son to Alexander Duff of Keithmore. (Rose MS.).

In 1691 Patrick Duff of Braco was factor for the Duke of Gordon.[1]

He fully maintained the family traditions of energy and aptitude for

---

[1] *Aberdeen Sheriff Court Records* He was also an elder of Grange, and in the kirk-session records we find, under date March 2, 1693, ' John Gall, elder, at the Nether Mill of Strathisla, reported that Patrick Duff in Braco in breadth of my face called me a warlock.'

business. He carried on the trade in corn and meal which had been so successfully established by his father and elder brother, and became a man of great wealth. He purchased the estate of Castleton from Sir John Guthrie in 1695; Knockleith from James Urquhart, father of his second wife, in 1702; Craigston from the Duke of Gordon in 1705; and Hatton from Meldrum of Hatton in 1709.

Baird, who must have known him personally, says, ' He was a man of strong natural parts, and a most active industrious spirit. . . . Though naturally of a very passionate temper, he could argue with the greatest coolness, and was a man of so much acuteness and sagacity that he was seldom outwitted in any transaction.' Baird also gives a tale of Patrick of Craigston and his brother-in-law, Captain John Urquhart of Cromarty · ' When the Captain came to Britain in 1723 to get three ships built at London for the trade of South America, in consequence of his Licence from the King of Spain, he called for the clearances between his father and Craigston upon the price of the lands of Knockleith. Finding the remainder due to him much less than he expected, he complained, but finding he could be no better, concluded with saying: " Well, Craigston, I 'll tell you one thing. Ill-won gear will not last." " Ha, man," says Craigston, " i' my saul, man, ye 're a' mistane; it 's only ill-guided gear that winna last." ' In the latter part of his life he gave up the trade of ' carrying meal and malt to the south of the Firth, and confined himself entirely to agriculture, which he understood to perfection in the common old method, and to buying and selling country bolls [1] of meal. He acquired a pretty little fortune from a small beginning, which enabled him to bring up and give education to a very numerous family of children, leave landed estates to the eldest sons of both marriages, and provide for all the rest; he alwise kept a most hearty hospitable house.'

The house must indeed have been well filled. Patrick Duff was married twice, first to Anne Innes of Edingight, by whom he had thirteen children, and, secondly, to Mary Urquhart of Knockleith, by whom he had twenty-three; thirty-six children in all.[2] He is said to have been complimented by George II. on the addition he had made to His Majesty's subjects in Scotland. Many of the children seemed to have died in infancy, as was

---

[1] The amount of a boll differed in different parts of the country, and for different commodities, from two to six bushels For oats in Aberdeen it was the latter quantity

[2] ' Patrick Duff of Craigston had thirty-six children. There was " Hatton " and twelve more by the first wife, Miss Innes, by the second wife, Mary Urquhart, twenty-three. The eldest son (of second marriage), James, married Helen Abercromby, sister of General Abercromby of Glassaugh, and had one daughter Helen, who married David Clerk.' (Note by Baron Clerk-Rattray, son of the last-mentioned Written (January 12, 1829) on a family tree belonging to Norwich Duff, grandfather of the present writers)

generally the case in those days, but it was current tradition that twelve sons carried Patrick to his grave, and four sons of the first family and two daughters, and six sons of the second and five daughters are known to us. Almost a complete generation must have elapsed between the birth of the eldest and the youngest child of this large family, and it is reported that the father having met a small white-haired laddie playing in the garden at Craigston, inquired, ' And wha's laddie are you ? ' To which the future Admiral Robert Duff of Logie and Fetteresso, fifth son, who survived and is known to us, of the second marriage, is said to have replied : ' Dinna ye ken your ain son Robbie, ye auld fool ! '

The complete table of the family of Craigston known to us is as follows (this Duff would appear to be responsible for about half of those of the name now existing in the north) :

PATRICK DUFF married, in 1687, Anne Innes (died 1700), daughter of John Innes, fifth Laird of Edingight, and had thirteen children, of whom the following six are known to us :

    ALEXANDER, born 1688, baptised January 5.
    JOHN, born 1689.
    WILLIAM, born 1690.
    HELEN, born 1691, baptised October 25.
    PATRICK, born 1692
    JEAN, born 1696 ; married, 1720, John Innes ; died 1778.

He married, secondly, on October 4, 1701, Mary Urquhart of Knockleith, and had twenty-three children. She died in 1764 at Banff. Some of her children were :

    JAMES, born *circa* 1702.
    THOMAS, born *circa* 1704.
    ARCHIBALD, born *circa* 1714.
    FRANCIS, born *circa* 1715.
    ROBERT, born *circa* 1721.
    ADAM, born *circa* 1725
    ELIZABETH, married J Stuart of Auchorrachan.
    MARY, married W. Leslie of Melross.
    MARGARET, born 1720, married A. Gordon of Gight
    Another married Davidson of Newton.
    Another married Benjamin Duff, an Irishman.

Patrick Duff died August 3, 1731.[1]

The family of Hatton must first be traced.

The eldest son of the thirty-six, Alexander of Hatton, was born in 1688.

---

[1] For Patrick Duff's sympathies with the Jacobite rising of 1715 see chapter xxxvi

To no one does Baird devote so much space, and a long quotation from this, the first historian of the family, must therefore be permitted here :

'As Alex. Duff of Hatton was my intimate friend and particular acquaintance for above thirty years,[1] and one who, during the whole course of his life, was really in the first class, as a man of the world and a man of business, I shall be the more explicit in giving an account of him.

'He had an excellent understanding—a retentive memory, a clear and distinct manner of thinking and of expressing his thoughts on every subject. He served an apprenticeship of five years to Thomas Boys, a Writer to the Signet in Edinburgh, which, with his application and quick parts, made all sort of business familiar to him, and gave him a superiority over most men. His abilities both for public and private affairs were such that he could have been a minister of state to any prince in Europe. And the Earl of Findlater, who died in 1730, used to say that in person, solidity of judgment and address, Hatton put him in remembrance of Sir Robert Walpole. . . . He was a blessing to several young Gentlemen to whom he was named Tutor and Curator by their parents, in directing the management of their affairs. . . . He did more than any man I know to introduce good husbandry amongst his own farmers and in the neighbouring parishes.

'He was alwise on the Commission of the Peace and a strenuous Protector of the Country by mitigating the Severity of the Excise Laws, and when any riot fell out between a farmer and a malt Gauger, which was frequent at the first introduction of that Tax upon Scotland, he had a singular dexterity of saving the Offender from punishment, and of this I remember one instance which had something ludicrous in it.

'A malt officer came to a Gentleman's house in that neighbourhood, and desired his servant, whom he found turning over a dunghill, to give him the key of his master's barn, because he was informed there was malt on the floor. The servant denied he had the key, and gave the Officer so much abusive language as provoked the other to strike him. Upon which the servant beat the gauger, who then made his complaint to Hatton, and was assured that he should have all justice if he summoned the rascal to appear at the Justice of the Peace Court at Turriff to be held in a few days. The Gentleman also came to Hatton asking protection for his man, and was " bidden attend the court and bring the Lad with him, but that he should get his whole head close shaved, with a wig upon it, in a suit of good cloths, with a clean shirt and cravat put on, and speak very smooth.

'They all came to court, and Hatton began by setting forth the heinousness of the Crime, and concluded with saying that the punishment for such a knave ought to be transportation. Then the lad was called, and the Gauger asked if that was the person who had struck him. He, who did not know him in his new figure, cried " By no manner of means. The fellow who struck him was liker to the Devil than to that Lad." His master said, if that was not the

---

[1] He was also his brother-in-law, the two men having married sisters, daughters of Dipple.

Criminal, he could not conceive who it could have been, for he had no servant at present, but him and a boy ; the officer found afterwards that he had been fairly bubbled (*i.e.* made fun of), but was obliged to sit down with the skaith (injury) and the scorn too.'

The obituary notice of the death of Alexander Duff of Hatton in the *Aberdeen Journal* calls him, among other things, ' The arbitrator and universal reconciler of differences.' He married, in 1709, his cousin, Catherine Duff of Dipple, who was ' elder than him by three years and survived him five years.' [1]

On his marriage, his father gave him Hatton and Knockleith, but, as he at the same time took Catherine's portion of 12,000 merks, and moreover left the Hatton estate bare of crops, Alexander was indeed, as Baird expresses it, ' brought up thro' the hard,' and was a poor man, comparatively speaking, for some years. He was able to add to his resources by obtaining, in conjunction with Alexander Achyndachy, the ' factory ' [2] of the forfeited estate of the Earls of Dunfermline,[3] which he managed with great success until the lands were sold in 1727. He very soon began the purchase of small estates adjoining his own. The first was Bogfontein in 1719. Some years later he bought Drumblair and some other smaller properties from Theodore Morison of Bognie, and in 1729 Balquholly from John Mowat for £4000, Downies and Auchinhamper from North Leslie, and Balnoon from Ogilvie. ' His last purchase was, in 1753, of about 2000 merks pr. annum of the estate of Kinnairdy, and after all he left 10,000 sterling settled on good security. In a word, I am convinced no man in his time conducted all his affairs with greater prudence, or, I believe, with more honesty, and gave a better example of all commendable industry ' (Baird). He died in 1753, and is buried at Auchterless. He seems to have been the only one of William, Lord Braco's brothers-in-law who did not come to him for pecuniary help. A few of his letters exist, but they are not of general interest. He appears to have taken no part in the political events of his time, beyond the following :

' Decreet against Alexander Duff of Hatton for £200 Scots, two years rent of a house in Banff, taken and possessed by him from Whitsunday 1746 to Whitsunday 1748, belonging to the deceased George Abernethy, convicted of high treason

' It was found proven that Alex. Duff the Defender took the house for one year from Whit 1746 to Whit. 1747 at £100 Scots of rent ; that the house was possessed by the Duke of Cumberland's army, the house as a Hospital and the Lower part as a Magazine, until the first of Nov. following, and that it was with

---

[1] ' Died on 20 Dec. 1758 Lady Hatton ' (*Aberdeen Journal*)   [2] Management
[4] These included Fyvie

difficulty they would remove and give the Defender access, and when he got
access he was put to extraordinary expense in mucking, cleaning, washing,
repairing, and fitting it up for being habitable. The Defender was eventually
allowed to retain his expenses for repairing and cleaning the house, amounting
to £16 14 6 Scots, out of the half-year's rent ' (*Scottish Forfeited Estates Papers.*
Scot. Hist. Soc).

By his wife, Catherine Duff, second daughter of William Duff of Dipple,
he had seven children ·

1. PATRICK, who predeceased his father. He married, in 1738, Mary
Ogilvie of Inchmartine, and she died in 1784 a widow. There were no
children.

2. ALEXANDER and

3. JOHN, who both succeeded to Hatton.

4. JAMES, Sheriff-Clerk of Banff.

5. MARGARET, who married her second cousin, Gordon, an officer of
Customs at Dundee. She is said to have eloped with him, and died 1750.

6. JANE, who married James Abernethy,[1] third of Mayen.

7. HELEN, died unmarried, in 1796, and the following rhyme was
current in Banff at the time, referring to the spinster of the family .

> ' Gin I 'd as many braw new gowns
> As Provost Dirom's Suffy [2] has,
> Gin I could walk the streets as clean
> As Mistress Gordon Goody [3] does,
> I wudna lain sae lang my lane
> As Hatton's Gley-ed [4] Nelly has.'

---

[1] ' James Abernethy quarrelled at an election dinner in Aberdeen with John Leith of Leith-
hall, and shot him dead in the street He effected his escape, but was outlawed and died abroad
(at Dunkirk, 1771) Lord Fife obtained a gift of his life-rent of Mayen for the benefit of Jean
Duff and her children ' (*Frasers of Philorth*).
These children were
   1 James, last of Mayen, died intestate 1785.
   2 John, 1759-1779, buried at Rothiemay.
   3 William, died young
   4. Jane, 1751-1805, married, in 1785, Alexander Duff of Mayen (*q v*)
   5. Isabella, married Lieutenant Graham of the 42nd Regiment.
   6 Helen, 1753-1787, buried at Rothiemay.
   7. Anne, died 1796
   8 Katherine *
And five others died young Jean Duff died 1780, and is buried in Banff
[2] Sophia Dirom, afterwards wife to George Duff, R N
[3] Miss Goodrich Gordon, an eccentric lady who lived in Banff, where she boasted much
of her connection with the Duke of Gordon, and habitually dressed in the family tartan
[4] Gleyd, cross-eyed, from which we infer that the lady squinted

* ' Poor Kitty Abernethy is dying ' (1774)

She is buried in Banff, where presumably she lived in her latter days. Her stone is still in the old churchyard, and on it, besides her own name, are those of Alexander, Sophia, and Mary, three children of her brother James, who died in infancy. There are no dates.

ALEXANDER the second of Hatton, born March 26, 1718, had married, in 1745, his second cousin by the father's and first by the mother's side, Anne Duff, eldest daughter of William, Lord Braco [1] (she became Lady Anne in 1759, when her father was created Earl Fife). By the contract of marriage, Hatton, Knockleith, and Balquholly were entailed on the heirs-male of Alexander and his brothers in succession, and he was given immediate possession of Balquholly, which he rebuilt, and changed the name of the house to Hatton Lodge. After his father's death he was very well off, and spent a good deal of money [2] on the education of the only child who survived infancy, Jean, married, at seventeen, to her mother's first cousin, Sir James Grant of Grant. She had fourteen children, seven sons and seven daughters, and two of her sons were afterwards Earls of Seafield.

She married Sir James Grant of Grant, M.P., at Bath in January 1763. Her fourteen children were :

1. Lewis Alexander, fifth Earl of Seafield, born 1767.

2. Alexander, born at Castle Grant 1772.

3 James Thomas, born 1776 ; a judge in the Indian Civil Service ; died 1804.

4. Francis William, M.P., afterwards sixth Earl of Seafield, and father of seventh and ninth earls,[3] and great-grandfather of the present earl.

5. Robert Henry, born 1783.

6. Alexander Hope, born 1784.

7. Dundas, born 1788.

1. Anne Margaret, died unmarried 1827 (see page 218).

2. Margaret, married Major-General Francis Stewart of Lesmurdie.

---

[1] From whom he had the salmon fishings at Banff, and in March 1749 writes thus to his father-in-law ' The fishing goes on bravely   We have catched a good many more than last year at this time, and all the old fishers say the Watter mouth was never so direct from the sea as it is now—which is a great advantage.'   To those who know the present mouth of the Deveron between Banff and Macduff, the quotation is interesting

[2] He has left the accounts of his expenses during a winter tour in England, which amounted to £1000

[3] Francis William, sixth Earl, 1778-1853

John Charles, seventh Earl, 1815-1881.   James, ninth Earl, 1817-1888

Ian Charles, eighth Earl, 1851-1884.   Francis W., tenth Earl, 1847-1888.

James, eleventh and present Earl, 1876

3. Jane, died unmarried 1809.

4. Penuel, died 1844.

5 Christina Teresa, died unmarried 1793.

6. Magdalene, died unmarried.

7. Mary Sophia, died unmarried 1788.

Jean and her husband, with several of their children, are buried in Duthil churchyard. There is a portrait of her by Zoffany at Cullen House, and a copy at Hatton.

Alexander Duff died in 1764, at the early age of forty-four, as the result of an accident in falling over a sack of coal in his own cellar. He broke his leg, and it was afterwards amputated, but he died a few days later from loss of blood.[1]

'HATTON LODGE, Oct. 29th, 1764

'MY LORD,—The Doctor determined yesterday that it was in vain to expect an effectual cure upon Mr. Duff's Leg, and that allowing him to linger on for four or five months longer, attempting a cure, was only unnecessarily endangering his Health, and that after all they would be in all human probability obliged to cut it off at the last.

'They therefore spoke of the uncertainty to himself, upon which he immediately took the hint, and with the utmost composure begd it might be cut off.

'He underwent the operation this morning and is in as good a way as could be expected. His magnanimity and coolness were remarkable through the whole and supported the spirits of every one about him.

'All this family join in kind compliments to your Lordship, Lady Fife, and all at Duff House, and I remain with the utmost regard, My Lord, Your most obedt. and affect. Servt.,   JAS GRANT.

'P.S.—Your Lordship will oblige me by communicating this to Mr James Duff as I have not a moment to write.

'To the Earl of Fife, Duff House, Banff'   (D)

Band thus sums up Alexander the second of Hatton. 'He was an honest, generous, sensible man, of a very candid, ingenuous disposition, a warm heart to his friends, and nothing sordid or unworthy of a gentleman in his nature, it was a great loss to all his connections, and I may say to the countrie in general, that his days were so few; his Tenants lamented his early death as if they had lost their father.'[2]

---

[1] It is almost impossible now to realise what such an operation meant at that date, and how great was the danger It was prior even to the days when Lord Nelson unconsciously advocated the sterilising of the surgeon's knife by previously plunging it into boiling water, because in the amputation of his own arm he had found the cold of the steel the hardest thing to bear

[2] He left one natural son, Alexander, afterwards Colonel 58th Regiment and proprietor of Mayen He married, and his family will be found in chapter xviii

The estates of Hatton, Knockleith, and the other entailed property then passed to John Dulf, brother of Alexander, but the latter had left all personal property and all estates not entailed to his wife and daughter, the estates being worth £25,000 a year. To Jean, Lady Grant, went also all the family pictures, plate, and china.

To Lady Anne was left a liferent of the mansion-house of Balquholly, to which she maintained her right until her death, forty years later. She died in Edinburgh 1805. Several letters of Lady Anne to her brother Arthur, late in life, show her as taking a great interest in the estate, price of crops, etc. She was very kind to her various nieces, particularly the daughters of Jane Urquhart, kept a hospitable house, and visited a good deal among her neighbours. When nearly seventy she writes : ' Mrs. Stewart and family have to leave me instead of staying till the month of October—however there is no loss, but there is some small profit, and it will enable me to visit some friends this season.'

There is one amusing letter from her to her brother James :

' *March 1st*, 1788.

' MY DEAR LORD,—I have just now a letter from Mrs. Duff, Housedale, requesting I wd. write your Lordsᵖ in favors of a son of Mr. Duff's minister of Monimusk, for his having your Interest for him to be apointed School Master of Keith in room of the Present School Master—who is apointed 2nd Minister of Old Abdn.—Mr. Duff has a large young familie—and I saw this young man last Summer—he seem'd modest and well behaved—Mrs Duff writes me that my Br. Alexr. was to write for James Grant—but left it to me to solicitate your intrest in favor of Mr. Duff.

' They do me a great deal of honor—but I have not the vanity, but to think Alexr. as well intitled to ask a favor as I am and rather better at Present, as he has not given you so much trouble as I have lately done—but alls well that ends well—(as the Play says) which I hope will be the present case. Lady Augusta Hay (Erroll) is to be married Tuesday next to Ld. Glasgow, I 'm glad, as the familie are so large of Dauglis.—the story goes thus—at the Peers assembly—Lord Glasgow was there—he hates dancing and never dances, he came up to Lady Augusta—who was sitting—ask'd her Lap. why she was not dancing—she say'd she was not found of Dancing and would not dance that night—he requested then, to have the honor of being of her Sitting Partie, which was agreed to—next that he might be admitted to visit her next day—this was also agreed to, and next day he offered to give her himself—which she accepted off.—Adieu, my Dr. Lord, with esteem and respects, yours, etc.,   ANNE DUFF.

' The Earl of Fife, Whitehall, London.'   (*R*.)

And one to her brother Arthur on the occasion of the death of her mother's brother :

'Hatton Lodge, *Wednesday afternoon*
(*circa* 1785)

' I was concerned but not surprised, my Dear Brother, when last Post brought me the acct^{ts} of our worthie Unkle's Death. My fears by the state I knew he was in for two years were great—yet as long as there is Life there is some degree of Hope, and so was my mind as to him. We both knew him so well that we need say nothing to each other as to him, Yet sure enough our residence in this world is so uncertain that those that Love each other, sh^d as far as they conveniently can, enjoy each others society as much as in there Power. I have done so all the well days of my Life. I depend as all of us does, upon Providence, if it pleases Him I w^d wish my Seck days to be short and to see then as few of my Friends, or of those that continues to Love my Driggs [1] as possible.

' I 'll assure you what I supposed my mothers feelings might be upon the occation gave me true uneasiness, the good accts Ld Fife gave me yesterday of her gave me much pleasure. I have not yet fixed a day for moving South-wards as I have various little matters to put into my ordinary method before I go, but at no time but that the sight of you will give Pleasure.

' I unite with you Perfectly in the old adage that we should live like Brethren but by no manner of means Count like Jews, for as I wrote you in my last from Edn. I gain'd twinty shillings by lending you £100. Instead of having it in the hand I took it from the ordinary Received interest in General is 2½ P.C. so with-out obligation upon either side it is but fair to Return a 20 sh^{lls} note and you can Calculate whether it is one shilling or Eighteen pence difference by the odd four months upon the ten shillings discount of the years ½ P.C.

' My Aff^{te} Duty to my Mother with warmest wishes for Comfortable and happy days to be her lote. Lord Fife talks of her as an evergreen, he say'd for many years he had not known her so well in health, strength, Intellect and memorie as Intire as in the best days of her life and that you was absent so that they were quit by themselves which enabled him to form a Perfect Judgement.

' I have wrote so much to-day that my write is wear to a hair and as I 'm convinced you have got enough of the goodness I shall only Request you to beheve me with my Duty to my Mother and Aff^{te} Regards to Frances,—Your truly Aff^{te} Sister and friend,　　　　　　　　ANNE DUFF.'　(O.)

Some extracts from her will show her in a very gracious light. ' Cer-tain testamentary dispositions of Lady Anne Duff of Hatton to Sir James and Lady Grant, dated Hatton, June 11th, 1805.'

Among minor legacies occur :

' To my niece Mary Urquhart, to two Miss Whartons, Jane Catherine Anne Brodie, Anne Duff, daughter of James Duff and niece to my

---

[1] Dregs, remains.

late husband, £50 each. Also to Anne Duff, daughter to my brother Alexander.

' Also to my faithful and esteemed friend, Colonel Duff of Mayen,[1] whose love and affection for me have been such as a child would possess for a parent, I bequeath his late dear father's miniature picture set round with pearls. At the back there is placed that father's hair, my hair, and Sir James and Lady Grant's hair ; this I know will be an acceptable present to him. I desire that he may receive my silver tea-kettle and lamp. I request that he will at my death give all the assistance he can in rouping (*i.e.* selling by auction) my house in George Square, and in the rouping of my furniture there and at Hatton Lodge.

' I bequeath £100 to my black servant.

' To Lady Sophia Wharton [*her sister*] a ring set round with diamonds with our father's hair, and another ring with Lady Gordon's [*her sister Janet's*] hair, set as an urn.'

JOHN DUFF, styled of Drumblair, possession of which estate and of Lensham he had enjoyed during his brother's lifetime, was born in 1727, and died 1787. He succeeded to Hatton 1764. He married, on January 26, 1762, his first cousin once removed, Helen Duff of Whitehill, and by her had sixteen children :

BATHIA, born December 8, 1762, died October 3, 1774.
ANNE, born February 17, 1764, died April 8, 1775.
ALEXANDER, born January 14, 1765, died 1791.
PATRICK, born June 12, 1766, died 1801.
CLEMENTINA, January 16, 1767, died *circa* 1845.
JAMES, born August 10, 1768, died before 1789.
ANDREW, born September 17, 1769, died 1819.
JOHN, born February 12, 1771, died before 1776.
KATHERINE, born June 22, 1772, died 1805.
JEAN, born July 6, 1773, died 1793.
WILLIAM, born October 12, 1774, died before 1808.
JOHN, born January 2, 1776, died before 1789.
BATHIA, March 13, 1778, died an infant.
GARDEN, born November 1, 1779, died 1858
ANN, born April 15, 1781, died young
ROBERT, born May 1, 1783, died 1854.

In 1776 ' the six sons of Hatton ' were made burgesses of Banff. These must have been the six eldest, aged eleven, ten, eight, seven, five, and two.

In 1790 the three remaining ' sons of the late John Duff of Hatton '

---

[1] See chapter xviii

were similarly honoured. They were John, Garden, and Robert, aged fourteen, eleven, and seven.[1]

All but two of these children died without issue, some in very early infancy (and a curious stone in Auchterless churchyard commemorates seven of them).[2] The family lived at the manor house of Hatton in Auchterless, and John seems to have acquiesced in all the arrangements made by his brother, which impoverished both the estate and himself. He lived quietly, saved money, and made some small additions to the estates.

As far as we know, only six of the sons lived to grow up—Alexander, Patrick, Andrew, and Garden, who all succeeded to Hatton; William, who died in early manhood, and Robert, who became a merchant in Glasgow and died unmarried 1854, and three of the daughters—Clementina, who lived to old age in Banff; Jean, who died in Edinburgh, aged twenty; and Katherine, who died at Peterhead in 1805, aged twenty-three.[3]

The daughters had £600 by their father's will, and the sons £700. Helen Duff succeeded her brother in Whitehill in 1786, and left it eventually to her son Garden, who sold it.

Like all the rest of the family, John Duff applied to Lord Fife for help, and writes on April 3, 1781 :

'My Lord,—I have seen you Lordship very oblidgeing and kind letter off the 14th to Mrs. Duff. We are both very sensible off your kind concern for the weelfare off our ffamily. Wee have resolved to give our children the choice of their trade—or business that seems most their own inclination, after sygnifycing to them what appears to be the business most advantageous to them. Petter our second son made two proposals ; the scaffearing life or to goe out to the East Indies as a Cadett. Att last he ffixed on the goeing out to the East Indies : And every step after has been taken to prepare him as ffar as the education here would doe and its now ffixed that he goe to an Academy in ffrance att Calmar in Upper Lusatica to learn the ffrench languadge and to compleat him in the Military line as it was mentioned to us a proper step ; and Delgaty's Eldest son Sandie Garden goes with him who also intends goeing into the Army in the British Service ; wee would only wish to have Petter readie to goe out the

---

[1] Children of well-known men were frequently made burgesses in those days, and the entertainment given was varied accordingly .

Thus to '4½ pints rum at making Captain Baird and Captain Lawson burgesses 15/9d , 1 dozen lemonds, 1 dozen biscuits and 3 lb loaf sugar at 10d =4s

'But to 2½ lbs. raisins for some boys made burgesses 1/3d. 1768, Sheriff Urquhart's children made burgesses, for confections to them 4s ' (Banff Records)

[2] 'Two daughters named Bathia, two daughters named Ann ; two sons named John, and a daughter named Katherine.'

[3] Peterhead was then a health resort, and the Aberdeen Journal of that time contains frequent lists of visitors to the baths and wells of that place. General Wolfe passed three weeks there in 1751 in search of health. See his Life by Beckles Wilson.

next Spring or with the first ships off that season for the East Indies ; May I presume to ask the favour of your Lordship to give your aide to procure a Cadett ship on the Bengale establishment and your ffriendly recommendating to any of your acquaintances in the East Indies ; wee should be happy to have my son in the same corner with my wife's brother Petter who has experience and is long their ; and a good hearted man , He is just now at Generell Godert's att Bombay.   But as he is upon the Bengale establishment, its more than probable that upon the pease with the Moratoes [1] he will return their.   The ffirst letter that his ffriends here getts from him possibly will inform them of the place he has expectation to be att, whether Bengale or Bombay.

'Mrs. Duff joins me in our best wishes for every ffelicity to your Lordship.— I have the honour to be, My Lord, Your Lordship's ver oblidged humble serv^t,
'JOHN DUFF.' [2]   (D.)

JAMES OF BANFF, fourth and third surviving son of the first Alexander of Hatton, was born in 1729, and died 1804.   As a boy of sixteen he ' went out ' in the '45, but was sent home after the skirmish of Inverurie, and owing to his extreme youth and the family interest the matter was hushed up, and he seems to have suffered in no way for what was considered his early indiscretion.

Lord Sempill, commanding at Aberdeen, to the Earl of Albemarle, C. in C. Scotland

'ABERDEEN, Aug. 21, 1746.

'MY LORD,— . . . Since I have been hear I have been Solicited by Sir Alex. Reed,[3] Mr. Duff of Hatton, and Mr. Reed, who each of them had a son about Eighteen Years of Age, printises in this place, and were unhappily Seduced to go with the Rebels to Inverurie ; as the above Gentlemen are well affected to his Majesty and Government, So soon as they had an account of their having Joind thoas Rebels, they Emediately Seazed them, which prevented them being any more concern'd.   Your Lordsp. will please observe they are younger Brothers and men off no Estate nor fortone.   I would not give them any passes such as the Common Sort of Rebels gets till I know your Lordsp.'s pleasure about them. .   .' [4]

Sir Harry Innes of Innes to Ludovick Grant of Grant

'ELGIN, Sept 10th, 1745.

'DEAR SIR,—We ar hear in a perpetuall alarm for Glenbucket ; he took sume of the Duke of Gordon's horses and arms this morning, at lest I am credably

---

[1] Mahrattas

[2] John's son Peter or Patrick was appointed Ensign in the 78th Regiment of Highland Foot, November 20, 1781, and writes from Tanjore, September 1, 1788, to thank Lord Fife for the many favours he has done him, for allowing Patrick ' a place in his friendship,' and for mentioning his name to Lord Cornwallis and Colonel Ross, and asks for assistance in purchasing his company   For ' my wife's brother Petter,' see chapter XIX.

[3] Of Bara   [4] *Albemarle Papers*, vol. i. p 134.

inform'd of it, and have no reson to question its beeing trew. I am sory to tell you that the Duke is quite wronge.

' This alarm and seearch for horses has determined me to send mine under your protection. Yow have the most of my cavalry, and God knows they ar but very indiferent. Was it not mor for humour that they shall not have them, then the reall valow, I should not send one out of the way. Lord Braco, his son Jamie, and Mr. Duff, younger of Hatton,[1] went to the west this day, to be free of Glenne. I met his Lordship as I was walking to Innes, and now I must walk, for the divell of a hors I have worth riding. News I have non   Our compliments to Lady Margaret, and behve me, yours, etc.,

' HARIE INNES.'
(From Fraser's Chiefs of Grant.)

' James Duff writers apprentice Hatton, Auchterless, Aberdeen, carried arms in the character of an officer at Inverury,[2] and was one of those who apprehended Mr. Maitland of Pitrichie, not known where he is ' (Rosebery's <i>Last of Persons concerned in the Rebellion, 1745</i>).

James Duff was afterwards, in 1761, appointed, by Lord Bute, Sheriff-Clerk of Banff (in those days a most important post), and Deputy-Keeper of Sasines 1765. He received £2200 from his father, and sasine from his brother Alexander on various crofts. There are many letters from James Duff in the family correspondence, but they are mostly on business and not of general interest. He was factor for the estate of Mayen, and did other business for the family. A few extracts are given :

James Duff of Banff to the second Lord Fife

' BANFF, 22nd Feby.

' Before leaving Duff House, I took the liberty of mentioning a communcing that had taken place twixt Mr. Abercrombie of Glassa and his Brother the Parson, regarding his office of Kings Painter ; the Parson, I find does not incline to resign and allow a new commission to be taken out, so that there is nothing to be done at present, but applying for the Commission in the event of his death, that is some times done, but I beleve not readily, and very uncertain it is, who may have the disposal when it comes to be open.'

---

[1] Alexander, elder brother of James.

[2] Skirmish of Inverurie, December 23, 1745 Lord Lewis Gordon, with about nine hundred men, Drumonds, Farquharsons, and Gordons, defeated a large body of Government supporters under MacLeod of Skye, to whom Lord President Forbes and Lord London were anxious to entrust some important enterprise to mark their appreciation of his adherence. The slaughter at Inverurie was not great, but about fifty prisoners fell into the hands of the Jacobite forces, amongst whom were a son of Gordon of Ardoch, Maitland of Pitrichie, Forbes of Echt, and Professor John Chalmers of Aberdeen University

JAMES DUFF OF BANFF.

Lord Fife's answer (noted on the back of the letter, in the convenient manner of those times) :

'If the Abercrombies had agreed to take a new Commission with him or his son included in it which, by the by, would not have been excentric. The only favour the Abercrombies could do would be to resign, if a new commission could be obtained for Mr. Duff's son.'[1]   (R.)

As early as 1765, James Duff was pining to get away from what he calls 'this corner,' *i.e.* Banff, where there was 'little work to be done in the business to which he was bred,' and hopes by Lord Fife's interest to obtain some Government post.

In 1794 he announces that Sir James Grant, his nephew, 'has now obtained new commissions for my son and me for keeper of the Register and Sasines and Clerk to the Peace.'

On February 3, 1802, he writes, referring to James, fourth Lord Fife :

'The anniversary of the Queen's Birthday was held here, on the 18th ult. with great splendour. We had an elegant dinner at Watson's Hotel, and after having a sufficient portion of wine went to a ball given by the Volunteers of the Trades Company, where we enjoyed ourselves till one in the morning, and then Sandy Milne and I supped at G G Robinson's with James Duff, the heir of Fife, where we set till 3 A.M., but this is not at all uncommon for ever since Mr. Duff came to this country we have not dined till 5, and seldom or ever went home before 2, 3, or 4 A.M. when he was of the party. He is very much liked here on account of his affability and agreeable manners.'   (R.)

James was twice married, first, at the age of twenty-six, to Helen Skene of Rubislaw,[2] who bore him a daughter, Helen, and two sons, Alexander and George ; dying when the latter was six weeks old, March 12, 1764.

And, secondly, on February 1, 1772, when forty-three, to Margaret Dunbar of Kincorth (aged eighteen), whose mother was Isobel Abercromby of Birkenbog, and had by her thirteen children, several of whom died young.[3]

First Family

HELEN, 1756.   ALEXANDER, 1758.   GEORGE, 1764-1805.

---

[1] The office of King's Painter was worth about £100 a year until the emoluments were reduced by Burke See page 123 The Rev. Thomas St Clair Abercromby seems to have held it until his death.

[2] 'On 12th Aug 1755, was married in this place, Mr James Duff, Advocate, to Miss Nelly Skene (daughter of George Skene of Robslaw, Esq), a young lady posesst of every accomplishment that can render happy the connubial state' (*Aberdeen Journal* of that date)

[3] In 1790, 'Three sons of James Duff, Esq , Sheriff-Clerk of Banff, were made burgesses of Banff ' No names given

Second Family

JAMES, 1773; his birth is mentioned by Baird, writing in 1773.	ISABELLA, *circa* 1780.
	CATHERINE, *circa* 1782.
MARY, 1774.	ANNE, 1784-1876
JAMES WILLIAM, 1776-1797.	SOPHIA, 1785.
FIFE, 1778-1800.	Another, died young.
JOHN, 1779-1801.	

Helen, the eldest, made a runaway marriage with Thomas Bell, a travelling actor, against her father's wishes, and the younger children were for long unaware of her existence.[1] In her father's will a sum of money is left to her, but in the event of her death, her husband was not to benefit

Ten days after the marriage Helen writes from Aberdeen :

'*May 9th*, 1782

' MY LORD,—I the more readily address myself to you in my present situation as your Lordship was not altogether unacquainted with an attachment I had formed when I had last the pleasure of seeing you in Banff, many causes have concurred to forward that atatchment into affection which has since ended in marriage. I shall be plain with your Lordship and relate a circumstance that pointed out the above conclusion as the most adviseable and indeed only step that I could take, which tho' it may not entirely efface your Lordship displeasure, I sincerely hope it may in some degree mitigate it. I must confess I ventured myself with Mr. Bell (as no clergyman could be found in Aberdeen who would marry us) as far as Montrose where we arrived late at night and were to have been married next morning had not his supposed friend who travelled with us at Mr. Bell's particular request, most maliciously and without provocation plunged a case-knife into his stomack and in so dangerous a manner that the whole of the Physicians there pronounced his recovery impossible, the event however has proved they were mistaken and as Mr. Bell concluded the accident could not have happened had I not been of the Party he imagined that having suffered so much entitled him in some degree to my hand which was given to him in the presence of some of my own Relations, it being now known that he is a Gentleman's son his father having been long an Officer in the 55th Regt. and now respectably settled in Ireland and his Stage profession was entirely owing to a temporary disagreement between them not a passion for it, well knowing the universal detestation in which it is held in this Country. Now, my Lord, permit me to explaine to your Lordship the reason of me thus troubling you—Gentlemen who have conversed with Mr. Bell have been pleased to think

---

[1] In the Register of St Paul's Episcopal Church, Aberdeen, appears :

'April 28, 1782. Thomas Bell, son of Captain Bell, Dublin, and Helen Duff were married', no witnesses given But the actual wedding seems to have taken place at Montrose, which is curious It was possibly a Scottish marriage only, followed by the church ceremony on the return to Aberdeen

favourably of him and say his education has been liberal and suits him for any employment, and I am certain your Lordship's goodness will plead in my excuse when I sollicit in his behalf, he is now my husband and I am anxiously desirous for his welfare and flattering myself that you will be pleased to think a little favourably of the connection I presume to offer him to your Lordship's consideration, as your Interest and Influence are both unquestionable permit me earnestly to entreat a small exertion of them in providing him with some small appointment many of which are in your Lordship's power which will ensure me happiness and prevent necessity from forcing him to his late profession, which at all events he is determined to relinquish untill such time as he sees if anything will be effected for his interest, and as my dependence is entirely upon your Lordship let me not sue in vain, and your compliance will put me in your gratitude to acknowledge your Lordship's favour while I have existence.—I am, My Lord, Your Lordship's most obedient and very humble servant,

'HELEN DUFF.' (D.)

And again from Edinburgh, January 23, 1788 (six years later):

'MY LORD,—I took the liberty to write to your Lordship some time ago requesting the loan of Ten Pounds for a particular purpose, but as I have not been favor'd with any answer I must conclude that either your Lordship is offended at my request, or if your Lordship wrote, the letter miscarried: the immediate want however of that sum induces me to apply again and to state the cause . I have two little white-headed boys the oldest is at home with myself running about, but the youngest is out at Nurse who is at present very clamorous for my arrear to her, which is almost eight pounds, and in consequence of my deficientcy I fear will use the Boy ill : I wish greatly to pay her and take him home. My Father (I must say) is an unjust unfeeling hardhearted man and consequently nothing cou'd move him to give me the least assistance : besides at present he's at law with my husband. I have only to say if your Lordship will condescend to listen to my application it will be ever gratefully acknowleded by your Lordships Truly Thankful Friend and humble Servt.,

'HELEN BELL.' (D.)

In 1793 James wrote to William Rose, ' Would it be prudent to cause try by some unconnected person if my poor daughter and her husband would upon granting bond for a certain sum discharge the claim of legitime. Mr. Lachlan Duff was employed for me in the dispute with them.'

Helen Bell had four children :

John, who went to the West Indies, where he did well, and died before 1837.

George Skene, whose baptism is registered in Aberdeen 1788 [1] (Register of St. Paul's Church), but of whom nothing more is known.

---

[1] He was probably not christened till he returned from his nurse. See above

Helen and Elizabeth, who married into a humble rank of life, and some of their descendants are still in Banff.

The children of these two daughters are enumerated as numbers 69 to 75 in the Fife entail of 1841. See chapter xiii.

ALEXANDER, eldest son of James of Banff, was at college in Aberdeen, but died young.

GEORGE was the distinguished officer killed at Trafalgar, and will be treated of in the next chapter.

Of the second family, the first JAMES died an infant, and is one of those buried in Banff. He was ' nameson ' to Lord Fife, and his mother writes thus to her husband's cousin, who was obviously a kind friend :

' MY LORD,—I had the honour of your Lordship's letter by last post and returnes you my best thanks for your kind enquairrys for me and your nameson who I thank God is very stout and thriveing. He was inoculated about ten days ago and is getting very easily over the small-pox. You shall have the direction of him whenever you wish.

' The pattern of paper your Lordship is so good as send me I do think is very genteel and pretty and very suitable to the furnitur in the room. The Dido round and painting below it I think will be a great improvement. Your Lordship is very good in remembering it. I should not have wondered from the hurry and bustel of the great world you are in had you not done it so soon

' Poor Mr. Abernethy who is with us is in a very declining state, his complaints are come on so rapedly that I much fear all remedys for his recovery will be ineffectual. It will always give Mr. Duff and I much pleasure to hear of your Lordships being in good health, we hope you will soon thinking of returning to Duff House ; he joins me in best respects and good wishes to your Lordship. Nelly begs her best respects may be offered you.—I am, your Lordships much obliged humble servant,   MARGT. OGIL. DUFF. (D.)

' BANFF, April 18th, circa 1775.'

Of the next three, MARY, JAMES WILLIAM, and FIFE, there is a charming portrait, now in the possession of Mr. Walter Blaikie. It is on the authority of their younger sister Anne, Mr. Blaikie's grandmother, that the portrait is said to represent these three.[1]

The second James lived to be twenty-one, and is buried in the Grey-friars church, Edinburgh. The following inscription was on his tomb-stone, but has now disappeared :

' James Wm. Duff, son of James Duff, Esq. of Banff, who died July 28, 1797, aged 21 years. To whose memory this stone is erected by his afflicted

---

[1] The dates of birth for some members of this family are only conjectural.

parents, as a tribute of their affection for a child whose conduct in life was such as to leave them ever to lament his loss.'

This James was educated at Aberdeen University (King's College), and appears in the Roll of Alumni 1789. He was afterwards articled to George Robinson of Gask, writer, and was then employed in the office of Messrs. Brodie, who acted for Lord Fife in Edinburgh. One brief letter of his has been preserved, and one from his father on his death:

'BANFF, *12th July* 1797

'DEAR SIR,—Your most friendly condolance for my dear Jamie I 'm certain is most sincere from you, as you always exprest a warm attachment to him, and he was ever gratefull, this severe stroke has much disconcerted me, and his poor mother to be pityed, I do what I can to conceal from her my feelings to support her, but nothing will do, but time and the assistance from Haven. I will be glad to see you at any time convenient, the visits from a friend gives pleasure. To you and all your friends at Montcoffer Mrs. Duff unites in good wishes.—I always am, D. Sir, Yours, JAMES DUFF.

'To William Rose.' (Mrs. Blaikie.)

FIFE was a midshipman, and died in 1800, when administration of his estate was granted to his father. (Registers at Somerset House.)

JOHN's death in 1801 is chronicled with regret in the journals of the period, and he must, therefore, have been 'a grown man,' and have come thus early in the family, but nothing is known about him.

ISABELLA died young.

CATHERINE lived long in Banff, and when over seventy went to Bath, and finally to Cheltenham, where she died before 1840. She took into her service Jane Suttie, granddaughter of her half-sister Helen, and was very kind to the rest of the family.

ANNE, the youngest daughter but one, married Mr. Walter Biggar, and died at the age of ninety-two, leaving one daughter, now Mrs. Blaikie, mother of fourteen children,[1] and numerous grandchildren and great-grandchildren.

SOPHIA, known to have been younger than Anne and one other, both died as infants.

James Duff died in 1804, and is buried in the old churchyard, Banff.

'To the memory of James Duff, Esq., 4th son of the first Alexander Duff of Hatton, who died 19 Nov. 1804, aged 75. As a just tribute of dutiful regard, this stone is placed over his remains by his affectionate widow, daughter of James Dunbar of Kincorth, 1805.

---

[1] The second son is Walter Biggar Blaikie, LL.D., author of the *Itinerary of Prince Charles Edward Stuart*, and other historical and antiquarian works.

' James, Isabella, and John Duff, their children are buried here. And Alexander, Sophia and Mary in the Grave with their aunt, Mrs. Helen Duff.

' Also Margaret Ogilvie Dunbar, Widow of the forenamed James Duff, died 1829, aged 75.'

TOWN HOUSE IN BANFF OF MRS. DUFF OF HATTON
(WHERE BYRON'S MARY STAYED WITH HER GRANDMOTHER)

To return to the main line of Hatton.

On the death (in 1787) of John Duff of Hatton, he was succeeded by ALEXANDER his third child and eldest son, 1765-1791. He married, in 1787, Mary Leslie of Glenmyre, of the family of Melross, and had three daughters: (1) MARY, born 1788 (Byron's Mary), afterwards Mrs. Cockburn; (2) HELEN, born 1789, afterwards Mrs. Tod; and (3) MARGARET, born 1791, died 1803.

In a letter from James Imlach, long resident and well known in Banff, written, August 16, 1879, in his ninety-second year, to the Rev. Dr. Blaikie, there is the following account : ' Byron is vividly in my mind, as a smart little fellow, exactly of my own age, when in Banff, end of last century, and I met him at his aunts, the Misses Gordon of Gight, and his mother, Dame or Lady Gordon of Gight was with him—the youth then visiting the young Duffs of Hatton. Mary, who became Mrs. Cockburn ; Helen, Mrs. Tod ; and Margaret, who died. All dancing school partners of mine. How bewitching was Mary, no wonder the young lord lost his heart.' [1]

And George Huntly Gordon, writing to *Notes and Queries* in 1858, says : ' I observe in the *Times* of March 10, the death of the lady, Mary Duff of Hatton, who certainly lighted the first flame in the too susceptible heart of my illustrious namesake. Byron told my father at Brussels, in 1816, that he was in love with her at Banff in his ninth year, that some of his earliest verses were addressed to her, mentioning that she was a year older than himself, though from her age as given in the obituary I think she must have been born in the same year, and that she was slightly his junior.[2] He never saw her after he left school in Aberdeen. . . . When I saw her she was in the zenith of her beauty.'

Byron himself writes : ' I have been thinking lately a good deal of Mary Duff. I have never seen her since we were both the merest children. I have been attached fifty times since that period, yet I recollect all we said to each other, all her caresses, her features, my restlessness, sleeplessness. My tormenting my mother's maid to write to her for me. . . . Poor Nancy thought I was wild, and as I could not write for myself, became my secretary. I remember, too, our walks and the happiness of sitting by Mary, while her lesser sister Helen played with her doll, and we sat gravely making love in our way.' (*See Byron's Journal of 1813 in his Life by Moore*)

Mary Duff married, in 1805 (when only seventeen), Robert Cockburn, a wine merchant of Leith and Oporto (of the family of Cockpen).

They had five sons :

Archibald and Alexander, who were in the family business, and died unmarried ; John Montague, who went to South Africa, where he married and left a large family ; Robert, a sailor, drowned in 1836 ; Garden Duff, who died young in 1819 ; and one daughter, Helen Clementina, married Admiral Hugh Dunlop, and had one son, James.

---

[1] After her father's death Mary lived for some time with her grandmother, Helen Duff, in the Hatton town house in the High Street, Banff, now demolished

[2] Byron was born January 22, 1788, and Mary Duff later in the same year.

Mrs. Mary Cockburn died in 1858, aged seventy.[1]

Her sister, HELEN DUFF, married John Tod in 1808, and had thirteen children, whose descendants are now very numerous :

1. Thomas, born 1809, married Amelia Cumming.

2. Alexander, born 1810, *o.s.p.*

3. Helen Clementina, born 1812 ; married David Muir, and had issue.

4. John Robert, 1814-1856 ; married Jemima Wharton Duff (*q.v.*).

5. Mary Jane, 1821-1901 ; married, 1843, G. Ross, and had issue.

6. Charlotte Joanna, 1823-1901 ; married J. Maconochie, and had issue.

7. Caroline Jane, born 1826 ; married Thomas Graham Murray, and was mother of Lord Dunedin.

8. Louisa Garden, born 1828 ; married, 1859, Charles Fellows, and had issue.

9. Joanna, born 1831 ; married, 1876, Thomas Abdy Fellows.

And four others died unmarried, and all before 1841, at which date the nine children above mentioned appear in the Fife entail (see chapter xiii.). Helen Tod died in 1873, aged eighty-three.

Alexander's father-in-law, Major Leslie of Glenmyre, was a man of large property, and settled on the children of the marriage £2000, and the succession to all his property, subject to their mother's lifer ent. Alexander died of apoplexy in 1791, at the early age of twenty-six, and the property passed to his brother Patrick.

Alexander's death is thus chronicled in the *Scots Magazine* · ' On November 3, 1791, death of Alexander Duff of Hatton. The estates go to Patrick his brother, now under the command of Earl Cornwallis in the East Indies.' PATRICK was at that time Captain in an Independent Company of Foot (transferred from the 72nd Highland Regiment) The company was disbanded in December of the same year, and he was placed on half-pay, but was brought into the 74th Regiment as Captain in 1792. On his return to Scotland, a dispute arose between him and the trustees of his late brother as to the unentailed estates. The trustees claimed the right to sell these estates and-pay all debts, and invest the money for the benefit of Alexander's three young children, while Patrick maintained that, subject to the debts, the estates should go to the heir-male, *i.e.* himself, but he had to give way on this point and all lands not in the original entail were sold for £15,000. That to which Patrick succeeded was indeed not much from a pecuniary point of view. There were three jointures to

[1] There is a portrait of her, reproduced from a crayon drawing, in the *Cockburn Family Records* Foulis, Edinburgh, 1913.

pay to the widows of his three predecessors. Lady Anne, his aunt, had £500 per annum, and the liferent of Balquholly. Helen, his mother, had £151, and still held her own property of Whitehill. Mary, his sister-in-law, had £200, and her children had the interest from the £15,000 quoted above. As actual income from the estate Patrick would seem to have received less than £300, but he lived on good terms with all the family, and managed to raise money by granting long leases, for several lives, of large portions of the estate, and receiving in return what were known as ' grassums ' from the tenants. He never married, and died in 1801, being succeeded by his brother ANDREW, who had been in the Navy, but ' owing to the effects of an attack of fever in the West Indies, he lost his reason, and was ever after incapable of managing his own affairs.' [1]

Admiral Robert Duff, shortly before his death, wrote to Lord Fife :

' BATH, 19th January 1787

' MY DEAR LORD,—On receipt of your letter of the 15th inst. I applied to two of my Naval acquaintances who were here but command Guard Ships at Portsmouth for their assistance to get Andrew Duff into a Coursing Ship, which I am persuaded they will do, and acquaint me when they have success. I did not ask them to receive him on board one of the ships they command as he could not improve in his profession there.

' Yesterday I wrote to Andrew Duff setting forth the difficulty of getting preferment in the Navy and earnestly recommending it to him to make choice of some other profession, but did not mention my having made any application to get him on board a man of war as that might have contributed to prevent his choicing another profession.'   (D.)

For eighteen years the estates were managed, in Andrew's name, by his younger brother Garden, who succeeded him on his death on August 12, 1818

GARDEN, the fourteenth child and eighth son of John of Drumblair and Hatton, was born in 1779, and died in 1858. He was a Major in the Banff, Moray, and Nairn Light Infantry Militia In 1805, his aunt, Lady Anne, died, and released her jointure, and in the same year he married Louisa Dunbar, daughter of Sir Benjamin Dunbar of Hempriggs (she died at Auchintoul 1865). In 1827, on the death of his cousin, Sir Benjamin assumed the title of Lord Duffus, but this was disputed, when he went to vote at the election of Scottish representative peers, by claimants in the female line, and he never proved his title, though he was called Lord Duffus to the day of his death. The title is now dormant. Louisa's brother was

---

[1] Andrew Hay of Rannes, his great-uncle, after whom he was named, left him £100 in 1789

Sir George Dunbar of Hempriggs (creation of Nova Scotia). He died unmarried, and owing to the special terms of the patent ' to his heirs-male whomsoever ' the baronetcy passed to the heirs of Louisa (see page 252).

Garden, who was the eighth Laird of Hatton, enjoyed possession of it for nearly forty years. He greatly improved the property, rebuilt

HATTON CASTLE

Hatton Lodge, formerly Balquholly, which Lady Anne had allowed to fall into disrepair, and named it Hatton Castle.[1]

He died, in 1858, in his eightieth year, from the effects of an accident, having broken his thigh in a fall, when rising from his chair in the

---

[1] Garden Duff of Hatton writes to Rose about engaging a servant February 19, 1808 Rose replies that the applicant ' asks £14 in the half year to furnish clothes for himself or £10 in the half year and to be furnished with a suit of clothes Coat, small cloths, a waist coat and jacket in the half year. Tea for breakfast after it comes from the table, as to other matters whatever is customary in the house Clothes washed '

Garden Duff writes again that the terms are too high ' I could get a thorough-bred house servant from Edin for very little more If my service is agreeable to him my terms are £12 10 in the half year, furnishing himself in every article of dress, and that he always appears clean and neat and proper in his dress He shall likewise have tea in the way mentioned, and his washing His work to be confined to the house entirely, but he is likewise to brush my cloaths, boots and shoes, etc. Should he not be inclined to accept of these terms I will thank you to get me his answer immediately in order that I may be upon the outlook for some other person '   (R)

dining-room.[1] He was much regretted. He had five sons and three daughters·

1. JOHN, 1807-1829

2. BENJAMIN, 1808-1897.

3. GARDEN WILLIAM, 1814-1866.

4. ROBERT GEORGE, 1817-1890.

5. JAMES, 1820-1898.

6. JESSIE ELIZA, 1806-1883; married Alexander Morison of Bognie, and died without issue.

7. HELEN, 1809-1889; married James Buchan of Auchmacoy· one son Thomas, 1836-1866; one daughter Louisa, died 1910; both unmarried.

8. LOUISA CLEMENTINA, 1811-1883, unmarried

JOHN, the eldest son, died at the age of twenty-one from rapid consumption, brought on, apparently, by a fall from the top of a coach. BENJAMIN, who thus became the eldest son, was disinherited by his father, who was dissatisfied with his conduct.[2] The estates were re-entailed on GARDEN WILLIAM, the next son, and Benjamin was left by his father's will only £400 per annum for life. Benjamin served in 92nd Highlanders, passed into the half-pay list as a Captain in 1835, and retired in 1844. He lived for many years at Duddingston, and died there in 1897.

He married, when quartered in Ireland, Emma Haines, sister of Field-Marshal Sir F. P. Haines, and had by her four children : GARDEN, 1838-1889; LOUISA, 1833-1845; HELEN EMMA, 1835; and JESSIE, 1843 (married to the Rev. Courtenay Moore, and had five children).

GARDEN, the only son, became an Ensign in the 79th Cameron Highlanders in 1855, served in the Indian Mutiny, sold out in 1860, and entered the Indian Woods and Forests Department. He married, in 1877, his first cousin, Louisa Duff, and died in 1889, leaving two sons, GEORGE, born 1878, and KENNETH JAMES, of the Royal Navy, born 1886. Garden succeeded in 1875 to the estates of his great-uncle, Sir George Dunbar, and assumed in consequence the additional surname of Dunbar. His son GEORGE was first in the Cameron Highlanders, and subsequently went to India and

---

[1] Falls would seem to have been specially fatal to the Hatton family·

Alexander (second) of Hatton died from the effects of a fall over a sack of coals, 1764, aged forty-four.

Alexander (third) died of an apoplectic seizure in 1791, aged twenty-six

Lady Duffus, mother-in-law of Garden Duff, died from a fall off some steps, March 15, 1857, aged ninety

Garden Duff died from the effects of a fall from his chair at the age of eighty, 1858.

John Duff, his eldest son, died from the effects of a fall from a coach

[2] The entail was invalid under the Entail Act of 1848, as it put no limit to the money which could be borrowed on the estate

joined the 31st Punjabis. He served in the Abor expedition. He married, in 1903, Sybil Tait (who died in 1911), and has one son, GEORGE COSPATRICK, born 1906.[1]

GARDEN WILLIAM, the third son, who thus succeeded to Hatton, was born in 1814, and died in 1866. He married, in 1850, Douglas Isabella Maria, daughter of Beauchamp Colclough Urquhart of Meldrum, and for the first nine years of his married life lived at Gask, where his seven elder children were born. His first wife died in June 1861, and in 1862 he married Jean, daughter of Walter Cook. He had in all ten children :

First Family

| Annie L., 1851-1906, unmarried | Louisa H., 1852 1908, m Francis Pollard Urquhart of Craigston | Garden A., 1853 | Beauchamp, 1855 | Janet Douglas, 1856 1908, m Alexander L Duff | George, born and died 1858 | Douglas Mary, 1859 |

Second Family

| Walter, 1863, Royal Irish Constabulary 1888 Resident Magistrate of Downpatrick, 1911, m Elizabeth Leith, | Mary Elizabeth, 1864 | Bertha Hope, 1866-1897, m Alan C. Duff, Indian Civil Service |

He did a great deal of rebuilding on the farms on his estate, and was much interested in the welfare of the agricultural labourers, founding the Duff Society for the Relief of Farm Servants. He died at Harrogate, September 17, 1866, having only held the estates for eight years.

He was succeeded by the present owner, GARDEN ALEXANDER, born in 1853,[2] who was educated at Harrow and Cambridge, taking a first-class History Tripos, and playing Association football in the first two Inter-University matches in 1875 and 1876. He was a Major in the Banff, Moray, and Nairn Militia. He is now a Director of the Great North of Scotland Railway, a Trustee of the Seafield property, and Convener of the County of Aberdeen. He married his cousin, Annie I Urquhart of Meldrum, and has two sons, GARDEN BEAUCHAMP, born 1879, Captain in the Cameron Highlanders, married, in 1913, Doris Lindsay Smith ; and BEAUCHAMP PATRICK, born 1891, who will succeed, in the right of his mother, to the estates of Meldrum and Byth. The only daughter was MARY, b. and d. 1881.

[1] Sir George Duff Sutherland Dunbar assumed the title of sixth Baronet of Hempriggs and Ackergill on the death of his grandfather in 1897, and obtained from the Lyon King of Arms, in 1899, a warrant for the matriculation, to him, of the arms which belonged to the first baronet in 1706

[2] Garden Alexander, born 1853, m 1878, Annie Isabel Urquhart of Meldrum

| Garden Beauchamp, 1879. | Mary, born and died 1881. | Beauchamp Patrick, 1891 |

ANNIE ISABEL URQUHART,
WIFE OF GARDEN ALEXANDER DUFF OF HATTON.

His brother, General Sir BEAUCHAMP DUFF, G.C.B.,[1] born 1855, entered the Royal Artillery in 1874, served in the Afghan War 1878 and 1879, and was with Lord Roberts at Cabul. He joined the Indian Staff Corps, and was gazetted to the 9th Bengal Infantry, now 9th Gurkha Rifles. In 1887 he entered the Staff College, from which he passed out first and returned to India, where he was employed at Army Headquarters, first as an Attaché, and subsequently as D A A G. He took part in the Isazai Campaign, and subsequently in the Waziristan Expedition, 1894-1895, including the action at Wano, being twice mentioned in despatches, and made a Brevet Lieutenant-Colonel. On return, he became Military Secretary to Sir George White, and subsequently to Sir Charles Nairne and Sir William Lockhart. He returned to England to take up the appointment of Assistant Military Secretary for Indian Affairs to Lord Wolseley. In September 1899 he accompanied Sir George White to Natal as Military Secretary, and was present during the siege of Ladysmith, as well as at the actions at Elandslaagte, Rietfontein, and other fighting which preceded it.

At the conclusion of the siege, he joined Lord Roberts' staff as Assistant Adjutant-General, and was present at the actions of Vet River, Sand River, the surrender of Johannesburg, and other actions up to the occupation of Pretoria. He returned to India in the beginning of 1901 as Deputy Adjutant-General. For his services in the South African War he was twice mentioned in despatches, and was made a C.B. and received the Queen's medal with five clasps. He was appointed Brigadier-General to command the Allahabad district in 1902, appointed Adjutant-General in India, and promoted Major-General in 1903. In March 1906 he was promoted Lieutenant-General, and on the same day was appointed Chief of the Staff to Lord Kitchener in India, and created K.C.V O. In 1907 he became K.C.B., and in 1910 K.C.S.I. He was promoted General in 1911, and created G.C.B. at the Coronation in that year. In 1909 he became Military Secretary at the India Office, which office he held for four years, and in October 1913 his appointment as COMMANDER-IN-CHIEF IN INDIA was announced. He is Colonel of the 9th Gurkha Rifles.

His elder son, BEAUCHAMP OSWALD, in the 1st Gurkhas, received the medal of St. John of Jerusalem for saving life, in recognition of his services at Dharmsala in connection with the disastrous earthquake of 1905. He

---

[1] Sir Beauchamp, G C.B , K C S I , K C V.O , C I E , born 1855, m 1876, Grace Wood, daughter of Oswald Wood, Punjab Uncovenanted Civil Service.

| Beauchamp Oswald, 1880, m. Mary Lander | Evelyn Douglas, 1877-1897 | Douglas Garden, 1886 |

had previously served in the Mahsud-Waziri Campaign 1901-1902, medal and clasp; and in the operations against the Mad Mullah in Somaliland, 1903-1904, medal and clasp. He married in 1908 Mary Lander.

DOUGLAS GARDEN is in the firm of Torr and Co., solicitors, London.

The third son of Garden William Duff, WALTER GARDEN, born 1863, was in the Royal Irish Constabulary, and is now Resident Magistrate at Downpatrick. He married Elizabeth, daughter of Major James Leith, V.C., and had two sons, ERIC GARDEN, 1892-1899, and GUY LEITH ASSHETON, 1893, now in the Royal Field Artillery.

Of the six daughters of GARDEN WILLIAM DUFF, ANNIE died unmarried in 1906.

LOUISA married her cousin, Lieutenant-Colonel Francis Pollard Urquhart, now of Craigston. She died in 1908 without issue.

JANET married her first cousin, Alexander Duff (q.v.), and died 1908.

DOUGLAS MARY and MARY ELIZABETH are unmarried.

BERTHA married her first cousin, Alan Duff (q.v.), and died 1897.

The immediate younger brother of Garden William of Hatton was ROBERT GEORGE, of Wellington Lodge, Isle of Wight, 1817-1890. He was a Captain in the 12th Regiment (East Suffolk), but retired in 1847 on his marriage with Mary Astley, niece of Thomas Assheton-Smith of Vaynol, who died at Tidworth in 1828, and had three sons : GEORGE WILLIAM, CHARLES GARDEN, and HENRY ASSHETON, and one daughter, LOUISA ALICE. On the death of Mrs. Assheton-Smith in 1859, the Vaynol estates and a large fortune came to Robert's eldest son George, born 1818, who took the additional surname of Assheton-Smith. He was a great lover of wild animals and kept a number of these, including wild bears and wild white cattle, in the park at Vaynol. He married, in 1888, Alice Stanhope Jones, and had one daughter Enid, born 1889 At his death, in 1904, the estates and name passed to his next brother Charles

CHARLES GARDEN, born 1851, married (1) Hon. Maud Frances Vivian ; (2) Mary Elizabeth Binsley Sheridan; (3) Sybil Mary Verschoyle. His only son, ROBERT GEORGE VIVIAN, born 1876, entered the 2nd Life Guards in 1900, married, in 1903, Lady Juliet Lowther, daughter of fourth Earl of Lonsdale, and has one son and one daughter. At the coronation of King George V. Charles Assheton-Smith was made a baronet.

HENRY ASSHETON, born 1862, married, 1896, Emily Alice Pauline Morgan, daughter of F. M. Morgan, Esq., and has one son Frank, born 1901.

LOUISA ALICE DUFF, born 1853, married, in 1876, the Hon. Hussey Crespigny Vivian, afterwards third Lord Vivian. He had a distinguished diplomatic career, and died at Rome, November 1893, while Ambassador there.

GENERAL SIR BEAUCHAMP DUFF, G.C.B.

From photograph by Maull and Fox

They had four children : George Crespigny Brabazon, fourth Lord
Vivian, 1878 ; twins, Violet Mary and Dorothy Maud (Doris), now
Lady Haig, maids of honour to Queen Alexandra; and Alexandra
Mary Freesia, 1890, now wife of Lord Worsley, eldest son of the Earl
of Yarborough.

The fifth son of Garden of Hatton was JAMES, born 1820. Became
Captain in the 74th Regiment, Colonel of the Banff, Moray, and Nairn
Militia.   He served in the Kaffir War, and at the close of one engagement
was in command of the regiment owing to the death of the Colonel and
other officers. He married Jane Bracken Dunlop, daughter of Alan
Colquhoun Dunlop of Edinburgh, and had fourteen children .

1. JANE LOUISA, 1856.	8. CHARLES EDMUND, 1863.
2. MARY CLEMENTINA, 1857-1867.	9. JOHN, 1864.
3. GARDEN LLANOE, 1858	10. HELEN, 1865.
4. JESSIE MARGARET, 1859-1910.	11 KATHERINE, 1866.
5. ALAN COLQUHOUN, 1860-1897.	12. ROSE MARY, 1868.
6. JAMES DUFF, 1860.	13. ALICE, 1869.
7. ALEXANDER LUDOVIC, 1862.	11 MABEL, 1871-1910

After his retirement, and until his death, he lived at Knockleith, in
Auchterless, where he built a house on the farm left to him by his father
on a thirty-eight years' lease. He acted as guardian during the minority
of his nephew Garden, and subsequently as curator for Miss Wharton
Duff of Orton. His eldest son is now rector of Turriff, and had one son,
GARDEN ANDREW, who entered the Army and died in India in 1906, and
three daughters, ENID, KATHLEEN and HELEN.

The second and third sons, ALAN and JAMES, who were twins, took
scholarships at Fettes from home in 1870.   ALAN entered the Indian Civil
Service, taking fifteenth place in the Indian Civil Service examination in 1878,
but as there were only thirteen vacancies he competed again in 1879, and
took first place ; he then took a Foundation Scholarship at Trinity College,
Cambridge, and was there until 1881, when he went out to India, and
served in the Central Provinces. In 1893 he was appointed Deputy-
Commissioner of Jubbulpore, and died there in 1897 of fever induced
by overwork in connection with the famine, his wife Bertha dying a
few weeks later. He left one son, LUDOVIC JAMES, born 1889

His twin brother JAMES was head of Fettes in 1877-1878, and gained a
scholarship at Trinity College, Cambridge, in the latter year, and in 1879
a Foundation Scholarship at the same College, took a first class in the
Classical Tripos in 1882, and was elected a Fellow of the College in 1883.
He still resides in Cambridge.

He married, in 1895, Laura Conyngham, and has three sons and two daughters ·

1. ALAN COLQUHOUN, November 11, 1896; scholar of Wellington.
2. JAMES FITZJAMES, February 1, 1898; scholar of Winchester.
3. PATRICK LUDOVIC, February 22, 1901.
4. MARY GERALDINE, 1904.
5. HESTER LAURA ELIZABETH, 1913.

ALEXANDER LUDOVIC DUFF, fourth son of Colonel James Duff, was born February 20, 1862. He entered the Navy in 1877, and has served on the China, South African, and the North American stations. He was promoted Commander in 1897, Captain 1902, Rear-Admiral 1913.

In 1906 he was appointed Deputy-Comptroller of the Navy   In 1909 he had command of the *Temeraire* in her first commission. He was subsequently Commodore of the Naval Barracks, Portsmouth, and in 1911 was appointed Director of Naval Mobilisation. C.B. in 1912.

He married, in 1886, his first cousin, Janet Douglas Duff, who died, after a long illness, in 1908. They have two daughters, HELEN DOUGLAS, born 1887, and DOROTHY ALEXANDRA, born 1890.

CHARLES EDMUND, the fifth son, born 1863, was first in the merchant service, then became a doctor, and finally took Holy Orders, being now the vicar of Sydling, Dorset. He married, in 1892, Mary Susan Smith, and has two sons, IAN ARCHIBALD JAMES, 1894, and COLIN GUTHRIE, 1895.

JOHN, the sixth son, born 1864, went to California, where he had a fruit farm. In 1897 he married Constance Evelina Pratt, who died leaving one daughter, FRANCES EVELINA, born 1898.

He returned to England, and in 1904 married Lily Clough, who died the following year, leaving a daughter, LILY KATHERINE, 1905.

Of the daughters of Colonel James Duff, the eldest, JANE LOUISA, born 1856, married her first cousin, Garden Duff, afterwards Duff-Dunbar, as already mentioned.

MARY CLEMENTINA, died 1867, aged ten.

JESSIE MARGARET, born 1859, became an hospital nurse, was night superintendent of Charing Cross Hospital for several years, and was then appointed matron of the Infirmary in Dundee, where she died in 1910.

HELEN, born 1865, married George Whistler Pratt, and lives in California.

KATHERINE, born 1866, married Cecil Robert Stevens, Indian Medical Service, and has two children : Cecil James, born 1893, and Mignonette Kathleen Jean Duff, born 1906.

ROSE MARY, born 1868, married, 1901, James Brignell Dand, 1st Innis-

killen Fusiliers (he died in Egypt in August 1904), leaving one son, Alistair James Duff, born 1902, and a second, born after his father's death, Richard Travers Middleton, 1905.

The two youngest daughters, ALICE, born 1869, and MABEL, born 1871, were unmarried. Mabel died 1908.

The descendants of the first Garden Duff of Hatton, the fourteenth child of John Duff of Hatton and Drumblair, now number nearly seventy.

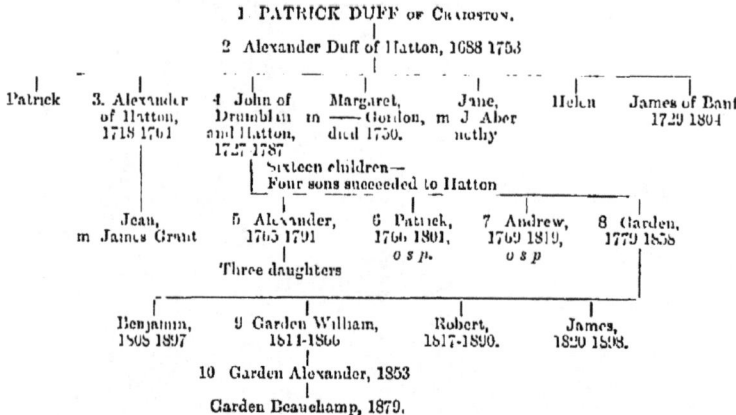

1 PATRICK DUFF of CRAIGSTON.

2 Alexander Duff of Hatton, 1688 1753

Patrick | 3. Alexander of Hatton, 1718 1764 | 4 John of Drumblair and Hatton, 1727 1787 | Margaret, m —— Gordon, died 1750. | Jane, m J Aber nethy | Helen | James of Banff, 1729 1804

Sixteen children— Four sons succeeded to Hatton

Jean, m James Grant | 5 Alexander, 1765 1791 | 6 Patrick, 1766 1801, o s p. | 7 Andrew, 1769 1819, o s p | 8 Garden, 1779 1858

Three daughters

Benjamin, 1808 1897 | 9 Garden William, 1811-1866 | Robert, 1817-1890. | James, 1820 1808.

10 Garden Alexander, 1853

Garden Beauchamp, 1879.

In the two hundred and five years since Hatton was purchased, there have been ten lairds :

1. Patrick, the purchaser, who held it for a few months only, and made it over to his son.

2. Alexander, who held it for forty-four years, 1709-1753.

3. Alexander, his son, held it for eleven years, 1753-1764.

4. John, his brother, held it for twenty-three years, 1764-1787.

5. Alexander, his son, held it for four years, 1787-1791.

6. Patrick, his brother, held it for ten years, 1791-1801.

7. Andrew, his brother, held it for eighteen years, 1801-1819.

8. Garden, his brother, held it for thirty-nine years, 1819-1858.

9. Garden William, his son, held it for eight years, 1858-1866.

10. Garden Alexander, his son, who entered upon possession of the estate when thirteen years of age, and has already held it longer than any of his predecessors

DUFFS OF HATTON

The complete genealogical tables of the Hatton family are given again in full for the sake of clearness.

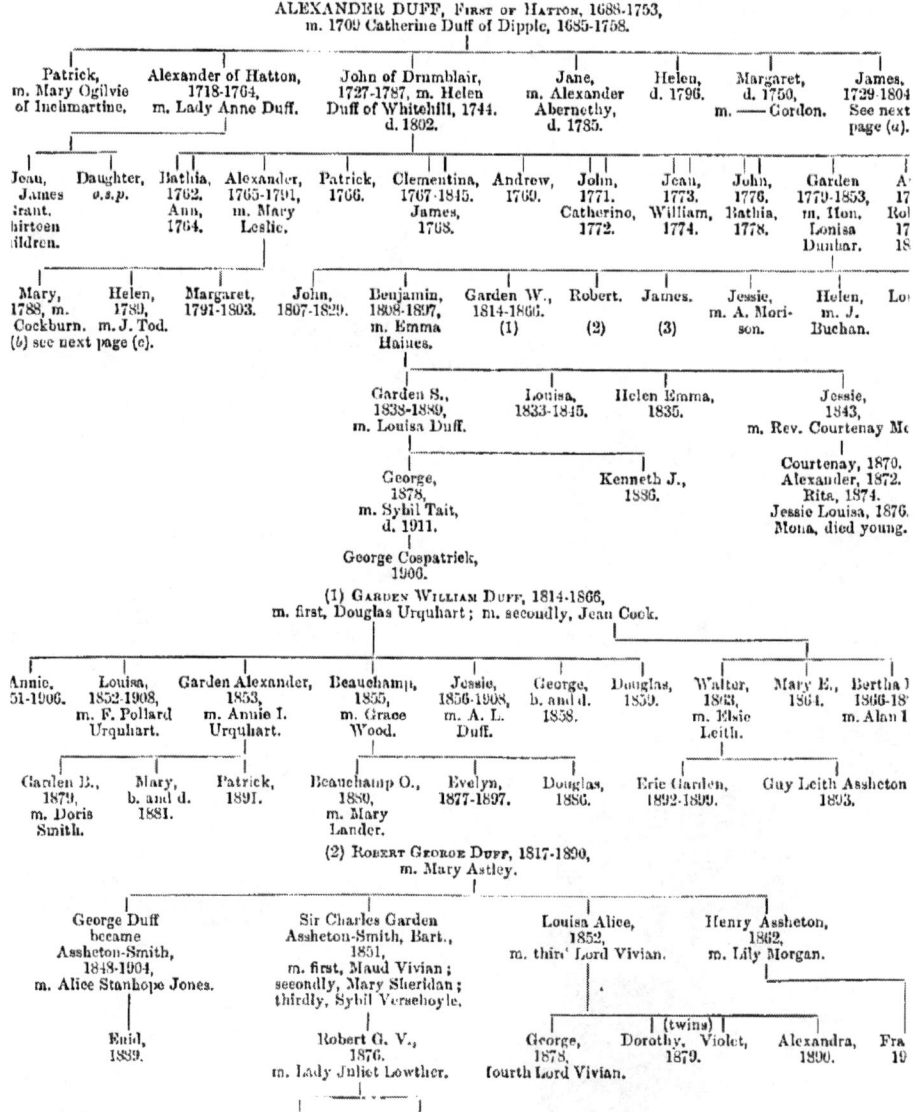

ALEXANDER DUFF, First of Hatton, 1688-1753,
m. 1709 Catherine Duff of Dipple, 1685-1758.

Patrick,
m. Mary Ogilvie
of Inchmartine.

Alexander of Hatton,
1718-1764,
m. Lady Anne Duff.

John of Drumblair,
1727-1787, m. Helen
Duff of Whitehill, 1744.
d. 1802.

Jane,
m. Alexander
Abernethy,
d. 1785.

Helen,
d. 1796.

Margaret,
d. 1750,
m. —— Gordon.

James,
1729-1804.
See next
page (a).

Jean,
James
Grant,
thirteen
children.

Daughter,
o.s.p.

Bathia,
1762.
Ann,
1764.

Alexander,
1765-1791,
m. Mary
Leslie.

Patrick,
1766.

Clementina,
1767-1845,
James,
1768.

Andrew,
1769.

John,
1771.
Catherine,
1772.

Jean,
1773.
William,
1774.

John,
1776.
Bathia,
1778.

Garden
1779-1853,
m. Hon.
Lonisa
Dunbar.

Mary,
1788, m.
Cockburn.
(b) see next page (c).

Helen,
1789,
m. J. Tod.

Margaret,
1791-1803.

John,
1807-1829.

Benjamin,
1808-1897,
m. Emma
Haines.

Garden W.,
1814-1866.
(1)

Robert.
(2)

James.
(3)

Jessie,
m. A. Morison.

Helen,
m. J.
Buchan.

Lo

Garden S.,
1838-1880,
m. Louisa Duff.

Louisa,
1833-1845.

Helen Emma,
1835.

Jessie,
1843,
m. Rev. Courtenay M

George,
1878,
m. Sybil Tait,
d. 1911.

Kenneth J.,
1886.

Courtenay, 1870.
Alexander, 1872.
Rita, 1874.
Jessie Louisa, 1876.
Mona, died young.

George Cospatrick,
1900.

(1) GARDEN WILLIAM DUFF, 1814-1866,
m. first, Douglas Urquhart; m. secondly, Jean Cook.

Annie,
51-1906.

Louisa,
1852-1908,
m. F. Pollard
Urquhart.

Garden Alexander,
1853,
m. Annie I.
Urquhart.

Beauchamp,
1855,
m. Grace
Wood.

Jessie,
1856-1908,
m. A. L.
Duff.

George,
b. and d.
1858.

Douglas,
1859.

Walter,
1863,
m. Elsie
Leith.

Mary E.,
1864.

Bertha
1866-18
m. Alan

Garden B.,
1879,
m. Doris
Smith.

Mary,
b. and d.
1881.

Patrick,
1891.

Beauchamp O.,
1889,
m. Mary
Lander.

Evelyn,
1877-1897.

Douglas,
1886.

Eric Garden,
1892-1899.

Guy Leith Assheton
1893.

(2) ROBERT GEORGE DUFF, 1817-1890,
m. Mary Astley.

George Duff
became
Assheton-Smith,
1848-1904,
m. Alice Stanhope Jones.

Sir Charles Garden
Assheton-Smith, Bart.,
1851,
m. first, Maud Vivian;
secondly, Mary Sheridan;
thirdly, Sybil Versehoyle.

Louisa Alice,
1852,
m. third Lord Vivian.

Henry Assheton,
1862,
m. Lily Morgan.

Enid,
1889.

Robert G. V.,
1876.
m. Lady Juliet Lowther.

George,
1878,
fourth Lord Vivian.

(twins)
Dorothy, Violet,
1879.

Alexandra,
1890.

Fra
19

(3) James Duff, 1820-1898, fifth son of Garden Duff of Hatton,
m. Jane Dunlop.

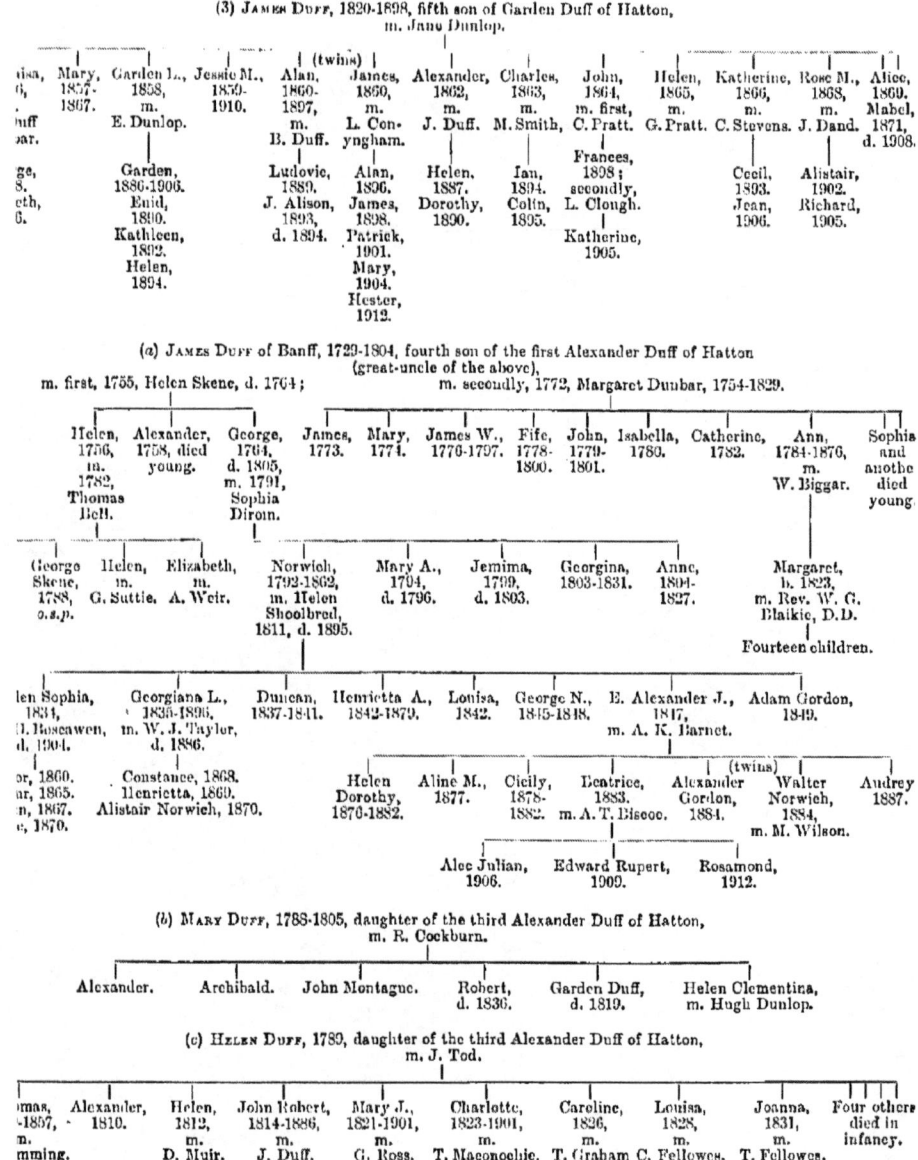

iisa,	Mary,	Garden L.,	Jessie M.,	Alan,	James,	Alexander,	Charles,	John,	Helen,	Katherine,	Rose M.,	Alice,
6,	1857-	1858,	1859-	1860-	1860,	1862,	1863,	1864,	1865,	1866,	1868,	1869.
.	1867.	m.	1910.	1897,	m.	m.	m.	m. first,	m.	m.	m.	Mabel,
nff		E. Dunlop.		m.	L. Con-	J. Duff.	M. Smith,	C. Pratt.	G. Pratt.	C. Stevens.	J. Dand.	1871,
ar.				B. Duff.	yngham.							d. 1908.
								Frances,				
ge,		Garden,		Ludovic,	Alan,	Helen,	Ian,	1898;		Cecil,	Alistair,	
8.		1886-1906.		1889.	1896.	1887.	1894.	secondly,		1893.	1902.	
cth,		Enid,		J. Alison,	James,	Dorothy,	Colin,	L. Clough.		Jean,	Richard,	
6.		1890.		1893,	1898.	1890.	1895.			1906.	1905.	
		Kathleen,		d. 1894.	Patrick,			Katherine,				
		1892.			1901.			1905.				
		Helen,			Mary,							
		1894.			1904.							
					Hester,							
					1912.							

(a) James Duff of Banff, 1729-1804, fourth son of the first Alexander Duff of Hatton
(great-uncle of the above).
m. first, 1755, Helen Skene, d. 1764 ;   m. secondly, 1772, Margaret Dunbar, 1754-1829.

Helen,	Alexander,	George,	James,	Mary,	James W.,	Fife,	John,	Isabella,	Catherine,	Ann,	Sophia
1756,	1758, died	1764,	1773.	1774.	1776-1797.	1778-	1779-	1780.	1782.	1784-1876,	and
m.	young.	d. 1805,				1800.	1801.			m.	another
1782,		m. 1791,								W. Biggar.	died
Thomas		Sophia									young
Bell.		Dirom.									

George	Helen,	Elizabeth,	Norwich,	Mary A.,	Jemima,	Georgina,	Anne,			Margaret,
Skene,	m.	m.	1792-1862,	1794.	1799.	1803-1831.	1804-			b. 1823,
1788,	G. Suttie.	A. Weir.	m. Helen	d. 1796.	d. 1803.		1827.			m. Rev. W. G.
o.s.p.			Shoolbred,							Blaikie, D.D.
			1811, d. 1895.							
										Fourteen children.

len Sophia,	Georgiana L.,	Duncan,	Henrietta A.,	Louisa,	George N.,	E. Alexander J.,	Adam Gordon,
1834,	1836-1896,	1837-1841.	1842-1879.	1842.	1845-1848.	1847,	1849.
0. Boscawen,	m. W. J. Taylor,					m. A. K. Barnet.	
d. 1904.	d. 1886.						

or, 1860.	Constance, 1868.		Helen	Aline M.,	Cicily,	Beatrice,	Alexander	(twins) Walter	Audrey
ar, 1865.	Henrietta, 1869.		Dorothy,	1877.	1878-	1883.	Gordon,	Norwich,	1887.
n, 1867.	Alistair Norwich, 1870.		1876-1882.		1882.	m. A. T. Biscoe.	1884.	1884.	
c, 1870.								m. M. Wilson.	

| | | Alec Julian, | Edward Rupert, | Rosamond, |
| | | 1906. | 1909. | 1912. |

(b) Mary Duff, 1788-1805, daughter of the third Alexander Duff of Hatton,
m. R. Cockburn.

| Alexander. | Archibald. | John Montague. | Robert, | Garden Duff, | Helen Clementina, |
| | | | d. 1836. | d. 1819. | m. Hugh Dunlop. |

(c) Helen Duff, 1789, daughter of the third Alexander Duff of Hatton,
m. J. Tod.

mas,	Alexander,	Helen,	John Robert,	Mary J.,	Charlotte,	Caroline,	Louisa,	Joanna,	Four others
-1857,	1810.	1812,	1814-1886,	1821-1901,	1823-1901,	1826,	1828,	1831,	died in
m.		m.	m.	m.	m.	m.	m.	m.	infancy.
mming.		D. Muir.	J. Duff.	G. Ross.	T. Maconochie.	T. Graham	C. Fellowes	T. Fellowes.	
						Murray.			

CHAPTER XVII

CAPTAIN GEORGE DUFF, R.N.

(TRAFALGAR)

GEORGE DUFF, second son of the first marriage of James Duff of Banff, was from his earliest youth passionately fond of the sea, and was always to be found among the boats in Banff harbour, near his father's house. At the age of nine he managed to conceal himself on board a small merchant vessel, and actually sailed to a neighbouring port. His father wisely realising that a bent so strong ought to be followed, had him shortly afterwards rated to a ship of war, and for four years he was carefully educated with a view to his future profession. At the age of thirteen he was sent to join his grand-uncle, Commodore (afterwards Admiral) Robert Duff, who commanded at Gibraltar with his flag on board the *Panther* of sixty guns, September 1777. During the next three years George Duff had the good fortune to be in thirteen engagements, in the American War, in the Mediterranean, and in the West Indies, and in consequence of his gallant services was made a lieutenant at sixteen. In 1780 he sailed with Rodney to the West Indies, in the *Montague*, seventy-four guns, and was in her when she was blown out of St. Lucia in a hurricane and nearly lost. On this occasion he was wounded by a falling spar. He was still serving in the *Montague* at the glorious ' Battle of the Saints,' April 12, 1782, when the Comte de Grasse, Commander-in-Chief of the French fleet in the *Ville de Paris*, one hundred and ten guns (then the largest ship in the world), and four other ships of the line were taken and brought to Jamaica.

In 1790, when on home service, Lieutenant Duff was recommended to Mr. Dundas, Minister for Scotland, by the personal exertions of the Duke of Gordon, and shortly after was appointed commander of the *Martin* sloop of war on the Scottish coast.

His father also wrote the following letter, which recalls the urgent requests of Lady Anne Barnard to the same Henry Dundas, afterwards Lord Melville, to obtain employment for her husband (see her Memoirs, *South Africa a Century Ago*, 1901).

Extract from letter from James Duff, Banff, to Earl of Fife at Whitehall, London, dated May 24, 1790 :

‘ . . . I shall be ever sensible of your protection, my Lord, to my son, the present bussle gives flattering hopes to those in his profession earnestly wishing promotion, I confess my expectations are only from the war being of some duration, and my son being in the fleet where most success may be, chance only can determine that, anxiety is not to be avoided, but its wrong to carry too far. In the meantime he has got employment, patience for the rest, this is my doctrine to him, yet he still points further, induced from a circumstance only made known to me a few days before he left this, of ane intended connection twixt Miss Sophia Dirom and him. I remonstrate to no effect further, than to prevent thinking of marriage untill it could be done with a prospect at least of decent competency; that was agreed too and there it rests, but Miss Diroms friends are most desirous to get George forward, with this view they have solicite the Duke and Duchess of Gordon who have wrote favourably of him, the Duke to Lord Chatham, the Duchess to Mr. Dundas, the consequences will in time appear, but Im not sanguine, the young ladys friends are. Before the application was made it was communicate to me, my reply, that I had no tittle or claim to solicite in that quarter, they might if they pleased, only I mentioned the moment made I would mention the subject to your Lops. I flatter myself your Lop. would not disapprove of it, but continue your protection. . . .’   (D.)

On May 6, 1791, George Duff married Sophia Dirom, to whom he had been attached since childhood [1]

After his marriage George Duff fixed the residence of his family at No. 9 South Castle Street, Edinburgh, now the well-known book shop of Douglas and Foulis, the house having been sold by his grandson.

There were five children—one son, NORWICH, born August 5, 1792, and four daughters:

MARY ANNE FOTHERINGHAM, born 1794, died 1796, buried in Greyfriars, in the grave of her uncle, James William; the inscription is now illegible.

JEMIMA, born 1799, died 1803, buried in Greyfriars.

GEORGINA HELEN, born 1803, died 1831.

ANNA MARGARET, born 1804, died 1827, in the same year with her mother.

---

[1] Mr. Alexander Dirom was laird of Muiresk, and had a town house in Banff. He was a solicitor in Edinburgh, but when he married the daughter of Dr Fotheringham he settled in Banff Alexander Dirom was Sheriff-Substitute for the county and Provost of Banff, and died in 1788

He had two sons John, born and died 1750; and General Alexander Dirom, who served in India against Tippoo Sahib In 1793 he married Miss Pasley of Mount Annan, Dumfries; in 1814 he retired to Mount Annan, and died 1830 He had several sons (to whom Thomas Carlyle was tutor), but the estate afterwards passed into the female line

The provost's two daughters were Grace, of whom a miniature still exists, and the above Sophia, both buried in Greyfriars churchyard, Edinburgh

'Upon the breaking out of the war in 1793, George Duff was one of the very few master-commanders appointed post-captains by Lord Chatham, who had known him at Gibraltar when himself a captain in the Army. At his lordship's desire, Captain Duff soon after relinquished the command of a frigate then fitting out for him (in which at so early a period of the war he would probably have made his fortune) to go on an expedition to the West Indies as captain of the *Duke*, ninety guns. This ship led the attack on the batteries of Martinique.

'His next appointment was to the *Ambuscade* frigate, in the North Sea, and upon the coast of Ireland, and subsequently to the *Vengeance*, seventy-four guns, belonging to the Channel Fleet, which was detached to the Baltic to reinforce the fleet off Copenhagen (1801). The squadron under Rear-Admiral Campbell, of which the *Vengeance* formed part, was then sent to Bantry Bay to protect the coast of Ireland, and during the mutiny which broke out there the crew of the *Vengeance* were found to be so much attached to their captain that they refused to join it, and in consequence were the only men allowed shore leave at Portsmouth when the squadron came there, previous to sailing for the West Indies.

'Upon the general promotion in the Navy which took place in April 1804, Captain Duff was appointed to the command of the *Mars*, seventy-four guns, and immediately joined her, off Ferrol. His ship formed part of Collingwood's small squadron off Cadiz. When Vice-Admiral Lord Nelson returned from England in the end of September to resume command of the augmented force, Captain Duff had the honour of commanding the small inshore squadron of four sail of the line, stationed midway between our frigates which cruised close to the harbour of Cadiz and our fleet which kept out of sight of that port. On the 19th and 20th of October, the *Mars* was kept almost constantly employed transmitting signals from the frigates to the fleet, relative to the movements of the French. On the memorable morning of the 21st, when it was certain that the enemy's fleet could not escape, the signal was made for the ships of Duff's squadron to return and take their places in order of battle, and the *Mars* was ordered to lead the lee division of our fleet and to break the enemy's line. Knowing his ship to be a slow sailer, Duff ordered every stitch of canvas to be instantly set and ordered his gunners not to waste their fire, as he would " take care to lay them close enough to the enemy." '—(Memoir by his son.)

Notwithstanding every exertion, the *Mars* was passed by the *Royal Sovereign*, bearing the flag of Vice-Admiral Collingwood, and the *Belle Isle*, both of which were in action a few minutes before her, each ship breaking through a different part of the enemy's line. The wind, which had before been light, now dropped, so that the rest of the ships were

prevented from closing immediately with the enemy, and these three were for a time isolated. The *Mars* was attacked by a French ship on either side, and had a Spanish first-rate on her bow. There was a fourth ship also within range. The ship on the starboard quarter, the *Fougueux*, was soon disabled, and it was thought she had struck, but her colours were only shot away, as she never ceased firing. She shortly after raked the *Mars*, and a cannon-shot killed Captain Duff and two seamen who were immediately behind him; his body fell upon the gangway, where it was covered with a Union Jack until after the action. The rest of the battle could not be better described than in the following letter from a young Banffshire midshipman:

'*Mars*, Oct. 29, 1805, GIBRALTER.

'MY DEAREST MOTHER,—Victory has at last given me an opportunity of writing you, a victory fatal and glorious, which you shall judge of by the following account. On Saturday the 19th of October the signal was made that the ennemies fleet consisting of 36 sail of the line, 5 frigates and a brig had put to sea. Admiral Nelson made our signal to look out during the night and by no means to lose sight of the enemy, we kept sight of them that night, and all the following day and night. At daybreak on Monday we saw them formed in a line of battle to leeward; at ten o'clock Nelson made a general signal to bear up and our signal to lead the van, but the breeze dying away, the *Royal Sovereign* got ahead of us; and at half past eleven commenced a dreadful fire. We followed her, the *Belle Isle* next; it unfortunately became calm, and left us three ships in the centre of the ennemies fleet. Judge of our situation, we engaged five ships at one time.

'Captain Duff walked about with steady fortitude and said, "My God, what shall we do, here is a Spanish three-decker raking us ahead, a French one under the stern." In a few minutes our poop was totaly cleared, the quater deck and forecastle nearly the same, only the Boatswain and myself and three men left alive. It was then the gallant Captain fell. I saw him fall. His head and neck were taken entirely off his body, when the men heard it, they held his body up and gave three cheers to show they were not discouraged by it, and then returned to their guns. We fought two hours and a half without intermission, and when the smoke cleared away we found five ships had struck. By this time the rest of our fleet came up, and at three o'clock the action was renewed and continued until sunset, at which time our fleet were in possession of 19 sail of the line of ennemies ships, besides two that were blown up in which perished 9 hundred men. It was a dreadful sight, nothing was to be seen but ships without masts, two were so bad that they sunk a little while after the action.

'The gallant Lord Nelson fell, and with him four captains,[1] we had an hundred and ten men killed and wounded, four midshipmen and Captain of Marines. We

---

[1] There were, in fact, only two captains of ships killed at Trafalgar, Duff and Cooke, whose monuments face one another in the crypt of St Paul's

unfortunately got very bad weather after the action and what was worse a lee shore which forced us to cast off our prizes to save ourselves from being lost. We sunk on purpose 9 of our best prizes to fear of them falling into the enemies possession again. 19 English and 1 hundred Spanish went down in the Saint [*illegible*] nearly double the number in the *Redoutable* French 84. I cannot exactly tell you what perished in other ships; in short, out of 22 sail of the line taken only three escaped the rage of the sea and elements, which we have now got in Gibralter.

'Our fleet has got 19 thousand prisoners on board not counting these that were killed and lost which are thought to be about 5 thousand, we have got the French Admiral Villenuve on board; the French lost four admirals and a General for they had troops on board. Never has there been such a action before. They came out on purpose to fight and were nine ships of the line superior to us. The wind was [*two words illegible*] Cadiz which port received the rest of their shattered ships, had the wind been otherwise we should certainly not have left a single ship of the combined fleet of France and Spain to carry home the news to Bonaparte of so compleat a victory. We are now laying in Gibralter and expect hourly to return to England as we are entirely disabled, having lost all our masts and rudder, our stern is all shot away. Were you to see the ship the look of her would make you shudder.

'We received the thanks of Admiral Collingwood who so nobley distinguished himself in the *Royal Sovereign*, and has command since Nelson's death.

'I am perfectly well, and Cuthbert Collingwood in good spirits. Norwich Duff is gone on board the *Donegal*. I shall have no more time, and for my own affairs you shall know more in my next letter.—I am, your affectionate son,

'T. ROBINSON.'

On board the *Mars* were killed, besides Captain Duff, Alexander Duff, master's-mate, acting lieutenant, Messrs. Corbyn and Morgan, midshipmen, and twenty-five seamen and marines. The wounded amounted to ten officers, five petty officers, and sixty seamen and marines, in all over one hundred killed and wounded. ' Captain Duff was a man of fine stature, strong and well made, above six feet in height, and a manly, open, benevolent countenance. During thirty years' service he had not been four years unemployed, and that was twenty months after his return from the West Indies in 1787, and not quite two years after the last war. Although he went early to sea, he lost no opportunity of improving himself in the theory as well as the practice of his profession, and acted the part of an instructor and a father to numerous young men who were under his command. By his wife he had five children, of whom a boy and two girls, aged one and two years, remained together with their mother to mourn his death. He was known in the Navy as "Worthy Duff."' (*Scots Magazine.*)

Monday Morng 21st Octr 1805

My Dearest Sophia I have just time
to tell you we are just going into action
with the Combined, I hope and trust
in God that we shall all behave
as becomes us, and that I may yet
have the happiness of taking my
beloved wife and Children in my
arms Norwich is quite well and
happy, I have however ordered him
of the Qr Deck yours ever and most
truly Geo. Duff

George Duff's son Norwich, thirteen years of age, had joined him as a midshipman just a month before the battle, and wrote the following letter to his mother two days later. At the same time she received a brief letter from her husband, written just as he was going into action :

To Mrs. Duff, South Castle Street, Edinburgh

'*Monday morning, 21st Oct* 1805.

'MY DEAREST SOPHIA,—I have just had time to tell you we are just going into action with the combined [*fleets*]. I hope and trust in God that we shall all behave as becomes us, and that I may yet have the happiness of taking my beloved wife and children in my arms. Norwich is quite well and happy, I have, however, ordered him off the quarter Deck.—Yours ever and most truly,
'GEO. DUFF.' [1]

'MY DEAR MAMA,—You cannot possibly imagine how unwilling I am to begin this melancholy letter. However as you must unavoidably hear of the fate of dear Papa, I write you these few lines to request you to bear it as patiently as you can. He died like a hero, having gallantly led his ship into action, and his memory will ever be dear to his king and his country and his friends. It was about 15 minutes past 12 in the afternoon of the 21st Oct· when the engagement began ; it was not finished till five. Many a brave hero sacrificed his life upon that occasion to his king and his country. You will hear that Lord Viscount Nelson was wounded in the commencement of the engagement and only survived long enough to learn that the victory was ours, "then," said that brave hero, " I die happy since I die victorious," and in a few minutes expired.
'I have written my uncle a long letter and have enclosed one to my Aunt Grace, containing a short narrative of some particulars of the action. We are now all aboard the *Euryalus* with the Hon. Captain Blackwood and in compliance with the wish of Admiral Collingwood are now on our way to England that we may have an opportunity of more readily knowing your wishes respecting the arrangement of our future conduct. Captain Blackwood has indeed been very polite and kind to me, and has requested Mr Dalrymple to let my uncle know that on account of his acquaintance with my papa he will feel himself very happy in keeping me on board his ship and to acquaint him that his annual allowance to young gentlemen in his ship and under his charge is fifty pounds, half of which he wishes to be deposited in the hands of his agent once in six months ; however I would much rather wish to see you and to be discharged into the guard ship at Leith for two or three months. My dear Mamma, I have again to request you to endeavour to make yourself as happy and as easy as possible. It has been the will of heaven and it is our duty to submit —Believe me, your obedient and affectionate son,   NORWICH DUFF.'

---

[1] Reproduced opposite.

P.S. by Mr. Dalrymple, afterwards purser :

'MRS. DUFF: DEAR MADAM,—It is with sincere uneasyness and regret that I have occasion to offer my condolence to you on the late unfortunate but glorious and honourable fate of our worthy and generous and brave Captain, whose name will ever be revered and whose character will ever be esteemed. Believe me, your ever respectful and ob humble servant,   W. DALRYMPLE.'

The originals, together with the fine portraits of father and son by Raeburn, the medal awarded to Captain George's widow, his sword and other relics, are now in the possession of Mr. Edward Alexander Duff, grandson of Captain George, and uncle to the present writers.

The following poem appeared at the time in the *Gentleman's Magazine*, December 1805 :

'AN APPEAL TO THE GRATITUDE OF BRITONS

'Say, say, my country, does a tear remain
To soothe the wives—the widows of the slain ?
Has Nelson's loss quite dried the lucid rill
Whence pity erst was wont her cup to fill ?
Let names less splendid claim one grateful tear,
The last sad tribute o'er their early bier.
Does Duff's, does Cooke's [1] brave death no pang impart,
Nor plant one dagger in the feeling heart ?
Alike they fell to guard their native shore,
Alike to be lamented—"When no more."
Let Duff's sad wife your fond compassion crave
A husband, son, enveloped in the grave ;
A husband whose unceasing kindness proved
How much he valued and "how much he loved "
Though no famed titles graced his transient span,
She mourns him equally, she loved the man
A son whose youth had been her constant care,
Whose life presented joy, whose death, despair.
Think what a sound the dreadful tale reveals,
Think what a helpless wife, a mother feels
Shall she not claim one drop from British eyes,
One cheering word which mercy's tongue supplies ?
Shall she, like Philomel, be left alone
To vent her anguish and to make her moan,
Unseen, unfelt, unpitied, e'en unknown ?
Shall Duff's, shall Cooke's bright stars refulgent blaze
Perish, in Nelson's more resplendent rays ?
Blush, blush, I say, and those whose blood was shed

---

[1] Captain Cooke of the *Bellerophon*, also killed.

CAPTAIN GEORGE DUFF, R.
(Killed at Trafalgar)

To guard their country, oh revere when dead!
To each their well-earned meed of praise apply,
Let each partake the tributary sigh.
Be Nelson's fame as Luna's fullest pride,
Theirs as the stars which twinkle by the side,
And that brave troop whose still inferior light
Is darkened in oblivion's deepest night
All, all demand your pity and your praise!
Though crowned with cypress, they deserved the bays.
All these should share affection's warm applause;
All perished nobly in their country's cause.
So shall succeeding tars with parting breath
Bleed with delight and glory e'en in conscious death,
Conscious that Britons should record their name
And future ages emulate their fame.

'PETERBOROUGH, *Nov. 25th*, 1806.'

The writer evidently imagined that the Alexander Duff, midshipman and master's mate,[1] who was among the killed was the captain's son. This Alexander, with his brother Thomas, afterwards Colonel Gordon of Park, were the sons of Lachlan Duff, W.S., youngest son of John Duff of Culbin and his second wife, Helen Gordon of Park. Thomas had joined the ship with Norwich just before the battle, and Alexander died in his arms.

A monument to Captain George Duff was put up in the crypt of St. Paul's Cathedral, adjoining the tomb of Nelson, and bears the following inscription : ' Erected at the public expense to the memory of Capt. George Duff, who was killed 21st Oct. 1805, commanding the *Mars* in the battle of Trafalgar, in the 42nd year of his age, and the 29th of his services.' There is a medallion portrait of him by J. Bacon, junior [2]

---

[1] George Duff had written to Alexander's father in May of the same year . ' H M S *Mars*, 5 May 1805 —I am happy to assure you that your son Alexander is in good health and as fine a young man as I have ever met with   I only regret he has not served his time, as soon as he has, we must get him made Lieut   At present I make him do the duty of acting Lieut , but that puts nothing into his pocket, only gives him more consequence and makes him see more of his duty   I would with pleasure receive your son Thomas and take all the care I can of him, but I fear they will send me abroad before either he or my son can join me, as you must have heard we are fitted for foreign service, and if the French send any ships abroad I suppose we shall be one of the party to follow them ' *

[2] At a meeting of the Patriotic Fund in January 1806 it was resolved ' that a piece of plate value £100 and adorned with a suitable inscription be presented to Mrs Duff and to descend to his son, now in His Majesty's navy, and annuities of £50 each to his two daughters, Georgina Helen and Anna Margaret '   They lived to the ages of twenty-eight and twenty-three respectively.   Two elder daughters, Mary Anne Fotheringham and Jemima, had died in infancy.

* Letter at Drummuir.

Norwich Duff, his only son, born on August 5, 1792, was thus aged thirteen years two and a half months at the date of Trafalgar, being, as far as is known, the youngest officer, and probably the youngest person, present.

His godfather was the fourth Duke of Gordon, who bestowed upon him the name of Norwich, after his own secondary title of Earl of Norwich, derived from his great-grandmother, Lady Elizabeth Howard, daughter of Henry, first Earl of Norwich, and afterwards Duke of Norfolk[1] This name, which seems to be quite unique as a Christian name, is preserved by two grandsons of the late admiral, and should go down to posterity in connection with the 'honourable augmentation' of the Duff arms, granted to the first Norwich Duff in commemoration of his father's services. See chapter xxxviii.

Norwich had always shown a strong predilection for the sea, and in July 1805, being then not quite thirteen, he had been sent on board H.M.S. *Aurora* lying off Spithead, under orders for the Mediterranean, for a passage to join his father's ship H.M.S. *Mars* off Cadiz, which he did on September 19, and appears in the ship's books as an A.B. After the battle of Trafalgar and the death of his father, he was removed by the directions of Lord Collingwood into the *Euryalus*, and later was transferred to the *Ajax*, eighty guns, commanded by Captain Blackwood, a friend of his father

Mr. Dalrymple, apparently purser and instructor on board the *Euryalus*, writes from time to time to Mrs. George Duff about her son. The year after Trafalgar he writes from Spithead, February 24, 1806 : 'Mr. Norwich, I am convinced, has good dispositions and abilities, superior to many of his age, and with delight I look forward to the time when, by his manly conduct and heroick services to his country, he will in a measure restore the happiness of his affectionate mother, and be a comfort to his friends, and by his endearing manners make himself a welcome and useful member of society. Mr. David Cleik [*a young relative who will appear again*], I am much pleased in saying, shews an example of economy and religion worthy to be copied by many of more advanced years '

---

[1] George, fourth Marquis of Huntly and first Duke of Gordon, married Lady Elizabeth Howard, eldest surviving daughter of Henry, first Earl of Norwich and Baron Howard of Castle Rising, who afterwards succeeded his brother as Duke of Norfolk

His son Alexander was second Duke of Gordon, and was succeeded by

His son Cosmo George, third Duke, called after Grand Duke of Tuscany.

His son Alexander was fourth Duke, who, in virtue of his descent, was created second Earl of Norwich, July 2, 1784, with limitation of the title to the heirs-male of his body. He was born 1743, died 1827.

His eldest son, George, fifth and last Duke, born in 1770, died 1856 The last Duchess died 1864 The earldom of Norwich became extinct in 1856 on the death of the fifth Duke

Three weeks later: 'Norwich and all the young gentlemen are making proficiency. We have got an excellent globe which we shall study occasionally; every morning . . . a certain number of words, learn English grammar once a week, and in the evening read geography, history, etc., after having poured over their navigation, French, arithmetic, etc., the greater part of the day.' [1]

The *Ajax* took part in the expedition to Constantinople, and on February 14 was completely destroyed by fire, off Tenedos, nearly three hundred persons being lost. Norwich was among the saved, as well as his preceptor Dalrymple, who writes a thrilling account of the incident to the anxious mother:

'*Feb.* 1807.—Lest my letter of the 17th should have miscarried, I do myself the honor of preparing another against the earliest opportunity. Before this reach you, the *Gazette* will have publicly announced the loss of the *Ajax* off the mouth of the Dardanelles on the evening of the 14th instant about 9 o'clock. She took fire in the starboard side of the Breadroom, and it is generally thought it was occasioned by the carelessness of the Purser's steward who was much addicted to drinking and was seen drunk a few minutes before the fire was discovered. Everything being dry, the flames raged with incredible fury and tho' repeated attempts were made to get them under every exertion availed us nothing: yet till I saw the flames rolling on the quarter deck and everything round me in a blaze I had not the most distant idea that the ship would be burnt, but then I was forced to rush forward to the forecastle and consult my safety. You will easily conceive how much I was rejoiced to find Norwich there (he was one of the midshipmen of the watch), but my joy was soon interrupted when he told me he had not seen Mr. David Clerk or Mr. Manners from the time the fire broke out. We stood on the sprit-sail yard for some minutes thinking we might discover them, lurking in some place which the flames had not reached, but no, the poor little fellows had leapt overboard, as we afterwards understood, soon after the accident happened.

'At this time there was no boat near us nor any prospect of our preservation, as neither of us can swim; however I bless God Almighty that I continued as cool and collected as I am at this moment, and exhorted the dear partner of my misfortune to keep up his spirits, depend upon the mercy of God and we might be saved. For since I had found him, I was resolved to save him or perish in the attempt. We shook hands and bid adieu to Captain Blackwood who at that moment plunged into the waves with a Mr. Sibthorp, a worthy young man who perished with cold, struggling against the current. We had not waited above ten minutes when a boat from the *Windsor Castle* came under the bows, into which I made Norwich immediately go down. Even then we were far from being safe, the flames had taken such full possession of the ship that the guns

---

[1] Thus we see that the junior officers of Trafalgar were only little schoolboys after all, and had their drudgery to get through like their fellows.

which were loaded being made hot, were discharging the shot in every quarter and several flew over our heads when in the boat rowing towards the *Canopus*, which ship we got safe on board, when we had the good fortune to find the Captain and several other shipmates among whom I am happy to include Mr. Thomas Duff, who was saved in the half of the Captain's boat, which in lowering was cut in two upon the anchor. From what I have said, I daresay you already perceive that my unfortunate young friends Mr. Clerk and Mr. Manners are included among the lost. I hope you will receive my first letter and answer it, as I am particularly perplexed what to do with Norwich after this service is finished. By going home he will lose much practical knowledge of his profession which he perhaps may never again have as good an opportunity of acquiring, and by staying here without a thread of clothes but what the generosity of a shipmate may bestow, is very inconvenient, and may in the end hurt his health.'

Two days after the burning of the *Ajax* Norwich joined the *Active* (Captain Mowbray), so that a friendly letter from Captain Blackwood to his mother must have been prior to the catastrophe.[1] He says : ' Norwich has latterly improved much in his attentions to Mr. Dalrymple and the care of his person and clothes.' [2] ' Thomas Duff, being older, is as steady, active, and attentive as any young man I ever saw.' [3]

The *Active* took part in the passing and repassing of the Dardanelles and various other actions off the Turkish coast, in which neighbourhood she remained for two years. In 1808 she paid off at Sheerness, but was in August of the same year recommissioned by Sir James Gordon, and Norwich again sailed in her, to the Adriatic, and had the good fortune to take part in many boat expeditions, in the capture of twenty-five vessels off Gras, 1810, and in the action off Lissa, March 13, 1811 He there had another narrow escape from fire when on board the *Corona*, a prize. In September,1811 he passed as Lieutenant at Malta, but continued on board the *Active*, and after the next action was sent to take charge of the *Pomona* (prize), and had another narrow escape from drowning owing to his boat being upset. In 1812 he was appointed to the *Seahorse*, and went to the West Indies. In 1813 he was appointed Flag-Lieutenant to the Hon. Sir A. J. Cochrane, G.C.B., then going out as Commander-in-Chief to the American station. On June 13, 1814, he was promoted Commander, and appointed to the sloop *Espoir*, and took part in the expedition up the Chesapeake and the destruction of Washington and the disastrous attack on New Orleans. After the conclusion of peace by the Convention of

---

[1] In which poor Blackwood himself lost all his prize money.

[2] Which again gives a glimpse of a very normal schoolboy

[3] All these letters are in the possession of Edward Alexander Duff, eldest surviving son of Norwich.

ADMIRAL NORWICH DUFF, R.N.

Ghent, the *Espoir* remained to protect the fisheries of Labrador, but returned to England and was paid off in October 1816.

He subsequently served as Commander in the *Beaver* and in the *Rifleman*, and in July 1822 was promoted Post-Captain, after which he saw no more active service, and retired in the same year. He became A D C. to the Queen in 1849; in 1852 he was placed on the reserve list of Rear-Admirals, and became Vice-Admiral in 1857. He had, at one time, some thoughts of buying the property of Blervie, but did not do so.[1]

In 1833 he married Helen Mary, only child of Dr. Shoolbred, and granddaughter of James Shoolbred, merchant, Auchtermuchty, Fife (to whom Helen was served heir at his death in 1818). He had four sons and four daughters :

1. HELEN SOPHIA, born 1833 ; married, 1857, Boscawen Trevor Griffith, late 23rd Welsh Fusiliers.   In 1875, on the death of his mother, he assumed the additional surname of Boscawen   They have issue :

> Boscawen Trevor, born 1860 ; married Lilian Bellers, and has issue.
>
> Arthur Sackville Trevor, born 1865 ; M.P for Tunbridge Wells 1892-1906, and Dudley 1910 ; knighted in 1911 ; married Edith Sarah Williams.
>
> Helen Evelyn, born 1867 ; married Hugh James Archdale, late Colonel Lincolnshire Regiment; one daughter.
>
> Alice Catherine, born 1870, married George Taaffe of Smarmore, Co. Louth, and has issue.

2. GEORGINA LUCY, born 1835 ; married, 1864, William James Tayler (see page 195) ; died 1896.   They had issue :

> Constance Jane Dorothy, born 1868 ; married Hubert Coulson, and has issue
>
> Helen Agnes Henrietta, born 1869.
>
> Alexander (Alistair) Norwich, born 1870.

3. DUNCAN ALEXANDER, born 1837, died 1841 ; buried in Père Lachaise Cemetery, Paris.

4 HENRIETTA ANNE, born January 1842, died 1879.   A poetess and novelist.

5. LOUISA JESSIE ELIZA, born December 1842.

6. GEORGE NORWICH, born 1845 ; died 1848, buried in Bath.

7. EDWARD ALEXANDER JAMES, born 1847 ; for many years General

---

[1] Archibald Duff to Colonel Thomas Gordon of Park, 1852 · ' You perhaps would hear that Blervie is in the market, and there is a talk that Norwich Duff is to be the purchaser at the price of £40,000 '

Manager of Lloyd's Bank, now a Director; married Amy Katherine Barnet, and has issue, two sons and five daughters:

HELEN DOROTHY, born 1876, died 1882.

ALINE MARY, born 1877.

CICILY KATHERINE, born 1878, died 1882

EMILY BEATRICE, born 1883; married, 1904, Arthur Tyndale-Biscoe, and has three children—Alec Julian, born 1906; Edward Rupert, born 1909; and Rosamond Mary, born 1912.

ALEXANDER GORDON and WALTER NORWICH, twins, born 1884. Walter Norwich married, in 1910, Margaret, daughter of Thomas Perceval Wilson. He is an engineer in the firm of Thornycrofts, Southampton. Alexander Gordon is a solicitor.

AUDREY LOUISA, born 1887.

8. The fourth son and eighth child of Admiral Norwich Duff was ADAM GORDON, born 1849; educated at Harrow and Cambridge, and called to the Bar.

There is a window in Bath Abbey dedicated to the memory of Admiral Norwich Duff, who died in Bath, April 5, 1862. His widow died in London in 1895, aged eighty-four.

CHAPTER XVIII

DUFFS OF MAYEN

Alexander 'second of Hatton' left one natural son, Alexander Duff, Colonel 58th Regiment, died 1816, who married, first, Rebecca Powell of Liverpool, died 1773. Secondly, 1785, Jane Abernethy of Mayen, 1751-1805.

Alexander Samuel, born 1773, Ensign 3rd Foot Guards 1799, m December 31, 1808, Mary Finlay. William A of Mayen, 1789 1857, unmarried.

William Higginson, 1811-1855, m Amelia Charlotte Marsham No issue.   Folliott, 1818 1872, m Eliza Anne Parker.   Robina Mary, m. first, Baron Ablomar   Secondly, Charles Wilkinson   Baroness Cary.

1 Mary Ada, died young
2 Nina, m Pierre Mouchot.
3 Eva Maud, m. Ottley

Two children.

ALEXANDER, natural son of the second Alexander Duff of Hatton, was born in 1743 or 1744, and obtained a commission as Lieutenant on October 12, 1760, in the newly raised 89th Regiment. Four years later the regiment disappears from the Army List, and he with it, but on March 21, 1765, he became a Lieutenant in the 58th Regiment, Captain in 1772, Major in 1783, and retired on half-pay in 1786. He married, while still a Captain, Rebecca Powell, daughter of Samuel Powell of Stanage Park, Radnor (her nephew was of Brandlesome Hall, Yorkshire), and sister-in-law of Ralph Higginson of Liverpool. He appears in the family correspondence of the Powell family as 'Sandy Duff.' Rebecca died in 1773, leaving him one son, ALEXANDER SAMUEL, to whom went the fortune inherited from her father and uncle.

Alexander thus announces her death to Lord Fife :

'MY LORD,—Since I had the honour of your Lordships favour I have sustained an inexpressible loss of a most valuable wife, who to all appearance was safely delivered betwixt eight and nine o'clock at night of the 12th instant, and for several hours seemed in as good a way as possibly could be expected, but about 2 o'clock in the morning she suddenly expired, without any friend in the room perceiving the least alteration. She has left me a very fine boy, who is, in all probability likely to do well. This is now become so melancholy a place that I intend setting out for the north in ten or twelve days, and as I shall have frequent occasion to write to my friends here, has made me take the liberty to

'BANFF, 10*th May* 1786.

'DEAR SIR,—I was unlucky the other day in missing you at Mountcoffer, as I had several interesting matters to communicate to you, which I must now defer till meeting, which I hope will be soon, tho' I am going for a few days to Glassa and Hatton Lodge, with intention to be at Mayen by the Term to receive servants and set them. I have much to do in getting the old House [1] made comfortable and taking furniture from hence, which puts me under the necessity of trespassing on the kindness of my friends at this time to request the assistance of their Carts. A few are prepared for that Business next Saturday, when, if your Carts can be spared at the same time, will be doing me a most singular favour, as I am anxious to have the greatest part transported altogether. If you are at the Roup of Mountblairy I shall have the pleasure to see you, in the meantime Mrs. Duff joins me in best compliments to you and Mrs. Rose, and I remain most sincerely yours,   ALEXANDER DUFF.'

From Mayen, on November 3, 1788, Colonel Duff writes to William Rose that he has 'determined on building,' which refers to the present mansion-house of Mayen.

And again to William Rose:

'MAYEN, 18*th Nov.* 1788.

'DEAR SIR,—In consequence of your favour of the 16th I have signed the Discharge for Lord Fife, but have at the same time to observe as 5 pr. Cent was allowed to last Whitsunday, that I expected it would have been continued to Martinmas 1787, and have sent you the accts. and letters relative to the different settlements, which makes a difference of £30, but if not allowed by his Lordship I shall give you no farther trouble on the subject, tho' perhaps I may mention it to him when I have an opportunity, as well as other matters formerly proposed. I am truly sorry for the Death of the King.[2] With Mrs. Duffs kind Compts I am always sincerely yours,   ALEXANDER DUFF.'

Alexander Duff's second wife was very delicate; in fact, all the Abernethys seem to have been consumptive. On several occasions he took her and her sister to the Wells of Pannanich, near Ballater, and also to England.

In July 1787 Colonel Duff writes to Lord Fife from Pannanich that his wife is rather better for the pure air of this place, and he hopes she will soon recover her appetite and usual spirits, and again from 'Hotwells, Bristol,' to William Rose: 'Mrs. Duff and Miss Abernethie are still poorly, but I have great expectations from ass milk, excellent water, pure air, and the approaching season, and shall be happy how soon I can bring them back, in perfect health, to the Land of Cakes.'

---

[1] Now the farm of Mains of Mayen

[2] Charles Edward Stuart died this year in Rome But as the event took place on the 31st January, if this is referred to it seems that news then travelled very slowly

Apparently Colonel Duff, his wife, and his sister-in-law, Miss Aber-nethy, were at Bath in 1787, as he writes to Lord Fife from there, as follows :
- ' My Ladies, I am sorry to say, retain so much of Scotch bashfulness that I find it a most difficult matter to get them to mingle with the crowd, but hope in a short time they will be more familiarized to the gay manner of this place. . . . We intend to see a little more of London, where we were only a few days, after which 'tis intended to visit my friends at Liverpool and to see my son,[1] as Mrs. Duff is most anxious to be acquainted with him.'

On October 26, 1787, Colonel Duff writes from ' Hulton Hall, Brent-wood, Essex,' to Lord Fife :

' I had the pleasure to acquaint your Lordship of the ladies being safe arrived at this place, after some alarms and frights and fatigues, but I am now happy to think they are pretty well recovered from those incidents that attend a sea voyage, tho' I believe it would be a difficult matter to persuade them to trust the watery elements again, but from what we have already experienced they shall never be desired by me. Mrs. Duff is certainly benefited by the jaunt, and I only hope the gay scenes will not give a disrelish for Mayen, which I left with much reluctance.'

Lord Fife replies as follows :

' Duff House, Nov 28th, 1787.

' Dear Sir,—I received your Letter, and am very glad your Ladies are well, and you will forgive me for not joining in your wishes, for I shall be very glad when they are most heartily tir'd of Bath which I think they must be, and very anxious to get home, resolving never to do the like again for fear of being punished. Mr. Stronach is here just now clearing his accounts, he has never showed me your memorandum, and I told him this morning he need not now, for I had heard from yourself, so he shall have no merit. To the first point I answer that you are most heartily welcom to bury where you please,[2] and I heartily wish it may be many years before you take up that habitation, but that I shall most certainly never lay one stone above another to confine you when there. As to the road, I told you I had very much inclination to oblige you, but that I had really seen so much altercation and dispute betwixt the Late Lord Fife and Mr. Abercrombie[3] (sic) about these roads, that I was very unwilling to do anything that could occasion any altercation in matters that had been settled with so much trouble. I shall enquire about the Minister's Demands and the vacant stipend and inform you how it stands. Lady Ann Duff is at Hatton Lodge very well, and I suppose goes soon for Edinbr. I shall leave this about the 16th of December. Kind Compts: to the Ladies with much regard, Yours, etc., Fife.

---

[1] Alexander Samuel.
[3] Probably a mistake for Abernethy.
[2] See page 278.

'Since writing my letter I find there is some agreement about the vacant stipend at Rothiemay for a bridge on the burn of Millegan which the poor people are often liable to be drowned in, and this is as great a convenience to your tenants as mine, that a Bridge be there.'   (*R.*)

Having purchased the rights of his sisters-in-law in Mayen, Alexander Duff settled down there, and subsequently became an Honorary Colonel of the Banffshire Volunteers By his second wife he had one son, WILLIAM ABERCROMBY DUFF, born in 1789. There is a portrait of Alexander in uniform at Hatton, as well as pictures of his wife, and his son William, as a child. These were left in Colonel Duff's will to Garden Duff of Hatton.

William was educated at Banff Academy and Marischal College, Aberdeen, and went into the business of Messrs. Morison of Riga, Archangel, and London By his father's will he inherited Mayen, Tillydown, and Cornyhaugh, which estates he sold before his death. He bequeathed to the town of Banff a sum of £700, either for the benefit of the hospital there or to found a Duff Bursary at the Academy. He died unmarried in 1857, and was buried in the old churchyard of Banff, near his mother and grandmother (the former Jane Abernethy who became Duff, and the latter Jane Duff, who became Abernethy). The earlier Abernethys of Mayen had been buried in the old churchyard of Rothiemay, near the river and below the house of Rothiemay. The following letter from James Abernethy of Mayen to 'Earl of Fife,' docketed by Lord Fife 'Mayen anent a wall he designed to build round his Burial place,' is interesting to those who know the neighbourhood :

'MY LORD,—As I heard your people were working on the old Church Yeard I went up and measured of my burial place conform to the agreement entered into betwixt your Lop and me, and as I design very soon to have a wall put round it, Have given you ye trouble of this to know if you have any objection to my taking the stones of the old Kirk for building the wall. If this is not agreeable, I must bring stones from my own hills, in doing which I am affraid the wheels of the carriages may break some of your new made ground below your house which I should be very sorie for. However, what is most agreeable to you shall be done. I shall expect an answer with your convenience. Having the honour to be, with the greatest regard, My Lord, Your Lop. most obedient and most humble servant,   JAMES ABERNETHIE. (*D.*)

'MAYEN, *Janry* 31st, 1761 '

On a single flat tombstone in this graveyard is still faintly visible :

' Among his ancestors underneath this stone is interred John Abernethy of Mayen, a young man of an amiable character. He died 2nd May 1779, in the

21st year of his age ; also Helen Abernethy his sister, who died April 1787, aged 34, also their nephew Charles Graham, who died Dec. 1800, aged 28.'

Good miniatures of John and Helen are in the possession of the present writers.

William Duff of Mayen would appear to have been the favourite son of his father, and was left sole executor and residuary legatee of the will. Colonel Alexander Duff, who died in 1816, expressed in his will the following desires as to his place of burial : ' Should I die at Mayen or Banff, and should there be sufficient space, I should wish to have my remains laid as near as possible to those of my beloved wife, Jane Abernethie (in Banff churchyard) ; if not space there, I should wish to be interred in the Mayen burying ground below the house of Rothiemay, unless Lord Fife or any of the family build a proper place in the churchyard of Rothiemay, close to that of Mr. Stronach, late factor to the said Lord Fife.' The last alternative was the one that eventuated, and the remains of ' Alexander Duff, Armiger, died 1816,' lie alone, under a fine stone in the churchyard of Rothiemay.

To return to Colonel Alexander Duff's elder son, Alexander Samuel. His birth took place on April 12, 1773. Of his education nothing is known save that he was at one time ' bound apprentice to Mr. Robert Richmond, attorney-at-law,' but in 1798 he joined the Militia, in 1799 obtained a commission in the 3rd Foot Guards, and on May 15, 1800, was promoted Lieutenant and Captain. In 1808 he married, in Dublin, Mary Finlay, daughter and co-heiress of W. Finlay of Gunetts.[1] Of this marriage there were two sons—WILLIAM HIGGINSON (so named after his great-uncle), born 1811,[2] and FOLLIOT, born 1818 ; and two daughters—ROBINA MARY, who married, first, the Comte d'Ablomar, by whom she had a son and a daughter ; and, secondly, Charles Wilkinson ; and a younger daughter, who was dead when Alexander Samuel made his will, and is only mentioned as Baroness Cary.

Alexander Samuel died at Versailles in 1852 ; he left considerable landed property in Denbigh and Shropshire. In his will he mentions the estates of Bangor, Marchwiel, Whitworth, Dodington, Edgeley, Tilston, and Whixall, but these were sold. His executors were Richard Jebb and John Lee. He mentions his wife, Mary ; his two sons William Higginson and Folliot, and the wife of the former ; his two daughters, Robina Mary,

---

[1] ' Decr. 31st, 1808, at Dublin, Capt. Duff, 3rd Foot Guards, to Mary, youngest daughter and co-heiress of the late W. Finlay of Gunnetts.' (*Dublin Registers*)

[2] ' March 8th, 1811   In George St. the Lady of Alexander Samuel Duff of a son ' (*Scots Magazine*)

formerly Comtesse d'Ablomar, and now wife of Charles Wilkinson; and Baroness Cary, 'now deceased'; also his grandson and granddaughter Ablomar.

The two sons, William Higginson, known as 'Billy,' and Folliot, enjoyed a good deal of notoriety in London in the early and mid-Victorian days. They were both, at one time, in the Army. Billy became a 2nd Lieutenant in the 21st Royal North British Fusiliers, July 6, 1830, promoted Lieutenant 1832, exchanged into the 10th Dragoons 1837, and retired 1839.

Folliot was an Ensign in 34th Cumberland Foot 1834, Lieutenant 1837, Captain 1843; retired 1844.

It was Billy who gave to the Army and Navy Club its nickname of the 'Rag.' Coming in to supper late one night, he found the fare so meagre that he declared it was only a 'rag and famish affair' This tickled the fancy of the members, and a button bearing the nickname and a figure of a starving man gnawing a bone was designed and worn for a time by many members when in evening dress. Ralph Neville, who relates the above, in his *History of London Clubs,* adds that 'Billy was a celebrated man about town at a time when knocker-wrenching and similar pranks were in favour. His exploits in this line were notorious.' Some of his escapades were, however, not so harmless. The *Times* of August 8, 1840, contained the following: 'The Earl of Waldegrave and Captain Duff, who were committed to take their trial at the Middlesex sessions for a violent assault upon a policeman at Hampton, have moved the proceedings into the Court of Queen's Bench. The defendants will in all probability be put upon their trial in the forthcoming Michaelmas Term.' The result of the trial was a fine of £200 for Waldegrave, and £100 for Duff, and a sentence of six months' imprisonment in the Queen's Bench Prison, from which the two gentlemen emerged on November 3, 1841. The inhabitants of Strawberry Hill, where Lord Waldegrave lived, held a fête with illuminations in honour of the occasion. Folliot Duff wrote to the papers during his brother's imprisonment, endeavouring to fasten the guilt of the assault on others of the dining party who had assaulted and injured the policeman, but as Billy Duff had already pleaded guilty the matter was, of course, concluded. The *United Services Gazette* of April 15, 1841 thus dismisses him: 'Captain William Higginson Duff, to whose exploit in half murdering a single and unarmed policeman, with the aid of three fashionable companions as dastardly as himself, we alluded in our last, is no longer in the Army. He appears to be one of those feather-bed soldiers who enter the Army solely for the purpose of wearing a red coat and being dubbed "Captain." He probably had good reasons for retiring altogether from the Army by the sale of his Lieutenant's Commission in 1839'

For many years Billy Duff continued to amuse London with his pranks. He had a museum of curious objects collected by himself on some of his excursions at home and abroad, including door handles and knockers, buttons and studs, walking sticks, signboards, and a French soldier's helmet. On one occasion he is said to have kidnapped the baby of a dog-stealer and held it as a hostage for the return of his dog.

He married, in 1842, Amelia Charlotte, daughter of Captain Mathew R. Onslow, and widow of S. R. Marsham, who long survived him, living at 15 Grosvenor Place. His death occurred at Versailles in 1855, and hers in London in 1870. They had no children.

Folliot Duff, born 1818, was more of a harmless eccentric. He married, in 1849, Eliza Ann Parker, and they had a house in Belgrave Road. It is still remembered how Folliot used to write his name in blue chalk on the pavement outside his house and on neighbouring walls. They had three daughters: MARY ADA, died young, buried with her parents at Kensal Green; NINA, who married Pierre Clement Mouchot, and had issue; and EVA MAUD, afterwards Mrs. Ottley. Folliot died in 1872, and his wife in 1883.

CULTER HOUSE

CHAPTER XIX

YOUNGER SONS OF PATRICK DUFF OF CRAIGSTON

JOHN DUFF, second son to Patrick of Craigston, was, according to Baird,
'bred at Elgin with his uncle Dipple, and became factor to the late Lord
Fife for his estates in Moray, and also a merchant; John came soon into
the magistracy and was also sometime Provost of that burgh (1746-
1749). He was a man of very shrewd, solid judgment, not ignorant of
the Latin, and well acquainted with modern history and trade, and the
present state of the world; of very entertaining, facetious conversation,
and I have heard good judges say that he was the best companion of the
four brothers (i.e. sons of Craigston's first marriage, who lived to grow up).'

Among the Drummuir papers and those of Mr. E. G. Duff there are
several somewhat illegible letters from this John Duff on the business of
William Duff of Braco, afterwards Lord Fife.

One, dated Elgin, May 20, 1734, addressed to Mr. Andrew Hay, W.S.,
of Mountblairy, at Banff, informs him that the suspension is closed against
Lady Linkwood and Mr. Rainy, and encloses Braco's charge to Kilrach
and accounts for disbursements and entertainment at Boat of Bog in
October last, 'delivered to my brother William, amounting to £421. 6.

Scots.' He asks Hay to 'look out what papers Braco hath anent the Thanedom of Alves and the thirlage [1] of the lands belonging to his Mills and Old Mills, and what payments of thirl-muller are to be made. This wants to be looked to with attention. The Laird of Grant may have these, because he was Dipple's author in these mills. I hope this will find all glade with you on Glassaugh's [2] election as parliament man for your county. I shall have the pleasure to write you, and now and then drink your health, till I have an opportunity to serve you.'

Another says : ' This will be delivered by my brother William, to whom give answer and receipts. The Lady Roscommon tells me she recommended Thomas Sinclair, Laird of Brodie's man, to serve Braco as a miller. I have known him from his childhood, and am of opinion that Braco could not get a more sober and honest servant. Write me if you think him proper.'

Among the Duff House papers there is an order, dated 1720, by John Duff, merchant in Elgin, to ' deliver one Boll of oat meal to ffindlay Duff at the latter's house at Longbride.' ' The latter ' cannot be traced.[3]

John does not seem to have been especially successful in business, nor did he leave his children very well off, but he is said to have spent a good deal of money upon their education. He married Margaret Gordon of Farskane, by whom he had seven sons and four daughters. He died in 1751, ' A gentleman well beloved and universally lamented.' [4] ' His family burying place is in the Cathedral in Elgin.[5] His sons were PATRICK, ARCHIBALD, WILLIAM, JOHN, and JAMES. His daughter ANNE married James Leslie of Bennegeith, near Forres.' (Baird.)

PATRICK, or PETER, the eldest son (according to Baird, but in reality the second), was ' bred to the Law at Edinburgh and entered Writer to the Signet. He would have been well employed, but he fell into a life of dissipation and pleasure, and at last into an itch of gaming, and kept company with some of the great folks at Edinburgh, and, after losing his own money, played away other people's entrusted to him, and was obliged to retire to North America. He married a gentleman's daughter in Fife, an agreeable, pretty woman, and had a daughter, but both are dead many years ago.' (Baird, writing in 1773.) The name of this lady was Grisell

---

[1] Obligation to grind corn at some particular mill

[2] General James Abercromby, M P. for Banffshire

[3] Though mentioned also in Lady Roscommon's accounts

[4] *Aberdeen Journal* of that date

[5] He is known as Provost Duff, the elder, to distinguish him from John Duff (father of Major Robert of Ladyhill), who married Janet Gordon of Farskane, niece to the elder John's wife, and was Provost five times. See chapter xxviii.

Balfour, and the daughter, GRISELL or JEAN, was served heir to her mother in 1752.

The eldest son was ARCHIBALD, Sheriff-Clerk of Moray, known as the 'Muckle Clerk' (to distinguish him from his successor Patrick, known as 'Little Clerk Duff,'[1] brother of the junior John Duff, Provost). Archibald married his own first cousin (his mother's niece), Jane Stewart of Lesmurdie. He resided at Bilbohall, near Elgin, then the property of George Duff of Milton, Convener of the County, to whom he probably paid a nominal rent.[2] At his death, in 1798, his assets appear to have amounted to £14. He had one son, William, who predeceased him.

The Provost's three younger sons are thus dismissed by Baird : ' James is in the planting way in Jamaica ; John was a factor in Holland, but died lately ; and William died some years before his father.'

According to the Elgin Parish Registers, John Duff's children were :

' Archibald, 1718. [His baptism is not recorded]
'Peter, baptised Aug. 19, 1719; witnesses, Peter Duff of Craigston, Peter Duff, writer in Aberdeen.[3]
' William, baptised Aug. 5, 1720; witnesses, William Duff of Dipple, and William Duff of Braco his son.
' Helen, 1722 ; witnesses, Helen Duff, Lady Roscommon, Helen Taylor, Lady Braco.
' Alexander, 1723 ; witness, Alexander Duff of Hatton.
' John, 1725 ; witness John Innes of Edingeith, brother-in-law to the provost.
' Margaret, 1726 ; witness, Margaret Duff, Lady Farskane, the child's aunt.
' John, 1729.[4]
' James, 1736.[4]
' Helen, 1737 ; witness, Helen, Lady Roscommon.
' Anne, the youngest. [Baptism not recorded.] '

There is one letter from Archibald Duff to Lord Braco :

' MY LORD,—By my Mothers orders I send this express to acquaint your Lordship of my fathers death this morning, as she knows it would have been very agreeable to the inclination of your dead friend, so it would to her, if your

---

[1] See chapter xxviii

[2] In the annals of Elgin there is a note of the summoning before the kirk-session of ' the people of Bilbohall, who were in the plew on the fast day, and said their master forced them to do so '

[3] The custom of having many friends and relations of the same Christian name as the child, present at the baptism, makes the old registers very useful reading

[4] In 1750 John and James Duff, sons of John Duff, late Provost, were made burgesses of Elgin. ' For regard to the said John Duff, senior, and for the good services done by him to the burgh '

Lops. occasions led you to this country that you honoured his Funeralls with your Company, but as the heat of the weather and the situation of the Corpse will admit of no delay, so she can hardly ask your Lop. to come on purpose. The Burial is therefore intended with all the privatness decency will admit of, on Saturday afternoon. I have the honour to be, my Lord, your Lops. most obednt. and most humble sert.,   Archd. Duff.

   'Elgin, *12th June* 1751

   ' To Lord Braco at Rothiemay.'   (D.)

    And another to William Rose ·

                                                      ' 16 *May* 1791.

   ' Dear Sir,—Immediately on receipt of yours of the 7th this day sennight, I sent over express to Pluscarden for Mr. Mepherson. He was gone over to Glass the day before, on Friday I met him accidentally on his way home and he promised to sett about making out the extracts you Desire without loss of time. . . . The Memorials and other Exhibits he has not yet Ingrossed in his Record. He is Directly to sett about Doing this, and how soon I can get them from him, you may be sure they will be Sent you. I wish you to look over the note of the Acct formerly sent you, and make up and Send me a Sketch of it from yourself Specifying what I'm to Pay Mr. McWilliam for his Trouble and if I'm to Pay Mr. Lachlan, or how much I'm to give him for his Exs. He says the Dues he is commonly Paid, and what he Received from Mr. Tod for the Duke was 2/6 the first and 1/6 for every other sheet, but he Declines making any Demand for Lord Fife expenses untill he have your Sanction for the Doing it. I Beg you not to fail in writing me as to this, as he has called on me Severall times already for your answers. As you Desire, I shall forbear sending your £10 and the same shall be Deduced from your Whitty Payt for the office. Burdsyeards Seasme was taken on Saturday sennight. I told him he was to pay you, as I was only acting for you and that I should write to you to Transmitt your acct. I think it will be best—if you please look at the Regulations and in case you are not to be over soon, make up the acct. and send it either to Peter Duff or me, as I have found these things paid as willingly when recent or otherwise. You are Sutherlands Debitor in half the chaise hyre. I have not seen Prov. Duff as yet, when I do, shall make Inquiry and tell you if he and I differ. I 'm sorrie the sprain in your leg has given you so much uneasiness. I wish you would make your writing a little more intelligible, as its difficult to read it.[1] Believe me alwise, Dear Sir, Yours,   Archd. Duff.' (R)

    Of John Duff of Elgin's son called William, Admiral Duff, writing to Patrick Duff of Premnay in 1744 says that ' my Brother at Elgin's son

---

[1] The present writers, who have struggled with a good deal of Rose's MS , heartily endorse this opinion.

was too old before he came to sea to learn to be a seaman, and the only office he can qualify himself for in our service is a Purser.'

Apparently William was not a very prudent or capable person Patrick writes back to Admiral Robert that it would be best if William would settle in Jamaica.

Of James we have the following further account. Lord Fife had indeed no sinecure in finding employment for all his young relatives.

Mrs. Duff, Oldmilns, Elgin, to Lord Braco

' MY LORD,—Its with Reluctance Im induced to give you this trouble, but in my present circumstances having my youngest son Jams upon my hand and without any ffriend ffitt to advise or able to assist or att lesst with humanety sufisent to befriend me in putting him in a way of making his living. The bussness he was bred to being that of a Wiver and that brinsh of tred being quit gone, and in learning it lost great pert of his patrimony, I could think of no way for him but making my appleeation to the Honble. Mr. Jams Duff solliciting his Interest, to procure him an ensigns Commission and as in my Husbands life-time all of us had a dependance on your Lordshipe, I have now presumed to beg your Lop use your influence with your son to effectuate this matter.

' As this is at present the only Scheme I can form to my self of the poor young lad's being provided for, I canot help flattering myself with the thoughts of your Lordships interesting yourself in Behalf of the son, whose father your Lop. always and with justice accounted one of your best well-wishers.—I am, with great Respect, My Lord, Your Lordships Most oblidged humble Servtt.,

'MARGRAT GORDON.   (D.)

'OLDMILNS, 29th June 1757 '

This James Duff did not, however, enter the Army, but went, like many of the family, to Jamaica, and his will, proved at Kingstown in 1782, shows him as leaving a considerable amount of money to his nephews and nieces.

' To John, Margaret, Alexander, Archibald, Robert and Ann Leslie, children of his sister Anne.   To William Duff, son of his brother Archi-bald, and in case of his death to Archibald himself.

' Also to Patrick, James and Margaret Gordon.'

(As far as is known, the family of Provost John Duff, in the male line, died out entirely.)

The ' immediate younger brother ' of John Duff, Provost of Elgin, was WILLIAM DUFF of Whitehill, born 1690. ' He settled a merchant in Banff about 1716 ; he was a very sensible, social, friendly, honest man ; while provost of that town he studied the interest of the place without any regard to person or party ' (Baird). William of Whitehill seems to have been

his father's executor, and had a good deal of trouble with the amounts left to his younger half-brothers who were abroad, and much correspondence with his brothers John and Patrick.

The following poem, published at the date of his death in the *Scots Magazine*, December 1740, shows the respect in which he was held :

'On the death of William Duff of Whitehill, late Provost of Banff. Ingens sui desiderium moriens reliquit.'

> 'Who can behold and shun to drop a tear,
> When all the town in sable weeds appear,
> For him who made the public good his aim,
> And by the city's thriving rais'd his fame ?
> Tho' great your grief and just your cause of woe,
> Your wound yet green, your loss you scarcely know
> No city e'er a better burgher had
> To guard her int'rest, or advance her trade
> No frowns or flatt'ry of the rich or great,
> No hope of sordid gain or private hate,
> E'er brass'd him to yield or join with those
> Who durst the city's publick good oppose
> Candid in commerce, once the word he spoke
> No man can say that word he ever broke
> I strive not here in pompous praise to shine,
> Or paint fictitious merit in each line ,
> Yet justly I can say, because 'tis true,
> Through a long tract of time, the man I knew
> Sincere in friendship, honesty his view,
> May angels waft his soul with endless joy
> To that bless'd place where pleasures never cloy '

'In Queen Anne's Wars, he went upon a trading voyage to the Levant, aboard of a merchant ship, was taken prisoner by an Algerian pirate and carried to Smyrna, where he lay a winter, till his ransom was remitted, and then came home. He was very successful in merchandizing, husbandry, and country dealings, and managed all his affairs with activity and prudence; he was a most candid, ingenuous man, had much of what the French call naiveté, and would sometimes, when half in his bottle, play upon his own industrious spirit, and say it was a bare muir where *he* could not find a cow.' (Baird.)

In 1718 he married Bathia Garden of Troup (who survived him till 1781), and had ten children : [1]

1. BATHIA, 1718; married, in 1738, John Gordon of Badenscoth; died 1753.
2. PATRICK, 1720.

---

[1] Register of the Episcopal Church of Banff

3. JAMES, 1722-1726.

4. JEAN, 1724-1733.

5. WILLIAM, born and died 1726.

6. JOHN, 1728-1732.

7. ANNE, 1730-1732.

8. WILLIAM, 1731-1732.

9. JAMES, 1735,[1] died unmarried in the East Indies 'As supercargo of the ship *Greyhood*, 1758,' *vide* Indian Registers.

10. MARGARET, 1738-1742.

There is one letter from William Duff of Whitehill to his brother Patrick Duff of Premnay :

'BANFF, *9th Octr* 1735.

'AFFECT. BROYR,—Our Broyr Francis came here and I advised him to goe forward to Elgine and gett his assignation signed by our Broyr John. I send you inclosed a letter I had from John on that subject. By yit I think he has mistaken what was designed, and Francis tells me he signed the assignation you sent out and kept it by him. It would be hard Francis should be detained by this mistake, and I hope you will order it in such a way as he may goe forward as was designed, and you may be sure, as I am fully satisfied, youll desyre nothing of me but whats right. I will readicly goe in to any methode you propose and John can be satisfied afterwards. My kind respects to Lady Braceo and my sister and I still am, Your affect. broyr, etc.,   W. DUFF.

'*P.S.*—Mind to cause Archibald Duff assigne all the accounts relating to Craigstouns[2] funeralls before he goe away.

'For Patrick Duff off premnay att Aberdeen.'   (*D*)

The only one of William's children to carry on the family was Patrick, the eldest son, born 1720, and, like his father, Provost of Banff. He married, July 13, 1743, Clementina Hay of Rannes, daughter of the famous giant, whose monster stockings were long exhibited at Duff House.[3] They also had a large family, many of whom died young, but in 1773, when Baird wrote, there were 'two sons and two daughters living.' 'WILLIAM bred with a Writer to the Signet in Edinburgh, now gone to North America ;

---

[1] 'John Gordon' was appointed 'Tutor' to James Duff, second son to William Duff of Whitehill, on February 2, 1741. James Duff must therefore have been under fourteen at the time, as between the ages of fourteen and twenty-one a boy had a curator The register of his baptism shows him to have been born in 1735, and therefore six at this time His eldest brother Patrick was twenty-one, and all the intervening children were dead John Gordon was no doubt Gordon of Badenscoth, the boy's brother-in-law. John, William and Anne, who all died in 1732, are buried in the churchyard in Banff.

[2] His half-brother James, died 1734

[3] Charles Hay's stockings are now in the Banff Museum, and a portrait of him at Hatton His son Andrew was 'out' in the '45. Charles Hay's wife was Helen Fraser

PETER, who is in the East Indies ; HELEN, married to John Duff of Hatton ; and MARGARET, to Mr. William Stewart, a grandson of old Lesmurdy's, and minister at Auchterless '

Provost Patrick Duff died in 1783, and his wife in 1752.

The births of two of their children are to be found in the registers of the Episcopal Church in Banff .

' HELEN, baptised June 22, 1744; name-mothers Mrs. Helen Fraser, Lady Rannes, the child's grandmother, and Miss Helen Innes.'

' WILLIAM, baptised July 16, 1745 ; named after Provost William Duff, deceased, the child's grandfather, and William Leslie of Melross, Esq.'

The other three were baptised at New Deer (after the church in Banff had been burnt by Cumberland), and the records were only discovered accidentally :

' May 24, 1748, Patrick Duff of Whitehill had a son baptised, named CHARLES.'

' March 29, 1750, Patrick Duff of Whitehill had a daughter brought forth by his Lady, Clementina Hay, baptised, named MARGARET.'

' March 28, 1751. Patrick Duff of Whitehill had a son baptised, named PATRICK WILLIAM ' (' Petter ').

Patrick Duff of Whitehill writes thus to Lord Fife soliciting help for his son William :

'CRUVIE, Sept 1st, 1775

' MY LORD,—I had a letter from my son William enclosing letters for your Lordship and Troup. Your Lordship's I send Inclosed. It seems, by the aid of one of the Clerks of the Treasury, he has got information, of the vacancy of the Collectorship of Port Antonio on the Island of Jamaica. My Friend Troup wishes this post for him and Coll. Morris left a letter with Wm. at London to be delivered to Lord North with the letters of other friends and I have taken the liberty to send this by express to your Lordship, beging your Lordship will send me a letter for Lord North in my sons favours that I may send him to deliver with the others. When your Lordship was here and exprest your wish to serve Wm. has made me take this freedome and will always have a just sense of your favours and has the honour to Bee, My Lord, Your Lordship's most obdt. and very humble Sert., PATT. DUFF.

' P.S.—In case your Lordship inclines to write and send it off yourself to Wm. his address is New Loyds Coffie House, London.' (D.)

Andrew Hay, Patrick's brother-in-law, to Lord Fife

'RANNES, Feb 24, 1775.

' MY LORD,—Its William Duff, Provost Duff's eldest son, my nephew by a favorite sister. The young gentleman has the Honr to be of your family and looks

up to your Lop. as father and protector of your cadets. As far as I can judge, he 's ane honest sensible fellow w^t out show and possesses the sentiments of a gentleman. He intends soon to return to the Island of Grenada where he was last three years. His business in this corner was in quest of a small creditt w^h he 'll obtain, and to request the intercession of friends if possible to obtain for him from Government some place in either of the W. India Islands either in the Customs or any other Branch of the Revenue. Of course the Climate occasions many vacancys, its useless to sugest to your Lop. If in the customs, nothing less than being a Contracker would be agreeable to himself or friends, or if in the Revenue a place equal in emoluments to it. I flatter myself his conduct may enable his friends w^t assurance to get something better in time. Your Lop. will eassily believe that every interest will be asked to serve our young friend in the laudable attempt of wishing to make a reasonable liveing, his ambition is to return to his country and friends w^t a decent competency ; What pleasure would it give me if he ow'd his promotion and good fortune to your Lop and I 'm certain it would equally gratifie Mr. Duff to be under obligations of gratitude to you. Troup and severall others will be addressed on this subject. I shall now beg leave to assure your Lop. that serving Wm. Duff will be obliging many of your friends in a particular manner who 's warmly interested for Mr. Duff. . . . I have the honour, etc.,   ANDREW HAY.' (*D.*)

And William Duff himself from Barbadoes to the Earl of Fife :

'BRIDGETOWN, BARBADOES, 27 *June* 1779

' MY LORD,—I wrote your Lordship some time ago. And takes the opportunity of an express that goes from this Island to inform your Lop. that the Island of St. Vincents surrendered to the French the 24th of June, the particulars of which we had this morning by an express from St. Lucia

' That St. Vincents was taken by several French Men of War thought to be Monsieur le Mothe de la Piquet's squadron from Europe, Two hundred of the Regt. of Martinica and sixty Grenadiers aided by the Curibs, Arms and Amunition having been brought them by the French ; Admiral Byron with the whole of the British Squadron have been off the Station for this sometime ; he having conveyed, it is thought, a considerable way to the Northward the homeward British West India fleet of Merchantmen. They sailed from St. Kitts the 16th June ; considering what a fine fleet Byron has in those seas, it is astonishing he should not have left a sufficient number of ships to protect the Islands which he had in his power to have done, every vessell even to a sloop of war is with him except a Bomb Ketch that 's within the Carinage at St. Lucia. The French finding the coast clear and so fair an opportunity, landed at St Vincents Monday 21st June. The Island surrendered Thursday the 24th. Several expresses have been sent by the Commander at St. Lucia in quest of Admiral Byron, of whom they had heard nothing on the 25th June. We have no account as yet of the Terms of Capitulation. St. Vincents lyes fifty miles-north west of Barbadoes and thirty south of St. Lucia is twenty-four miles long and eighteen broad.

The Island of Carriacow [1] is closs by, the one being seen most distinctly from the other. St. Vincents is a most valuable Island. It made better than 15,000 h-hds sugar this year I remain, with all due respect, My Lord, Your Lops. most devoted and most ob^dt Sert, WILLM. DUFF.

'*P.S.*—It is imagined Grenader has likewise fallen.' (*D.*)

From William's father, Provost Patrick ·

'CHOVIE, *9th Aug.* 1780

'MY LORD,—I had a letter from my Son William from Barbadoes dated Aprile, Informing me that Henry Smith, Colector of his Majesty's Customs, on the Island of Saint Vincent, is dead. The Island is presently in the hands of the French. But, at Barbadoes its thought it will be soon retaken by Britain, and he begs of me to apply your Lordship to solicite in his Favour, to have Lord North's Promise that if the Island fall to Britain, my Son shall have the appointment of the Colectorship. A promise of this kind is the more ready to be obtained from the uncertainty, and if William is presently apointed, he can wait untill we see if shal have the good luck of retaking it. May I beg the favour of your Lordship to write a letter to Lord North in favour of William, and transmitt it to me, and I will cause a friend there Deliver it, in doing of which your Lordship will much favour both William and me. I beg to hear from your Lordship by the Bearer, and I have the honour to be, My Lord, your Lordship's most obedt. and humble servt., PATT. DUFF.' (*R.*)

In April 1784 William died at Barbadoes (unmarried), and his brother PETER or PATRICK is mentioned in the Decennial List of Heirs as being heir-at-law both to him and to their father on July 20, 1785, Peter's death early in that year, apparently not having been yet reported from India. Administration of William's estate was granted to his brother-in-law, John Duff of Hatton, 'as lawful attorney,' for the use of his sisters Helen (John's wife) and Margaret (Mrs. Stewart).

Of Patrick [2] not very much is known, save from two letters still existing at Hatton. From these it appears that he went out to India in 1769, when the other Patrick Duff ('Tiger') of the East India Company's service returned to Bengal after his temporary suspension.

The first letter is dated

'CAMP NEAR SOURFN, *Mar* 15, 1780

'MY DEAR FATHER,—I have not received a letter from you this season, which makes me very uneasy, nor one from my grandmother nor any other person excepting Mr. Garden, Troup, and Delgaty, each of them one letter, Troup's enclosing one from a Mr. McPherson at Kensington to Mr. Hastings which I don't believe will be of any service to me as he cannot forgive any adherent of General Clavering's. I was one, and though not the most powerful

---

[1] Curaçao.   [2] Called 'Petter' in the family letters, see page 239

of whose estate, value £1000, was granted in 1807 to Mrs. John Duncan, his only relative, was the other child, and is by name mentioned in the will.

Admiral Robert Duff of Logie, his great-uncle, then in the Mediterranean, had made interest for 'Petter' with General Coote, and otherwise helped him. 'Petter' seems to have had a keen eye to his own advantage, and to have been anxious to make money. He is known from the second letter at Hatton (from John Grant, and chiefly concerned with money matters) to have gone 'up country in command of a battalion of sepoys in the first brigade' in December 1784, and to have died or been killed early in the following year, as a commission of factory given to his brother-in-law, Mr. Stewart, minister of Auchterless in 1783, was produced and acted upon in 1785, and Helen Duff was served heir to both her brothers William and Patrick in 1786.

Patrick Duff's name does not appear in the list of Indian cadets published in this country, which proves him to have gone out as a volunteer, and probably to have waited for some years before being appointed Ensign. At that time the Bengal army was organised in three brigades, each consisting of one European regiment, several sepoy battalions, and some artillery. The sepoy battalions were usually commanded by captains.

From papers at the India Office, the following facts as to Patrick Duff's services have been ascertained :

In the Muster Roll of the first brigade, 1778, appears 'Patrick Duff, Lieutenant, age twenty-eight years. Corps—Sepoys. Ship in which arrived—*Deptford*.[1] Native of Scotland.'

He was probably appointed Brevet-Captain in this year, though he appears as Substantive Captain only in 1785, the year of his death.[2]

His will is in the Registers at the India Office :

'The Last Will and Testament of Captain Patrick Duff, decd., Filed and Probate granted to Lt.-Col. Patrick Duff, one of the Exors., reserving power, etc : the 21st day of April 1785.

'I, Captain Patrick Duff, in the service of the Honourable East India Company, by these presents, make my later Will and Testament, as follows :

'It is my will that the Estate of Whitehill, the lands and houses in and about the town of, and the farms and lands of Crovie, which fell to me on the decease of my Father,[3] shall on my decease descend agreeable to the meaning and intent of my said Father, as is expressed in his Will.

'Further, it is my desire that all sums of money, debts and movables which

---

[1] The *Deptford* was a company's vessel which had started for India in February 1769.

[2] In the Burgess Roll of Banff for the year 1774 the names of both Major Patrick Duff and Captain Patrick Duff of the Honourable East India Company's service appear In both cases the rank was Brevet For Major Patrick Duff ('Tiger') see chapter xxxi

[3] His father had died in 1783, and his elder brother in April 1784.

shall belong to me, both in Great Britain and in India at the time of my decease shall be disposed of as follows, after having first paid all my lawful debts.

' First, I bequeath unto my housekeeper, Newajee, the sum of sicca rupees 3000 ; secondly, unto my adopted son, commonly called Peter, sicca rupees 2000, and the remainder in equal shares between my illegitimate son James, and the child with which my forementioned Housekeeper Newajee is now pregnant, and that in case of the death of one of these, the survivor shall inherit the share of the other, and in case of the decease of both of them it is my will and desire that my second eldest sister, Margaret, spouse to the Rev. Mr. William Stewart, and the heirs of his body, do succeed to and inherit the shares of both.

' And I do hereby appoint the Rev. Mr. William Stewart, Lt.-Col. Patrick Duff, and Capt. John Grant exors. and trustees for my affairs in Europe, and I do further appoint Lt -Col. Patrick Duff, Major William Duncan, Captain Robert Baillie, and Captain Robert Lennard, Exors. of this my last Will and Testament, for the purpose of transacting my affairs in India, and to them I also recommend the care of the children before mentioned, and that they may be sent to Europe at what time they may judge proper.

' In witness whereof I have subscribed and set my seal to these presents at Futtyghur, where no stamp paper can be had, this fourteenth day of January 1785.   PATRICK DUFF.' [1]

HELEN, who married John Duff of Hatton and Drumblair, had sixteen children ; these will be found in the chapter on the Duffs of Hatton. She succeeded her father and grandfather in the estate of Whitehill.[2]

Although there were two Provosts of Banff of the name of Duff in the eighteenth century, it is difficult to identify the host of Chevalier Johnstone.[3] He gives the following account of his visit. A week after the date of the battle of Culloden, since when he had been in hiding with Sir William Gordon, Gordon of Cobairdy, and Gordon of Avochie, he went with Sir

[1] General Sir Beauchamp Duff points out that this is the will of a man at the point of death, but no actual details as to the circumstances or day of his death, nor of his place of burial, are known

[2] There is among the papers in Mr. Edward G. Duff's possession a long letter, dated October 7, 1793, from Helen Duff, widow of John Duff of Hatton, to William Rose, factor for Lord Fife, complaining of the way her own and her ' dear departed son Sandy's affairs ' have been mismanaged, and the same Alexander's confidence in regard to his lawsuits with his aunt, Lady Anne, betrayed by George Robinson, brother-in-law to Rose, who had, on Rose's recommendation, been employed as man of business to the family   In this letter Helen mentions the matter of a ' Submission betwixt my brother's children and me '   This must refer to Captain Peter or Patrick's sons and daughters, as William died in Barbadoes without issue   She also mentions that ' Mr Stuart was there to take care of his own interest and the children's '   This is the Rev William Stewart, minister of Auchterless, husband of her sister Margaret   She also mentions that her own son Patrick ' was bred a soldier and left the country at fourteen years of age, and was therefore unacquainted with business '   (Patrick succeeded to Hatton 1791.)

[3] Memoirs of the Rebellion, 1745, 1746, by the Chevalier de Johnstone, A D C. to Lord George Murray.

William to pass the night ' at his castle of Park,' from whence he proceeded to Banff to have an interview with his brother-in-law, Mr Rollo:

' I went straight to the house of Mr. Duff, provost of Banff, where I had been so agreeably entertained a short time before. He was a secret partisan of the Prince, but being prudent and discreet, he only avowed his principles to his particular friends. He was one of the most amiable men in the world, endowed with every possible good quality, and possessed of true merit. Mrs. Duff resembled her husband in everything, and their two daughters, the youngest of whom was a great beauty, were the exact copies of their father and mother. There was but one way of thinking in Mr. Duff's house, and I shall regret the loss of their delicious society as long as I live. The servant who opened the door did not know me on account of my disguise.' (It was that of a farm-labourer, the servant of Mr. Stewart, minister of Rothiemurchus, with whom on the previous day he had exchanged clothes, and comments plaintively on the smell of those he had to wear.) ' Mr. Duff came downstairs and did not recognise me, any more than she had done, but having fixed his eyes on me for some moments, his surprise was succeeded by a flood of tears. As Mrs Duff and her daughters were in bed, he conducted me to a room, and sent a message to my brother-in-law, who however could not be found. Early next morning, the servant-maid suddenly entered my chamber and told me that I was undone, as the courtyard was filled with soldiers, come to seize me.[1] I flew to the window, when I saw in reality the soldiers which the maid had told me of and returned to my chair perfectly resigned, and considered myself as a man who was soon to end his days, keeping my eyes steadfastly fixed on the door, ready to spring on the soldiers like a lion the moment they should appear. Having passed about a quarter of an hour in the most violent agitation, the door of my chamber at length opened, and I sprang forward with precipitation to the attack But what was my surprise when, in place of the soldiers, I saw the beautiful and adorable Miss Duff the younger, burst in, out of breath, to tell me, like another guardian angel, to be no longer uneasy, that the disturbance was occasioned by some soldiers fighting among themselves, who had entered into the court to elude the observation of their officers. Miss Duff the younger was very beautiful and only eighteen. I seized her in my arms, pressed her to my bosom and gave her, with the best will in the world, a thousand tender kisses.

' In an instant, the whole family were in my room to congratulate me on my happy deliverance, the noise of the soldiers having raised every person in the house, though it was hardly six o'clock. Fully convinced of the sincere friendship and esteem of this respectable family, my greatest uneasiness during this adventure was lest from their excessive anxiety for me, some of them should have innocently betrayed me. Mr. Duff was the only person on whose coolness and presence of mind I could fully rely.

---

[1] The house with the courtyard still exists on the Banff Low Shore There is no actual record as to whom it belonged ; it is now a tenement house

' My brother-in-law called on me a few minutes after the alarm was over
and made me many protestations of friendship, but excused himself from contributing in any manner to assist me in procuring a passage to some foreign
country, which as he knew all the masters of the trading ships in Banff he could
easily have done, but he would not expose himself to the least risk for me.
Having passed the whole day at Mr. Duff's, in as agreeable a manner as was
compatible with the unfortunate situation in which I was placed, I took my
final leave of that amiable family about nine o'clock in the evening, to return
to the castle of Gordon of Park, and our tears at parting were reciprocal and
abundant.'

Now, William Duff of Whitehill, who was Provost of Banff from 1732-
1733, and would therefore still have kept the title (' once Provost, always My
Lord '), died in 1740, and his only daughter who lived to grow up, Bathia,
had married, in 1738, John Gordon of Badenscoth.

While William's son Patrick, who was afterwards Provost in 1764-1767
and 1773-1776 was only twenty-six at the date of Culloden, and the only
daughter then born to him, Helen, afterwards Mrs. Duff of Hatton, was
two years old.

The Provost from 1744 to 1748, whose wife was Jean Duff of Craigston
(married in 1720), was John Innes of Edingight. It was most probably
in his house that the Chevalier Johnstone stayed. In that family there
were several daughters, of whom the youngest, Helen, died in 1806 ; or Jean
may have had some of her young half-sisters staying with her, some of
Patrick of Craigston's second family of twenty-three children, of whom
the younger ones would have been under twenty (Elizabeth and Mary,
the two eldest daughters, were married before 1737, but the youngest
son was born about 1725, or later) ; and the lovely Miss Duff about
whom the Chevalier waxes so eloquent may therefore have been one of
the unnamed younger daughters of Patrick of Craigston.

The fourth son of Patrick Duff of Craigston was his namesake, PATRICK
or PETER DUFF of Premnay, ' so called from an estate in the Garioch which
he first purchased and afterwards sold, but retained the title. He served
an apprenticeship to George Keith, advocate at Aberdeen (presumably of
the same family as Keith of Bruxie with whom Dipple and Braco afterwards
had so much litigation, as seen from their letters), at that time the most
eminent man of his profession in the north of Scotland He was afterwards much employed by his uncle Dipple, and his cousin William Duff
of Braco, in their business ' (Band).

He was appointed factor, or as it was then called ' doer,' to his cousin
William of Braco, and would seem to have taken an unfair advantage of
the position, for three years after his cousin's untimely death he married

that cousin's only surviving child, Margaret, then aged eleven, as to which event he writes the letter given in chapter viii.[1]

The greater part of William of Braco's property went at his death to his uncle, William of Dipple, as heir of entail,[2] Margaret receiving £3000 as a bond of provision 'But Premnay being advised that her father's entail was liable to several objections, served his lady heir of line to him, and got her infeft in every part of the estate' (Baird), and they had to be bought out. In 1721, the year of her marriage, she also appears in the Decennial List of Heirs as heir to her father (who had died 1718), and her grandmother, who died that year. The estate of Eden belonged to Margaret, and only at her death passed to the descendants of her aunt Helen (married Gordon of Farskane), now represented by the Grant Duffs (*q.v*).

'Premnay acquired, soon after (in 1729), the estate of Sir Alexander Cumin of Culter, by buying in the debts; and after that, most of the low country estate of Drum; but both these families, especially the last, complain of a train of fraudulent and unfair steps taken by him in accomplishing these purchases' (Baird).

Patrick died in 1763 at Culter, which he had made 'one of the most beautiful and best finished gentleman's seats in the North.' He left it to his half-brother, Admiral Robert, in whose family it remained until it was sold in 1908 by R. W. Duff of Fetteresso to Mr. Theodore Crombie of Aberdeen. The mansion-house has unfortunately since been burnt down, and rebuilt.

Patrick is buried at Culter, and the following inscription adorns his grave:

'To the memory of Patrick Duff of Culter, Esq. He was born Nov. 16, 1692. He dyed Oct. 20, 1763. He examined Christianity, believed it firmly, and loved it warmly. From Christian principles, he practised social virtue; in relieving distress and promoting useful arts he delighted. The affection of his widow raises this monument.' [3]

His widow married, on Christmas Day 1768, Alexander Udny of Udny (he died 1789 at Culter), and was afterwards known as Mrs. Udny-Duff. She died 1793, aged eighty-three.[4]

---

[1] From constant messages in letters to him from members of the family it would appear that his notable mother-in-law, who long survived him, dying at the age of over a hundred, lived with him during all his married life   Patrick and his wife had no children

[2] See chapter vii

[3] The obituary notice of Patrick Duff concludes by saying : 'We can with justice affirm that in no place was the man of law more usefully blended with the character of the country gentleman than in this worthy person.'

[4] In Peterculter church there are two silver goblets, bearing the Duff arms and motto with the monograms H D and M U. D., presumably presented in memory of Helen and Margaret Duff, wife and daughter of William Duff of Braco   The plate marks show these cups to be of London manufacture and date 1809   (*Aberdeen Notes and Queries*)

PATRICK DUFF OF CULTER

By W Mossman

Of Patrick of Craigston's daughters by his first wife, only one is known to have reached womanhood: JANE, born in 1696; married, in 1720, her cousin, John Innes of Edingight, Provost of Banff, and died in 1778, aged eighty-two. He died in 1790. She had three sons and several daughters, of whom the youngest, Helen, died unmarried in 1806; many descendants of Jane exist to-day.

Among the Banffshire sasines there is one, dated 1720, to Jean Duff, spouse to John Innes of Edingight, of two hundred merks yearly on the estate of Edingight.

The baptism of HELEN, Patrick's eldest daughter, is found in the Parish Registers of Grange, under date October 25, 1691, but nothing more is known of her.

Of Patrick of Craigston's daughters by the second wife, Mary Urquhart, five are known to us:

1. ELIZABETH, born 1702; married William Stuart of Auchorrachan, a younger son of Lesmurdy's, and her own cousin.

2. MARY, who married William Leslie [1] of Melross (died 1776), and had one son, Major William Leslie, who became heir to his uncle, Adam Duff of Stocket. She died in 1773.

3. MARGARET, born 1720, died 1801; married Alexander Gordon of Gight.[2] She had nine sons and three daughters, and the eldest son, George, born 1741, who married Catherine Innes, was the father of Catherine Gordon, married to Captain John Byron, and mother of the poet.

4. A fourth daughter married to Davidson of Newton.

5. A fifth daughter married Benjamin Duff, an Irishman, and was the great-grandmother of William Duff, minister of Grange (q.v.).

The sons of Patrick's second marriage were JAMES, THOMAS, ARCHIBALD, FRANCIS, ROBERT, ADAM.

JAMES of Craigston, born about 1703, married Helen Abercromby of Glassaugh (contract of marriage dated June 22, 1732), and died in 1734.

---

[1] William Leslie, Banff, writes thus to Patrick Duff of Premnay ·

'SIR,—I 'm very well pleasd to hear of our Broyr ffrances's good settlement, and I hope he will alwise have a gratefull sense of the service you and Capt. Urquhart have done him   As to what you write concerning Thos. portion the free stock to be divided after all deductions amounts to Nyne hund and twelve pound eighteen shill and four pennies Scots money w^h sum you know is presently liferented by the Lady Craigstown   It comes as youll see to £10 18 Str each share and a very small fraction more.'

[2] The death of Alexander Gordon is thus chronicled in the *Aberdeen Journal* of January 24, 1760 'We hear from Fyvie of the death of Alexander Gordon of Gight, much regretted.   He was an honest, unoffensive gentleman, an affectionate husband, etc   He having frequently found benefit to his health by using the cold bath, had the misfortune to perish in the Waters of the Ythan while bathing, the water being suddenly swelled by melted snow.'

He had two daughters—HELEN, born 1733, who married, in 1761, Dr. David Clerk, and had four sons, of whom the eldest was afterwards Baron Clerk Rattray, and married Jane, only daughter of Admiral Duff of Fetteresso; and MARY, born 1734, died an infant.

At James's death, Craigston, being entailed in the male line, passed to his brother Thomas, while Castleton remained the property of his daughter. Helen would also appear, at her father's death, to have legally represented her grandfather, Patrick Duff of Craigston, as Thomas Duff, her uncle, claims from her ' the balance of a sum of 4000 merks Scots contained in a bond of provision granted by the deceased Patrick Duff of Craigston to Thomas Duff, his lawful son, and to the other children of him the said Patrick, dated 29 Aug 1726.'

An inventory of the goods, etc., of James Duff shows that he died in the month of June 1734, and was buried in Drum's Ile in the church of Aberdeen. William Duff of Whitehill (his half-brother) was discerned executor and had charge of all his debts, etc.

A sum was paid to ' Helen Abercrombie for her own aliment and the aliment of Helen and Mary Duffs her children, both then alive, and of two men servants, and two women servants, and one nurse, besides those who served in harvest, and besides those who were employed for labouring the Mains A further item of £63 Scots (£7, 10s. sterling) was paid to the said Helen Abercrombie for the expenses of the birth of Mary Duff, her posthumous child, and for the funeral expenses of the said child ' (Another of the Mary Duffs whose sojourn on this earth was short and sad See chapter xxxii., note, page 501.)

A further entry shows that the sum of £128, 14s. Scots of money belonging to James Duff was found in the said James Duff's ' Cloach bag after his death,' and Archibald Duff, who was by the said defunct in his sickness and at his death, accounted for the same to the executor. Archibald, it must be remembered, was afterwards a doctor, and is described in the will as ' Student of Physick in Aberdeen.' There was a further sum allowed for the entertainment of the doctors.

THOMAS DUFF was the second son of Patrick of Craigston's second marriage. In his own testament-dative, dated 1737, he is described as elder son of the second marriage, but that was after the death of his elder brother James. The edict of executry grants warrant to summon, warn, and charge Archibald, Francis, Robert, Adam, Elizabeth, Mary, and Margaret Duff, his brothers and sisters, and the husbands of Elizabeth and Mary as executors-dative and nearest of kin. Thomas was in possession of Craigston for a little over two years, but as ' neither he nor his brother James had owned it for three years, titles in their names were never made up.'

Thomas died unmarried, and was succeeded in 1737 by his brother Archibald.

There are several allusions to Thomas Duff in the letters of William, Lord Braco. He seems to have been drowned. The only other reference to him is in the following letter from his mother:

Mary Urquhart to Captain John Urquhart

'MY DEAREST BROTHER,—Yr kind obliging leter was sent me from Haton yesterday. Blessed be God that I have such a true frind as you ar that puts me on my geard to shun whats wrong and derects me to doe what right, good God enable me to doe that which is right in the sight of God and pleassing to my frinds perticularly, for which is the sincer deser of my heart. Im much grived and ashamed at the great expence I have put you too, tho you ar so generious as to forgiv itt. If ever I should truble you mor that way I would be wors then a brut. Dear brother Im much obhdged to Premna,[1] and would be glead if he would be so good as notice me in yr abescnce, only I most beg off you and him and all my frinds to leave an ear to the abescnt and not to belive all thats said. Pardon for God sak my writing to offer to you and tho I will not presum to writ to you again till you deser me yet if you would be so good as writ me the never so short a lin ether under Meldrums cover or Premnas I would tak it as the greatest favour that could be don me for yr leters will be the welcomest presents I can receive, and if you doe not writ me it will be long or I know how you ar. My Dearest Brother, if Premna cause get for his Brother Thomas three hundred marks a year it will be an act off great frindshipp and kindness and I hop Thomas will contmow in the steat of liff he is in and never be so foolish as desire to go to law. I shall God willing give him the best advice I can for I would wish all my children to please ther frinds and much oblidged am I to you that minds them. Thomas wrot to you som tim agoe and I wrot seen affter to you to Byth, but I was so seek that wick that they war not sent, I bless God I 'm better now, and while I live Ill ever contmow with a heartfull of sincer esteem.—My Dearest Brother, Yr most affectionatt sister and obedent oblidged humble servant, MARY URQUHART.' (D.)

The third surviving son, ARCHIBALD, was born about 1714, as he is found as a student entering King's College, Aberdeen, in 1728, and the normal age at that period was fourteen. He was at Leyden University in 1736, and studied medicine both there and in Paris.

'He was long in the service of the Swedish East India Company in Bengal; from thence he went to Cochin China, of which kingdom it was said in Europe he was made a Mandarine. He sold Craigston to the late Captain John Urquhart of Cromarty, his uncle. He died in 1758 while

---

[1] Her stepson Patrick.

on a trading voyage from Cochin China to Batavia, in poor circumstances' (Baird). He wrote a history of Cochin China, said by Band to have been printed in London, but there is no copy in the British Museum. His voyages in the East would seem to have been adventurous, and both his early and later letters are among the most interesting in the whole of the family correspondence.

Archibald Duff, Paris, to Captain Urquhart, his uncle

'PARIS, 27 *March*, N.S., 1736.

'MY DEAR UNCLE,—We received your kind letter of the 12th March from London yesterday, after I had wrote you and Premnay fully, anent Francy and myself: We 're sorry Premnay is offended that we did not write him sooner; it is not, I assure you for want of affection and Esteem, for considering his carriage towards us and the favours he has done us it would be the hight of Ingratitude and stupidity if we did not esteem and love him. I shall not clear us of careless-ness and Laziness, however if I were to give you a journal, how one of our business thats to pass only six or seven months here ought to spend every day in order to improve as he may, you would see he would be sufficiently imployed: But thats not the reason, if one had a mind he could ay find time to write a letter: We were sensible it was our duty to write Premnay a letter of thanks since its the only mark we 're in a condition to give, that we have a sense of the great kindness shewn us by that Family, but we did not think if we did that the first time we wrote, that the circumstance of time made any odds. Because we did not understand the Language the imperfect remarks we could make in travel-ling to Paris were not worth the while. All the time we have been here, because we have not made it our business to go into Company or to see places as yet we don't know much of the People or many things worth taking notice off We were not allowed to stand in need of anything, we wrote our Mother to write us of our friends. For the future we shall write our friends frequently and we begge to be excus'd for what 's past. . . . We hope you 'll be so kind as pardon us and that you 'll make an apology to Premnay for us the first time you have occasion to write him Its very comfortable to us to hear of our Mother and other friends weelfare. I have nothing to add but that I ever remain, with great affection and esteem, My Dear Uncle, Your very much obliged and most obedient humble servant, ARCHIBALD DUFF.' (*D*)

Archibald Duff, Paris, to Patrick Duff of Premnay

'PARIS, 28 *March*, N S , 1736.

'AFFECTIONATE BROTHER,—We were favour'd with your's of the 29th Nover. last from Edinburgh and in consequence of our Uncle's letter at that time to Mr. Alexr. my Broyr and I have each of us received the twenty Pound str. As Francy wrote you last week we will have finished our courses of surgery and

anatomy in two or three weeks hence, and so will not have occasion to stay here longer on that account. But as I can now live here pretty cheap and the Business my Uncle was so kind as propose for me, does not require that I go immediately to Sweden, I believe it will be thought proper for me to stay here some time after that. I'm now in a good way of learning the French, and when its my principal business I shall be able to make a considerable progress in a short time. As for Francy, now he has finished his education, he wants as soon as possible, to get business and beggs his friend's assistance and advice in what way to apply himself whither they think the Army, the Navy, a Merchant Ship, or to follow his business in any oyr way, wch they would advise him to—he would chuse small business rather than wait. He intreats and depends on your advice and how he'll dispose of himself in the meantime and that you'll reccommend him to any of the Members of Parliament and any others of your acquaintance at London that can be of use to him and that, if you think recommendations from any of the rest of his fuends can be of use to him, you'll be so good as procure them. I think Mr. Bell a Chirurgeon at London got ships to two of the young lads that went from Abdn. last Spring, on Mr. Dyce's Reccommendation. Dear Brother, your kind and affectionate carriage towards us hitherto incourages us to give you all this trouble. Our dear Father's Death and then our Brother's,[1] were Dispensations of Providence very grievous and afflicting; yet such has been the goodness of our surviving friends and brothers, I may say Fathers,[2] that we have scarce as yet felt that great loss. Your kindness towards us all has been very great, particularly the Instance of it to our mother is ever most obliging, the great trouble you put yourself to and the expence in serving us on our leaving Scotland; the affectionate care you had of me in my dangerous illness and the continued train of your kindness to us, we can make no reccompence for any of them only our best wishes and thanks, which we render you most heartily. Likewise Hatton: he has been very kind especially I lye under many obligations to his Family: and all the rest of our Brothers and Sisters have been all very kind. We design to write our Master under your cover what we have been doing when we have finished our Courses and therefore shall not trouble you with that at present, only in general I belive there is not such anoyr place in the world for Learning Anatomy and all the Branches of Surgery. Because the best way of remitting money is by Bills from London, please with your conveniency remitt £22 Str. of the money that should answer me at Whitesunday and the £27. 6. 10½ that should answer Francy, in our Uncles absence; to Mr. George Auchterlony to answer us as we have occasion to call for it. I belive Francy will have use for £32 Str. including the £12. 5. of his £50 before he leaves Paris, tho' he leave it three weeks hence, so ther's occasion for remitting his money that should answer him at Whitsunday to London immediately. I have not as yet taken any kind of cloathes here and so have a little of my money remaining, but will have occasion for more shortly and therefore have of this date wrote my Uncle to remitt me £17. 5. Str. the remainder of my £50. I

---

[1] James   [2] Archibald's four half-brothers were a great deal older than himself.

belive it will do much to serve me whilst I'm here. The reason that Franey needs more money than I, is his being very ill provided of necessaries when he left Scotland. We have not gone to see many remarkable places as yet, and cannot form a Judgement of either the people or place only in general the People seem to be very polite and easy in their cariage, only they use a Plaguey dale of useless Compliments. The common people make a great show of Religion. I cannot tell if the better sort be less religious, but they seem to have a great dale less superstition. We saw a great many things both in our way to Paris and since we came here that we thought remarkable ; but I belive considering we have seen but very little of our own country and know but little about it, together with our not speaking French would make them appear triffling and not worth mentioning to anybody that knows better, and therefore I shall trouble you but with a few of them. At Rouen we saw a fine house of salt sellars belonging to the King (there is nobody sells salt there but the King, and he sells it very dear). Churches are everywhere very numerous and magnificent : we likewise saw several fine houses but not any country seats, except one, after we had pass'd Normandy, in the Isle of France, that we thought comparable to Culter. In the beginning of Nov. they were just about as far advanc'd in their labring and the beir as long as it will be with us just now. They plough not half so deep as with us, but the furs are nearer to one anoyr : their ploughs are drawn by two horses only and go on wheels ; they differ in little else from ours, only the stilts are longer because in working the man who holds the plough goes with his back strait. Ther 's a great dale of wood all through the Country, mostly oak and fruit trees, very few Firs and what I saw were Pines. All their fire here is wood, except some coals that are imported from Britain that the smiths burn : they have mostly windmills : on two or three bridges over the Seine that we had occasion to cross we saw two or three Watermills of a different fashion from ours. I cannot tell if there be any of them in Scotland, but because I think they would be usefull in some places where thers big Rivers and scarcity of burns and convenient places for building our Mills, the first one I have occasion to see again I shall write you a particular description of them. It apear'd to be a very simple engine, instead of having two wheels moving in a circle perpendicular to the Horizon it has but one moving horizontally to the Needle that turns about the running Milstone for its axis. We begg you 'l excuse all this trouble and have nothing more to add at present, but our best wishes to you, your Lady, and the Lady Braco, to whom and the rest of our friends and Benefactors we begg to be kindly remembered when you have occasion to see them. I ever remain wh. great affection and esteem, My dear Brother, Your most oblidged and obedient humble Sert., Archibald Duff.

' *P.S.*—When you have occasion to see my kind old Master, Mr. Burnet or Mr. Rait, please make my compliments to them. If there were any thing here that we could be of use to you in, it would be a very sensible pleasure to us to do it. We wrote some time ago to our Mother to hear of our friends, and are conserned we have not heard from her yet.'   (*D.*)

Archibald Duff, Leyden, to Patrick Duff of Premnay

'LEYDEN, *ye* 16*th Octor* 1736

' MY DEAR BROTHER,—I wrote you last from Paris of ye 15th Augt. I have been attending the Colleges here now some weeks but have the prospect of business soon ; and tho it is not worth any body's while to come to this place on purpose to hear the Professors only for a few weeks, yet as it is to fill up some vacant time, and having been att Paris, I 'll profite by it considerably, and if after this I shall have an opportunity of returning here to study, my being here now will be a great advantage to me. My Uncle wrott an exceeding kind letter in my favours to Mr. Campbell, however soon he got notice of his being seen on this Coasts weh I hope will succeed : he wrote the week before he left Paris and expects an answer now every post and tho' it should not be favourable he has so much Intrest and is such a kind hearty friend that he 'll soon get some oyr business for me tho' it is indeed difficult : there are so many that have been disbanded from the Fleet, oyrs that have been voyages and at same time so many new ones (almost all Scots). I believe a Kirk is easier got than any tollerable business in our way, at present. I hope ere long I shall be at greater distance from Abdn. than at present. Perhaps I 'm a very great fool that might have been geting in half a year or a year after this fifty and perhaps a hundred pounds a year and the most of my Patrimony remaining and been at my own ease and in a capacity of doing perhaps a little good, but I 'm sure you would reckon me stupid or mad if, after leaving that and spending so much upon my Education, I should expose myself to certain hardships and eminent danger without endeavouring to have it in my power, even supposing it may please God that no misfortune happens to me, to make myself a bit the better for it ; weh must certainly be the case if I carry adventure out wt money. Three pound a month (Surgeon's Pay) after taking on trust and consequently at the Druggest's price a Chist of Druggs to furnish the crew with and buying Instruments to be keept off from the first end of ye day, is but poor business, or any oyr business that I can expect were it not for the advantage I 'll have of tradeing, weh is not worth a farthing to me if I have nothing to trade with   After I 'm fitted out I will not have much of my money left and tho' I had more I would incline to venter it as well as myself : I hope it will be of more service to me now than ever twice as much would be again. My Dear Brother, I hope when you know the circumstances you 'll likewise think it reasonable. I 'm very sensible you would do nothing against my Intrest. I have experienced your kindness too much not to be intirely perswaded of that. As I know but too little of the world and have but very little experience, I am sensible how lyable I am to commit mistakes and how much need I have of good advice and I hope and earnstly intreat youll do me that very kind office of letting me know my faults and favour me with your good advice : and I sinserly promise you I shall endeavour to mend them and follow it. I heartily wish it were anyway in my power to show that I have a gratefull sense of your favours. I am very happy of having the good fortune

to be so much with your friend my Uncle.[1] Such an opportunity in my opinion
is the greatest happiness and advantage that a young lad can meet with : and
he is so good humour'd and kind as to use me with the affection of a parent and
familiarity of a friend or Broyr. I heartily wish he were settled to his liking in
Abdnshire and I dont doubt but you 'll do what lies in your power to promote
it and procure him an estate [2] that good and convenient, and as I know he has
an intire friendship and very great esteem and regard for you I believe you 'll
have a good dale of influence with him. I the rather wish he would settle
amongst our friends because I 'm sure he would not himself give in to a great
many of our pernicious customs and I believe he would have influence upon
several of his own relations to give them over likewise : perhaps oyrs seeing ye
advantage of the method might imitate them : Besides I don't believe it would
be disagreeable to himself and certainly a great satisfaction to all his friends. I
heartily wish long life and all manner of Happiness to you all and ever remain
wt the greatest love and esteem, My Dear Brother, Your very affectionate
Brother and much obligd obedient servant,   ARCHIBALD DUFF. (*D*.)

One letter is of much later date, from

'CANTON IN CHINA, 31*st January* 174⅔

' Patrick Duff of Premnay, Esqr.

' SIR,—It gave me great satisfaction to receive your ffavours by Mr. Elphin-
ston ; when I found my Relations so free from being involved in their country's
ruin.[3] I have taken money at Bottomry [4] One thousand thirty pounds Str on
the English China Ships, York and Lin, and have discounted 30 and 28 pr. ct.
for my chance of their miscarrying, which God forbid ; and I have ordered
George and Wilm. Catanach to pay it, so that I shall be in their debt if both
these ships get home safe. Messrs. Pye and Cruickshanks have laid so long out
of their money, and please not to order any of my money for any other Account ;
except that my Mother or any other near Relation may be in straits, and in
that case please to relieve them on my account as the exigency of the case
requires. I pray to be kindly remembered to your Lady, Lady Braeco and all
my relations. I am sory for poor Adam's ill luck, if he is not at his ease, for
God's sake send him abroad. I shall write to him from Batavia and to you likewise at greate length. In the mean time and alwise I ever am with exceeding
great respect and esteem, My Dear Brother, You most affectionate Brother and
obliged humble Servt.,   ARCHIBALD DUFF.' (*D*)

Archibald Duff was at one time a rich man, as his affairs in the East

---

[1] Captain John Urquhart.

[2] He subsequently bought Craigston from Archibald himself

[3] *i.e.* the Jacobite rising.

[4] Bottomry, a contract by which a ship is pledged by the owner for the money necessary
for repairs to enable her to complete her voyage   The debt is repayable only if the ship arrives
at her destination.

piospered, and the lucky opportunity he had of curing the Emperor of Cochin China of a dangerous malady, which had defied the local medicine men and the Jesuit missionaries, went far to make his fortune;[1] but while in Canton his house and all his property was burnt, and he died, as has been said, quite poor. This will was made before he left Europe, and did not take effect :

'I, Archibald Duff, lawful son to umqle Patrick Duff of Craigston being certain of Death and willing to settle my affairs to avoid disputes when it happens, I name Robert Duff my Broyr. german my Exor, and failing him by decease, I name Adam Duff my Broyr. my Exor. Item, I leave to the said Robert Duff ten thousand pound scots and to the sd. Adam Duff two thousand pound scots and In case of ye death of ye sd. Robert I leave the sd ten thousand pound left to him in that case is to fall to the sd. Adam. Item, I leave the fourth of my residue of my effects to Capt. John Urquhart my Uncle to be by my mother and all ye remainder to be divided equally amongst ye sd. Adam and Robert Duffs, Mary, Margt. and Elizabeth Duffs my Sisters equally, and this I declare is my latter will. In Witnes quof written by Patrick Duff of Premnay I have subscribed this at Abdn the third day of November seventeen hundred and thirty-eight years before Wittnesses, James Black Mert. in Abdn, and the sd. Pat Duff and John Duncan his servant, ARCHIBALD DUFF. (D.)

'3rd Feb. 1739.'

FRANCIS DUFF, son of Patrick Duff of Craigston, born about 1715, was also a doctor. In the year 1731 he bound himself as apprentice to Doctors John and James Gordon, physicians in Aberdeen, for the space of four years. In 1735 he appears to have decided to go to Paris with his brother Archibald to study, and got his discharge from Dr. James Gordon. In 1738 he was living at Cape Coast Castle in Africa, and was factor for the Royal African Company there, as well as being a doctor. In the same year he went to Whydah in Guinea, where apparently he died. Two letters of his give a good idea of some of the difficulties he had to encounter.

Francis Duff to Patrick Duff of Premnay

'LONDON, 21st May 1736

'SIR,—I shall be glad this find you, your Lady and Lady Braco in good health, to whom I wish all manner of happiness.

'I arrived here a fortnight ago, but delayed writting you untill such time as I could give you some account of what I now designe to follow, tho' I can not say the footing on which I go is Intearly certain for Captain Renton with whom I sail is bound for Jamaica. But as he is not yet certain if he gets into the South Sea Company's Service I have no pay allowed me from this to Jamaica, but have

---
[1] See letter from Sir James Kinloch, chapter viii.

the Capts. promise, if his project takes, to have the same pay other surgens in the Company's service have, or if I find any tollerable encouragement there, I propose to stay some time.

' No dout youll be surprised at my Draught on Brother John. But as I had myself to put in Cloaths and furnish Instruments and other necessarys for my voyage with the small adventure of stockings [1] I carry wt me, I most own the small stock I had is now near exhausted —Sir, I remain wh the greatest esteem, Your most obedient humble Servtt.,   FRANCIS DUFF.' (D.)

Francis Duff, Whydah, to Patrick Duff, Premnay

' WILLIAM'S FORT, WHYDAH, Nov 14, 1738

' SIR,—Having this opportunity of returning you my most hearty thanks for the innumerable favours I have already received from you when I am very sensible it was out of my power of repaing, I beg leave to offer my self a Petitioner to you for this last favour which I hope yowl be so good as giant, my unforseen necessities obliging me to it, but be assured that the former with this shall be faithfully remitted to George Auchterlony merchant in London in six months' time.

' My Delay betwixt Cape Coast and Whydah being so very long forces me to trouble you in this manner. A Gentleman named Crabb and I, in our passage from Cape Coast to Whydah, in a thirteen hand canoe were taken by three large canoes belonging to Champo off Quytah the 7 of Agust who striped us of all our necessaries and detained us prisoners for ten weeks three days. Champo being then Defeated by the King of Dahome, the Dahomes released us and carried us to their King, who behaved in a very civil manner to us, and sent us to Whydah, my not having so much as a shirt, stocking or shoe on my arrival at Whydah, or any necessary whatsomeever, but two cloths the King of Dahome give us to hid our nakedness, forced me to draw upon you for Sixty-one pound fifteen shillings payable in three weeks after sight. The King of Dahome promis's to pay us for all our things in two months we lost which amounts to two hundred and forty-six pound stirling which I do assure you shall be remitted to George Auchterlony for the repaing of you, I hope my necessities will make you take compassion upon me and now allow my Note of Hand to lay unpaid. In compliance wt this, you will for ever infinitly oblige me. He to whom the Note of Hand becomes due being an Englishman and knowing Geo. Auchterlony makes me give the order upon him to whom I hope youl be so good as order to pay. My being very much indispos'd after my long journey so far by land, hinders me from writing my Uncle and the rest of my relations, hoping yow 'l be so good as write them. How soon I am indifferently well, I shall write you more fully. I now beg leave to offer my most Dutyful respects to you, your Lady and Lady Braco and all the rest of my relations. Wishing sincerly this may find them all in good health is the earnest desire of, Sir, your most obedient and most humble Servt,   FRANCIS DUFF.' (D.)

---

[1] Probably the woven stockings from Aberdeen, at that time a novelty in the north

The date of Francis' death is not known.

The next surviving brother, ROBERT of Logie, founded a new branch of the family, and will be found in the next chapter.

The youngest son was ADAM, born about 1725. He was a merchant, and baillie of Aberdeen, and subsequently Provost of that town. He apparently did business for the family, as there is a bill—Archibald Duff of Drummuir to Adam Duff in Aberdeen, 1753, for ' printed papers @ 3/- a piece,' and ' entry and carriage of a large trunk ship'd aboard Captain Martiner for London,' receipted at Aberdeen 1754.

In his later years he owned the property of Stocket, now part of Aberdeen, and took some interest in agriculture. He was also a freeholder of Morayshire. He arranged loans for Lord Fife and managed the provision for the admiral's children, the mutual nephews and niece of himself and Lord Fife.

Lord Fife gave him a qualification to vote for Ludquharn in Buchan (for which apparently he paid), but in May 1791 he was struck off the roll, presumably on accepting some government office

In the historical papers of the New Spalding Club it is recorded, from the *Aberdeen Burgh Records*, 1745-1746, that when the town of Aberdeen was to be put in a posture of defence, Adam Duff, merchant, was appointed one of the twelve ensigns. He died unmarried in 1795, and left his money to his nephew, William Leslie of Melross.

Provost Adam Duff of Stocket to the Earl of Fife

'*Jan 12th*, 1759

' MY LORD,—Mr. Osborn, Comptroller of the Customes here died yesterday afternoon. I have taken the liberty to solicit your Lordships Interest for that office, I know several are applying to their friends, but if your Lo/ will be so good as to interest yourself for a relation that never likes to be troublesome to friends there's little doubt of success. Sincerely wishing your Lordship the Compliments of the season, with many happy returns I have the honour to be with great respect and esteem your Lop. Most obedt and much obliged humble servt.,

'ADAM DUFF.' [1] (*R*)

---

[1] William Duff in Turriff, who in 1747 married Isabel Urquhart in Banff, and had two daughters—Isabel, born 1748, and Sarah, born 1750, may have been another son of the second family of Craigston No descendants of his are known These details are taken from the Registers.

END OF VOL. I.

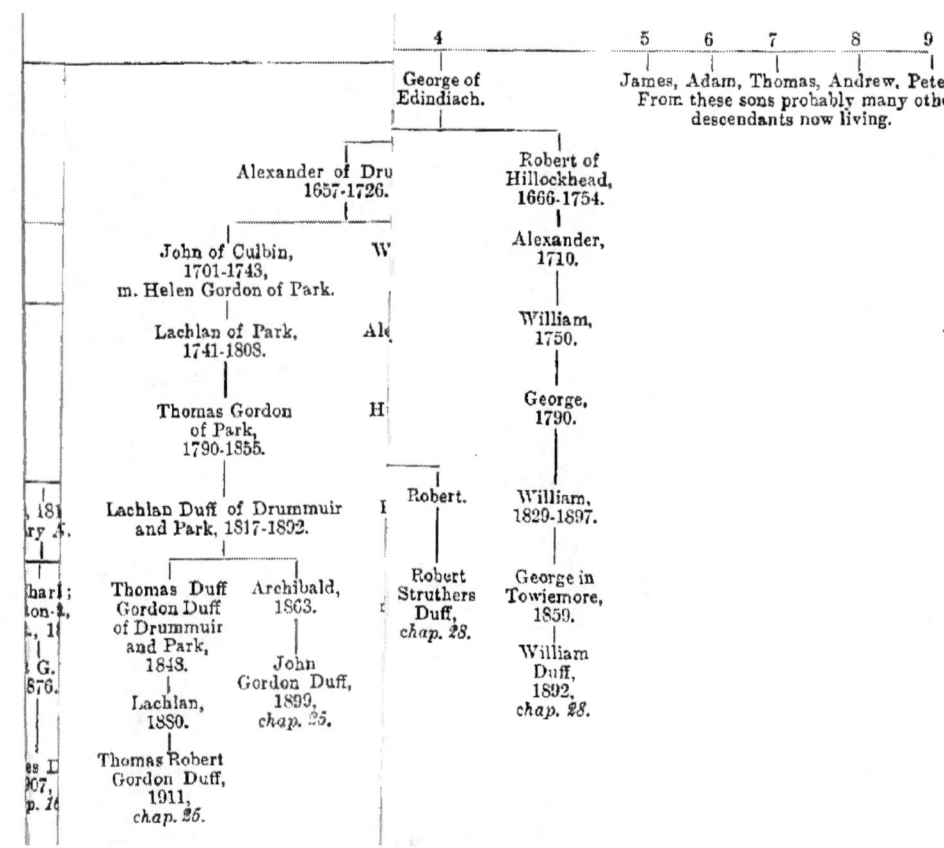

4   5 6 7 8 9

George of
Edindiach.

James, Adam, Thomas, Andrew, Peter.
From these sons probably many other
descendants now living.

Alexander of Dru
1657-1726.

Robert of
Hillockhead,
1666-1754.

John of Culbin,
1701-1743,
m. Helen Gordon of Park.

W

Alexander,
1710.

Lachlan of Park,
1741-1808.

Al

William,
1750.

Thomas Gordon
of Park,
1790-1855.

H

George,
1790.

Lachlan Duff of Drummuir
and Park, 1817-1892.

Robert.

William,
1829-1897.

Thomas Duff
Gordon Duff
of Drummuir
and Park,
1848.

Archibald,
1863.

Robert
Struthers
Duff,
chap. 28.

George in
Towiemore,
1859.

John
Gordon Duff,
1899,
chap. 25.

William
Duff,
1892,
chap. 28.

Lachlan,
1880.

Thomas Robert
Gordon Duff,
1911,
chap. 25.

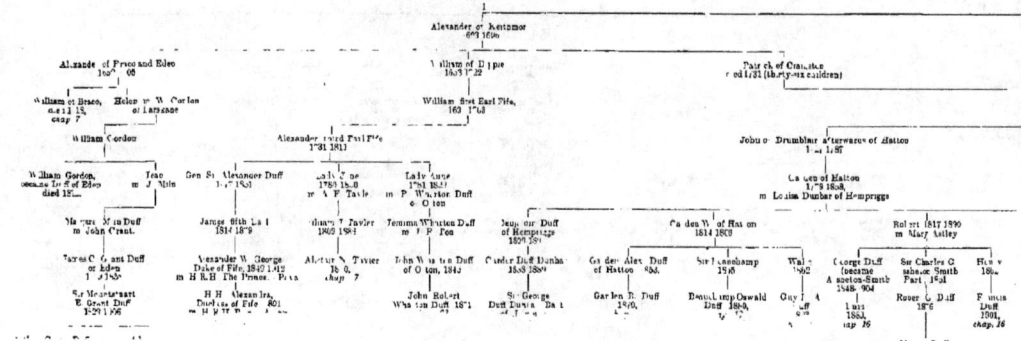

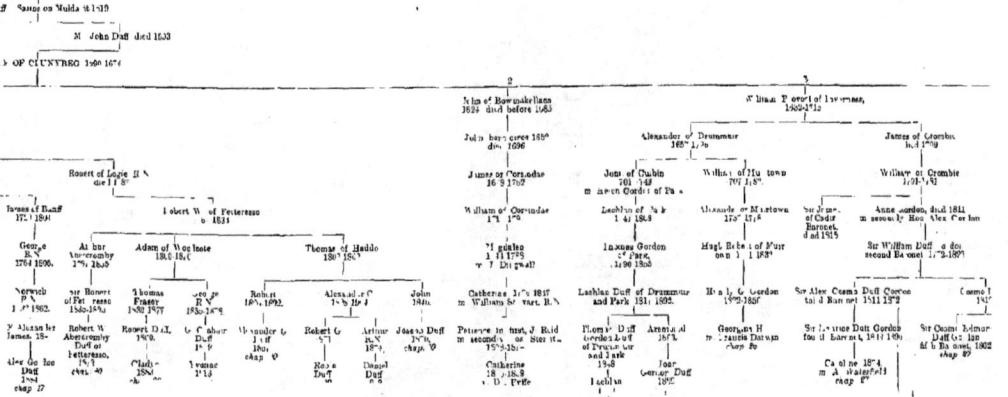